WHEN Robertito's father, Roby, set up the puzzle, Robertito quickly withdrew all the pieces. "Good, *papito*," Roby whispered, a grin overwhelming his face. "Find the place. Go ahead, find the place," he urged his son, giving him a hint with his finger.

Within seconds, Robertito had replaced the form. To celebrate, Roby gave him some food.

As they resumed the puzzle, Robertito remained focused on the cup of tuna. "Do you want food?" Roby asked him. "Just say '*co*.'"

No response.

They continued working with the puzzle forms. Then Robertito made a peculiar circle shape with his lips. Another crude sound bellowed from his larynx. He repeated the grunt a third time. Finally, in a loud voice, Robertito said "*co*."

"Oh my God," Carol gasped as Roby proudly fed the little boy, and wiped the tears from his face.

"Heartwarming story...overwhelming proof that love can work miracles."
—*The Literary Guild*

"THERE are at least eight places to cry for joy in this book, and at least one place to laugh out loud. Barry Neil Kaufman's story of the way his family loved a child back to life is a feast for the heart."
—*The Boston Globe*

"MANY thanks for the privilege of reading your account of the remarkable adventure with Robertito and his family. Love that comprehends and respects an inner sanctum of being without violating its uniqueness has always produced miracles—human miracles. Your story reminds us once again of our underused power to celebrate and ennoble life."
—Norman Cousins

"INTIMATE and awe-inspiring story."
—*Christian Bookseller*

"THE child whom readers came to know intimately in the bestselling SON-RISE, later made into a television drama, serves as a catalyst and teacher in this miraculous story of help...a new miracle begins."
—*Los Angeles Times*

"A POWERFUL, painful, joyful and true story of a boy's rescue from autism."
—*Minneapolis Tribune*

"A BEAUTIFUL and healing journey. The Kaufmans' message is one of peace, hope and possibility. Through their work they have demonstrated and continue to demonstrate in very tangible terms the power of love and acceptance."
—*New Age Magazine*

A MIRACLE TO BELIEVE IN

Barry Neil Kaufman

FAWCETT CREST • NEW YORK

A MIRACLE TO BELIEVE IN

THIS BOOK CONTAINS THE COMPLETE TEXT OF THE
ORIGINAL HARDCOVER EDITION.

Published by Fawcett Crest Books, CBS Educational and
Professional Publishing, a division of CBS Inc., by arrangement with Doubleday and Company, Inc.

ISBN: 0-449-24496-2

Everything that is said or depicted in this book is absolutely
true and exactly as it happened. However, the names and
other irrelevant details of some of the lesser characters have
been changed in order to respect their right to privacy.

Printed in the United States of America

First Fawcett Crest Printing: April 1982

10 9 8 7 6 5 4 3 2 1

To Suzi,
you knew from the very beginning
...you lit the first candle.

To Raun Kahlil, our loving little Buddha
...you dared to take the hand of another child
to cross a bridge you once crossed alone.

To Francisca and Roberto (Roby)
...you dazzled us and inspired us,
you kept climbing the mountain despite
all the evidence. This book is a testament
to your special love.

To Laura, Carol, Jeannie, Chella, Patti and Ginny
...a little boy learned to fly on your wings.

To Bryn and Thea,
you nourished another little boy
like you had once nourished your brother.

To Robertito,
you kissed us with your awesome calm and softness
...we had to grow to kiss you back.

And to the attitude, "to love is to be happy with,"
without which this story could not exist.

To Bryn, my daughter and teacher,
who, like a rose, shares her beauty in seasons.

A MIRACLE
TO BELIEVE IN

Prologue

An early morning mist varnished the weeping vineyards and the tops of our heads. An orange sun crept over the hillside, drawing the first beads of sweat from our foreheads. We were together, Suzi and I, listening to our pounding feet tap out their own heartbeats on the macadam road; each morning engaged in the ritual of our six-mile run. Though I could sense her form fading almost a quarter mile behind, I denied my impulse to turn, compelled by the hypnotic momentum of my legs and by my private race with the rising sun.

As I completed the fourth mile, I no longer had to push, merely to control the forward glide. This was the special part of each run, when the landscape, my breath and my body became one, when my vision seemed to disappear though everything remained in view, something like the long-distance driver who steered his car expertly over one thousand miles of road, but barely remembered the journey. Only Suzi's presence behind me remained vivid.

I felt kind of high and silly this morning, joyful and humble. I could hear myself thanking the universe for the cornfields which appeared at the crest of the road. Thank you, I mumbled, for the leaves and the trees, for the grass and for the gravel beneath my feet, for the lady I love, for the children who bring joy into our lives. I didn't feel sad, yet my eyes filled with tears and my vision blurred. The roadway before me suddenly flooded with the familiar faces of people I had taught and counseled.

Then the soft, smiling eyes of young Robertito Soto fluttered before me. "¡Hola!, Robertito," I whispered. I thought of him and the special family; once a group of strangers, who came together and journeyed to a place none of us ever quite imagined. Yet, the sheer physical energy needed to support our pace for the past year and a half never dulled the sunshine in Suzi's eyes; but it took its toll. So we had taken the time, this time, to remove ourselves from the hustle, to breathe mountain air, to slow the motors, to attend to our inner thoughts.

The facts had been catalogued; thousands of pages of notes, endless hours of tape recordings, reams of test results, sketches of the most personal experiences, photographs of special moments—more in-depth preparation than for any previous book I had written; yet, here, running down this path, I sensed something beyond the notations, something unstated but definite which happened to each of us in having touched and been touched by each other and this special child.

I inhaled deeply and held my breath. My mind cleared, a response to my decision to work on the book by leaving myself open, empty, receptive to whatever thoughts filled that vacuum.

The slapping of sneakers along the road echoed in my ears once again. The smell of freshly cut grass sizzled in my nostrils. Suddenly, I became aware of a crow skirting the treetops above me. He flew just in front of my running form, about fifteen feet above my head. The bird matched my pace exactly. As he glided easily forward, his head cocked beneath his body; he seemed to watch me, something strangely purposeful about his manner.

I turned to catch a glimpse of Suzi, still running behind, though the distance between us had increased. I threw my hands over my head, a gesture she mimicked. Although I couldn't see her face, I felt her smile.

At the point where the road dead-ends, I cut across a recently harvested hay field. The fifth mile completed. My legs felt lighter and lighter. Then, the gnawing feeling of being watched returned. The fields beside me; empty. The perimeter of a pine forest; unoccupied. Though I focused on the grass just ahead of me, I sensed someone, some thing. My eyes felt drawn immediately to a cluster of trees in the distance. On a branch, silhouetted against the sky, stood the crow. I couldn't keep my eyes off him.

I tracked his form, craning my head, unwilling to look away for a moment. As I moved beneath him, passing under the tree, he cocked his head in that same funny manner and watched me; then, effortlessly, he glided off the branch and flew above me. I stared at his graceful form, never seeing the root in the path ahead, only feeling the tip of my sneaker caught, knowing at once that I had lost my balance. Rather than fight the fall, I let my body go limp. My shoulder took the initial impact as my legs tumbled over my head; my knees bouncing against the earth as my body rolled through the grass.

I couldn't determine whether it was from the fall or not, but I began to feel lightheaded; not dizzy, not out of control, just released slightly from the pull of gravity. I considered stopping the run, but somehow I knew to continue.

"Do you believe in miracles?" a voice suddenly asked. My eyes darted quickly across the fields, searching for some hidden ventriloquist. The words were so clear, so very clear, yet not quite spoken. "Miracles," the voiceless voice said again, and then I knew the words had come from within my head. I'm talking to myself again, I chuckled, though this pronouncement sounded very third person, rather than me speaking to me. The question hung there...no answer, just the wind.

Little Robertito's face floated before me again, his blissful enigmatic visage confronting me. "¡Hola!, Bears Kaufman," he said in that wonderful, peculiar, whispering voice of his. "¡Hola!, Tito," I found myself mouthing. I love that little boy, once so inaccessible, so lost, so hidden behind an invisible wall. Robertito tilted his head and stared at me out of the corner of his eyes. I wanted everything for him, everything I had ever wanted for my own son. For all of us who worked with him, he had become a magnet, the human forum through which we searched and found more of our own humanity. He became a reaffirmation of the loving and accepting lifestyle we taught—more than a vision with specific therapeutic and educational applications, but a trusting way to embrace ourselves and those around us.

As I continued to run, the question about miracles lingered. Did I, indeed, believe in them? No. Of course not. I'm too pragmatic, too grounded. But then I stopped myself. I reconsidered this story and the journey of our extended family. Different realities, oftentimes peculiar and inexplicable, punctuated this experience. Miracles? Suzi and I had worked with so many other supposedly "hopeless" cases; our son, Joanna, Kevin, Teresa. Each time, the progress defied the prognosis. I heard the word "miracle" in regard to them and now, again, in reference to Robertito. Was that a way for others to dismiss the experience, minimize the evidence and deny the relevance? Miracles happen over there, to other people. Or, as one university professor once said, "If you can't substantiate it by scientific factors, then it doesn't exist"...or, he smiled sardonically, "you have a 'miracle' on your hands."

But we could explain it, not necessarily in terms of logic and science, but in terms of logic and love. We presented one human being with the most caring, stimulating, exciting, accepting and loving environment we could create. We tickled him, teased him, invited him to join us. In the process, twelve of us changed our lives, emphatically, irrevocably in order to set the stage for ourselves and for Robertito...and then we lived the lessons of accepting, really accepting and trusting what this child chose to do with our offering and what we chose to do with the mysteries we uncovered within ourselves.

Suddenly, I felt closer to understanding what I hadn't written in my notes. Running had always been a special time; I felt myself letting go, high on the rhythm of my moving limbs. I thought of Robertito's incredible parents, Francisca and Roby, crazy and wonderful Laura, intense and dedicated Carol, giving and giggly Jeannie, Chella, Patti, Charlotte, Ginny Lea; remembering when Suzi and I first created the program, how our children became part of it; Thea helping, Bryn, at twelve, assuming a role as teacher, Raun, at five, leading another child out of the darkness which had once enveloped him. We didn't just work together, we made a special universe for ourselves, a special extended family. While others stopped with what was, we attempted to pursue what could be.

My eyes refocused, like a motorized camera, whipped across the landscape; momentarily holding freeze-frame images before my mind; scrutinizing the components of each picture; searching. The bird was gone.

Again I felt lightheaded, freed from gravity. That same

12

question blared in my ears. "Do you believe in miracles?" I knew I hadn't put it to rest. I initiated another conversation with myself. If a miracle meant trying to make the impossible possible, if it meant trusting yourself despite all contrary evidence and trusting an experience before you could rationally explain it...then, yes, I guess I did believe in miracles. The dreams, the telepathic-type exchanges, the reversal of a physical illness and the words from the lips of a little boy that went beyond anything he could have possibly known defied explanation; but those events were as much a part of this story as a kiss or a flower. From such everyday miracles, we, perhaps, had learned our greatest lessons.

The moment that thought occurred, I had the sensation of being airborne, though I could see my feet touch the ground. I kept running, only moments away from completing the sixth mile. And then these words danced in my head as if spoken by someone other than me:

"Miracles happen to those who believe in them."

A hot sensation enveloped my entire body, then evaporated, leaving my skin and muscles incredibly subtle and relaxed.

Within seconds, the crow reappeared, angled in a wide, graceful curve; then pivoting to his left on a different air current, he dove toward me. I kept running those last years, willing to meet him head-on; no fear, no sense of confrontation, just respect for the flow of nature and the events that greeted me. As he soared at me, I found myself lowering my head. When a loud cry bellowed from the bird's throat, I veered to the left, narrowly missing a metal animal trap partially hidden in the grass. A second later, only five feet in front of me, the crow changed directions and disappeared amid the trees across a distant field.

*   *   *

It used to be so hard—to open my door, to love each hour, to celebrate each activity, to freely embrace those who crossed my path. It used to be so hard to smile easily at a stranger or thank someone for extending his hand. It used to be so hard to see myself as powerful and powerless at the same time.

The grueling years of psychoanalysis, the endless graduate courses in psychology, Eastern philosophy, Zen, the experiential seminars in Freudian, Gestalt, Rogerian, Primal and

13

Humanistic therapy, the dives into hypnosis and meditation gave me some answers, but never satisfied my appetite for wanting more communion with myself, with the people around me.

Later, after encountering a wonderfully lucid and loving teacher, Suzi and I began to learn and live what we came to call the Option Process; this book being a classic example of the possibilities of an Option experience. We discarded years of self-defeating beliefs and behavior through joyfully simple, direct and illuminating dialogues—dialogues devoid of judgments, expectations and conditions.

From that endeavor evolved a very special and accepting attitude: to love is to be happy with. A friend of mine protested immediately that such acceptance, such unconditional acceptance, breeds impotence and an unwillingness to change what we see. Our experience has been quite the contrary.

As we tried to live these themes more and more each day, we felt inclined to share them with others by teaching in small groups and on a one-to-one basis. We continued to learn and explore. Yet, it was only after the birth of our third child that we realized fully that the loving and accepting attitude we lived and taught was more than the basis of a therapeutic approach and an educational technique, more than even a lifestyle vision, but a gift for us and for those we loved.

Our son, Raun Kahlil, the third little person to be born into our lives, becomes a haunting undercurrent in this book, not only because of his active involvement and enigmatic insights, but also because his own journey had become a demonstration of possibility which affected our lives and Robertito's life as well as others who have been confronted with situations viewed as "depressing," "tragic" and "hopeless." When Raun was formally diagnosed as having a condition considered to be the most irreversible of the profoundly disturbed; severely impaired developmentally, neurologically and cognitively, Suzi and I waded through the quicksand, trying to extract the secrets beneath the complex terms which damned our child.

Why us? We had finally moved through the turmoil of our first years of marriage, we had grappled with some of the miseries and confusions and put them to rest. We had finally begun to experience our lives as an easy, mellow movement. Why? It was almost as if the universe shouted out to us: "Ah ha, so you think you have it all together, you think you know—well, well, my friends, try this situation on for size."

14

Eventually, we would come to know, through our journey with Raun and others who would follow, that this little boy came into our midst as an opportunity to be either diminished, saddened and defeated by our own unhappiness or to thrive, explore and be enriched by our encounter with this very special human being.

By Raun's first birthday, we noticed his growing insensitivity to sounds and voice; he no longer responded to his name. During the following months, this behavior became compounded by his tendency to stare and be passive. He preferred solitary play rather than interaction with his family. In our arms, he dangled limply, like a rag doll, never attempting to hold or hug. Tests, coupled by visits to doctors and hospitals, produced no definite answers except vague reassurance that he would outgrow his peculiar mannerisms.

By seventeen months of age, Raun withdrew from all human contact and slipped behind an invisible, impenetrable wall. He spent endless hours immersed in self-stimulating rituals; rocking, fluttering his fingers in front of his eyes, spinning every object he could find, finally spinning himself. No language development. No words, no pointing gestures. No expression of wants. He never cried for food, never indicated he wanted to be changed or lifted from his crib. Sometimes he appeared blind; other times, deaf. Silent and aloof, frozen in his own aloneness.

Eventually, he was diagnosed as being a classic case of infantile autism, traditionally considered to be a sub-category of childhood schizophrenia, though more recently viewed as a brain-damage situation of indeterminate cause with profound, lifelong cognitive and communication disabilities. "Hopeless." "Incurable." These were the underlying messages of the literature and the professionals we consulted throughout the country. One physician suggested institutionalization for Raun, then barely one and a half years old.

Most of the programs we viewed were little more than experiments. Whether based on psychoanalysis, sensory conditioning or behavior management techniques, the ratio of children reached was dismal, perhaps only a few in each hundred; those successes being defined as the child who learned to perform minimal tasks on a primitive level.

We encountered doctors who administered electric shock treatments with cattle prods on children under five because some professional, teacher or parent deemed their behavior unacceptable. Other boys and girls were locked in portable

15

closets without windows as part of aversion therapy. Still others murmured weakly, their hands and legs bound to chairs to prevent them from rocking and flapping. Even in the most "humanistic" programs, the therapists, despite their avowed sensitivity, approached these children with disapproval.

We turned away, refusing to relinquish our good feelings, refusing to extinguish the life of this delicate and different child by placing him behind the stone walls of some nameless institution. We decided to create our own program based on the philosophy of Option, grounded in a loving and accepting attitude. Our movement would respect his dignity instead of forcing him to conform to our ideals or behaviors. Our awareness suggested that in terms of his present abilities, Raun, like all of us, was doing the best he could.

After observing him for endless hours, cataloguing all his actions and reactions, we decided to join our son in his world with love and acceptance, to understand and know his universe by participating. Our major thrust began with imitating him, not just as a tactic or strategy, but sincerely being with him; rocking when he rocked, spinning when he spun, flapping when he flapped. Several physicians labeled our efforts as tragic since we supposedly supported our son's bad behavior. Yet for us, good and bad had no useful meaning in our endeavor to reach this very different little boy. We just wanted to somehow find a way to say: "Hey, Raunchy, it's okay wherever you are. Hey, Raun, we love you."

Both our daughters, Bryn, then seven years old, and Thea, then four years old, participated as loving teachers for their brother. We trained others to help, using the principles and attitude of Option as our tool. Piece by piece, bolt by bolt, we began to build bridges.

Although we worked with our son for three years, a total of almost ten thousand hours on a one-to-one basis, within the first year, this totally withdrawn, mute, self-stimulating, functionally retarded, autistic and "hopeless" little boy became a social, highly verbal, affectionate and loving human being displaying capabilities far beyond his years. Today, at just seven years old, he attends a regular second grade in a regular school. More socially and verbally sophisticated than many of his peers and exhibiting no traces of his earlier disability, Raun Kahlil loves life and life loves him back. In many ways, he has been a great teacher and mover of us all.

* * *

What our son came to learn, respect and trust in himself, we seem to have to relearn continually. In entering our lives, Robertito Soto not only challenged his parents and each member of the group we forged together, but became an unscrutable mirror from which none of us could hide. Helping him meant loving and accepting him for who he was, not for who he might become. But before we could accept him, we had to first learn to face and accept ourselves...perhaps the most crucial yet least visible part of our journey, without which we could not have hoped to reach this little boy and trust his choices...or dare to trust our own.

Chapter 1

It had become almost ritual for Roberto (Roby) Soto. After lunch with his family, he returned to his shoe store only to watch the second hand of the large wall clock advance spastically, recording the passage of time in apparent slow motion. At precisely four o'clock, he smiled nervously as he turned his store over to his cousin. The waiting Thunderbird, polished once a week at a local garage, used to be a source of great pride, a symbol of his social and economic arrival after climbing out of the gutter in a small village in central Mexico and attending school with pesos scrimped and saved from menial jobs. After several more years of employment, sometimes maintaining several jobs simultaneously, he moved north with his young wife and used his savings to open a small business.

His mind drifted as he drove down the crowded streets of Encinada, a small fishing village on the west coast of Mexico. Quaint Spanish-style buildings mixed awkwardly with glass-faced discount stores and supermarkets. Music blared from busy twenty-four-hour bars. Old school buses, belching black clouds, carried residents through the town filled with tourists from the United States. Negotiating through the traffic, Roby's soft eyes registered a fatigue which did not come from hard work. The joy of living had been compromised. Though he tried to maintain his traditional focus on family and business, he found himself increasingly consumed by what he had once anticipated would be a beautiful, natural and easy experience.

Maneuvering the final stretch of heavy traffic, Roby envisioned the last daily mail delivery from the "States." For nine consecutive working days, he had come to the post office in search of a package. He parked his car in front of a donkey painted like a zebra with black and white stripes. The car behind the animal contained a family of smiling tourists who posed for a color Polaroid portrait. A uniformed postal employee waved and called to Roberto Soto when he entered the building. The package had finally arrived.

He waited until he sat alone in his car before stripping off the wrapping paper. His eyes filled with tears. There had been so many unfulfilled promises, so many painful dead-ends. From a psychiatric research center in Houston where they had last taken their son for help, a young graduate student, remembering the Sotos, forwarded an article to Roby which had appeared in *People* magazine. It detailed the story of a young family that had successfully developed a unique program for their special child, who had similarly been discarded by the professional community as incurably ill. Hope or another false start? Having the article translated into Spanish, Roby and his wife, Francisca, read and reread the piece. A notation about a book written by the father led him to further research. Another month passed until a friend had acquired the book for him in the United States.

Roby opened the package with great care. A little boy's porcelain-like face filled the cover of the book. His dark penetrating eyes mirrored those of Roby's own son. Large, bold type and various quotations filled the front and back cover. He cursed his inability to read English as he threw his car into gear. His heart pounded. Tiny beads of sweat gathered at his hairline. He drove slightly south of the city to reach the house of Maestro Jaime Ankrom, a teacher and translator.

Señora Ankrom invited him into the entrance hall and offered him a cool drink. Roby shook his head. Within minutes, Jaime Ankrom appeared, greeting Roby with great formality and respect. He had grown to care for the Sotos and their strange little boy. On many occasions, he had translated papers and articles for them. The magnitude of this project considerably escalated his involvement. Jaime nodded his head, reaffirming his commitment to translate the book within six weeks as agreed. Six weeks, Roby thought to himself, six weeks is another lifetime. Propriety squelched his inclination to request faster delivery. But Jaime understood Roby's sense of urgency and canceled some of his own students in order to translate the book within three weeks.

* * *

The neatly typed pages contained a story and message radically different from everything else they had read and been told. Instead of pushing and pulling the child to conform to appropriate behaviors designated by some doctor or text, the couple from New York entered their son's world; joined him in his so-called bizarre behaviors with a loving and accepting attitude which defied any previous notions about dealing with such a situation.

As Roby and Francisca read the translated manuscript, they took a roller-coaster ride through someone else's life. They felt inspired and enriched for the first time in three years. Their own plight had taken them first to Mexico City, then to hospitals and universities in several American cities, including Los Angeles, Chicago and Houston. Their son, Robertito, had participated in three programs which ultimately yielded no results.

Though labeled alternately as brain-damaged and retarded, the diagnosis most frequently suggested was infantile autism. Many of these children, the Sotos discovered, spend their lifetimes drugged on Thorazine as they rock back and forth in their own feces, alone and forgotten on the cold floor of some nameless institution. The prognosis for Robertito conformed to that dismal picture.

Yet the Sotos kept looking, kept trying. Though confused by the regimen and disapproval techniques of behavior modification, they entered Robertito in such a program after numerous professional recommendations. The year of involvement yielded no visible or lasting results. They tried "patterning," a method of sensory conditioning which attempts to have a child relive all the developmental stages in the hope he might regain some lost step. They watched with discomfort as doctors wrapped their young son, then three years old, in a rug, pulling it back and forth across a room. They viewed Robertito being forced to crawl like an infant, his screams ignored by a staff dedicated to executing a textbook treatment for autistic and brain-damaged children. Again, no differences could be detected with the exception of a noticeable increase of anger and unhappiness. The Sotos also tried orthomolecular medicine (mega-vitamins) without success.

Francisca and Roby decided to try to contact the people in New York, determined to fully understand and, perhaps, institute what appeared to them as a very special and unusual alternative.

Jaime sent a telegram on their behalf. Weeks passed with no answer. Another telegram also yielded no response. They followed up the wires with two letters. Finally, they resorted to the telephone, uncomfortable about so directly invading someone else's privacy. A house-sitter answered. She acknowledged receipt of the telegrams and letters, but explained that the family had never received them since they were out of the country. She assured the Sotos an eventual response when they returned at the end of the month, though she cautioned them about expecting a fast answer in view of the rapid accumulation of mail from around the world which also awaited a reading and a response. At the beginning of the following month, they received a response from New York offering assistance.

Huddled around the phone, these two eager parents sputtered in Spanish while Jaime translated everything into English for their long-distance recipient. "He says," Jaime told Roby and Francisca, "the attitude is the most important consideration. He wants you to know they will do what they can to share with you and teach you whatever you want to learn, but...and the emphasis is strong on this point...there can be no promise of miracles, no assurance there will be any changes whatsoever. The child is the unknown which we all must respect."

Francisca held her hand over her mouth, wanting to shout her response. She had always felt so isolated in her love and affection for the little boy most others regarded with disdain.

"Yes, yes, they understand you exactly," Jaime declared, straightening his back authoritatively as he continued to talk loudly into the receiver.

Elaborate preparations were made for the New York journey. Roby hired Jaime to accompany them as their translator.

21

The maestro shifted his teaching schedules, making himself readily available. Roby then arranged for his cousin to handle the store in his absence. Francisca bought little Robertito new clothes, anxious to do everything possible to ensure her son would be liked and accepted.

They drove to San Diego for a direct flight to the East Coast. Staring eyes, pointing fingers and hissing whispers marred their short delay in the airport terminal building.

Robertito's dazzlingly large dark brown eyes rolled from side to side like marbles in their almond-shaped sockets, finally resting to stare absent-mindedly at his own hands flapping like a bird beside his head. High cheekbones accented the width of his face. All his features seemed sculptured to perfection; the strong chiseled nose, the delicately arching lips, the copper-colored skin; even the straight black hair neatly trimmed in bangs formed an expertly styled bowl shape around his face. Robertito could have been an exquisite picture postcard for his native Mexico, a beautiful four-year-old boy with a startlingly handsome and haunting presence.

Yet all this beauty, all this physical perfection cast a very different shadow after only a few minutes of contact. Sitting in the chair beside his parents in the San Diego airport, Robertito Soto never once looked at anyone in the room. Robertito Soto never once moved his lips to speak; never once stopped flapping his hands beside his head. When his mother tried to adjust his four-button vest, he shrank away from her touch, seemingly lost behind vacant eyes. From time to time, he made loud, peculiar, infantile sounds like a ventriloquist, hardly moving his lips or altering his fixed facial expression.

SUNDAY EVENING

The fire licked the bricks behind the mesh screen. The easy, muted horn of Miles Davis filled the room with its special melody; an old jazz aroma from an early nineteen-sixties' album. Our daughters played backgammon. Intense and competitive Bryn, just eleven years old, dangled her head and arms over the side of the couch as she energetically threw the dice, converting an otherwise mellow game into the mini-Olympics. She threw her arms into the air and shouted in response to the high score of double sixes. Then she turned to me, smiled her sultry victory smile and returned to the game. Thea, poised gracefully on crossed legs, ignored her sister's outburst. Though she participated enthusiastically,

22

she maintained only a limited investment in winning. Thea embraced her world in a more ethereal and mystical manner than her sister. The moment-to-moment involvement excited her far more than the outcome.

A small city of wood blocks jutted majestically skyward from the shaggy rug. Raun, our four-year-old architect-in-residence, busily constructed houses and towers and office buildings just west of the coffee table and south of the fireplace. His eyes beamed at the rising structures. Occasionally, he solicited our help for his more delicate designs. Suddenly, Raun paused, looked directly into my eyes with a silly grin, then charged at me like a bull. I intercepted his thrust with my arm, tossing him gently into his mother's lap. Immediately consumed by Suzi's kisses, Raun giggled and screeched. On his feet within seconds, he asked me to "slap him five," which triggered a short series of comic antics.

The piercing ring of the telephone cut through the music. Suzi motioned to me, indicating Jaime Ankrom as the caller. We exchanged a smile, knowing we were about to embark on another journey with another special child.

"Hello, Jaime. Welcome to New York. How was the trip?"

"Good, the plane ride was very pleasant," he said.

"And the Sotos and little Robertito?"

"They, too, had an enjoyable flight. We have made hotel accommodations for tonight at the airport. The Sotos would like to know what time after work would you be available to meet with them."

"Oh, wow," I said, awed by the realization they had traveled thousands of miles for, perhaps, an evening meeting of only several hours. "Suzi and I will be available for you all day tomorrow and if you want, the next day and the next. We've cleared an entire work week." I listened to him translate my words.

"The Sotos are very grateful to you and your wife for your kindness. They say we can arrive any time. What is most convenient for you?"

"Nine in the morning would be fine. And, Jaime, please tell them we will try to share what we know and are happy, very happy to do it," I said. Again he translated the words, then closed our conversation with a rather succinct good-by.

Something about the tone of their telegrams and their letters excited both Suzi and me. To translate *Son-Rise* into Spanish, then hire an interpreter and fly with their son to New York represented a special determination. Though I

23

have carefully responded, in some personal form, to each letter amid the hundreds we received each month, the process of making ourselves available to teach and help by sharing our vision and attitude formed the most difficult task. Without the support of funds and grants, which we continued to solicit, our involvement in this area began to seriously drain our financial resources. Nevertheless, we chose to continue as long as possible, also working with schools and early childhood developmental centers wanting to adopt our perspective and techniques.

Before the Sotos' arrival, Suzi and I spent hours discussing optimum conditions for working with them and Robertito. Since they had traveled over three thousand miles to see us, we decided to try to be with them on a marathon basis, which differed from our previous involvement with special children and their parents. Usually, our input with them was limited to single visits or a series of full day sessions spanning several months. Although we had witnessed immediate and spectacular changes in some children, in most situations we felt hampered by limited time or the lack of consistency in the child's total environment.

A grant might have enabled us to help parents surround their children with a network of loving and accepting mentors capable of giving sensitive and responsive input around the clock, seven days a week...a critical component of the program which facilitated our son's rapid and amazing rebirth. An idea evolved, but not yet consummated; a fantasy composed, but not yet delivered. For the moment, with the Sotos, we would do what we could...not by mourning what wasn't, but by celebrating what was.

MONDAY—The First Day

Sasha arrived first, her black shirt tucked neatly into her black pants, a green knapsack strapped tightly to her back. She might have been a pallbearer in a military funeral or a renegade bohemian from a Greenwich Village which no longer exists. Yet a soft, almost vulnerable smile tempered her harsh appearance. Sasha had volunteered to help with meals and the care of our children while we worked with the Mexican family. Since Bryn, Thea and Raun attended school until three in the afternoon, she delighted in having the opportunity to observe.

Several minutes later, a taxi deposited the Soto party at

our front door. Jaime Ankrom bowed slightly as he shook my hand, then Suzi's. His plaid sports jacket framed a starched white shirt and tie. Wisps of hair barely covered his huge head, which sheltered deep-set eyes and offset thick jowls. With great dignity, he introduced Roberto Soto, a tall, handsome man in his late thirties. Dressed more casually in a walking suit, he bowed his head humbly as he took my hand.

Francisca, tall and full-figured, waited with her son. Long, silky black hair dipped just beneath her high cheekbones, accenting her classic features. She searched our faces carefully while being introduced. Her penetrating eyes peered boldly into ours. A hesitant, half-smile fluttered across her face.

Robertito bounced rhythmically up and down on his toes. He made a clicking sound with his tongue as he pulled at his mother's hand, obviously trying to release himself from her grip. Francisca resisted, knelt down and addressed him with great affection. Her subtle eyebrows and animated face accented each thought. But her words fell on deaf ears, her warmth never penetrating the invisible wall encapsulating her son. A great sadness clouded her eyes as she rose to her feet. Holding back tears, she avoided looking at us directly.

Still unresponsive and mute, Robertito continued flapping his free hand in the air.

Our guests seated themselves stiffly on the couch in the living room. We faced them in silence. Only soft smiles passed between us for those first minutes. Their sensitive faces rippled with moments of anxiety. Francisca tried self-consciously to stop her son's flapping hands on several successive occasions.

Suddenly, Roby swallowed noisily, then cleared his throat. He pulled a pile of documents from a large leather briefcase which he carried, then began to recount in detail their experiences with Robertito. Jaime meticulously translated each word, each detail, even the implicit attitude between the words. Roby gestured emotionally as he spoke. Each time he glanced at his son, his voice cracked, his eyes watered.

In combination, the papers presented a confusing computer-like smörgåsbord of conflicting reports and diagnoses. Three described Robertito Soto as definitely autistic with a grim prognosis. Two labeled him authoritatively as severely retarded; one further suggested the boy was uneducable. Another hypothesized brain damage resulting from an undetected case of encephalitis. The most recent report talked vaguely about an atypical schizophrenic condition complicated by unknown bio-chemical irregularities. Pages and pages filled with complex four- and five-syllable words; abstractions grounded in theoretical judgments, several of which were concluded after only fifteen minutes of testing. Yet, not one of these clinical work-ups clearly suggested a mode of treatment. Not one analysis captured by description or inference the particulars of the child facing us.

As his father spoke, little Robertito sat awkwardly on the couch. He moved his body like an infant just learning to sit upright. An occasional murmur erupted from his throat. The incessant hand-flapping continued unabated. And yet, his face appeared serene.

"Señor Soto says these reports have not been very useful," Jaime translated. "No more useful than all the programs the boy has participated in."

"Ask him why he chose to show them to us in such detail?" Another pause for the necessary translation.

"He says he wanted to illustrate that they care very much for their son and did not come here as...how do you say, as...as innocent or naïve people."

I nodded my head, peering first into Roby's eyes, then into Francisca's. We, too, had once jumped through the same hoops to no avail.

Quietly, like a cat, Sasha slipped into the room carrying a tray of coffee and tea. She also brought a large glass of juice for Robertito. Francisca immediately led her son into the kitchen, fearing he might suddenly decide to throw the glass or dump it on the couch. Often, when he finished drinking, he would relax his hand in an absent-minded fashion, allowing the cup or glass to drop to the floor. When they returned to the living room, Suzi sat on the rug beside Robertito. She stroked his leg very gently. When he pulled away, she smiled, slowly withdrawing her hand. Robertito seemed to increase the flapping motion.

As I turned to address Jaime, I realized when any of us spoke, we looked at the maestro instead of each other. Bending forward, I purposely faced Roby and Francisca as I talked. "Jaime, tell the Sotos that I very much would like to look at their faces when we talk, that our eyes carry very important messages for each other. Tell them our words are just one way to speak."

As Jaime translated, they smiled, nodding their heads affirmatively.

"And I will address you directly," I continued. Then I turned to Jaime. "Instead of saying 'they say' or 'Señor Soto says,' would it not be more direct just to speak their words?"

"Señor Kaufman, the role of interpreter is new for me," Jaime said. "I usually translate written matter. Your suggestions are helpful. I will learn these fine points...ah, on-the-job." He smiled, enjoying his own ability to use idiomatic expressions.

"Okay," I laughed, deciding to make one last suggestion. "I want to address you by your first names. Please feel free to do the same. Most people call me Bears, a nickname Suzi and the children gave me. In our home, we're very informal. For the next few days, we will be one family with one common purpose."

Jaime considered my words, but insisted on addressing me and Suzi more formally as a sign of respect. The Sotos welcomed the warmth.

We decided to work directly with Robertito the remainder of the day, at least until dinner. Then, in the evening, we could deal with Roby and Francisca...exploring their feelings and attitudes, all significantly related to any program they would institute for their son. We preferred to be alone with Robertito, without any distractions. We offered the Sotos our car to transport them to a local hotel. Jaime gallantly doubled as chauffeur.

Suzi led Robertito into the bathroom, the same one we used with Raun. It provided us with a simple non-distracting environment...no dazzling wall pieces, no busy windows, no mesmerizing lights. The confined space also kept the child in close contact with us.

We sat opposite each other, our backs planted firmly against the wall. Robertito walked aimlessly around in circles. His body seemed clumsy as he tiptoed on the tile floor. Both his hands flapped vigorously. We began to note several distinctive particulars.

Robertito never looked directly at anyone or anything yet he obviously could see. When Suzi lifted an oatmeal cookie from her pocket and held it in front of him, he either did not see it or ignored it. Yet, when she brought it around to his side, he immediately turned and grabbed for it. Robertito absorbed much of his environment using peripheral vision. In that manner, he could easily watch his flapping hands at the side of his head.

Despite his preferences for perceiving the world tangen-

27

tially, we did notice that he looked directly at the cookie when he grabbed for it, though he maintained that focus only momentarily. In another instance, when Suzi sensed him preoccupied with the faint sound of a distant siren, she snapped her fingers right in front of his eyes. No response. Not even a flutter in his eyelids or eyeballs. Apparently, he had the power to blind himself, to shut off his vision in order to concentrate on his other senses.

Although generally unresponsive to most sounds, this little boy paid careful attention to soft, almost imperceptible, noises. We turned on the tape recorder which we had placed in the bathtub. The room filled with the melodic and lyrical piano music of a Chopin's nocturne. Robertito moved his head from side to side. He made the strange clicking sound with his tongue. An awe-struck expression lit up his face. Something about his gaze reminded me of the peaceful, wide-eyed stare of a Tibetan monk.

We watched him be what he could be, do what he could do, and wondered about the doctors who once tied his hands to stop him from flapping, the psychologists who wrapped him in a rug and dragged him screaming across the floor, the behaviorists who slapped his hands and finally his face because he did not conform to a specific task. We thought of the physician who suggested electric shock treatment to correct all the "bizarre" and "intolerable" behavior. And so most everyone in little Robertito's world had played judge and executioner.

They defined certain behavior as good and other behavior as bad. Using those distinctions as commandments, they then took that as license to forceably extinguish the so-called "bad" or inappropriate behaviors ... as if Robertito was not, in fact, at two and three and four years old doing the very best he could based on his abilities and limitations. To treat a dysfunctioning child, who already displays dramatic difficulties in relating to our world, in such an abusive and hostile fashion raises serious questions. But the issue is side-stepped by the professional, who does not examine his own methods in the face of "no progress," but simply dismisses the child as uneducable or incurable.

At no time did we intend to manipulate Robertito physically, either to stop or to encourage any movement or response. The attitude of "to love is to be happy with" created the foundation from which we approached him. We had no conditions to which he must conform, no expectations which he had to fulfill. Most important, we would make no judgments about good and bad, appropriate or inappropriate. In effect, like all of us, this strange little boy did the best he could.

Respecting his dignity and his world as we had respected Raun's, we decided if he, too, could not join us, we would join him...build a bridge through the silence, if possible, and motivate him to want to be here, to want to participate. Thus, we would, within the limitations of one week, try to create the same kind of easy, beautiful, responsive and loving environment as we had once done for our own son.

In joining him, we did what he did. When he flapped his arms, we flapped our arms. When he made the clicking sound with his tongue, we made the same clicking sound with our tongues. He toe-walked; we toe-walked. He grunted; we grunted. With the exception of defecating in our pants, an activity he still maintained, we followed him, taking our cues as he presented them. We were really there, moving in earnest, participating as caring friends, trying to say, "Hey, Robertito, we're right here; we're with you and we love you." The session continued to the point of exhaustion. Eight hours later, a little after six o'clock, Suzi, Robertito and I emerged from the bathroom. The Sotos had already returned. They looked at us expectantly.

"Wait," I smiled, anticipating their questions. "We all had a very beautiful day together...in the bathroom. After observing for several hours, Suzi and I joined Robertito. We did everything that he did with a loving and accepting attitude."

Francisca took her son's hand and led him to the couch. "*Sienta-te. Sienta-te,*" she said firmly, yet affectionately. Then, turning to us, she asked, "Did he respond? And did he know you were there?"

"I know how much you want things for Robertito. We do, too," Suzi said. "At no time did he respond in a way we could understand. So we don't know if he was even aware of our presence." Suzi tapped her chest. "Somehow, deep inside, I know it counts. We have to trust that and allow what happens."

Francisca nodded her head, trying to camouflage her disappointment.

Roby began to speak rapidly and Jaime waved his hands to slow the burst of words. "We have met your lovely children. Bryn and Thea are quite beautiful and loving. Raun, well...Raun is unbelievable. I never thought he would be ... be so, so normal. He introduced himself, sat on my lap, and asked to see Robertito. When I said you were with him in the bathroom, he shook his head like an old man and asked if Robertito was autistic."

Tears filled Suzi's eyes. "Wait," she said, "I want to get the kids. I know how much they wanted to meet Robertito." She called to them at the staircase. Little feet rumbled across the ceiling toward the stairs.

Bryn appeared first. "Oh, Robertito," she exclaimed, "you're so cute." Thea and Raun followed. The children gathered around their strange new friend. They smiled and chatted with great excitement.

"Look at his fat cheeks," Raun shouted. "I just lov'em." Any child in the universe with chubby cheeks is automatically adopted by Raun as a special friend. Some children are excited by ice cream, others by toys—our son manages to be quite different most of the time. After a couple of minutes, Raun, visibly confused, turned to his mother. "Mama, why doesn't he talk to me? He never answers. When I tried to take his hand, he pulled away."

"Remember our talk, Raun," Suzi replied. "Robertito doesn't speak. Maybe one day he will, but right now he can't. He also doesn't like to be touched, but don't think it means he doesn't like you."

"Joanna and Brian didn't talk either," Raun declared, pondering his association. "Robertito's autistic like them!"

"Yes," I said. In a hushed voice, Jaime translated our conversation into Spanish.

Thea stood beside little Robertito and laughed warmly as she flapped her hands the way he did. It was her way of saying hello. For a moment, just a fraction of a second, he paused. It seemed as if, in that instant, Robertito actually looked directly at Thea.

As previously arranged, our visitors left for dinner and returned at eight o'clock. Raun had been put to bed. Sasha, with Bryn and Thea's help, guided Robertito into the den. The girls wanted to work with him; to join him in his world as they once did with their own brother.

As I stoked the fire, Suzi offered them organic grape juice, turned and mellowed like a fine wine.

"Are you still with us, Jaime," I said jokingly to the maestro.

"Yes, definitely, Señor Kaufman." This warm and unpretentious man seldom smiled.

I leaned forward, peered directly into Francisca's eyes, and asked, "How would you feel if Robertito never changed, if he could never do anything more than you see here today?" Jaime's eyes jumped back and forth, registering surprise at my question. Then, mimicking my tone, he translated it. Roby sighed. Francisca's face flushed; her eyes narrowed. An expression of great sadness and pain overwhelmed her face. Anger curled her lips. She fought her instinct to cry or scream or shout.

Again as gently as possible, I asked the same question. Jaime hesitated, then repeated it. This time, Francisca gave in to the feeling and sobbed heavily. Roby held his wife, barely containing himself.

When she regained her composure, she faced me and said: "It would be awful, terrible. Don't you think so?" And so began our first Option dialogue.

"Well," I said, "what I think is not as important as what you think. It's your son, it's your pain. What is it about being this way that is so awful, so terrible?"

"He can't do anything for himself."

"What do you mean?"

"He does not feed himself. He cannot dress himself. He is not toilet trained. He does not talk. I could go on and on."

"All right, what is it about all those things which he can't do that gets you so upset?"

"I want more for him," she said, crying again.

"I understand that, but wanting more for someone we love is different than being unhappy about not having more. What is it about all those things he can't do that upsets you so much?"

"Most children his age do many things. Although he's four, he's like an infant. People stare at Robertito, make fun of him. I can't stand it."

"Why?"

"He's not a freak. I don't want him treated that way."

"What do you mean?" I asked.

"The whispering. The pointed fingers. The laughter."

"What about that makes you unhappy?"

She glanced at Roby, who remained silent but obviously involved. "I...I..." she stuttered, "I'm afraid it will always be that way."

"Why do you believe that?"

"Because I don't see any changes," she answered. "Because he gets older and older without learning new things."

"Since your fear is about the future, why do you believe if, up till now, he has learned very little or even nothing, that it means it will always be that way?"

Francisca looked at me, confused. "I don't know," she said. "I guess it doesn't have to mean it'll always be that way." She paused to rub her eyes. "Okay," she continued, grinning self-consciously, "but I'm still unhappy about the way Robertito is."

"What are you afraid would happen if you weren't unhappy about his condition?"

"Then, maybe, I wouldn't do anything about it."

"Are you saying by being unhappy, you stay in touch with wanting to change the situation?"

"Yes," she said.

Roby's face lit up, but as he raised his head to speak, I held my finger to my lips.

Directing myself back to his wife, I said: "Why do you believe you have to be unhappy in order to pursue what you want?"

"I don't," she answered, quite clear on that point. "But I guess I act like I do." She shook her head. "This is all very new for me."

"What is?" I asked.

"Well, if my son is sick and I am not unhappy, then maybe it would mean I did not care about him," she concluded.

"Okay," Suzi interjected. "Let me give you back your statement as a question. If your son is sick and you do not get unhappy, would that mean you don't care?"

"I don't know. I'm not sure any more," Francisca mumbled.

"What would you guess?" Suzi continued.

"The more I think about it, the sillier it is. Why do you have to be miserable when someone you love is sick? Sometimes you are so busy helping them, there is no time to feel sad…and yet, you still care. I know, I had that situation once with my mother when she was very sick." Francisca smiled fully for the first time since her arrival. She kept shaking her head up and down.

I apologized to Roby for my curious finger, but thanked him for holding his comment.

He had understood. "Bears," he said, "I want you to know that each time you asked a question, I tried to answer it for myself. Each time, I found my own thoughts in Francisca's answers. Often I have worried about whether this will go on forever. Now, I feel different."

We continued the dialogues until three in the morning. Roby further explored his fears about the future, his concerns about who would care for Robertito when he died. He uncovered the belief that if he wasn't afraid of these possibilities, he might not do as much as he could. When I asked him why he believed that, he answered that he didn't know. So I asked him what he was afraid would happen if he no longer believed it. Immediately, he laughed. His answer was the same as before; the fear he might not do all he could. At that moment, as he came to understand how he frightened himself into moving, the belief and the fear disappeared. No, he assured himself, he did not have to scare himself to make sure he covered every base. In fact, he became aware that the fear of the future had actually diverted him from fully attending to all that he could in the "now."

I quoted to him the words of a wall poster in a friend's office. It read: "I'm an old man now. I've worried about many things in my life, most of which never happened."

Francisca reviewed her thoughts and feelings about being responsible for Robertito's condition. When she could not give one concrete example illustrating how she might have caused his problem, she blamed it on heredity. Why did she believe that? She didn't know. What was she afraid would happen if she no longer believed it? Her answer surprised both her and her husband. If she no longer believed it, then she would have another child. And how would she feel about that? Badly. Why? Because she did not want to stop trying to help Robertito. Why did another child mean that? It didn't ...necessarily. And so, piece by piece, she unraveled some of her fears.

At ten minutes to three, Roby suggested they leave. He carried his son to the car as I followed with his briefcase. Francisca, Suzi and Jaime joined us on the sidewalk.

"It has been a most enlightening evening," Jaime said, shaking my hand.

"Perhaps, later in the week, I will ask you some questions," I said. The others laughed as the maestro smiled awkwardly.

Roby grabbed both Suzi's hand and my hand. His arms trembled as he said: "*Gracias. Muchas gracias.*" Without warning, Suzi kissed him on the cheek. Obviously very touched, he turned quickly to hide his emotions and slid into the driver's seat. Suzi then hugged and kissed Francisca. Jaime stepped back, anticipating her next move. Sensing his discomfort, she threw him a kiss.

"Nine in the morning," I shouted as the car left the curb. Time was so short, so limited. We wanted to cram as much into this week as possible.

Suzi looked at me with a knowing smirk, then she consulted my wristwatch. "I know exactly what kind of crazy week this is going to be. Okay, superman, if you can do it, I can too."

TUESDAY—The Second Day

The Sotos arrived at nine o'clock. Jaime bowed when I opened the door. Before entering the house, Francisca and Roby, both red-eyed, began chattering simultaneously. The maestro put up his hand like an umpire, slightly embarrassed to hush his employers. Francisca indicated Roby would speak.

"A very strange and wonderful thing occurred in the hotel this morning," he said. "Normally, when Robertito rises, he sits on the bed, flaps his hands or clicks his teeth. Always, he appears listless, confused, like he does not know what to do. He'll just stay in that position until someone comes for him. This morning was very different. Robertito sat up in bed as usual, but his expression appeared more thoughtful than at most other times. He didn't flap or make sounds. With great determination, he slid off the bed and walked directly into the bathroom. And waited there...in the bathroom!"

I nodded. Awed. Dazzled by the information. In the midst of Roby's narrative, another significant event occurred. Little Robertito had left us standing in the doorway while he toe-walked through the living room, down the hallway and into our bathroom. A connection established and reaffirmed.

Suzi beamed like a proud mother, her blue eyes ablaze. She waved to us as she jogged through the house to greet the waiting student. "*Buenos días*, Robertito," she said cheerfully as she closed the door to our tile classroom.

Addressing Roby and Francisca, I said, "We'd like both of you to observe today, one at a time. The only place possible is from the bathtub. With the glass doors closed, you won't be distracting. I put a stool in the tub so you can look over the top of the bath enclosure."

"I would like Francisca to go first," Roby insisted, tapping his wife on her shoulder to bestow on her what he considered an honor. We all agreed.

"One more thing," I added, looking at Jaime. "We decided if Robertito has some receptive language, some awareness of the words which have been used around him, it would be all in Spanish. So, in view of that possibility, Suzi and I decided to speak only in Spanish when we're with him. Can you give us a fast lesson, a list of familiar words or even short phrases?"

"Of course," the maestro replied. "I will sit with the Sotos and we will write the words for you in both English and Spanish."

"Write big," I said. "I want to tack that paper up in the bathroom for both Suzi and me." Talking through Jaime had become much easier. He had learned to mirror the tone and inflections of our voices.

"Also," I continued, "Suzi knows some Spanish. She already was speaking to Robertito in Spanish yesterday. She's a natural with language. Me? Well, I'd want to review the pronunciation with you. I'm an enthusiastic student, but with a tin ear."

When they finished their list, we carefully reviewed the words and phrases together: *agua* (water), *la música* (music), *habla* (talk), *mira* (look), *jugo* (juice), *leche* (milk), *los ojos* (eyes), *las manos* (hands), *la boca* (mouth), *diga-me* (tell me), *un besito* (a little kiss), *aquí* (here), *pongala aquí* (put it here), *yo te amo* (I love you).

With Francisca positioned behind the glass doors, we began our day in the bathroom with Robertito. Suzi had already turned on the music and sat with him on the floor. They rocked together, from side to side. A peculiar smile dawned on Robertito's round face. If I wanted to jump beyond what I could definitely know, I might speculate that this little person appeared to be enjoying himself. One activity gave birth to the next. Whatever he did, we did.

At lunch time, Roby replaced Francisca. Having been closeted in the bathtub for hours, her hair, her face and her shirt dripped with perspiration. Nevertheless, she left the room smiling.

Sasha slipped in food for Robertito. We fed him organic peanut butter and jelly on stone ground wheat bread. Normally, he would feed himself with his hands sloppily, depositing food concurrently in his lap and on the floor. Since we wanted to develop eye contact, we fed him ourselves, morsel by morsel. At first, we had to hold a piece of bread beside his flapping hand to draw his attention to us. Then we placed the food between our eyes, inches in front of our faces, and smiled. We also used soft, verbal cues to try to maintain his attention. Robertito grabbed the food awkwardly, moving his hands

35

lethargically as if they were only vaguely attached to his body. "*Mira*," Suzi said each time she held up another piece of food.

"Oh, Robertito, Robertito," she suddenly exclaimed, "*Yo te amo*, Robertito." Suzi whipped her head around, barely able to control her excitement. "Bears! Bears! He looked directly at me for a fraction of a second. He really did. I'm positive. Right at me!"

For the next several hours, we sensed Robertito observing us observe him. On one occasion when we flapped together, he stopped abruptly, leaving Suzi and me still shaking our arms. From his peripheral vision, he watched us curiously. We stopped flapping. Then, he shook his hands again. We followed. An incredible smile dawned on his face. He had it. I couldn't believe it, but he had it! And only in a day and a half. How could it be moving so fast? I thought to myself. Ah, I chuckled, fast and slow; they're only judgments and expectations.

We offered him puzzles and other simple toys, which he discarded immediately. Suzi and I stroked his legs on and off during the entire day. Robertito moved away each time. Finally, toward evening, he allowed physical contact. I moved from stroking his legs to stroking his arms. Very, very slowly and gently, I eased my hands across his belly and around his back. The little man stopped flapping while being touched. Suddenly, he jumped to his feet and walked in circles again. We followed.

Dinner was also served on the bathroom floor. I put each morsel of food between my eyes and smiled, repeating our luncheon ritual. He seemed more directed this time. On four occasions, he stared boldly at me, though only for a few seconds at a time. Real and spontaneous eye contact! These movements originated within him. They were beautiful and profound steps.

A child coming from himself, motivated from within, is significantly more powerful and effective in growing and in getting what he wants. If Robertito could ever climb the mountain, we knew he would have to do it himself...not as a function of anyone's commands, but as an expression of his own wanting.

After the Sotos returned from their dinner, Sasha and the children took Robertito into the den again. In the distance, we could hear Raun's enthusiastic voice: "I just love his cheeks. Thea, look! They're so cute, those fat cheeks." Jaime translated his words.

Clearing his throat and swallowing noisily, Roby faced me and asked: "Will you teach him how to eat with utensils?"

"Oh," I smiled, "in a way, Roby, we aren't trying to teach him anything specific at the moment. What we do is not important right now. We want to create connections, build bridges. Eye contact is so essential. Children learn by copying, imitating. If Robertito does not look at us or hear us, then, of course, he will not learn how we move in the environment and how he can move in the environment." I paused, wanting them to digest everything... and to question everything if they wanted.

"Since it's so, so much more difficult for him to do that than the average child," I continued, "we have to take special care, create a special environment. For example, he's hypersensitive to sound. When he's bombarded, he closes his hearing down to protect himself. For you and me, a cough sounds like a cough. Perhaps, for Robertito, it sounds like an earthquake. So, we try to bring music and our words to him in a gentle, soft manner."

"Yes, yes," Francisca said. "I've noticed his tendency to flap his hands more or pull away when there are many people in a room with him. People make much noise."

"Also," Suzi interjected, "people are visually very bombarding."

"Things begin to fit," Roby said with great excitement. "Now that you have said that, I remember watching him look directly at a small red truck we once gave him. Also at a doorknob. Also at the chrome leg of our dining room table. But, usually, he would never look directly at a person. In fact, he is much more relaxed alone. He seems confused when a lot of people move around him; it's his most difficult time. I never realized that before."

"And what could you know from that?" I asked.

Roby nodded. "That if we want to make contact or teach him something, it's best to do it without a lot of people around—one to one like we are doing here. Now I really understand about the bathroom."

"Beautiful," I commented. "Your observations, ultimately, are more important than ours. Roby, Francisca—it's you who will be putting this together. In a couple of days, you'll be on your own. You'll be watching for cues and deciding how to respond. You said you wanted to work with Robertito all day, every day. Okay. Your attitude is still the key because if you're loving and accepting, you'll also be a better observer. When we have expectations or need things to happen, we're distracted by our goals, by our fears. Being here moment to moment is essential."

"Look at all the professionals who told you Robertito was unresponsive," Suzi said. "Yet we've noticed many small statements...with his eyes, with his varied responses to being touched, with the imitation games. It's incredible, but some people discard such tiny bits of information as insignificant. But we know, if you're sensitive to all those cues, big and small, you create opportunities to make contact in a meaningful way."

"He's very into eating," I added. "You can use it—use everything! Anything! I'm not talking about bribing or conditioning. Each morsel of food can set the stage for possible eye contact. Our smiles, our warmth is just a way to say hello. He doesn't have to perform to eat. Yet when he takes the food, he might look past it and find our faces. And in that moment, we can be there saying something with our eyes, our expressions, our voices."

"Suppose he doesn't look?" Francisca asked.

"Then we wait," I suggested. "It makes all the difference in the world if we let it come from him. There's quite a distance to travel before we would try to teach him specific things like eating with forks and spoons."

"Yes, I see," Roby said. "You are talking about being there with him and for him."

"Even more than that. We're talking about going with him," I emphasized. "First: acceptance, contact, joining his world. Second: with our attitude and the responsive environment, we want to draw him out...have him be motivated to try. Then, and only then, would he be ready to really learn many different things. And there's a bonus. If he's motivated, in touch, finally watching us, then he'll learn much by himself."

"In a way," Suzi said, touching Francisca's hand, "it's trusting the child. And trusting yourself to trust the child."

"But he has very definite...ah, how, ah, can I say it properly?" Roby stuttered.

"It doesn't matter how you say it," I assured him.

"Well, he has a specific handicaps. The on-and-off hearing."

"I don't know if that's a handicap," I said, "as much as it's a way to take care of himself. He can certainly hear and see."

"What about memory?" Roby asked. "He can't remember from one moment to the next. Every day he looks at his hand like he's seeing it for the first time."

"I've noticed that, too," I said. "Especially with food, which we know he likes. He follows the food ferociously until it goes out of sight—behind my hand, in my pocket. Once it's out of sight, he doesn't pursue; it's as if he can't remember it or retain it without having it in front of him. It's a kind of memory dysfunction."

"There's nothing we can do for that," Roby concluded.

"Let's look at it in terms of motivation. Research illustrates that doctors will often predict that two people with identical brain damage resulting from strokes will never be able to talk or walk because the centers in the brain which control those functions have been destroyed. Yet, a year later, one stroke victim is speaking and moving about easily; the other is still mute and bedridden. When you ask for an explanation, the doctors say: 'Well, it's will-to-live.' In effect, the person who learned to speak and move again had to find new pathways in his brain, create new connections amid the debris. Since it required an incredible thrust, the person had to be highly motivated. And there's the key. Call it 'will-to-live' or motivation, but that's the power and energy we give ourselves to do what others might label as impossible. And that's what I'd love to see Robertito do. But you can't give him the spark. You can only be there, like a mid-wife, helping him find it within himself."

"Do you think he will find it?" Francisca asked.

"We can't really know that," I said. "We can only stay in touch with what we want for Robertito, for ourselves, and then do what we can to get what we want. Part of acceptance is allowing him to come our way or not come our way. Which leads me to a question. Francisca, how would you feel if Robertito never changed, never learned more than he knows at this moment?"

Jaime peered at me, his head cocked slightly to the side.

"Maestro?" I called.

"Ah, Señor Kaufman. I wondered why you were going back to that question."

"I'm not, Jaime, I'm going forward to that question," I said. Jaime became very pensive, then translated my words.

39

The Sotos looked at each other. Roby sighed. Francisca turned to me and said: "Still, it is a difficult question."

"Why?" I asked.

Her face became flushed. Her eyes reddened instantly. Tears flowed down her cheeks.

"What are you unhappy about?"

"Being a mother was something I wanted more than anything, more than anything else in the world. To love a child and have him love me. It's not..." Francisca stopped herself. She glanced at Roby, touched her fingertips to his face and said: "I know it's the same for him, too. We try to love Robertito and he rejects us."

"Do you believe that?"

"Isn't it obvious?" she said.

"How do you see it as obvious?" I asked.

"If I go to hug him or kiss him, he moves away."

"That's a good question," Roby interjected, leaning forward on the edge of his chair. "I think I always believed that's what his moving away meant. But if he's oversensitive, he could be protecting himself... like with the hearing. So when I call him, the switch isn't even turned on. Then, of course, he would not respond. And maybe, in some way, he's frightened." He rubbed his forehead nervously. "I guess I was so busy being hurt about being rejected, I never questioned why."

"And now?" I asked.

"And now," Roby said, "there are other possibilities. I can see it differently."

"Let me ask the question again. Do you believe moving away means rejecting?"

"I don't think I do any more," he answered.

"'Don't think' sounds like you're not sure."

Roby smirked self-consciously. "I guess I'm still deciding."

"About what?"

"About what this all means. If Robertito is doing what he can to take care of himself, that would be more than just okay with me. I would want him to be able to do that for himself." A huge grin radiated on his face.

"What are you smiling about?" Suzi asked.

"Oh, I guess, at how you assume things without ever questioning them. Somehow, I thought Robertito's action meant something about me... like if I were a better father, he'd let me touch him."

"Do you still believe that?"

40

"No," Roby affirmed.

"And you, Francisca?" Suzi asked.

"I can see how Robertito is trying to take care of himself...in the only way he knows how. I can accept that. It doesn't have to mean we're not good parents. But, Suzi, you know. I want to hug my son. I want to hold him close. I want him to hold me close."

"I know how much you want those things. I was once there, too," Suzi said gently. "But being unhappy about not having them is different than wanting them. What is it about not having that exchange of affection that's so painful?"

"I feel so empty."

"What do you mean?" Suzi asked.

"Like something is missing. There's supposed to be more."

"In what way?" I asked.

"Between a child and its mother," Francisca said, "there is a whole relationship which does not exist between Robertito and me. There should be so much more."

"Why do you believe that?"

"That's why I had a child."

"I understand what you wanted in having a child. But why do you believe there's supposed to be any more than there is right now with Robertito?"

"Because I want it!" she insisted.

"Why does wanting it mean it's supposed to happen?"

"I don't know. I don't know," Francisca said, shaking her head from side to side. "When I think about it, it sounds foolish. What is, is...but I still want so much more."

"That's what you want. But how do you feel about 'what is' right now?" I asked.

"Okay," she said with a touch of hesitation. "I feel clearer. You can really drive yourself crazy trying to make your life fit your dreams. I see that now."

"That's what we mean when we talk about expectations, shoulds and supposed to's," I added. "We get into needing things to be a certain way in order for us to be happy. If they're not, we're miserable. And so, while we look anxiously for what we don't have, we frequently miss what we do have."

"I'm proof of that," Francisca grinned, pointing to herself. "I have barely allowed myself to be excited about what's happened in these past two days because I'm still so concerned about Robertito's being toilet trained, feeding himself, talking. All the normal things a child is supposed to do."

Francisca stood up and turned away from us.

"What's the matter?" Roby said, jumping to his feet.

"I'm all right," she said. "I just realized something. In a way, I've never really loved Robertito for what he is; I've always loved him for what I hoped he would become, what I thought every little boy should become."

"That's not true," Roby insisted. "You've loved him and given him so much."

"Yes, I know, Roby, in a way that's true. I have given him everything I could. Tried to touch him, sing to him, talk to him, teach him and...and even discipline him. But maybe now, I can give him even more by accepting him, loving him as he is."

WEDNESDAY—The Third Day

The Sotos arrived at exactly nine o'clock. Before anyone could be seated, Francisca started talking very rapidly. Jaime put both hands up, trying to slow the avalanche of words. Suddenly, she started crying. Roby held her, then spoke quietly to Jaime, who turned to us.

"Señor Soto asks me to explain to you what happened last night in the car. Robertito and his mother sat in the back seat, which is usual. Always, the child pulls his arms into his body and falls asleep wrapped up in himself. Last night, quite specifically, he did something he has never done before. Never! Robertito edged across the seat until he sat right next to Francisca. Then, several seconds later, he rested his hand on his mother's arm, leaned his head against her shoulder and fell asleep."

Jaime, our dignified and very formal interpreter, drew a handkerchief from his breast pocket and put it to his eyes.

We all stood there. Together. In silence. Smiling through moist eyes for the mother who had waited four years for such a gesture from her child. Francisca hugged Suzi, then put her arms tightly around me. Her son walked easily across the room and headed for the land of toilets and tubs. Suzi kissed Jaime, then followed her student. The maestro beamed.

"I don't understnad," Francisca began. "You and Suzi have been working with Robertito and yet, he is different with us."

"Because you're different with him, Francisca," I said. "By working on yourself, you've been working with him. Each night, you've looked at some of your unhappiness and the beliefs which caused it. Every time you've changed a belief, you've changed your attitude and your feelings about yourself and your son. Your eyes, your smile, the touch of your hand, your body language—it all has begun to change. Remember, we're not talking about poses or strategy. When we're more accepting, Robertito knows. When we show him he can move us, he takes more risks."

"I don't know whether we're fully accepting yet," Roby admitted.

"Wherever you are now, your attitude has obviously made a difference already. We can explore it more tonight. Today, we'd like both of you to start working with Robertito. Okay?"

Roby and Francisca nodded their heads enthusiastically.

"You'll start right after lunch."

Eye contact with Robertito had improved dramatically. From time to time, he would look directly at us, sometimes for as long as eight to ten seconds. We noticed he stopped and started flapping more often in an effort to control us. He smiled much more easily. Though he still watched us peripherally most of the time, he seemed to understand we were there for him; without demands, without conditions. When Suzi out-flapped him, shaking her hands faster than he did, Robertito burst out laughing. They both giggled for several minutes.

Roby and Francisca took over the session in the afternoon. Suzi and I worked with them alternately. By early evening, we stood sweating behind the glass doors of the bathtub.

Robertito's spontaneous eye contact increased significantly all day. Francisca fed him dinner eye-to-eye. But we segmented half the meal for an experiment. Roby placed pieces of vegetables in all different parts of the room. Robertito watched carefully, then reached for the food as his father deposited it. One time, Roby put some carrots on a ledge too high for his son to see. At first, Robertito just stood immobile. The blank stare returned to his eyes. Then, very slowly, very methodically, he raised his arm and felt along the inside of the ledge. Within seconds, he stuffed the food into his mouth. A mind-boggling feat for this little boy. We could actually watch him develop before our eyes, actually witness his unfolding from moment to moment. His flowering made the movement with our son, Raun, suddenly seem like slow motion. It took eight weeks or seven hundred hours until we had developed observable eye contact. It took many months until Raun could retain objects in his mind without concretely seeing them.

Our excitement consumed us. We decided to try to make

the interaction between Robertito and his parents slightly more sophisticated. Roby placed plastic containers of juice and water in different parts of the room, out of his son's reach, but clearly within his line of vision. Robertito stood below the medicine cabinet and scratched on the mirror. He looked frantically at the can of yellow liquid beyond his reach.

"*Jugo. Jugo, Jugo*," his father repeated. "*Diga-me*, Robertito, *Jugo*." Allowing five seconds for any kind of response, he gave his mute son the juice. These games continued throughout the remainder of the day.

As Robertito became more attentive, wanting more from us and his parents, we tried to place ourselves in positions of use. Each time he indicated his desire for food, by grabbing or even by standing and looking at the objects, we came to his assistance immediately.

In the last moments of the session, Francisca introduced a simple stacking toy designed for six-month-old infants. Each time her son knocked it down, we rebuilt it. Just as we left the bathroom, Robertito bent down and placed one block on top of another. The roar of our applause and cheering chased him from the room.

After dinner, we continued the dialogues with Roby and Francisca. They explored more of their discomforts, unearthed more of their beliefs. We dealt with their questions about their own abilities to continue the program in Mexico. As they became more accepting and trusting of themselves, they began to realize they could have the answers if they allowed themselves to look freely.

THURSDAY—The Fourth Day

The morning session with Robertito signaled another movement. The Sotos accented physical contact, but not as a designed strategy. It evolved naturally during the first minutes they spent together. Roby imitated and tickled his son. Francisca hummed and stroked him while he stood stiffly like a figure cast in bronze. Then, quite casually, as if he had done it a thousand times, Robertito suddenly plopped into his mother's lap. Her mouth opened wide in delight. When she embraced him instinctively, he pulled away and jumped to his feet. Five minutes later, he dropped into her lap again. This time he remained seated for several minutes. Francisca handed her son insertion cups. He flapped the colorful plastic toys by the side of his head, then dropped them on the floor.

44

They repeated this exchange many times. We noticed Robertito's increased agility with his hands, though he still moved them with considerable awkwardness.

Roby presented lunch to his son in the same fashion as the previous dinner. He fed half to him eye-to-eye and placed the remaining food around the room. Little Robertito did not follow his father. Instead, he grabbed the juice container off the floor and held it. He put it to his mouth, but the cover cheated him of a drink. Roby moved to seize the can, but stopped himself and waited. His son walked up to him, dropping the container right in front of his feet. Roby gave him a drink quickly. Unwilling to assume Robertito knew what he did, he duplicated the situation with the water container. The little boy picked up the can and this time literally dropped it on his father's shoes.

After lunch, we coerced Jaime into taking a position in the bathtub. He declined at first, but the outcry from all of us persuaded him. The maestro leaned against the tile wall, watching the child he had grown to love.

Continual talking to Robertito about what we did and naming every item we touched formed an important aspect of the program. We suggested that Roby and Francisca shorten words and language forms. *Jugo* would become *ju*. *La música* would become *moo*. In other areas, such as expressions of love or excitement, they maintained the full richness of speech.

During early afternoon, we had a change of guard at our home. Sasha returned to the city and Elise, a dear and loving friend, joined to help. Her bubbling, new-age, astrology-oriented vision added another specialness to the texture of moods and energy at the house. Until our crew returned from school, she positioned herself outside the bathroom door. Later, she shared with us her endeavor to envision the room filled with white light so that Robertito might see an even clearer path.

We spent our last full evening together with the Sotos trying to lay to rest any remaining beliefs which caused them to be uncomfortable or disturbed about their son or themselves. Francisca discussed a problematic relationship she had with a dear friend. In the midst of a dialogue, she apologized for dealing with material she thought irrelevant to her son and our common purpose.

"Everything in your life is relevant, pertinent," I suggested. "How often have people expressed anger toward someone they loved as an outlet for the anger they actually felt

45

in another frustrating situation. And so, the frustrating situation or other problematic relationships affect other aspects of our lives. We're not compartmentalized, split into neat little sections. So, as we don't have set mechanics for helping Robertito, neither do we have set subjects for helping ourselves."

FRIDAY—The Fifth Day

Although we used our last day to continue observing and exploring, we also reviewed and embraced the events of the past week. The visible movement had been dramatic. The totally withdrawn and inner-focused little boy now sat on our laps and giggled in our faces. The child who never pursued anything or expressed his wants now found hidden objects and brought containers of juice and water to people in order to solicit their assistance. The staring, hand-flapping Robertito deviated from his well-entrenched patterns to hold cups and stack blocks. Though he continued to retain old behaviors, most of the time, his non-distractable commitment to self-stimulating activities, such as hand-flapping and rocking, had dwindled. Robertito had taken huge steps across the bridge, to meet us in a way that he had never done before in his life.

In this day's session, Francisca began by handing the insertion cups to her son. He turned them in front of his eyes, then tossed them across the room. Smiling, she gathered the plastic containers and inserted one into the other. Robertito, flapping slightly, watched from the corner of his eye. Quite often, he looked directly at his mother. She gave him the cups again. Robertito dropped them to the floor. They continued this exchange for almost twenty minutes with Francisca talking and demonstrating how one cup fit into another.

Roby served lunch in the usual manner; some pieces placed and others hidden around the room. They positioned the liquids within Robertito's easy reach. Their son brought the juice can to his father. "*Diga-me,* Robertito. *Ju. Ju,*" Roby repeated as he filled the glass. The little boy sat on the floor and rocked from side to side after the meal. Roby joined him. They both smiled...at each other.

Although the conversations were kept hushed and subdued, we noticed Robertito's growing tolerance for louder sounds. He also made a definite statement about his interest
46

in music by fingering the tape recorder until Francisca switched it on.

We ended the session in mid-afternoon and gathered in the living room. Bryn arrived minutes later from school. She kissed everyone in the room. Jaime blushed, flattered by her affection. Thea and Raun entered the house noisily. Within seconds, our son ran to Robertito and stroked his cheeks gently. Laughter bubbled throughout the room in response to Raun's infectious giggle.

Although Jaime still translated the conversation, we all talked together easily, intimately. With Thea on my lap, with Raun touching Robertito, with Bryn sitting ladylike beside Roby, with Suzi smiling warmly at Francisca, we had become, for these moments, a loving family of people sharing and enjoying one another.

After playing a game of "thumbs" with my son, I ushered the children into the den beside the kitchen. Bryn and Thea took charge of Robertito authoritatively. Returning to the living room, I smiled at Roby and Francisca, who had busily composed an elaborate list, complete with numbers and indentations. Reflections of a college outline.

"Why the list?" I asked.

"So we make sure we remember," Roby asserted.

"What is there to remember?"

Roby laughed. "Bears, are you serious?"

"Uh-huh."

"All the games we have established with Robertito, things to watch for, cues to catalogue."

"Is that all?" I asked.

"Yes, that is all," Roby said.

"How come you don't have to make lists of all the things we explored during our long evening sessions?"

"Those are part of us," he answered.

"Are you saying what we did with Robertito isn't part of you?" I questioned.

Grinning broadly, he said, "I...I guess so."

"Do you believe that?"

"No, I don't," he said. "Everything we've done here has become part of us." Roby put his pencil down.

"Roby, you can still make your list. I only wanted to clarify why you did it. Sometimes we can observe ourselves doing precisely the same behavior—one time from unhappiness, another time from our good feelings."

I took Suzi's hand and looked into her bright eyes, then

turned back to Roby and Francisca. "The reason I raised the questions about the list is because I want each of you to know you are your own best expert on yourself and your situation. Don't see the list as a guide to the future; at best, it's only a record of the past. If Suzi and I suggested turning left and, tomorrow, it seemed apparent to you to turn right, then trust yourself and turn right."

"There aren't any rules of conduct," Suzi interjected. "Only your choices, your decisons. And you can know better than anyone else, including us, what there is for you to do."

"I'd like to pose one more question, specifically to you, Francisca. It's one I've asked you almost every day. How would you feel if Robertito never changed from the way he is today, never learned anything more?"

She smiled broadly. "Bears, when you asked me that on the first day I met you, I became so upset, so angry. I wanted to run out of your house and never, never come back. How could I have traveled over three thousand miles to be asked such a crazy question? I thought there was only one possible answer...that, of course, I had to feel terrible if he didn't improve." A long, relaxed sigh echoed from her throat. "Now I can say it would be okay. I never realized by not accepting Robertito as he is, I was disapproving of him."

"It's like saying to a person it's not okay to be who you are; you must be something else to be acceptable," Suzi commented.

"Yes, I understand," Francisca said. "Although I want more for Robertito and we will work for more, I can see my son clearer now and can enjoy him now...really enjoy him. Oh, God, I feel so much easier with myself." Her face glowed; her eyes emanated a peacefulness which had never been apparent before.

Bryn charged into the living room wide-eyed. She held her index finger in front of her lips, hushing our conversation, and motioned for us to follow quickly. We gathered at the kitchen door. A bottle of juice balanced precariously near the edge of the counter. On tiptoes, little Robertito stretched his arms as high as possible, but missed his mark. A strange, throaty sound oozed from him. And then it became apparent. "*Ju. Ju. Ju.*" Francisca laughed and cried as she quickly poured the juice into a plastic glass.

Raun pulled on Suzi's pants. "Mama, can I have juice, too?"

"I'll give him some," Thea offered.

When we turned to re-enter the living room, I saw Roby

sitting by himself, his face flushed. Francisca sat beside him quietly, then talked softly to Jaime. "Francisca," he said, "believes Roby would like to be alone." The Sotos rose from the couch.

"Tell them to stay. We'll be in the other room." I asked Elise and the children to keep Robertito in the kitchen while Suzi and I sat in the den. A man's muffled sobbing filtered through the walls.

Within the next hour, Robertito used two more words in order to communicate his wants.

Later, we reassembled in the living room. Roby and the maestro completed a rather intense conversation. Jaime directed his words toward me.

"Señor Soto would like to say something, but he is concerned you might get insulted."

I laughed. "Tell him I doubt it. If I get insulted, I do that to myself. And since I don't want to feel uncomfortable or upset, there's no risk. Let him say what he would like."

Jaime spoke again for Roby. "The Sotos would like to pay you. They have calculated that you have worked with them and their son for almost eighty hours during the past week. They realize you and Suzi had to stop many other things in order to do this. They wish to compensate you for teaching them."

Leaning forward, I put my hands on top of Roby's and Francisca's hands. I searched their sensitive faces. "First, I'm not insulted. I understand your intentions. If we wanted to be paid, I would have told you that in the beginning. We chose to be here, to help. I don't know if we could always do this, but we wanted to do it now. We've been enriched by knowing you, your son, and witnessing his movement. It has been a very beautiful week, a very complete week. Your joy stands as our payment."

Roby nodded, acknowledging my words. Francisca's eyes sparkled. Caring thoughts passed from person to person in the silence. Suddenly, the blaring horn of a taxi invaded the room. Jaime excused himself, stepping outside to ask the driver to wait. Roby checked his passports and plane tickets.

Suzi fought back tears as she hugged Roby, Francisca and little Robertito. I embraced each of them as did our children. Then I turned to Jaime, refusing to say my good-by to him with a formal handshake. As I reached to hug him, he reached to hug me. We patted each other on the back and laughed.

"Señor Kaufman, I am slow at changing, but this has been

a great learning experience for me. On the day we met, you asked me to call you Bears. I am ready now."

"Peace, Jaime," I smiled.

"And to you, Bears. *Adios*," he said. Then the maestro embraced Suzi.

"I have no more words," Roby whispered. "My feelings are too strong for my words." He bowed his head and led his family down the walk to the waiting car.

Chapter 2

The infantile, siren-like whine of the little boy penetrated every room in the house. The rapid tap of feet prancing through the hall, then into the living room, then back again, provided a base accompaniment to the bizarre two-note symphony.

Alicia listened intently as she had always listened, except, this time, without any panic visible on her face. She munched on refried beans and tacos while on her lunch break from the store, Roby's store. Her eyes scanned her sister's home. She admired the dark wood table, the bureau chiseled with markings of ancient Spain, the old iron pitcher placed neatly on a doily, viewing them almost as if for the first time, freer now in Francisca's home to smile and to enjoy.

"Eee-o, eee-o, eee-o," Robertito droned. His verbal persistence filled the dining room, distracting Alicia despite the walls between them. Then she heard Francisca: "Eee-o, eee-o, eee-o." Clear sounds. Happy sounds. She started to laugh, sitting there, alone, feeling released, if only momentarily, from the weight of Robertito's illness. Maybe this is the way...maybe.

Suddenly, Robertito wandered into the room flapping a piece of tissue paper rapidly at the side of his head. Francisca accompanied him, holding her strip of tissue paper in front of her eyes, pulsating it in the same rhythm as her son. When she saw Alicia, she automatically straightened her blouse with her free hand and smiled awkwardly.

"*¡Hola!*, Robertito," Alicia said boisterously as she fumbled with her napkin, raising it to the side of her head and flapping it. But the little boy looked at her for only a couple of seconds, then his glazed and vacant eyes indiscriminately floated from side to side in their sockets. Nevertheless, she persisted. "It's my turn, Francisca," she chimed, mimicking the child.

Francisca watched her son and sister. So much had changed since her visit to New York. She couldn't believe the difference she felt inside. The weird, unearthly noises that had kept her in a state of controlled panic for years now became signals for imitation games. The strange, frantic body motions, the rocking and flapping that had confused and frightened her, now became opportunities to make contact. Strange ideas for her; difficult to digest. And yet, this new vision enabled her to recapture the old strength. Before Robertito, Francisca had been the rock. Before Robertito, the world made sense. As she watched her sister, especially her sister, the embarrassment of the past five years suddenly disturbed her. She had been groomed to respond and succeed. Tall. Statuesque. Athletic. Talented. Attractive. Competitive. But all the standards had collapsed around her in dealing with her son. She felt like a rabbit born in the land of wolves. What ingredient was missing? She had tried so hard, so desperately hard to please, to be useful, to be effective. The role of mother meant more to her than all the childhood triumphs, but the specifics of motherhood eluded her, at least, until now.

She straightened her hair, not as an act of vanity, but in an effort to assert control. Be strong! She had played that same scenario all her life. For Francisca Soto, some things had not changed, especially the demands she made of herself. Alicia's laughter diverted her. Robertito and her sister sat on the floor, rocking together.

"Okay, don't do too much, Alicia...I'll take over now," Francisca declared like an overprotective mother. But her sister shook her head and continued flapping the paper. "A few minutes more, Alicia, and that's it." Francisca could not explain the incredible tenaciousness of her sister, but she admired it. Be strong or, at least, act strong. The fact that Alicia, once crippled by rheumatoid arthritis, could bend and move with Robertito reaffirmed that credo. How else could her sister have survived an adolescence marred by pain and self-consciousness? How else could she have endured operation after operation? Was the illusion of strength the same as strength? All of her life, Francisca had suppressed the tears with a forced smile as if the flaunting of such a mask, itself, had special healing powers. Alicia had kept her head high in the face of a crippling disease, but Francisca, when put to the test with Robertito, had broken like a weak and sad old woman.

Francisca vowed not to cry. Other people cried. She vowed not to lose her way. Other people lost their way. A pulse pounded at her temples. These were the same promises she had made before her marriage... and she did cry and did lose her way. She wanted desperately to accept her vulnerability. Her experiences with Suzi and me in New York opened that door. But Francisca refused to forgive herself totally. If she said okay to her weakness, would she get weaker?

She focused her attention back to Alicia and her son. Their happiness in performing an absurd, incomprehensible ritual astounded her. Everyone had caught the fever. Nothing had changed, not really... except, of course, their attitude. Again, Francisca pounded herself lightly. She viewed the venting of emotions as an almost unpardonable diversion from helping her son. What had she been doing for over four years if her son could change in five days in New York? Rather than answer the question, she smothered it. Be strong! You can do it now! A scared little girl suddenly whimpered deep inside. She knew she had to let go, even more, but she couldn't. Francisca knelt down and hugged her sister tightly. Hold on! Please hold on to me! But the words which surfaced in her mind never found their way into her throat.

Francisca's eyes riveted on the child who stood at the center of her world. "I accept you. I do!" she insisted. An attitude which had evolved naturally suddenly had the unmistakable characteristic of a commandment. A rule supplanted her inclination. Her head jerked back slightly, throwing the hair off her forehead. She managed a full smile, then resumed her role as mentor to her son and followed him down the hallway toward the bedrooms.

Alone, again, with her food, Alicia let her hand fall slowly as she continued to jerk the paper spastically. Was that the right movement? she wondered. She wished she had been in New York with them, to see and understand what apparently revolutionized Francisca and Roby's perspective about their son. When she had been sick, the problems were concrete, capable of being itemized and described. The remedies were within familiar boundaries: operations, medication, physical therapy. For Robertito, the concept of illness barely applied; his dilemma, though couched in concrete symptoms, had an unknowable, frightening quality about it. The solution often appeared more bizarre than the problem.

And now this—watching her sister do all those things which the doctors had tried to stop; in fact, moving in a direction contradictory to their advice. Alicia wanted to stay open, but she couldn't deny the strange sensation quivering across her skin as she watched Francisca and Robertito on the floor in the hallway; four hands twisting in funny, repetitive gestures and the endless drone of eee-o, eee-o, eee-o.

She never hesitated when Francisca asked for her assistance, though both of them knew what it meant for her to leave Las Mochis, the small, quaint city hugging the Pacific Ocean on Baja California. Francisca had left when she was only nineteen, marrying Roby after a carefully supervised courtship during which time they were never allowed to be alone.

Being in her sister's house required Alicia to adjust her vision. Francisca had become very cosmopolitan. Though her skin stretched tight across her strong and attractive face, her eyes had grown old. It scared Alicia to imagine what her sister had seen.

As she opened the refrigerator to prepare lunch for Robertito and his mother, she was confronted with a new challenge. Obviously, someone had cleared the shelves of all recognizable foods and filled the bins with unfamiliar items from a San Diego health food store. Now she remembered; her sister said they had learned to consider everything which influenced Robertito, including food, all part of a more holistic view of their son's world.

"I'll leave two sandwiches for you," she called to her sister.

"Oh, Alicia, thank you," Francisca yelled back, her voice strained and surprisingly wispy.

Alicia stepped into the street, locking the door behind her. Somehow, she and her sister had switched positions. She had always been in need of help; now it was Francisca's turn. Illness and disability had been Alicia's constant companions

54

for so many years; now Francisca's whole world was enshrouded in it. What a cruel joke the universe had played on her sister...to have given her a son, damaged, as she herself had been delivered damaged, but with one essential difference. God had given her, Alicia envisioned, tools for her battle. Robertito came empty-handed.

Roby couldn't move fast enough. Distrusting the leather soles of his shoes, he continually denied his impulse to run. Every minute, every second counted. With Alicia tending the store, he could use this extra hour before his session with Robertito to try to finish constructing what would soon become his son's workroom. He kept remembering Robertito in our bathroom in New York; the limited non-distracting environment in which he had watched his son make his first gestures in contacting the world outside of himself. He could still hear his son's guttural, barely distinguishable cry for juice.

He catapulted himself up the front steps, then fumbled with his keys. He rocked his head slightly in anticipation of the most exciting event in his day—seeing his wife and son. Once inside, he tiptoed through the house, finally locating his family in Robertito's room. He pushed the door slightly ajar until he could see them clearly as they flapped the curtains together. Robertito jumped off the bed and paced the floor rapidly. His mother followed; smiling, laughing and talking constantly throughout the entire period.

For a minute, she stopped speaking. Her voice, which had created a gentle melody continually expressing her acceptance of his world, was replaced by the echo of their pounding feet on the linoleum floor. She tried to ignore her memory of New York, when Robertito had been more responsive. He would come around again, she reassured herself. She had to be patient, had to wait. Realizing she had drifted, walking beside her son momentarily like a zombie, she refocused on his angelic face, found the softest part in herself as Suzi and I had suggested and felt the surge of words flow from her lips once again.

Roby stared at his wife, never noticing the two minutes of tension apparent in her face. He nodded his head and confirmed to himself that in spite of his son's moment-to-moment responses, this was the way...it must be the way; everything else seemed so barbaric and so cold.

From a distance of ten feet, he examined every familiar feature of Francisca's face; twelve years since that festive wedding at her house; twelve years since their honeymoon in Mexico City and Guadalajara; twelve years since he first saw her naked with her hands covering her breasts and a silly look of embarrassment on her face. She had grown more beautiful, the slight lines at the corners of her eyes accenting her added warmth and depth. She was more special than he had ever imagined; through her, words like love and family had come alive. And he felt blessed to have his son; the sounds and flapping no longer signs of terror and tragedy. He wondered whether they would be able to retain all they learned in New York. It did work, he assured himself; when he explored and let go of the fear, the anxiousness, the judgments, he felt more relaxed, more accepting, more loving. It had been so easy, almost too easy—like his feeling about Francisca; sometimes scared to lose what he believed he hardly deserved.

Suddenly, Francisca noticed him. She beamed with a new energy. They waved to each other, neither wanting to disrupt the session, to diminish, even for a second, their pilgrimage to meet their son. They exchanged hugs and embraces through the tips of their fingers. Roby watched for several more minutes, then turned away. He felt filled, like a mountain river surging with the tides of melting snow; not depleted or exhausted by his son; not devastated by the life of this, perhaps, imperfect creature. He recognized that throughout their searching, he had never felt so confident, though, admittedly, some fears and doubts still lingered. He believed if they had had more time, more Option sessions, they would have cleared the path completely. At least for now, they had turned the corner, seen another way.

After changing into old clothes, Roby entered the bathroom, equipped with tools and lumber. Both he and Francisca had assessed the room as being too large; so, on the first night of their return home, he started to build a new wall and door, significantly diminishing the square footage of open area. But his lack of experience in construction slowed the process. Today, he moved with a new sense of urgency. He, too, had noticed that Robertito had been more responsive at our house in New York, deducing that their lack of a confined, nondistracting work area was the problem. Roby used the hammer more precisely. He drove each nail with two strikes, rather than the customary six necessary two days before. "This is for you, Robertito," he chanted silently in his head every time he swung his hammer.

Roby backed away from the doorway and celebrated that

moment of completion as the muscles in his shoulders eased from their state of readiness. In the afternoon, they would begin to use this area as their workroom. Perhaps his son, like Raun Kaufman, would be reborn in the confinement of the bathroom. He drew support and encouragement from such parallels. Perhaps, he teased himself, he had avoided sectioning one of the bedrooms for that very reason. No shame. No embarrassment. He used every piece of ammunition at his disposal to bolster his and his wife's confidence.

Twenty minutes later, Roby and Robertito sat together beside the bathtub, rocking side to side with their legs stretched across the floor. Roby had carefully set out several toys; an insertion box filled with different shapes, a five-piece wooden puzzle board with knobs; plastic boxes which fit one within the other. During those moments when his son stopped his repetitious behaviors, his isms, Roby would try to introduce a game. Each time he gave him a puzzle piece or geometric shape, his son would flap it by the side of his head.

As they continued to rock, Roby moved his hand very slowly until it came within inches of his son's thigh, then he set his fingers down on the boy's leg. Robertito looked at his father's hand and became very still. For four incredible seconds neither of them moved; then Robertito jumped to his feet and began twirling his fingers in front of his eyes.

"Four seconds, Robertito, that's very good," he said softly to his son as he rose to his knees and began twirling his own fingers, duplicating the activity with great precision. "Four seconds, my son...that's a beginning." The bathroom would make the difference. It would. He wanted to tell everybody; it would happen here.

At eight o'clock, Francisca slipped into the room, armed with her son's pajamas and a diaper. She had combed her hair and put on fresh lipstick. A light line of eyeliner had been expertly applied to her eyelids. Francisca not only trusted such formalities, but counted on them. She relied on the dignity she could see and assumed other people did the same. Her eyes scanned the bathroom. She smiled self-consciously, kissed her husband, then dove for her son.

Roby sat on the edge of the bathtub, watching his wife gently wrestle Robertito in an effort to remove his pants. Both he and Francisca laughed at their son's antics; twisting, turning, curling and rolling in a casual, rhythmic manner; no sense of urgency or malice in his soft, elastic form. Although he never once looked at her, Robertito's face suggested

57

a tacit approval of her efforts; almost as if he wanted what his mother wanted without really understanding how to co-operate; her signal misrouted chaotically through his neu-rological system, never creating a picture before his mind's eye which he could decipher; responding bodily, like an infant, to her hands. A big sigh filled the room as she threw her arms in the air, then let them fall heavily to her side. She picked at her tooth unconsciously, squinted her eyes and drifted to a place deep inside herself. Suddenly, her expression changed, a smirk exploding onto her face. She whipped a piece of toilet paper off the roll and handed it ceremoniously to her son...

"*Voilà*," she said proudly, using one of the few French words she knew; unaware that, at best, she had grossly mispro-nounced the word, muddling it with her very heavy Spanish accent.

Robertito grabbed the paper hungrily, ripped it quickly into long, thin strips and, using both hands, flapped them in front of his huge staring eyes. Having successfully diverted his attention, she undressed him; his body limp and pliable to her touch. A clever ruse, she thought, having beaten him at his own game.

"Go with him, not against him." My words had stayed with her. Two weeks ago, before their visit to our home, she would have fought with Robertito, depriving him of the paper while forcing his arms and legs into the garments. He would have whined and cried, kicked and pushed until the task had been completed. Then he would have huddled himself into a fetal position. Francisca would try to touch him; then hesitate, an apology pasted on her lips; not knowing another way to talk or touch, feeling impotent and abusive in her attempts to love her son.

"He's so peaceful now," she said aloud, "so gentle and so peaceful."

As she led Robertito out of the bathroom, she knocked against a shelf which Roby had not yet secured. A vitamin bottle tumbled to the floor. The plastic container splintered into several pieces, scattering hundreds of little pills all over the room.

"You go, I'll take care of it," Roby assured her as he bent down. The scene seemed so familiar, too familiar, as he re-membered another incident, one of many, when he was ex-actly his son's age.

His father, a stern and autocratic man, had five illegiti-

58

mate children with his mother; this being one of several different families he sired. He viewed his children as a source of labor; denying them education and friends so that one day they would work hard for him in his store or grainery. One morning, Roby played with several dishes in the kitchen while his mother prepared lunch. When his father appeared, he scolded both his common-law wife and the child, quickly returning with a ten-pound sack of rice which he spilled on the floor. He then commanded Roby to pick up the pieces. The little boy filled his hands with the rice in order to return it to the burlap bag. The old man kicked little Roby's arms, throwing him off his feet. Terrified, Roby tried to camouflage his trembling hands as his father's face flushed and his mouth stretched wide while he screamed, instructing the boy to pick up, under the threat of severe punishment, each grain of rice individually...one by one. Roby worked diligently throughout the entire day until he completed the job, his four-year-old mind unable to digest the brutality and unwilling to accept it. His mother's pained, blood-shot eyes watching from the side of the room frightened him almost as much as his father's aggression.

As he gathered his son's vitamins, he looked around the bathroom, thankful for his home. He could still see the old man; thick white hair, strong, tall, light-complexioned and dressed in one of his many white suits and matching white leather shoes; a polished, studied and misleading exterior. When he died, over forty children descended on the little village where he lived, seeking to grab their portion of his money and his businesses. But Roby made no claims. He had run away just after his eleventh birthday to live with his brother. He never returned to the house or the village. At seventeen, he went off by himself and lived on his own, trying to maintain some contact with his brothers, each of whom had also run away and were now scattered throughout Mexico.

What seemed so natural for his own father, the cruelty and the abuse, seemed so foreign to him. The pain and loneliness of his youth had softened with the years, but two other specific incidents remained vividly imprinted in his mind.

Just before his eighth birthday, when a rain and wind storm hit the village, his father forced him to join him on the roof of the house to fix several loose tiles. As he shivered in the cold, frightened by the wind which threatened to upset his balance, he watched and listened to the old man instruct

59

him in the art of tile repair. Roby tried to remember all the instructions, but details were muddled. After resetting one piece, the old man left the roof, tossing the tools and materials in front of his son. The young boy dragged the metal cases across the slippery tiles until he settled directly beside another loose piece. He tried to cement it back into place several times, but it would not hold, constantly sliding out of its position. His father peeked his head above the roof line, immediately becoming furious with his son's apparent incompetence. He climbed up the ladder with a raised fist, telegraphing his intention. Rather than walk carefully along the supported ledges, he plunged across the tiles, breaking the surface with his forceful step and falling halfway through the roof. Dangling precariously between floors, he screamed obscenities at Roby, who quickly scooted off the roof and disappeared for two days. When he returned, tired and hungry, his father beat him with a belt.

A year later, when the old man escalated his expectations for more services from his young son, he sent the boy into the fields to bring back a bull. "Don't come back unless you come back with the bull, you hear!" Those instructions lived in Roby's memory. He hiked several miles, crossing roads and wading through muddy creeks. Finally, he located the bull grazing on a sun-baked knoll; Roby was fully aware it would be impossible to approach the animal without being seen. His fingers rubbed the outer skin of the lasso draped across his chest. Impossible, he reasoned, he could never hold the bull; his slight figure was dwarfed by the heavy, muscular, black-skinned hulk. Tie him to a tree. That's it, he would tie him to a tree. Gingerly placing one foot in front of another, he circled the animal. The cluster of trees behind them would serve as a perfect corral. He filled his lungs, closed his eyes and charged the bull, yelling and waving the rope. The animal barely lifted his head. Roby kept coming, his high-pitched screams ricocheting off the rocks in the field. The bull eventually turned his full concentration on the young boy just at the moment Roby opened his eyes and faced his prey directly. Eyes met eyes. Breathless and frightened, Roby stopped short, his legs frozen, his pulse racing, his chest rising and falling uncontrollably. The boy turned away and started to count. As soon as he recited the number ten, he bit hard on his lip, shifted his body and pushed himself, approaching the animal slowly this time. Surmising the child was not a threat, the bull returned to his casual meal.

Once Roby had come within four feet of his prey, he slowed his pace and inched his way closer and closer. The thick neck and soil-stained horns took his breath away. He began to feel dizzy, but clenched his teeth, fighting the lightheaded feeling. With great precision, he slipped the noose of the rope over the animal's head and then ran in the opposite direction at full speed. Having first wrapped the rope twice around his waist, the impact of his body hitting the end of the cord snapped the noose tightly in place as he had planned. But the same impact also threw him head over heels, unraveling the rope from his waist.

The bull darted across the field, dragging Roby's lasso. Realizing the animal could choke himself with the rope, Roby pursued on foot. He had never intended to harm the creature. After crossing several acres, the bull lumbered into a clumsy walk, finally returning his attention to the grass.

More desperate than before, the boy approached again, grabbing the rope. The bull, responding to the tug at his neck, began to trot once again across the open field. This time, Roby hung on, running until he could run no more. Even as his legs began to sag and buckle beneath him, he refused to give up. His fingers locked around the cord. The animal dragged him almost a quarter of a mile, burning his hands and scraping the skin off the exposed parts of his body. Finally, his strength gone, he let go.

Eventually, Roby and the bull were rescued by a group of farmers and returned home. In the midst of his mother's cleaning the cuts and burns on her son's body, the old man arrived, interrupting the emergency treatment for only several minutes—time enough to drag the boy into the yard and give him a beating.

Roby shook his head uncomfortably. He wanted to eradicate all the details which still danced in his head; the grimace plastered perpetually on his father's face, the anguish indented in the lines around his mother's eyes, the cold, bare, unforgiving walls of their stone home. What had he lacked to have brought out such rage in his father? What deficiency in him supported his mother's eternal passivity? For years, he had scrutinized all his actions, all his motives, waiting to uncover the hidden dishonor. At first, he feared becoming like his father, as if the anger and violence might have been transmitted through the blood. Then he suspected the persistent whack of the belt had compromised and depleted his strength. But then, after courting Francisca for a year, he discovered within himself other motives and other sensibilities never permitted to surface in his early childhood.

He flipped the light switch in the bathroom and stood alone in the darkness. Twenty-nine years had not dimmed those memories. The questions still haunted him, even now... questions which he thought had been laid to rest.

Chapter 3

Since their return to Mexico, Francisca and Roby lived for their special time in the bathroom. They made requests, through church groups, local organizations and public service radio broadcasts for people willing to participate in their program to reach their special child. The urgency for help escalated as Roby's business demanded more of his time, especially during the busy season. Despite Alicia's input, his availability decreased. Francisca assumed more and more responsibility for the day-to-day sessions.

By the end of the third week, Robertito became more irritable, crying when he saw food. Francisca grew frantic in her attempt to feed him more rapidly. She wanted to intercept what she supposed was his fleeting unhappiness, remembering his first year of life.

For the first fifteen days following his birth, Robertito had been very quiet and unassuming. Then, on the sixteenth day, he began to cry day and night. Nothing soothed him. The doctor reassured Francisca, but she became petrified, plagued by a feeling of inadequacy not easily dismissed. Though she cuddled him in her arms, loved him, even cried with him, he never seemed satisfied.

Now, at four, his tearless, inexplicable sobbing on the bathroom floor awakened that old horror. Fears tensed the muscles in the back of her neck. "Don't judge it," she commanded. "This doesn't mean anything." Nevertheless, she felt herself faltering. She would get through it for her son. As he devoured food, the contorted expression disappeared from his face, leaving his features smooth and undisturbed.

She watched him chew and felt drawn again to the past, to another face; more peaceful, more relaxed, more infantile. The crying during Robertito's first month of life stopped as abruptly as it had started, replaced by an incredible calmness which enveloped every aspect of his behavior. When she picked him up, he never reached for her or grabbed her hands. He never indicated a desire to leave his crib or have his diaper changed. She did not question his passivity until the crying began again during his fourth month and continued, without interruption, for almost sixteen weeks.

When it stopped this time, Francisca and Roby cherished every moment, every expression of contentment on their son's face. His increasing lethargy didn't disturb them. During his ninth month, he said five words clearly. Yet, he never recognized his parents; there were no smiles when they appeared in his room. One person seemed interchangeable with the next.

At eleven months, he stopped talking and preferred to be alone, growing insensitive to sound, no longer responding to his name. His godfather, a pediatrician, noted the peculiar lack of desire for contact and decided to give the baby a complete physical examination. The physician found no signs of any pathology, but concluded there could be a problem of deafness. Francisca disagreed. Though Robertito did not respond to his name or the door slamming shut, he came running for food when she cooked with utensils in the kitchen. She also noted a similar response when he heard the unraveling of a candy wrapper.

Neither the Sotos nor the pediatrician recognized that little Robertito had begun his slide behind an invisible wall. As with other similar children, whether they be born in Japan, India, China, Russia, England, Sweden or the United States, this child's inconsistent signs and peculiar symptoms confused and misled even professionals. Robertito would behave, ultimately, in specific, bizarre ways, exactly duplicating the specific, bizarre behaviors of other autistic children around the world...as if he and they shared the same genes or had, indeed, come from another planet.

At fourteen months, he broke a toy helicopter, then isolated the propeller carefully from the other sections and proceeded to spin the blades, hour after hour, like an accomplished expert. He glanced at people peripherally, rather than directly, no longer responsive to physical contact or affection. At eighteen months, an ear-nose-throat specialist insisted Robertito could hear. The physician admitted, however, that he could not adequately assess the extent of that hearing. Two other pediatricians told them to wait another year until their child was more "testable." During this period, Robertito began to stare at his hands and fingers, often flexing them at the side of his head.

Francisca and Roby brought their son to the United States just after his second birthday. Francisca cried often now, wanting to understand but dreading the answers.

A hearing specialist in San Diego confirmed the child's ability to receive and respond to sounds through a complex series of tests. He suggested a psychiatrist at another hospital. The next physician diagnosed Robertito as autistic with a dismal and dark prognosis. Both Francisca and Roby rejected the diagnosis, refusing to believe their only child had a hopeless condition.

They shut themselves off from the world for the next year. They kept Robertito cloistered, away from the scrutiny of others. They lavished attention on him, trying to convince themselves he would develop normally. But Robertito's strange and different behavior increased: spinning objects for longer periods of time, rocking even more frantically than before, pushing people away without ever having any eye contact.

Francisca tried unsuccessfully to distract him with toys. At times, she fought with him, trying, as gently as possible, to dislodge the objects he flapped. When she hid the strings and strips of paper he twirled in front of his eyes, he became hyperactive. Most of all, Francisca dreaded the trips to the market, where she shrank from the eyes of other women, an easy target for their whispers and disapproving glances. They viewed her son as more than just an oddity. They pulled their own children close to them as if Robertito might infect them with his terrible disease.

Both Francisca and Roby tried desperately to hold on to

their dreams. Roby had wanted to give his son what his father had never given him, yet this little boy withdrew from his contact and his love. Francisca wanted a normal child for herself and for Roby, believing that in order to be happy, Robertito would have to become normal. She loved him passionately, trying to protect both of them from a reality she could not accept, from a future she did not dare contemplate.

One night, after almost a year of silence, a year of avoiding discussions about Robertito, Francisca and Roby faced each other across the dinner table.

"I want to talk about Robertito," she said, almost shouting her request, refusing to let her fear silence her any longer. "I want to talk about Robertito," she said again as the tears flowed.

Roberto Soto took his wife's hands and squeezed them as tight as he could. He felt his arms trembling as he, too, gave in to the pain and disappointment. He had waited until she was ready, not wanting to force her to look until she had decided. He had waited, holding back his own awareness, hiding the books on schizophrenia which he had begun to read six months before. She tapped the top of his hand as she gained control over herself. She smiled sadly through the wetness of her eyes.

"Roby, I've been unkind and stupid. I knew over a year ago, in San Diego, that the doctor was right. I just wanted the illness to go away." Again, she broke down. Roby could not find the words. He comforted her with the strength of his hands.

"You've been a good mother," he insisted. "Mommy, you have," he repeated, addressing her with an endearment he never had the opportunity to use as a child. "Robertito couldn't have better than you." He knew she had delayed, as he had too... but he also knew she needed the time to come to this place.

"We have to get help," she said. "We just have to." She held her breath for several seconds, then continued. "I don't know what to do anymore. I thought it would be so easy, so beautiful to be a mother. But it's not, not with Robertito." She held her hands in front of her face.

"Are you okay?" he asked.

She shook her head. "I will be strong. I will," she declared, more for her own ears than for Roby's. At that moment, she decided to suppress her fears and doubts in an effort to deal with the situation. Though she would cry many times in the next year, she would wait until that visit to New York before permitting herself to face any of the ghosts of the future.

They began their journey with the help of a close friend who suggested a child psychiatrist in Guadalajara. The doctor sounded hospitable on the phone, but when they described Robertito's symptoms in detail, he, suddenly, asserted that he only dealt with adults and abruptly ended the conversation.

Another physician gave them an interview in the same city. He told the Sotos that these children were a lost cause. He added, hesitantly, that all the other autistic youngsters he had seen were far more advanced than Robertito.

"Did we wait too long?" Roby asked.

The doctor leaned back in his chair and peered at the little boy rocking against the wall. "No. No, Señor Soto. It doesn't really matter. These children never come out of it." His casual manner infuriated Francisca, though she remained silent. Her son did matter.

Three days later they flew to Mexico City, marking the first step in depleting their life's savings, which they had accumulated by working together, side by side, for twelve years in their store.

Francisca stared through the dusty window of the taxi as it sped them from the airport to their first appointment in the capital. She and Roby made love for the first time in this city. They had walked arm in arm down the great boulevards and chased each other down narrow, ancient streets. She remembered everything, including the wine and the laughter; especially the laughter. One drink, that's all, and her serious, very serious Roby would become giddy and silly. She loved that little boy part of him which he kept under tight harness. She turned to him now and watched him watching his son. Had his soft, sensitive eyes grown sadder? Was she still pretty? Did he feel cheated in their marriage because of their son? Had she, in fact, failed in some unknowable way? She tried to block the questions. She wanted to give Roby everything he never had. Especially children. Especially a son. Francisca looked at Robertito twirling his fingers and humming in an eerie, high-pitched voice. What happened? She would do anything to make it right. Anything. His little fingers fluttered in front of her face, then tapped repetitiously on the back of the driver's seat. She tried to touch his arm, but he pulled away.

When they arrived at the clinic, they visited with a physician specializing in neurological rehabilitation. The doctor classified Robertito an autistic and instituted an elaborate program in patterning. This process, based on the thesis that the child has missed some important developmental stage, seeks to have him relive various developmental milestones—beginning with the birth experience. After Francisca and Roby watched the therapists wrap their son in a blanket and drag him across the room, ignoring his screams in their effort to simulate a womb experience, they discontinued coming to the clinic.

Several days later, the Sotos met with a team of neurologists and psychiatrists who suggested they could, perhaps, work with "the boy" and facilitate some elemental responses. Francisca asked about the rationale of their program. Complex and confusing medical terms rendered their answer unintelligible. Could they observe the program? One physician indicated that would be impossible. Under those conditions, Francisca and Roby declined their input.

A child psychologist prescribed a behavior modification program for Robertito. They observed her staff work at a nearby hospital. The interaction with the children appeared so mechanical, so robotized, so unloving. The most advanced child had learned to feed himself and stack four blocks on top of each other. The somber expression on his face clouded his accomplishment for the Sotos. After disengaging from the strict ritual of the session, he never looked directly at anyone, never once initiated human contact as he wandered around the room aimlessly. Francisca and Roby wanted to search further, though growing more sensitive to the passing weeks and months as they traveled from clinic to clinic.

At a hospital in Pueblo, a doctor, after extensively examining their son, said the boy was possibly a victim of an undetected case of encephalitis, but certainly was not autistic. He recommended an associate physician and college professor in the United States who directed programs at two major institutions. This man, in turn, disagreed with the recommending doctor, positively identifying Robertito as severely retarded and autistic with only a possible complication of encephalitis. He put the child through his sixth psychiatric work-up in addition to ordering an EEG (brain scan). The evaluation disturbed him visibly. Robertito's brain waves in the left frontal lobes were weak and intermittent, suggesting irreversible brain damage. Since this area controlled cognition, memory, language and communication, he asserted

68

there could be no hope for speech, thinking and processing of information.

The room began to spin for Francisca. The acid in her stomach gurgled and backed up into her throat. She steadied herself on the chair. Too numb to shout or feel pain, she turned inward. The room disappeared. Sounds no longer penetrated. In the privacy of her mind, she saw herself as a little girl again. She raced through a vineyard, trying to find her home. "Mama, Mama," she cried, but no one answered. "Please, Mama, please...where are you?"

Francisca's lips never moved. Her eyelids blinked only once. Beads of sweat dotted her forehead as her hands clenched the arms of the chair.

Roby nudged his wife. "Mommy?"

She looked at him through melancholy eyes. Somewhere deep inside she heard a voice scream: "God, why do you leave me so empty-handed?"

In the United States, Francisca and Roby visted other doctors, other clinics. Though disturbed by the methods of behavior modification they, nevertheless, enrolled their son in such a program for almost a year with no results...except for a notable increase in anger and unhappiness.

Two years of waiting, hoping and searching; precious time irrevocably lost. But at least, now they had found something special. For the first time, in New York, they met a child who had come the whole distance. For the first time, they listened to a program and life approach which felt so right not only for Robertito, but for themselves. Only one fact troubled them. They recalled that we had started our program when our son was under one and a half years old. Their own child had already passed his fourth birthday. Had Robertito's mind lost its elasticity? Had he spent too many years behind the wall?

*   *   *

Their attempt to develop their own home program entered its second and third months. The new ads and radio announcements, which skirted the issue of autism and offered modest payments, attracted many applicants. Most of those interviewed became mysteriously unavailable after the initial meeting with the Sotos and Robertito. Three young women survived the first shock of close contact with a special child and still offered to participate.

Marie, a graduate student at a neighboring college, studied all areas of abnormal psychology. The practical experience of working with an autistic child fulfilled some of the requirements for her degree.

She watched Francisca imitate her son and feed him at eye level. The outrageous and startling behavior of both mother and child fascinated her. Marie sensed the boy enjoyed his mother's parallel motion, although he never acknowledged her presence. His uncommon beauty and self-stimulating passion hypnotized Marie. She tried to suppress her immediate attachment and affection for Robertito. Her psychology professor championed the aloof and objective professional as if caring and helping were incompatible.

She had once viewed so-called psychotic children from the safe side of a two-way mirror, never within breathing distance. Her textbooks froze them amid statistical data. No warm hands, dirty diapers and silent stares. No flesh and blood people with real tears. Suddenly, Francisca and her son frightened her. Marie longed for the refuge of her classroom. Panic seized her when her turn to work with Robertito arrived. To watch a child perform "crazy" actions seemed simpler than to do them herself. She fought her impulse to flee, forcing herself to flap a wooden block when he did and to mimic his hand movements. Her voice echoed his bizarre whine. But her rigid body language and the odor seeping through her garments betrayed her attitude.

Francisca observed her son become more hyperactive, noting his tendency to move away from this petite, pretty young woman...as if avoiding an energy field surrounding her. Robertito increased the pace of his activities; his motions sped into high gear like a cartoon character dancing wildly through a nineteen-thirties' movie. Marie backed away.

The two women stared at each other. Francisca squelched her disappointment and touched Marie. She tried to remember the questions we asked her in New York. Her mind went blank. Nothing. A void. She admitted defeat, annoyed at her own ineptitude as a teacher. She knew Marie had not been prepared for the session and had not even been comfortable with it.

The young woman put her hands over her mouth, but her effort to abort her announcement failed.

"I...I just can't, Señora Soto," she whispered. "He's really a wonderful boy, really and truly." Marie glanced at Robertito, then squeezed her eyes shut.

"What can't you do?" Francisca asked.

The young woman swallowed noisily. "I want to help you. I just can't. I feel so...so stupid doing those things."

Francisca withdrew her hand and sighed. She wanted to love this girl and shake her at the same time.

"No, no, señora. Please. Do not look so sad. You will find others much better than me." Marie jumped to her feet. "Forgive me," she mumbled as she raced out of the room, leaving Francisca alone, very alone, with her son.

Within days, the other two volunteers quit. People came quickly and left quickly. Francisca had stressed technique and sheer hours as her fortress. Not once did she confront directly her doubts as a teacher or her discomfort about making decisions affecting her son. Instead, she extinguished her own questions as well as the ones she might have asked Marie and the other helpers. Again, Francisca relied on the dignity of form and technique. Rather than face and, perhaps, dissolve the anxiety and fears, no matter how embryonic their beginnings, she tried to avoid them and when she couldn't, she tried to drown them with bursts of energy and enthusiasm.

Francisca worked eight hours steadily each day. No complaints. No regrets. Roby contributed during his lunch hour and in the evenings. Though Robertito's crying escalated whenever his mother introduced food into the room, he appeared generally less frantic, less hyperactive than in the previous months. Their loving and accepting attitude still prevailed toward their son, but their trust in themselves began to dissipate.

Three months whizzed by; no signs of progress, no task-oriented accomplishments to be checked off on a standard educational chart. Francisca's energy ebbed during the fourth month. She remembered Suzi's bright aqua eyes and the bubbling energy which must have sustained her during those three years working with Raun. She recalled my prodding questions, my constant effort to prepare them and to teach them. "Before the Kaufmans had trained others, they did it alone." Francisca imprinted that notion in neon before her mind's eye, using it as a constant reminder and inspiration. To date, she had spent one hundred and twelve incredible days in the bathroom with her son and he still had not even demonstrated some of the skills he had exhibited with Suzi and me months before.

An early morning sun seeped through the windowpanes, bathing the room with soft yellow light. Mother and child threw their heads and shoulders from side to side, a rhythmic body dance punctuated by soft guitar music. Robertito snapped his body into a rigid position and surveyed the toys which littered the floor around them. Francisca turned the tape recorder off immediately. She gathered five blocks between her legs and performed the ritual of building a tower in front of her, initiating her seven-hundredth attempt to teach her son how to stack blocks. She called attention to each piece in the structure, neatly disassembled it and then rebuilt it again. Each time she gave Robertito a block, he flapped it beside his head.

She decided to alter her strategy after six fruitless attempts to engage him. She placed her hand over his, hoping to direct his movement. To her amazement and delight, he did not resist. She placed a block in his opened palm, then closed his fingers around it. Francisca guided his hand gently, ever so gently, to a point directly above another block. She shook his wrist until the wood form dislodged from his grip, landing on top of the other. Francisca nodded and applauded.

"Good, Robertito. Good. You're getting the idea, aren't you?" Oblivious to her words, he stared at the doorknob and hummed.

"C'mon, we can do it again." She repeated the exercise several times. Now she had to pry his fingers open in order to release the block. Nevertheless, she cheered him and coaxed him to try again and again. Finally, he pulled away from her, twisting his body and head from side to side. She followed him into his world of repetitive motions.

Toward evening, Francisca brought his meal into the bathroom. The shouting and crying began again. She fumbled with the spoon and upset the container. Food fell on the floor. They both dived simultaneously for the pieces of fish, but her hands moved faster than his. Robertito screeched his dissatisfaction. Francisca, in response, stuffed his mouth repeatedly.

"I'm sorry. Please, please don't cry, don't be unhappy." She whipped another spoonful into his mouth. "Here. See. Everything's all right now. That's a good boy. No more crying."

During the calm, when he chewed, Francisca repeated the block-on-block ritual.

"Okay, take this!" she said, placing a block between his fingers. No resistance. She showed him a banana slice. "C'mon, put the block here and I'll give you the banana." She pointed while guiding his hand. Suddenly, beneath her fingers, she felt his movement joining hers. She held her breath. When both of their hands arrived at a point directly above the other block, Robertito opened his hand spontaneously, letting his block settle on top of the other. Francisca screamed, filling the room with her applause.

"I don't believe it. Oh, God. You did it this time." She shoved the fruit into his mouth. "That's great, Robertito! Just great!" She tried to hug him, but the force of her arms jolted him. He pushed her away, grabbed a puzzle piece and flapped it.

The following day, Francisca could not get Robertito to repeat his accomplishment. She offered him bananas, apples, pears, peaches. With single-minded concentration, he rocked frantically throughout the entire morning and afternoon. She followed him like a pied piper, ignoring her own disappointment and dizziness. Be strong! Like Alicia! Like Roby! Like the Kaufmans! She remembered our discussions about acceptance, comfort and understanding being a source of power. Yes, she had experienced that sensation after our sessions, but now, alone, without external support, her strength came from an act of will...a declaration. She faced her son erect and determined as she duplicated his actions studiously. The tension of her posture competing with the intense, rapid rhythm of her arms sapped her energy. She fixated on Robertito's dark, hypnotic eyes. Wasn't there strength in love? Francisca could not imagine loving any human being more than she loved her son. "I'll stay with you, Robertito. I promise." The more she feared her fatigue, the weaker she felt. Her diaphragm tightened, suppressing the full expanse of her lungs. "I'm here," she said reassuringly to her child. "Mama's here."

Roby returned home with Alicia at five o'clock. In accordance with his custom, he tiptoed down the hall to spy on his favorite people before working a shift with his son. He pushed the door open slowly. Robertito, barely awake, flapped a paper strip in slow motion. Francisca, her hand clutching a piece of tissue, lay on the floor beside her son...fast asleep.

Having mastered the art of turning doorknobs, Robertito Soto roamed the house freely during the following weeks, refusing to stay in the bathroom. They taught him to insert one circular form into an insertion cube. He stacked several blocks and, inconsistently, on request, he touched his nose. He took three months to learn to put one cup inside another. Yet, one time, he placed a puzzle piece into its rightful slot with apparent ease while actually looking in the opposite direction...as if his hand could be more exactly guided by some internal radar system rather than with the aid of his vision.

He looked in the direction of people more often, but with no observable frequency. Occasionally, he peered directly into his parents' eyes for several fleeting seconds. He chose to be alone whenever possible, exiting rooms occupied by other people. And yet, in dramatic contrast, this strange little boy began to allow his mother and father to touch him. A soft smile often radiated on his face. Only the appearance of food provoked a grimmer mood.

The Sotos wanted more progress and decided to feed him less at meals in order to use the food as a learning incentive. They noted, for limited periods, Robertito would definitely respond more. But as the quantity of his meals decreased, his random crying during the sessions increased, especially in the presence of any food whatsoever.

Francisca resisted his tantrums at first. Then Robertito began to hit his chin, cutting the skin with his nail and drawing blood. The image of a little girl tied to a chair, her head encased in a football helmet, assaulted Francisca's memory. Boxing gloves had been strapped onto another child in the same hospital, preventing him from chewing the flesh on his hands. Would her son become self-destructive like them? Her diaphragm spasmed against her rib cage. No. Impossible. Please, God, not Robertito...never Robertito! They were extreme cases, she assured herself. And those children had not been treated lovingly. Not the way she and Roby treated their son. Nevertheless, she began to feed Robertito excessively in an effort to compete directly with his chin-banging. Instead of subsiding, it increased. Francisca went with her fear, rather than with her son.

Robertito, despite his tangential contact with the outside world, had learned something very special which had gone unobserved by Francisca and Roby. Food, delivered out of anxiety, had become the immediate response to crying and chin-banging. In effect, food rewarded and supported the very behaviors they dreaded.

The following five months brought new additional accomplishments. They felt ill-equipped to respond productively to each new situation with their son, clutching nervously to the few specific techniques they had learned. They defied the mechanics. A non-judgmental attitude toward their son stayed with them, more often as a strategy rather than a vision of seeing and embracing themselves. They responded to an idea, a rigid and inflexible notion they fixed like gauntlets between their eyes.

They hesitated calling us in New York, believing they had already received more than they deserved.

Chapter 4

Roby. Francisca. Robertito. Their faces, their tears and their wanting haunted me. Though Suzi and I had worked with other parents and professionals, loving and caring for them during those moments of contact, Francisca and Roberto Soto left a special imprint under our skin. They had grabbed for everything they could. They had even faced their own demons during their visit with us in order to reach their child. And Robertito had dazzled everyone with incredible changes within the single week they had spent with us. My words to Francisca and Roby had been clear in our last meeting: "Call us, write us, use us in any way you can." And yet, ten whole months of silence greeted my offer.

During that period, hundreds of people passed through our home. Many came in search of miracles. Others wanted us to perform the "magic" on their children. Sight-seers and skeptics arrived. A noted physician took two days of our time, asking to learn our approach, and then, in a public forum, he ridiculed our attitude of acceptance as nonsense and unscientific. A leading psychologist and educator called our work the most significant advance in psychology in twenty years. An organization concerned solely with the welfare of autistic children attacked us privately, then publicly, without having met us or observed our work. What we had done for the love of one child inspired some, but frightened many others, especially those people with an emotional and economical investment in depicting these children as hopeless and using techniques which supported those beliefs.

Sometimes I wanted to turn away. We tried to live a lifestyle based on love and acceptance, not combat. Fight the devil and you make him stronger. Our energy focused on teaching Option to adults and young people, who used their own experiences and triumphs to substantiate their happiness and power. Before designing a successful program for our son, no one screamed at our doorstep: "Prove it according to this standard or that standard." We had nothing to prove; no offering of nirvana or a way to live which everyone should embrace. We had found something that had altered our lives dramatically and wanted to share it with those who wanted to know.

Raun's young life and his journey through autism became a demonstration for Suzi and me and all those who worked with him. Had he had cerebral palsy or multiple sclerosis or leukemia, we would have turned our energy toward him with the same attitude and clarity of purpose. His autism was not nearly as relevant as the fact that he had been dismissed as "incurable" and "irreversible." Though we believed others might profit from understanding his rebirth, we presented no instant cure for autism, schizophrenia or brain-damage syndromes. What we could point to was the impact of labels and judgments as self-fulfilling prophecies. Had we listened to the pronouncements of others and not trusted ourselves, Raun would still be autistic, stranded behind a steel door, a forgotten statistic confined in some nameless institution for the remainder of his life.

One person's opinion or belief can be another person's death sentence. That had been the message for us.

Rather than attend conferences and debates, we worked with people...one at a time, putting our energy out there in a caring environment instead of spending hours defending ourselves or confronting other people's bitterness. "Talk to those who want to listen," I repeated to myself over and over. "And let the rest be."

Each time I said enough to autism, another couple like the Sotos entered our lives for an hour or a day. Whether they came from Japan, France or Minnesota, their soft voices and sincerity drew me back; other parents, other children ...other mountains to face. But a time limit always confronted us. I knew we had only walked with them for that first step. Was it enough? Francisca and Roby and the promise of that special week revived that question continually. We had lost them to their own silence...and, then, finally, a letter arrived.

"We're writing you," they began, "hoping you are in good health, in the company of Bryn, Thea and Raun. We remember every one of you with love, in that atmosphere of affection and understanding that prevails in your home.

"Thank you...thank you very much for being with us and Robertito, for sharing with us your care, your special vision and love in this beautiful task that we have undertaken."

They described the months of work with Robertito. They believed he enjoyed their imitation of him. Small portions of "organic" cookies and slices of fruits had been used to improve his eye contact. He demonstrated an ability to stack one block, withdraw a puzzle piece and move to music. Diet changes had been dramatic, feeding him all natural foods.

Although they noted lack of language development and the continuance of self-stimulating behaviors, they never mentioned his crying at meals or chin-banging.

"We consider that we've made some progress and, of course, we continue like the beginning, with much enthusiasm, love and acceptance, offering him the best of ourselves...motivating him, stimulating him, loving him immensely and always alert to help him even more."

Elated, Suzi and I wrote them an extensive letter, with suggestions and a series of questions. Several months passed before we received an answer. Their correspondence acknowledged ours, but did not deal directly with it. Since they knew I would be in southern California as part of a national tour for my second book, *To Love Is to Be Happy With,* they asked me to visit them and give them additional assistance.

When I embraced Francisca and Roby in Mexico, I realized the strong, almost passionate, attachment I felt for both of them. Their eyes gave me so much more than just a hello. Time had intensified our bond. We conversed clumsily using sign language and single Spanish words. Jaime joined us within the hour, surprising me with a hug and smile.

"Bears, it is good that you are here, even for an overnight

visit. They need your help. And, ah, how do you say it; ah, yes...I am at your service until you leave."

I tapped his cheek. "Maestro, you're a special person." Jaime blushed. "A red face is a sign of humility," I assured him. Everyone laughed. "Please tell Francisca and Roby that I want to use every minute to work with them, even if we have to stay up all night. Okay?"

As Jaime translated, Francisca smiled like a little girl. Roby hugged her, barely containing his huge grin. "Yes, yes, all night," he said. "If necessary, all night."

The beautiful little boy I observed seemed less responsive than the one who left our home over a year ago. The patterns of crying and chin-banging infiltrated every session. His weight gain had made him lethargic. And yet, he often reminded me of Raun with his far-off angelic expression. We worked until four in the morning, using extended dialogue sessions to unravel some of their fears and anxieties, which had compromised their attitude significantly.

The next morning, I concentrated on concrete suggestions for changes in the program and in diet. I tried to give their niece, who had just volunteered to help, a quick orientation.

Their smiles waned quickly as we said good-by. Somehow, we all knew there had not been enough time. At best, we had plugged a hole in the dike. Or had we? Be glad for the time spent, I reminded myself. Francisca squeezed me so tight that she trembled. I knew she didn't want to let go. If I could have left part of myself there, a hand, a talking mouth, anything...I would have.

* * *

My overnight visit rejuvenated both Roby and Francisca, leaving them with thoughts and ideas to ponder. Roby had listened carefully, taking elaborate notes. That night, he scribbled my answer to one of his questions on a large piece of cardboard and pinned it to the wall.

"The teacher and the student draw from the same well; they know the same things...only the student is not aware of what he knows."

After his wife fell asleep, he left his bed and sat in the kitchen. He played the tape recordings of the overnight discussions and studied his notes. He wanted desperately to have the presence of mind and depth of understanding to help his

79

son. Roby tried to memorize the truth rather than find it within himself.

Francisca, awakened by the drone of the recorder, rolled onto her back and stared at the shadows on the ceiling. She knew Roby wanted to absorb it all, inscribe each insight permanently into his brain. Her fingers slid across the cool sheet until they encountered the warm, lingering imprint of her husband's body. She rolled over, squeezed Roby's pillow to her bosom and pressed herself against the lightly heated portion of the sheet. Her limbs were like lead weights, yet she felt aroused. Francisca wanted to drag her husband out of the kitchen, but she buried the impulse as she had done before. Robertito. First Robertito. Her eyelids closed slowly. She concentrated on visualizing her son's lips; how they might move if he could talk. But they remained sealed, even in her fantasy.

The Sotos continued working for several more months. Robertito allowed some physical contact. He permitted Francisca to hold his hands as they jumped together on the bed or rocked to music. He did not resist his father, who lifted him off the ground and swung him in circles. Yet he pushed them away if they tried to hug him. Robertito learned to flip a light switch and did it automatically whenever he entered a dark room. The Sotos cheered their son's modest movements until they judged them, seeing these victories as insignificant conquests for a year and a half of intense input. They pushed themselves and their son for more. Food, given and then withheld, became a growing dynamic in the sessions. He rebelled against the pressure. The program became less regulated and more chaotic. Robertito ran through the house for hours until they could contain him in his room. He smiled and giggled, but did not direct any energy toward learning. He still viewed the world from the corners of his eyes and still flapped objects. Francisca and Roby's confidence eroded. Embarrassed to ask us for more help, they began to search elsewhere.

The doctor that Roby contacted in Russia sent data on his experiments with B_{15} and autistic children. Interesting, but inconclusive. Roby's correspondence with professionals in England yielded volumes of literature. Their techniques to his dismay, mirrored key elements of behavior modification. But then, in the course of his research, he uncovered an article about a special clinic in the Southwest which riveted his attention. The doctor theorized that autism came from an allergic response to food. The facility focused on nutrition related to maladaptation of food, metabolic malfunctions, enzyme deficiencies, neurological allergies and the like. The physician claimed successes from their experiments. The biochemical aspect fascinated Roby. Could it be so simple? Delete a certain food and Robertito would become normal? Give him an injection and he would look directly at people?

He didn't remember his annoyance, almost contempt, for a parent group that championed such a concept. While they lobbied for legislation for research and prayed for the penicillin of autism, their children drifted away, finally being placed in residential settings, a hip, Madison Avenue medical term designed to camouflage the stone walls, barred windows and locked doors of an institution. He didn't recall his research into mega-vitamin utopias that could not present him with one successful patient in the flesh. Rather than be choked by the memory of such information, Roberto Soto inflicted himself with a minor case of amnesia so that he could chase the rainbow. An instant cure! Images of Robertito talking, riding a bicycle, playing baseball. Why not? Hadn't he and Francisca paid their dues?

Quickly and efficiently, Roby made all the arrangements; Alicia and a cousin to cover the business, plane tickets to Kansas, new clothes for their son, duplicates of all Robertito's evaluations and tests. The clinic required six weeks for their study, six weeks to experiment with a wide selection of foods while monitoring the child's blood and urine. Six weeks! For Roby, that was an instant and yet...forever.

* * *

Francisca watched her son lying on the table. He flapped a string which she had provided. He smiled as he rolled his head from side to side, obviously content; Robertito, a dreamer adrift on his own fluids. The bubbling sounds reverberating in the stainless steel tray distracted her. A nurse, her eyes obscured by heavily tinted glasses, slid two hypodermic needles into the boiling water. She appeared so precise, so disciplined to Francisca, though her efficiency verged on the point of rudeness when she neglected to greet Francisca and her husband as they entered the examination room with their son. The woman spoke to one of the doctors in the room. He, too, seemed efficient; no wasted motions, very professional. He squinted his dark, beady eyes as he watched their son;

the young doctor was somewhat aloof, but scientific in his posture. His layered haircut, tanned skin and impeccably pressed uniform exuded success, affluence and respectability; traits that Francisca had been taught to trust. Yet, some of the very aspects which reassured her simultaneously alienated her; the cool, white tiled walls, the chrome cabinets, the plexiglass tubes, the digital scanners and the two cushioned tables neatly enshrouded in paper—everything so antiseptic, so impersonal. She dredged up her fantasy of a morgue, then erased her vision, frightened by her own imagination. When two additional nurses and another doctor arrived, she moved toward the side of the room. Though she did not understand one word of English, she followed their conversation intently, hoping to sedate her nervousness with the tone of confidence and authority in their voices.

A second doctor kept pushing his gray unkempt hair out of his eyes. He never looked at the others as he talked; his eyes jumping in their sockets as if punctuating his phrases and sentences. He picked at his Walrus mustache constantly. Roby had met him when they first arrived. He liked this man for what he considered to be silly reasons; this physician was less than perfect—disorganized and idiosyncratic, rather than rehearsed and mechanized.

Dr. Dugan turned to Roby and Francisca suddenly and smiled. He had forgotten about the boy's parents, never once surveying the room beyond the specimen on the table. Roby nodded several times, flattered that this man departed from his intense conversation to be courteous. Francisca felt momentarily relieved.

The other doctor and nurses, under the direction of Dr. Dugan, proceeded to check Robertito's eyes, ears, heart, blood pressure, and reflexes. The little boy pulled away sharply several times, cuddling himself into a fetal position as protection against the probing. Then he relaxed, preoccupied again with the string while his body remained passive, his arms and legs seemingly disconnected and limp. He made a soft, gentle cooing sound as he smiled at his fingers.

The preplanned activity in the room, orchestrated and executed in a precise ritual, was disrupted by the noisy entrance of a portly, jovial woman in her late forties.

"I mean, after all, first the car, then the traffic, then no parking place...one catastrophe after another. You know, I'm not a negative person, but..." She stopped as soon as she became aware of the serious expressions on the faces around her. "I'm real sorry if I've..."

"It's okay, Mrs. Andrews," the well manicured doctor said. "We'll make out just fine, won't we? Good. Now if you would just introduce yourself to Mr. and Mrs. Soto, we can continue."

The woman spoke to Roby and Francisca in Spanish, explaining she had been hired as a translator to help them. Francisca complimented her on her accent, at which point Mrs. Andrews began telling her life story.

Dr. Dugan interrupted her. "Now if you could ask the father to help us hold his son while we take blood."

Roby, in response to the request, fixed his hands over his son's shoulders as the other clinicians placed their hands over the boy's arms and legs. Using a special instrument, the nurse with the tinted glasses lifted the hypodermic needle from the tray and held it aloft until it cooled. Her heels clicked on the ceramic floor as she approached the table. Her movements had all the grace of a wind-up toy. Roby stared at the reflection of his son's face in her lenses. She whipped a small rubber strap from her breast pocket, wrapped it tightly around Robertito's biceps and then inserted the needle into his arm. The little boy lunged forward, jerked his head spastically and screamed. His fingers grabbed the waxed paper beneath him. Francisca gouged her fingers into her thighs as she forced herself to watch.

The nurse shook her head. She hadn't located the vein. Dr. Dugan nodded as he locked the child's leg between his arms. Roby, obeying an implicit command, pressed his son tightly against the table. The boy struggled and cried as the technician probed his arm six times, still unable to locate the vein.

When they finally released Robertito, he whimpered like an infant. His lips puckered, sucking and kissing the air. His delicate fingers gently scratched the material at the bottom of Dr. Dugan's shirt. Mrs. Andrews watched the boy's hand, mesmerized. Was this disconnected, almost loving, gesture his way of pleading for no more? She turned to the nurse, then to Dr. Dugan. They ignored her. She had been hired to translate, that's all, to translate. Her eyes focused back on those little trembling fingers. Mrs. Andrews called herself a coward and closed her eyes.

The Sotos tried to calm their son. Roby picked up the string from the floor and deposited it back into Robertito's hand. The little boy flapped the string faster and faster, oblivious to everyone in the room. His eyes glazed as he withdrew from the hostility of a world he did not understand and found a place deep within himself to hide.

The young physician consulted his watch and sighed loudly, purposely communicating his displeasure. Dr. Dugan heard nothing, preoccupied with examining both of Robertito's arms, then the bottoms of his feet and his neck. He decided they would take blood from his neck, from the bulging, pulsating vein in easy view. Mrs. Andrews translated the doctor's intentions.

Roby glanced at his wife. Their eyes locked. They begged each other for some alternative, but their lips remained sealed. Somehow, they could not let go of the rainbow. The nurse indicated that Roby should reapply pressure and hold his son. The other nurses and two doctors fixed their grips. Robertito squirmed, responding to the pressure immediately. The first nurse checked the needle against the light.

"We don't have all day," the young doctor snapped at the nurse. Dr. Dugan eyed his associate, then twirled his mustache, immediately drifting into his own thoughts, which took him far away from the examination room.

The nurse glared at the young physician. She slowed her movement in obvious defiance. In a haughty gesture, she snapped her wrist and, using the hypodermic needle like a fencing saber, she pierced through the skin in the child's neck and punctured his vein. Robertito's terrified eyes swelled from their sockets. He screamed at the top of his lungs. The world inside that he sought to control, the internal universe that he called his home, had been invaded. The muscles in his neck and along his arms spasmed as he tried to free himself; he panicked without understanding the panic, scared, alone, trapped by an octopus of hands and arms he could not comprehend. Roby tried to talk to his son, but his voice failed him. Francisca began to cry.

The nurse withdrew the needle once the glass tube filled. The little boy continued to tremble even after they released him. He gasped for air as his weak, raspy voice chanted eee-o, eee-o, eee-o. He rubbed the edge of the table with a desperate repetitive motion. His eyes remained wide open.

Without words, without the tools to help him understand, Roby agonized over his realization that his son was trapped with the horror and the pain inside. He could never explain it to him. Robertito would never understand. Would his son always wait now, frightened and defenseless against a violence which would just randomly, nonsensically, without warning, attack his soft, gentle, self-contained world? Roby could protect him from the outside, he assured himself, but what about the demons they let loose inside?

Dr. Dugan checked the child's pulse, then prepared another needle.

"What's that for?" Roby asked. He waited precious seconds while the translator repeated his question.

The physician mumbled his answer to the floor without looking at Roby.

"The doctor says it's a tranquilizer. To help calm your son," Mrs. Andrews restated in Spanish. Then, daring to go beyond his words and add her own, she continued: "He's concerned about the rather extreme reaction, I think."

As Dugan approached the boy, he sprayed some liquid from the tip of the needle. He stood over Robertito, dazzled by his constant motion. The nurse rubbed the child's arm with alcohol. Francisca brushed past the technicians. She placed her hand on the prepared spot and shook her head.

"*No más inyecciones.*" Her voice quivered in contrast to her aggressive body language. Mrs. Andrews translated the words instantly in apparent support of Francisca's position. The doctor nodded, shrugged his shoulders, then retreated to the medicine counter.

In the motel, later that same day, the Sotos watched their son pace the room. His lip curled. He kept slamming his chin with the back of his hand. He pushed his parents away every time they approached. His legs moved awkwardly, jerking in a peculiar, frenzied fashion. His chest still heaved. His eyes fixed in a frozen, wide-eyed stare. When they tried to dress him in pajamas, he ran to the other side of the room and pushed himself into the corner as if trying to hide. Occasionally, they heard a small, infantile whimper escape from his throat.

Francisca kept speaking to her son. No more needles in his neck or arms, she promised. No more restraints. She knew he could not understand, but she couldn't stop herself from talking. Roby watched her. He wanted to wish the day away, to erase it forever. He knew they had violated all the trust and acceptance that they had worked so hard to establish with their child.

The tests began the next day. They drew blood only from the tip of Robertito's finger, which he accepted passively. But the trauma of the first day lingered, the calm, peaceful expression gone from his face, the gentle, rhythmic motions thrown into a frenzied high gear. Using three test foods each day, they recorded his blood, urine, behavioral changes, color of face and other factors deemed a reaction. The seventeen foods out of sixty which tested reactive were stripped from his diet.

When they returned to Mexico, they observed their son diligently, hoping for changes which never came. Despite an altered diet, Robertito's response to the world remained the same. They tried to reinstitute the Option program, but felt inadequate to the task.

Robertito's anger and unhappiness distressed Francisca. She cringed when he began hitting his chest as well as his chin. When she put a towel under his polo shirt, the little boy found another part of his body to assault. Both she and her husband noted, unhappily, all the black-and-blue marks in both areas. His erratic behavior unnerved her. Some days, she watched him cry for hours, feeling her own helplessness again like those months following his birth. On other days, he smiled suddenly, then giggled and laughed for four to six hours.

After additional observations, Francisca and Roby decided to provide Robertito, once again, with an accepting and non-judgmental environment. At times, they mimicked him and followed him. When he did something they judged as self-destructive, they felt "unable" to go with him.

Eventually, the little boy with dark eyes and perfectly sculptured features relaxed, but he no longer ventured out from behind the impenetrable wall.

Chapter 5

Toward the back of the huge lecture hall, a young man in green leotards raised his hands and shook them sporadically. A blind man in the second row cocked his head sideways, angling one ear toward the stage. The sound technician, his earphones barely visible through his long hair, tapped his foot nervously each time he adjusted his audio equipment. An impeccably dressed professor, sucking on his pipe passionately, smiled and nodded his head. Suits and ties mixed with panchos and jeans. Though my talk had been sponsored by the university, concerned individuals from the immediate community had also been invited.

I tried to humanize the nine hundred faces by focusing on one individual at a time and giving my thoughts directly to him or her. Vibrant eyes called to me from the fourth row. A soft smile beckoned from the front of the balcony.

"Could you explain in more detail what you see as the connection between attitude and health?" asked a spunky woman in her seventies.

"Perhaps the most effective way to answer your question," I began, "is to share the experience of one woman.

"Her voice trembled at the other end of the phone, as she discussed her traumatic visit to the doctor earlier in the day for abdominal and lower back pains. The physician diagnosed, after elaborate tests and X-rays, a huge kidney stone obstructing her urethra. Her fury and anger focused on the professional for treating her like a 'piece of meat' and on her fear of operations and hospitals. Her self-indictment formed the most intense part of her unhappiness; seeing herself as a bad person who abused her body through improper diet.

"As I might do with anyone, I asked her questions about her unhappiness. Though she did not eradicate all her fears and judgments, within an hour, in an accepting environment, she uncovered and discarded some old beliefs. As a result, her unhappiness dissipated and the panic disappeared.

"'Now that you feel more in control, more comfortable, what do you want?' I asked her.

"'I want the whole situation to just disappear, to just go away,' she snapped.

"'Okay,' I acknowledged. 'If that's what you want, what could you do to get what you want?'

"Following a minute of silence, she asked, 'What are you saying?'

"'I'm not saying anything...I merely asked a question.'

"She never answered the question in that moment. When we ended the conversation, she decided to read more about what we discussed, particularly a section in one book which raised questions about our personal power in terms of body balance and well-being.

"A week later, her husband appeared at the door. 'I have to tell you both something very incredible about what happened to my wife. After you talked to her she stayed up all night. In the morning, well, she was different...not hysterical. The difference stayed with her several days; right up until I checked her into the hospital. When she walked into the doctor's office, she kind of elbowed him and said, "I took care of it, Doc." Then she winked. Now I gotta tell you how out of character that is for my wife. Well, it gets even wilder. When the doctor returns with ner new X-rays, he compares them with the pictures he took four days ago. You had to see his face. The stone was gone...the one he said could not pass. Not only that, he couldn't believe that the urethra had a perfectly normal curve. The infection was completely gone. He kept shaking his head, saying it would have taken weeks and significant doses of antibiotics to have eradicated that infection.'

"A miracle? Perhaps, if that's the word we choose to use for things we don't understand. This lady could not specifically account for what happened, but the phenomenon she did discuss later was her change in attitude about seeing herself so impotent and her body disconnected from her will."

A woman in a business suit stood up rather abruptly. "You are obviously adept at telling inspirational stories, but I seriously question the practicality of your 'attitude,' as you call it, and your methods. I'd like to go back to another one of your inspirational stories...about your son, Raun. As the mother of an autistic child and a member of the National Society for Autistic Children, I think your story does a disservice to all parents of similarly handicapped children who could not do what you did. You have now placed upon their shoulders an added burden of guilt." Everyone's eyes riveted on this woman and the open hostility changed the mood in the lecture hall.

"We have always shared the story of our son, Raun, and his journey, in an effort to show other possibilities, never meaning to, in any way, suggest that what we did is or was a commentary on anyone else or what they might have done with their child. Each person does the best he or she can. The choices other parents of autistic children made for their families are certainly not diminished by what we did. In some ways..."

"Are you suggesting," she interrupted, "that other parents who didn't sit in the bathroom with their child from morning to night didn't love them as much as you?"

"He never said that," a young woman in the balcony shouted.

"I'm not sure I would ever want to compare people's love," I continued. "What we did came naturally from our attitude and understanding. Other parents, wanting the very best for their child and themselves, might choose completely different alternatives. The reason we share our story is because it worked for Raun and, in varying degrees, with other children we've worked with."

"What about the guilt? What about all those parents who will think they haven't tried enough or that they did the wrong thing? Don't you think that's a terrible burden to inflict on them?"

My head bobbed up and down. What am I doing here? Stay

with it, I counseled myself. "I think guilt is a very personal matter. Nobody makes another person feel guilty. People decide that for themselves. If I said to you that you did something wrong and you disagreed, you would not feel guilty about it. Only you have that power to make such a decision based on your beliefs. The suggestion implicit in your comment, I guess, is not to tell the story. But if one person, in Des Moines or Denver, looked at her child and felt she could love him easier or more freely, then for that one person it was worth telling."

A woman sporting a huge Afro leaped to her feet. "I'm a special education teacher working with profoundly disturbed children at one of the city clinics. Several of us have been influenced by your work. I've been working with one little boy for three years with no eye contact. The day after I read your first book, I thought to myself...Jesus, this is so simple it's stupid. I came into work the next day, threw all my books and materials aside and just loved Kevin and joined him. That was three months ago and his eye contact and other skills have improved dramatically since that time—more things happend for him in the past three months than in those past three years."

The chairman of the psychology department stood up. He smiled at me, then spoke very softly.

"What you have presented here is quite fascinating, certainly an alternative to confront existing positions and therapeutic approaches. Though I understand the implications of our attitudes and judgments in working with others, I find the absence of a strong theoretic base to be quite disconcerting. Rather than argue polemics, I'd like to ask you a simple, straightforward question stimulated, in fact, by the comments of the lady in the audience who has an autistic child." He turned toward her and nodded. "Have you ever worked with a self-destructive child?"

"No, I have not," I replied.

He smiled; a minor victory. "Your method sounds possible enough to implement with children like your son, who are peaceful and withdrawn. But what about the violent child? What would your approach be for a self-destructive child?"

"No different than with any other child."

"I am asking you what you would do?"

"I don't know," I said.

"You don't know. How could you help others when you

yourself have no firm grounding as to how to handle situations other than those which you have already dealt with?"

"One of the things we've learned is to be open, to trust ourselves and the children we work with. I cannot tell you in advance what I would do with a child. Our whole perspective begins with watching and acting on the child's cues, being responsive and respectful of that other little person. There are no theoretical abstractions for that...each person is different."

"Yes, yes..." Dr. Brewster said impatiently, "but if a child came into the room and banged his head against the wall, would you let him do it and then, in accordance with your 'perspective,' would you do it with him?"

"Again, I don't know. And it's okay with me not to know. To have an established plan before you see the child is not to see the child."

Brewster raised his eyebrows, obviously disconcerted. "I'm a man of science, Mr. Kaufman. And psychology is a science whose premises are comprehensible and provable. Perhaps, we are speaking different languages."

"Miracles, again, Dr. Brewster," I said. "My experience has taught me not to limit myself only to what I understand. To be able to prove something tells me much about the tenacity of my own mind, but does not necessarily tell me about all there is and all there could be."

Though I had enjoyed the talk, especially the questions of Dr. Brewster, the woman with the autistic child became my focus of attention as I crossed Waverly Place in Greenwich Village. Gusts of wind whipped my face when I turned south along Seventh Avenue. Air currents looped and whistled through narrow alleys like a shrill chorus of nervous witches. Old posters, clinging limply to the walls of unoccupied buildings, flapped in the stiff breeze. I kept thinking about that woman. She wanted to make it ugly so she could dismiss it. I reviewed my answers to her. Somehow, I knew she hadn't heard them. Then why did I persist in responding? Why?

A tall, statuesque woman holding the leashes of two white Russian wolfhounds guarded the entrance to the building. A man wearing black leotards leaned against a nearby brick wall. Several groups of well-dressed people huddled together like teams preparing for a football scrimmage. I climbed the steps rapidly after nodding at familiar, but nameless faces.

In the darkness, I found a seat by the center aisle. The whispers and hushed chatter ceased as the lights abruptly illuminated a rather stark, impressionistic room. A gray-haired woman, named George or Sister George to be precise, dominated the stage with her aging, plump form clothed in a drab, sexless dress. Deep lines around her eyes and mouth cut bitter gullies in her face. She glared at the other two women beside her, particularly the younger one, who recoiled instinctively.

"Don't, George...don't..." she whimpered.

"Look at you," Sister George snapped with seething contempt. "Whimpering and pleading! Have you no backbone, can't you stand up like a man?"

"I can't...help it."

George raised her eyebrows and mimicked her young friend sardonically. "'I can't help it!'" Then she turned to the other woman. "She'll never change—feckless, self-indulgent—" She fired the words from her mouth like deadly bullets, heightening the verbal combat as the scenes progressed.

The play ended with a strange, heart-wrenching sound emanating from the major character. Applause enveloped the theater. The actresses paraded back onto the stage. The stiff, matronly walk and stern visage of Sister George mesmerized me. Only when she smiled and removed her gray wig, revealing her long blond hair, did I begin to recognize the softness of Suzi. Her ability to submerge herself in that character dazzled me.

Even when we left the theater, I had to keep looking at her, unable to find any traces of the sad and bitter woman she had just portrayed. As we walked crosstown, the Sotos and their early morning telephone call pierced my thoughts, but I decided to wait until later before broaching the subject. I didn't want to break the spell for Suzi, who seemed especially beautiful tonight. Though only five feet three inches tall and barely one hundred and ten pounds, the power of her stride gave her a much taller appearance. Her peasant outfit, which had been lovingly fashioned by a friend, outlined the prominent curves of her breasts and clung to the inside of her thighs as she walked. Suzi smiled and laughed each time she looked at me; little girl giggles surfacing on sensuous lips.

She had waited thirteen years to return. The highlight of her adolescence focused on her dreams of acting, which helped her survive the pain and bitterness of warring parents who ultimately divorced and created new families, depriving both her and her sister of a sense of belonging. Having lost her home at twelve years old, she shuffled between different houses clinging to her invalid grandmother and to her dreams.

Alone, in an empty room, she recited speeches and acted roles from famous plays. The characters she portrayed became her friends.

When she applied to the High School of Performing Arts in New York City, she confronted her fantasies. She watched her reflection self-consciously in the mirror as she practiced day and night for her audition. The nausea and vomiting began two days before the performance, curtailing her private rehearsals as she sat on the floor in the bathroom hugging the toilet bowl. The day of her presentation, she felt exposed, naked and vulnerable in front of strangers. She had risked her dreams. Without them, she had nothing. A week later, the committee notified her of her acceptance.

The fantasy finally had more substance. She studied and worked at developing her skills until her early twenties. Then, in a dramatic decision, she walked away from everything she had worked so hard to develop. Marriage and a professional acting career seemed incompatible. Suzi still wanted the family and the home, the sense of belonging so long absent in her life. Following the birth of our son, our third child, Suzi decided to go back to her studies and training. But within a year, Raun drifted into the pit of autism, diverting her for yet four more years until she could again take up the banner of an old dream.

Tonight, with her performance of Sister George, she celebrated her return. Although she segmented her time between the theater and working with adults and children, her commitment to acting had found a practical outlet in school, workshops and experimental presentations.

We walked in silence, but the intensity of our clasped hands kept us close. I knew what this night meant to her. I almost didn't want to tell her about the Sotos. As we turned into Spring Street, a man in hunting boots, carrying a worn knapsack, waved to us with a silly grin. Old factory structures mixed easily with health food stores and art galleries. Modern glass and metal façades blended with the ancient stone and chipped bricks of another century. The mecca of Soho charmed us.

Sawdust cushioned our feet in the small restaurant. Joshua, one of the chefs, greeted us by bowing with clasped hands from behind the simple butcher-block counter. We sat at a corner table by the front window. Across the street, a

93

neon plaque blinked its message: "Learn to drive to get away."

Suzi pushed the vegetarian menu aside. "Let me call home and check on the kids," she said.

"Everything's fine. I already did that before I met you at school."

She rubbed the top of my hands. "Bears, do you think I could do it? If I really tried and put energy toward acting, do you think I could establish myself?"

"Uh-huh," I said, "but do you want to?"

She eyed me cautiously. "Of course." A pause. "Why did you ask that?"

I picked at my beard, collecting the words, trying to choose the exact phrase. "Somehow, it's an old dream. But you're a new Suzi, a very new Suzi. Everything about you has changed in the last four years."

"I know that." She bent over the table and peered directly into my face. "I always feel you don't quite think acting is up to snuff."

"The problem I've always had with acting is that you're saying other people's words."

"But I'd pick and choose," she insisted.

"If you have the chance," I said.

The waiter interrupted, taking our order.

Suzi shook her head. "I never asked you how the talk went today."

"Good. But I had to cancel four sessions today to make it into the city on time."

"So?"

"So maybe spending four hours with four people who want to learn and help themselves would be more fruitful than making presentations to nine hundred curious people," I said.

"Anything happen?"

"No, not really—except a parent of an autistic child who was very uncomfortable happened upon me." We shared a look of recognition. "Autism," I sighed, then I thought about Roby and Francisca again. "Suz, the Sotos telephoned today."

Her eyes opened wide. "Really? God, I'm so glad they finally called." She searched my eyes. "Okay, tell me."

I told her of their journey to Kansas, of their inability to continue working with Robertito and about the little boy's further withdrawal.

"Bears, they're such wonderful people. I really thought they could do it."

"Wait, I'm not finished. They feel that our approach is the only one which ever produced real changes in Robertito. They want us to help again. In fact, they want to come to New York, put their life savings on the line and live here, literally, so they could have our input. So I asked them what kind of input they wanted. Roby suggested several hours per week, if possible. I refused."

"Bears!" Suzi exclaimed.

"I didn't feel that would be meaningful. I told him we would only do it if we went all the way. Set up a program seven days a week. Do sessions with both of them as well as train a staff of five others. Observe everyone throughout the week. Do everything we did for Raun." I smiled at Suzi. "I guess what I offered was all or nothing. Then I told them I'd have to think about it."

Suzi's eyes glazed. "You're such a wonderful fool."

"But we can't afford it," I retorted, challenging my own suggestion. "Between us, it would take at least fifty hours a week. I'd have to cancel a lot of students. I couldn't start working on another book. It doesn't make any sense."

"That's why I like it." She winked. "What about the grant? This time, they're really receptive. Bears, they practically wrote the proposal with us. If we get the grant, then we'll make it."

"If. But if we don't, not only will we have trouble paying the mortgage, but we'd have to send them home."

"Suddenly you're the pragmatist," Suzi countered. "That didn't stop you from dumping your business when you wanted to work more with Raun and teach Option."

"Somehow, that was different," I said.

"Somehow, it's the same."

"Suz, you want to do it, don't you?"

"I think so," she said. "The acting is really important...God knows how important it is to me." She sighed and forced a smile. "I've waited thirteen years to go back. I guess another six months won't kill me, but another six months might just bury that little boy." Suzi stared down at the table. "It's hard to imagine withdrawing from school again. Sometimes I get scared I'll never go back."

The following day before school, we had a breakfast conference with Bryn, Thea and Raun. We tried to explain all the possible effects the program might have on our time and resources.

"Daddy, if we don't help them, nobody else will," Thea said.

"That's probably true," I replied. "But hundreds of people call and write us each month. The most important thing is that it has to feel right inside...for all of us." Thea tucked her little eight-year-old hand under her chin as she considered my answer.

Bryn looked back and forth between Suzi and me. She grabbed her mother's hand. "Whatever you guys think. We trust whatever you'd decide."

I shook my head, awed by the presence of my own children. Suzi kissed her daughter's hand; then bestowed the same affection on Thea and Raun. "How about you, Thea?" she asked.

"I think we should help them," she replied.

Noting Raun's pensive expression, I said: "Hey, Raunchy, what are you thinking?"

He turned, giving me one of his starry-eyed, penetrating glances. "Could I work with him too?"

"Sure," I answered.

"And," Raun continued with a mischievous smile, "could I squeeze his fat cheeks?"

Chapter 6

We told Francisca and Roby of our decision. We would train them and a staff to provide a continuous, consistent input with their son. There would be no Sundays or holidays in our attempt to give Robertito everything we could, every chance, every possible opportunity. Again, we stressed the importance of a loving, accepting and nonjudgmental attitude. Our only concern was for a period of time four months in the future, when we had obligated ourselves to lecture and teach in England for six weeks during the summer. Since the Sotos could only commit themselves for three months, that eventuality did not pose a problem.

They expressed their willingness to leave their home within a few days. We discouraged them from coming to New York too quickly, not wanting them to deplete their funds while looking for a place to live...too much had to be accomplished before their arrival. Suzi and I would do whatever was necessary; rent a house, find furniture, interview volunteers, and then locate a facility that could give Robertito a developmental and psychiatric work-up in Spanish so that we could form base lines and external reference points against which we could check and monitor our program. Though the Sotos would bring a translator, a student who traded her bilingual talent for an opportunity to learn, we decided that the actual working program with Robertito had to be in Spanish. Perhaps, though distant and unavailable, he had absorbed some receptive familiarity with his own language. But more important, Robertito would return to Mexico. If we succeeded in teaching him anything, we did not want to confuse an already confusing world by introducing a second language. Suzi had a minimal grasp of Spanish. I had none. How could we learn another language in three weeks? Suddenly, to our relief, we realized that we did not have to become fluent, just capable enough to speak in some simple one- and two-word sentences... an ability which far outstripped Robertito's evident skills.

We laid aside our plans to develop an Option teaching center. I referred most of my students and clients to others I had trained. Suzi, after forcing a funny smile on her face, left for Manhattan and withdrew from school.

And so we began. Suzi searched for a house, calling forty real estate agents and answering countless ads. I canvassed doctors, teachers, universities and hospitals looking for professionals capable of administering the appropriate developmental tests and studies. We put signs up at six colleges in our hunt for volunteers. By the end of the first week, our hypothesized weekly input of fifty hours had already toppled the one-hundred-hour mark. The yield for all our energy: no house, no volunteers, no Spanish-speaking professional to give the tests.

After an early morning session with one of the students that I had retained, I came down from my little windowed house on the hill and entered the kitchen. Suzi shifted her papers excitedly.

"I think I found something. After running my butt off all week, I think I've hit it. They were hesitant at first because the Sotos can't sign a year lease, but I explained everything. I think they're anxious to have the house occupied. We have an appointment at ten."

The small modest house, painted in battleship gray, sat on a narrow strip of land, sandwiched tightly between its neighbors. The real estate broker, sporting a nineteen-fifties' pompadour, waited at the front door. As we walked toward him, he discreetly ran his eyes thoroughly up and down my body, then Suzi's, giving himself several additional moments to assess the condition and value of our Jeep. Momentarily satisfied, he permitted his face to give us a small, rehearsed smile, then he ushered us into the living room. We toured the house quickly. No long term lease. Completely furnished. Perfect.

As Suzi checked the refrigerator and the inside of the stove, I peered out the back windows. I felt the agent's eyes again feeding the little computer in his brain. I had purposely changed my dungarees and sweatshirt for slacks and a jacket...mostly due to Suzi's request. But I did not cut my rather longish hair, which flopped over my ears and neck. He studied my head, then my beard; not in a manner dissimilar from that of an artist studying his model...only the man had not brought his paints and easel.

"Excuse me," he began, "this Mr. and Mrs. Soto are from Mexico. Did you say whether they spoke English?"

"They don't," Suzi offered innocently. "They're wonderful people. We will help them to communicate. Besides, they'll have an interpreter with them."

His eyes wandered before she finished speaking, as he formulated his next question.

"What part of Mexico are they from?"

"Encinada. Are you familiar with Baja California?"

The broker shook his head. "Actually...no." He cleared his throat again. He tapped his pencil on the pad nervously. "Are they of Spanish descent?"

I glanced fleetingly at Suzi and said: "As versus what other descent?"

"Well," he began, "Mexico has different heritages I guess...the Spanish, the Indians...ah, people from other continents."

"They're two human beings trying to help their son by coming to New York," Suzi offered tensely.

I squeezed Suzi's shoulder. "We'll take it. I'm willing to cosign the agreement. You can certainly check my references."

The real estate broker peered at us blankly.

"We'll take it," I repeated. "Just send us the agreement in the mail."

The following day Suzi barged into the den and dropped limply into the chair. "Our friendly real estate agent just called."

"Are you surprised?" I asked.

"No, Bears...." she sighed. "How could he? His client mysteriously decided not to rent the house. How convenient! You know, at first, I thought we weren't hitting right. Now, well, my vision has cleared. Every time I've called on an ad, as soon as I mention Mexico or the Spanish language, the apartment or house is unavailable."

"Maybe if we just become slightly less articulate...not dishonest, just give them less information instead of a family biography. They're our friends. Period. They live on the West Coast. We don't have to define which side of the border."

"I'll keep at it," Suzi sighed. Just as she left the room, she turned and said: "I'll bet you that man goes to church every Sunday."

"Now is that very loving?" I said.

Suzi picked a paperback book off the shelf and tossed it into my lap.

"Catch, knuckle-head!"

Living within easy access of the city, I presumed finding bilingual psychiatrists and psychologists would be a relatively simple feat. Though the universities had no recommendations, the psychological association of three counties referred eleven professionals fluent in Spanish. The first seven felt ill-equipped to perform the tests on a young autistic child. Two psycholgists, who knew of our work, said their busy schedules would not permit them to participate. Another did not want his tests published or reviewed by others. A rather caring physician asked me why I would want to spend all this energy on a child whose medical profile illustrates the hopelessness of his condition. I remembered other doctors with similar pronouncements four years before when we searched for help for our own son. Nothing had changed.

I exhausted my list in two days. By the end of the week, after gathering more references, I spoke with thirty-one professionals without finding one willing and able to see Robertito Soto.

Next, I focused on hospitals and teaching centers. One clinic wanted to do a language scale on Robertito despite the fact he's a non-verbal child. Though each of these facilities I contacted had Spanish-speaking clientele, one, in fact, servicing the huge Spanish population, none of them had Spanish-speaking professionals capable of administering childhood developmental tests and none of these institutions seemed to view the fact with any deep concern. In effect, English-speaking psychologists and psychiatrists routinely tested Spanish-speaking children. Obviously, they would form opinions and diagnose from their findings—labeling, prescribing and, perhaps, even institutionalizing little people they could not fully understand.

As I sat in my little house on the hill, shuffling through papers and jotting notes from my last telephone conversation, Bryn appeared at the window. She smiled a goofy, cartoon face. I motioned her to come in.

"Bears," she began as she slipped through the doorway. "I knew you weren't working with someone, so I thought I would come up. Is it okay?"

I nodded, which became her signal to pounce on me and kiss my nose. I tickled her until she jumped off me. When Bryn stood up straight and bent her head, her long brown hair flowed around her shoulders, almost reaching her elbows. Though only twelve years old, Bryn had the carriage of a mature woman.

She withdrew a small box from her back pocket and placed it in my hand. "Here," she said. I looked at her, then eyed the small container. Inside, I discovered a varied assortment of dollars, quarters, nickels and pennies.

"There's eighteen dollars and ninety-seven cents there. I thought since we're gonna be poor, I wanted to help. I know it's not a whole lot, but it's everything I've saved for the last two years."

I hugged my little friend, who, despite her moments of unreasonableness, had always shared with us the best of who she is. "Brynny, I'm really glad for your offer . . . it's wonderful to want to share. It's a real good feeling, for you and for me." I patted her belly. "There's more than a stomach in here; there's a beautiful person."

Bryn smiled self-consciously. "Daddy, c'mon, don't say you won't take it."

"Let's start with the idea of being poor," I suggested. "I didn't say we would be poor. I just said we would have less for a while; perhaps, a lot less. For the moment, we're okay . . . really, we're okay. Now as far as your offer to give me your savings . . . how about knowing that I will definitely remember your offer, that if something happens, Bryn has tucked away eighteen dollars and ninety-seven cents for this family. Okay?"

She nodded. "Bears, is it gonna be like this when they come?"

"Like what, babes?"

"I don't mean to sound selfish, but you guys have been so busy since you told the Sotos to come."

"Brynny, I know. We'll be jammed just a couple of weeks more...until we pull it all together. Even so, we'll always have time for you, for Thea and for Raun. If you think you're not getting enough, you just shout it loud and clear."

She seemed relieved. "Lov'ya," she said as she kissed me and opened the door.

"Hey, I think you forgot something," I said, holding out her little case. She removed it from my hand and did her little girl walk-skip down the stairs.

*　　*　　*

The second week bore a different harvest. On Monday, I located someone to do the video tapes. Gratton, a bright, articulate and idiosyncratic man, had once taped a session with Raun years before. He would be available.

The following day, Rita Corwin, a fellow Option mentor and therapist, called with the name of an associate, a psychiatrist, who volunteered to help. Paul Goodman's retiring manner contrasted dramatically with that of other physicians I had spoken to the previous week. Since his area of specialty was pediatric psychiatry, he expressed his own interest in seeing us work first hand and in assuming the possibilities of an Option approach with a severely dysfunctioning child. Though Paul's time usually translated into significant fees, he offered his time and expertise without charge. When the Sotos arrived, he would do the first psychiatric evaluation and then successive ones at intervals I specified.

Toward the middle of that week, we located Dr. Carl Yorke, a pediatric psychologist with a specialty in administering a battery of developmental scales and studies for children with suspected developmental, cognitive, neurological and emotional problems. The word autistic did not scare him. He had tested hundreds of autistic and retarded children. Our wanting to dissect all aspects of the examination did not insult him. He welcomed that participation with a full awareness of our needs in terms of the program. Even the Spanish-speaking aspects of our situation did not upset him. Carl had tested many Spanish children and, though he himself was not bilingual, he performed numerous tests with the help of a Spanish special education teacher. They worked as a team, with Carl directing the activity, cataloguing and interpreting the findings. I crisscrossed my references on this psychologist since his role was crucial in providing us with an external yardstick. The feedback was unanimous: highly regarded, seasoned, sensitive and very knowledgeable.

We had managed to secure all the significant trimmings...but no house. On Thursday, Suzi and I split the chore of house-hunting. We had used up half our time. Francisca, Roby and Robertito would arrive in ten days.

By midday, I had seen seven apartments; all unsuitable—either because of size, lack of privacy or serious noise problems. My monologue with agents about my friends from the "West Coast" followed the simple format Suzi and I had decided upon after our previous encounters. Ironically, no one probed beyond the few details.

As I drove into the driveway, I spotted Suzi squatting Indian-style on the front curb. She smiled broadly and jumped to her feet like an excited teen-ager bustling with news about her first date. She brushed her hair out of her face as she sprinted toward the truck.

"C'mon," she shouted, whipping the door open and catapulting her small form into the Jeep. "We've got to put a lot of white light around this one. Oh, Bears, there's a tiny house available only five blocks from here...it came on the market this morning."

The little house, snuggled between small shrubs and sheltered by a tall white birch tree, faced an Italian restaurant; the exterior color—battleship gray. Traces of New England in an earlier century echoed along the sloping roof and around the dormered windows on the second floor. Though houses have no voices, this building exuded a peaceful, mellow energy. The Sotos could live here! We could work here. The owner, draped in paint-stained overalls, invited us inside. He had begun to paint the living room, but the floors, the kitchen and all the other rooms needed significant cosmetic work. He rubbed the tip of his bulbous nose, leaving streaks of pastel green on his cheeks. We told him about Raun and about our work. Without hesitation or censorship, we talked about our Spanish-speaking Mexican friends whom we wanted to help. He kept smiling throughout the whole story.

"We'll take it," I declared. "The house...we'll take it. Right now."

"Fine," he answered casually.

Suzi hugged the man, paintbrush and all. Startled, he

103

smiled, obviously flattered by her affection. "When would the house be ready?" she asked.

"Well, I'd say maybe four weeks."

"How about eight days?" I asked.

"No. No," he said adamantly. "I'd do it if I could, but I have a full-time job."

"How about if we get it done; paint the house, clean the rugs, fix the floors, work on the bathrooms and the kitchen," I countered.

"In eight days? Impossible!" he said, shrugging his shoulders.

"You don't know us," Suzi said with a giggle.

Supervising a painter, a carpenter, a rug cleaner and a plumber consumed a significant portion of the next five days. Suzi and I, with the help of Bryn, Thea and even Raun, cleaned the house in the late afternoons and evenings.

Sitting on the floor, I scrubbed the bins in the refrigerator. I felt Suzi's eyes and turned to confront her smiling face.

"This is the best part, really," she said, laughing. "To see you parked on the floor, scrubbing away—it just breaks me up."

"I thought about that a few minutes ago," I admitted. "In that other lifetime...you do remember, right?" Suzi dipped her head affirmatively. "Well, with twenty-seven people working for me, I did all the cerebral tasks without getting my hands dirty...not that dirty hands are any less attractive than clean hands." I smiled. "Why doesn't what I'm saying sound right?" I rubbed the Brillo pad along the metal rim of the drawer. "When I waited tables during school," I chimed, "I could never reconcile studying Plato, Kant, Hegel and Sartre every day and cleaning pots every night. I never wanted to scrub anything ever again. So this is my karma, of course...scrubbing again."

Suzi crouched theatrically and framed me between her cupped hands. "Click," she said. "I like the portrait. Gives you a wholesome look of humility."

Sandwiched between our activities to refurbish the house on Thelma Street, we started our trek through a series of stores, trying to create an instant home inexpensively with dishes, silverware, garbage pails, a toaster, towels, soap, pots—an endless array of items. Our next major project centered on furniture. We had rented an empty house. The limitations of time and expense suggested furniture rental as a suitable solution. With only six days left, Suzi and I trotted,

104

literally, through a warehouse on Manhattan's upper West Side, picking this couch, that chair, those two tables, a bed, a second bed, three bureaus, four lamps and one mirror. We had to return the following evening with a bank check to cover security and a month's rent.

That night, Suzi and I crawled through the eaves in our attic, withdrawing over twenty paintings and framed posters we had stored since I closed down my advertising company. We could fill the blank walls of the rented house easily with my works from this era. First, we chose a poster containing a multiracial group portrait of babies designed for a save-the-children campaign; then we picked a startling hand-held eyeball created for an eye safety program. We included an updated art deco illustration that I conceived and designed for a reissue of *A Duel in the Sun*. Old dreams faded in the forgotten faces of Jennifer Jones, Gregory Peck and Joseph Cotton. We pulled pieces from other campaigns I directed; the mirrored ballroom globe with frozen images of Jane Fonda and Red Buttons dragging themselves one more time around the dance floor in *They Shoot Horses, Don't They?*, the comic portrait of Arlo Guthrie seated at a table with knife and fork in hand prepared to consume his own head for *Alice's Restaurant*, the haunting presence of Liv Ullman's face from Bergman's *Persona*, the racy cartoon graphics of the Beatles used for *The Yellow Submarine*.

I stared at the art and posters, then rummaged through a box filled with television commercials. They represented years of my life, yet now they had no meaning. Raun, Robertito and Option didn't exist when I turned twenty-four and started my own advertising/communications corporation to the hisses and boos of some who considered my experience flimsy at best. Nevertheless, my company thrived, despite the fact that I experienced business as combat, never able to justify the pain and fatigue as I watched people threaten, compete and, sometimes, destroy each other.

The photograph of a mother wearing a gas mask as she clutched a naked child to her breast loomed at me from the darkened recesses of the closet. In the late sixties, before it was fashionable, I supported the October 15 moratorium against the Vietnam war with an ad placed in several major publications. The following day, half my clients withdrew their accounts. The loss almost toppled the agency, but we survived. I felt caught in quicksand as the company grew again. But then Raun's presence overshadowed everything.

105

At first, I flirted with selling the business until I realized that by withdrawing myself, I had depleted what a prospective buyer viewed as a major asset. So when I chose to work more intensely with my son and be more available to teach, I had to walk away empty-handed. A part of my life was finished; over, completed. There were other things to do.

The decision to work with Robertito did not seem as clear. As Suzi and I stacked the posters and paintings against the wall, I fantasized about the house on Thelma Street in which they would hang and daydreamed about all the activity that might occur within those walls. What was different? Sure, this was someone else's child. Certainly that changed the circumstances drastically. The grant. We needed the grant, but there was more. We hadn't committed ourselves to "cure" little Robertito Soto, though I suspected that fantasy lingered in the minds of his parents. I found myself asking questions which never occurred to me when we worked with Raun. Did Robertito have to progress? And if we provided this special little boy with a roadway out, but he chose, for his own reasons, not to take it . . . would we trust his choice? The thoughts bombarded me. For the first time since our decision, I considered the possibility of Robertito Soto's choosing differently from us.

* * *

The north wind whistled through the trees, bending the branches and dislodging the loose leaves from their stems. A squirrel scurried across the driveway in front of me as I walked toward the Jeep. The glow from the lamppost pierced the darkness of early evening, allowing me to peek into my pockets as I probed for the keys. Then, on the ground beside me, I noticed the shadow of a looming figure. A quarter-turn of my head enabled me to confirm a dark form poised on the roof of my truck. Instinctively, I swiveled to my right and lunged away from the driveway. But my quick movement did not abort the impact of an airborne body, which catapulted onto my back. Wild hands grabbed at my clothing. I threw my arms out to maintain my balance, but floundered, falling first to my knees, then rolling to the side. Just as I twisted out from beneath my attacker, I heard a loud, silly laugh. Laura rolled onto her back skillfully, then flipped herself upright like a gymnast, landing squarely on her feet. She flashed a huge, mischievous, chimpanzee grin while arching her hip like an old burlesque queen. A two-second tease without intent. Laura always flirted her hellos.

She anticipated my leap toward her as she turned and ran across the lawn. Her laughter drained my thrust, but I followed her small athletic form, duplicating her jump over the hedges. The distance between us diminished. Her thick, long brown hair danced behind her. Her racing form reflected hours, days and years of intense input, tuning and exercising herself like an instrument. The jangle of her egg-shell beads and the soft thumping of her conspicuous engineer's boots did not compromise the aesthetics of her antique, nineteen-thirties' maroon dress.

She attracted attention. She demanded attention. It was no accident that Laura played a large, golden tenor saxophone, that her improvised jazz statements included very beguiling body movements which throbbed with her notes. It was no accident that Laura drew the audience's eyes to her, compelling them to join her in a musical journey that somehow seemed sexual. Yet, in spite of all the dazzle and invisible neon, she earned the applause with an abundance of talent and finely developed skill.

When I grabbed her, her body went limp with more laughter. I threw her up onto my shoulders and began to spin around...faster and faster.

"Bears," she shouted. "I give up. I'm sorry! Bears! C'mon, let me down."

I kept twirling her around until I lost my own equilibrium, sinking slowly to the ground. The dizziness cemented me into the earth; a warm floating punctuated by our panting breaths.

"I've always wanted to do that," she giggled. Lifting herself into a sitting position, she brushed off her dress and stared into my eyes playfully. "We finished rehearsals early, so I wanted to see you and 'my' Suzi."

"Is that a statement of desire or ownership?" I asked.

"Both," she said coyly. "I really came for another reason."

"Hey, Rha," I responded, using the nickname we affectionately called her, "you don't need a reason to be here."

"You guys are so jammed lately, I don't want to interrupt. I know you finally got a house for the Sotos, but what about helpers?"

"That's our soft area. Nancy's still in San Francisco. Marie is too busy at school. We have the parents, a volunteer translator and Suzi and myself. And I have six more interviews this week." I flashed on my watch. "I have to go to the city to pay for the Soto's rented furniture, want to come?"

Laura nodded and we left immediately. The sparse traffic allowed me to arrive in Manhattan within thirty minutes, but then our movement spurted and jerked in the crosstown crawl.

Just as I depressed the accelerator for a clear run, a bag lady pranced off the curb directly in front of the Jeep, forcing me to slam on the brakes. The woman pushed an old rusted supermarket cart containing brown bags filled with all her worldly possessions. Her matted hair, heaped haphazardly into a bundle on top of her head, fell partially in front of her face, obscuring one eye. She wore an old army coat and torn combat boots. Her pock-marked face created little craters filled with the city's grime and soot. The woman turned, ever so casually, to observe my screeching tires until they came to a complete halt within a few feet of her form. She waved her arm affirmatively as if to compliment me on my driving skills. Laura hunched over the dashboard, disturbed at seeing some flickering similarity between this woman and herself. A hulk, a shell, a carcass, she thought to herself. Burnt out. Battered. Worse than dead. Compassion, she insisted, as she watched the bag lady bend down in the middle of Madison Avenue, pull up her baggy pants and adjust her red-and-white checkered argyle socks.

The old lady peered at me blankly. I smiled. She tipped her ancient chin with great dignity, grinned emphatically and then resumed her afternoon stroll. Laura giggled uncomfortably.

"Only in New York," I whispered.

"It's the place where the freaks aren't freaks. When I'm in the city, I feel really at home, especially in my art classes." Laura began a reflexology massage on her foot, applying pressure carefully to all of the acu-pressure points. Then, almost routinely, she said, "You know, what you're doing with the Mexican family...reminds me of my time working with Raun."

"Somehow, Rha, it's very different."

"Yeah, I know. But for me, well..." She dropped her foot and stared out the window.

"Do you want to finish the sentence?" I asked. When I noted her hesitancy, I added: "I'm not lobbying for a complete sentence. How about I ask you something?" She nodded without looking directly at me. "We're pressed for time. I wouldn't ask you...only if I had to. I know how involved you are with your music. But could you help us out for a couple of weeks working with Robertito...until we train the others. You were a great teacher for Raun. I know you'd be the same for Robertito."

Tears began to stream uncontrollably down Laura's face. "God, Bears, I thought you'd never ask." She sighed and smiled. "Working with Raun was the best time in my life...really, it was. I love what I'm doing now, but then, I felt so alive, so connected." She paused and looked down. "You know, you and Suzi taught me how to be soft."

I double-parked in front of the furniture store, then turned directly to her. "It'll be good to work together again. I'd want that for both of us, for all of us. And these people are very special to do what they're doing." Laura nodded and planted a soft kiss on my cheek. In that instant, she was neither sexual nor theatrical...just Laura.

Laura mounted the front hood of the Jeep. She draped her legs over the fender and let them hang conspicuously apart while she watched the traffic whiz by. A middle-aged man stopped within five feet of her form and leered at her. His eyes scrutinized her body. Laura toyed with the attention for several seconds, then caught herself, angered by his invading eyes and her own vulnerability.

She whipped her legs together and said: "Buzz off!"

"Maybe next time," the man snickered as he walked away.

Her face flushed. Her voice had had a deadly cutting edge. Maybe those who had accused her of being tough were right. Sometimes, deep down, she felt hard. Cold. Aloof. Anything but soft, feminine, motherly. Those qualities came to life in working with Raun. But that was different. He was special. Could she work with Robertito? Could she feel maternal again? The chorus from her childhood argued against it. Everyone accused Laura of putting Laura first. She knew it was true, even now, but was it wrong? She thought of Molly, her twin sister...her greatest comfort and her greatest burden. They had shared games, secrets, even friends. She depended on their relationship. But then the unexpected fractured the balance. Molly matured first, not by weeks or months, but by years. Her body blossomed fully within a short period. Womanhood came to her breasts and the curves of her hips. Laura remained small, undeveloped and boyish. She waited impatiently for years, inspecting her flat chest and eying the straight lines of her body. Her large hypnotic eyes, her strong Mediterranean nose and her prominent chin did not offset the missing attributes. Unable to compete socially, she had made herself tough and strong, a survivor whose music and art gave her special distinctions. Even when her womanhood finally flowered, Laura could not retrace the steps. Physical contact as well as expressions of joy and anger had been implicit taboos in her home, so boldness and self-confidence became her trademarks. And yet, she wanted to be tender, gentle, caring, especially with a child. Would she find that softness in herself again?

For a second, she wanted to withdraw her offer to help with Robertito. Suppose she didn't feel it again? Then the truth would be undeniable, once and for all.

Chapter 7

As the passengers disembarked from the plane, Francisca Soto struggled to put her son's jacket on him. Robertito pulled his arm away, thoroughly entranced with the string he flapped in front of his eyes. Roberto Soto gathered the hand luggage into his arms, fully attentive to his wife and son while being jolted by the people passing him. Several businessmen paused in the aisle for a closer look at the strange boy. His actions mesmerized two stewardesses, whose whispering voices easily reached the Sotos. Francisca tried to ignore them, but her growing self-consciousness made her more rigid in her insistence for her son to co-operate. She maneuvered his jacket into place and sighed her relief.

"Bueno, mi amor," Roby said to his son, talking as if the little boy understood every word. He touched Robertito's head and smiled proudly at his wife. She returned a tentative grin, then whipped a brush through her son's hair, carefully straightening his jacket.

Charlotte Medina, who had volunteered to accompany the Sotos as their interpreter and to be trained as a teacher, peeked out of the small oval window, trying to catch additional glimpses of New York from the grounded plane. She saw only other planes and glass-walled reflections. Disappointed, she turned and smiled at Roby. He nodded to her, wanting her to feel their excitement, to see the same hope that they saw in this journey.

"*Ven*," Francisca said to her husband, tipping her head to include Charlotte. She and her son were ready. She led him into the aisle, then hesitated. Her hand flipped the latch on an overhead compartment. The door sprang open revealing an insertion box game they had taken on the plane with them. She grabbed the toy and rattled it in front of her son, hardly distracting him from his string twirling.

"*Mira*, Robertito. *Esta es especial*." All she wanted was a sign, a tiny recognition she could record and share with us upon her arrival. But her son maintained his aloofness, stimulating himself happily to the exclusion of others. Everything would be okay now, she promised herself. New York meant hope, opportunity, salvation. She had forgotten my caution and my words. "Francisca, I know how much you love him, but we can't make any promises or predictions. We'll take one day at a time." But as she looked at her son, she fantasized about all the possibilities. The memory of their first visit to New York remained vivid. The changes in her son within less than one week had been dazzling. "Imagine three weeks or three months," she assured herself, ignoring the past two years and discounting the intensity of her son's present preoccupations. Francisca gaped admiringly at those finely chiseled features, held her breath and stoically exited the plane.

Suzi stood on her toes by the railing, searching for a glimpse of at least one familiar face. Raun sat on my shoulders, scanning the crowd, designating himself as the "lookout." Bryn and Thea stood beside me and waited.

"I see them, Bears," Suzi shouted. As she watched them walk up the ramp, her eyes filled with tears. She wanted everything for these people and their only child. At last, she thought, perhaps now, we can all work together and make it happen. Francisca looked exactly the same, spirited, walking tall, a determined expression on her face. The lines around Roby's eyes had grown deeper, adding to the soft, gentle quality of his appearance. And Robertito, beautiful, enigmatic Robertito. Although significantly bigger and bulkier, the infantile expression remained familiar. Robertito had not aged. He remained pure and untouched like a magnificent porcelain sculpture never weathered by time or daily concerns. His right hand tirelessly flapped a string beside his head. His legs carried him forward a little stiffly, as if he had been programmed to walk. Suzi pressed her hands against the railing like a young colt anxious for the race. To begin! A rapid pulse surged through her limbs. Waste no more time, she counseled herself and the Sotos in a silent dialogue. Then, unwilling to wait any longer, she slipped under the barrier and embraced Francisca.

Roby waved to me, his head bobbing not only in recognition of our presence, but somehow, for the very first time, acknowledging what we were all about to do...or try to do. Francisca's face tremored when she held Suzi. Thea jumped into Roby's arms and hugged him. Raun and Bryn waited their turn to be embraced. My arms enveloped Roby and Thea at the same time. When I looked into his eyes, I realized that we had moved closer to each other again. I felt like I had loved them all my life. We patted each other's backs, grunting and laughing like a couple of silly old ladies.

When I turned to pick up Robertito, Raun had already intercepted him. He stroked the little boy's cheeks. "You know, Robertito, we're all going to take care of you. Even me." Raun smiled at me and tugged at my sleeve. "Maybe he won't be autistic any more...like me." I knelt down and pulled my son close to me. Every word from his lips was a gift. "Maybe, Raunchy...only maybe." He smiled like a seasoned professor, full of thoughts and ideas, all of which significantly outpaced his five years. I put my hand out to Robertito. He pulled away and increased his flapping. His tongue laid lazily over his bottom lip. "Robertito Soto. ¡Hola!, Robertito." Blank. Expressionless. In the midst of this busy terminal, an unearthly calm permeated his face. Non-distractable. Self-contained. Spinning on an internal merry-go-round, the mesh of inner optics combined with his willful body motion. I watched him in silence, amazed at the completeness of his withdrawal. Robertito was less available now, at this moment, than during the first minutes when we had encountered him almost two years before.

The tapping on my shoulder distracted my attention from Robertito. A young woman, tall, thin, stylishly dressed in Scottish plaids, smiled at me. She would have to be Charlotte. As I went to embrace her, she moved back, finally extending her cheek for a quick, antiseptic kiss.

"We're glad you can be with us," I said.

"Well, I've heard so much about all of you. And I do want to do my best for the child."

Raun hugged Charlotte without hesitation. She held him awkwardly. "You look just like your picture," he said to her, "but I didn't know you'd be so big. You're big like a man."

"Not really. Tall like a woman would be more exact," she corrected him, visibly unbalanced by Raun's candid little commentary. She spoke with the barest trace of an accent, more European than Mexican. But Charlotte Medina didn't view herself as Spanish or Mexican-American. She considered those labels an indignity. Her American passport gave her a new birthright, allowing her to pull away from the shadow of her own heritage.

I said a few words of welcome in perfect Spanish to both Francisca and Roby. All eyes opened wide. My fingers located my teacher. Bryn, who had just begun second year Spanish in the sixth grade, had taught Suzi and me some idioms and vocabulary during the past two weeks.

Francisca put her arm over Suzi's shoulder with great pride and said, in very broken English, "My girl friend." Everyone applauded except Robertito and Charlotte Medina.

*   *   *

Suzi and I arrived at the house on Thelma Street at eight in the morning. Francisca's neatly combed hair framed her well-scrubbed face. She had prepared for our arrival. Her modest, but expertly applied, make-up suggested a certain formality. But when I hugged her, she gripped me tightly, neither withholding her warmth nor subduing her sense of urgency. Suzi embraced Roby, then Charlotte, who still withdrew instinctively from the contact. After we exchanged our hellos, Francisca pulled Charlotte deeper into our affectionate huddle, asking her to translate.

"This is a wonderful home," Francisca exclaimed. "It's just impossible to think how you did it. Everything's complete. The furniture, the paintings on the walls, soap in the bathroom and a refrigerator filled with food. I can't begin to thank you."

"You don't have to," Suzi insisted. "We're a family now."

Charlotte looked at Suzi as she converted the words into Spanish. Her pretty face softened with an unexpected smile. The comment had touched her and, for a moment, she relaxed her guard. Her cheeks glowed with a sudden warmth. Fran-

114

cisca and Roby listened intently and concurred. A family. Yes, a family. That's what they had both wanted.

"I don't know if you noticed," I said to Charlotte, "but all those strange items in the kitchen aren't poison. The food is all natural, grown organically. And we didn't buy sugar, salt or any chemically ridden products."

A groan erupted from the young woman's throat. She threw her hands over her mouth, then dropped them conspicuously to her side, wanting to minimize her exposure. "Well, I understand all this . . . for the boy, I mean. But I have to have my coffee in the morning and my coffee has to have sugar in it."

I laughed. "Sure. We would only want you to do what you wanted to do. Since we'll monitor everything in Robertito's environment, including nutrition, we thought you might want to do the same for yourself."

"No, thank you," she said, grinning.

Francisca asked for the exchange to be interpreted. Afterward, she reaffirmed her own sensitivity to food, citing concrete changes in her son's behavior after she modified his intake. He became more relaxed, less hyperactive and irritable when they eliminated sugar and foods with artificial flavoring and coloring. She herself experienced a more even energy since stripping sugar out of her own diet. This had been the legacy from their first visit to New York. Then, with great emphasis, Francisca assured Charlotte that if she wanted sugar, they would definitely provide it for her. The young woman appeared relieved.

Roby ushered us into the living room, where we encountered his son, pacing back and forth across the rug, screeching to himself and gurgling loud infantile sounds. His toe-walking became obvious immediately. I set up my cameras as Suzi opened our notebook. This would be the first of eight volumes. I felt the warmth ooze from Suzi as she observed Robertito. It made me remember, in a fleeting thought, the past few years when we had taught Option together and worked with other children and adults. But my lectures and writing had segmented our activities. This lady had become more than just my wife and the woman who shared my bed. We had walked a path together, undressed, without pretensions or barriers. Often, we anticipated each other's thoughts and feelings. She had become part of the creature I called me. I had become part of the creature she called Suzi. Separate, yet in concert. And now Robertito, like Raun, had brought us even closer.

"He's a gift," I whispered to myself. In that second, the jarring words of another writer, also a father of an autistic child, bombarded me. "You're the kind of person I dislike the most," the man said without hesitation after reading the book about my son. "You take something that's ugly and make believe it's beautiful." But Raun and his disability had been special, inspiring and, indeed, even a beautiful experience for us. We had allowed him to be our teacher, our guide into his world. We had been enriched by walking beside him.

"You take something that's ugly and make believe it's beautiful." I wondered why those harsh words stayed with me. In some ways, that other father had been correct. We had found beauty in what he experienced as despair and he had found pain in what we experienced as joy. His vision was no more or less accurate or grand than ours. His son, my son, the son of Roberto and Francisca Soto had no inherent, absolute qualities. Our feelings mirrored the judgments we made about them. At some point, we had both wanted the same things for our children; only we took very different paths.

While facing Robertito Soto, deviant, alien, a perplexing enigma, I found the beauty overwhelming again...not only in this child, but in those who journeyed with us; Francisca, scared and hoping beyond hope, yet here to watch, to learn, to find a more effective way to express her love to her son; Roby, jeopardizing twelve years of hard work for an ideal completely foreign to his own childhood—the love of family; Laura, willing to reconnect again and challenge her remaining fears; Charlotte, withheld and guarded, but taking a chance; Bryn and Thea, who wanted to give more at a time when their friends championed the vision of "hurray for me"; and Raun, deep and endless Raun, the student and the teacher who wanted to help another child climb the mountain. And, of course, Suzi, with her baritone Tallulah Bankhead laugh. She consolidated her strength on her inherently frail frame, never once hesitating when the Sotos asked for more. Unselfish? Sacrificing? No. Nobility seemed the lesser impulse. The last five years had brought her many opportunities to follow herself, plot her own path, listen to her old dreams, despite the doubts, despite the pressures of others. Robertito had given Suzi another chance to be more of Suzi. And what about me? What was my private destiny in being here and confronting the mountain again? Somehow, I knew it had to do with letting go...but of what?

The hiss of the motorized camera filled the room, capturing frozen moments, creating portraits of suspended animation. A busyness pervaded every aspect of the little boy's activity. His awesome commitment and conscientiousness framed every behavior. Robertito flittered quickly across the floor, ripping pieces of paper into identical lengths and then twirling them at the side of his head as he stared at their contortions from the corners of his eyes. Yet, despite this intense, consuming concentration, he maneuvered easily around the furniture, never once bumping into a chair, a table or a lamp. I off-centered the couch only to watch Robertito circle around it without once diverting his eyes from the twirling paper...like a finely tuned machine let loose on automatic pilot.

We called to him in seventeen different voices. Each reflected a contrasting mood. He didn't respond. Even his parents failed to attract his attention. Exhausted, they sat on the floor, huddled by the doorway. They strained to digest every moment, trying to understand more about their son's distinctiveness. Charlotte munched on a vanilla yogurt, alternately watching us and flipping through a magazine.

Several times I blocked his path. He glided around me without any acknowledgment of my presence. When I lifted him, he resisted at first. His muscles tensed, although his face remained placid. Then he went limp, his arms and legs dangling in the air. The smooth, unblemished texture of his skin reminded me of an infant. I stroked his hand, touching each of his fingers. For a moment, he cocked his head and stared at the fluorescent fixture visible through the open doorway. He moved his hand ever so gently against mine. Skin caressed skin. Four seconds passed. Then two more. And still another two more. Suddenly, his body tensed, becoming rigid in my arms as he flapped his fingers in front of his eyes. I set him carefully on the floor. He swayed for a second, turned and then continued his endless march around the room.

Food highlighted his day. Although he never indicated his wants, when Francisca placed food in front of him and put the first morsel in his mouth, he jumped at the remaining portion, consuming it with a fiery passion. Only after the food had been presented did he acknowledge it and show his wanting. At times, he ate with a spoon, but, more often, shoved his meal into his mouth with his hands. He drank juice and milk from a glass, but when he had his fill, he simply released his grip as he had done two years before, letting the cup drop to the floor and, sometimes, splinter into hundreds of pieces.

Laura arrived in the late afternoon. She embraced both Francisca and Roby easily, but hesitated momentarily with Charlotte. Ms. Medina, more accepting of the physical contact she saw freely exchanged, returned the embrace more enthusiastically than in the morning.

Francisca appeared prettier than Laura had imagined. Her erect posture and firmly structured face externalized an unswerving determination. What a tough lady, she thought, complimenting the other woman with the same words she leveled at herself as criticism. To her surprise, Roby had such a gentle quality. These people loomed bigger than life to her...putting their life savings and their business on the line for their son. Laura's language lesson with Suzi and her first Option session with me gave the program some reality. But, until today, the Sotos had been fictional characters, make-believe people about to enter a make-believe world.

She avoided concentrating on Robertito for a long time, half-expecting some final answer about her feelings in those first glances. Finally Laura forced herself to face him directly. "Oh, God, is he beautiful!" But as she watched his antics, her awe subsided. The project seemed so impossible. He was definitely more bizarre than she had expected. She tried unsuccessfully to imagine a little Raun contained within Robertito's substantial form.

I watched Laura watching us and the child. She rubbed her fingers together nervously, withdrew a saxophone reed from her pocket and sucked on it, her eyes glued to Robertito. I could hear her breathing from across the room.

As I observed Robertito, I began to see a pattern. By the end of the day, my conviction increased. Ninety per cent of the child's repetitive movements, including his finger twirling, originated with his right hand. He also tended to shake his right leg when he lay on his back. Did a body function preference reflect a brain function preference?

When we presented food to him, he grabbed it. But if a piece of paper was inserted between the food and his field of vision, he would not pursue. Once out of sight, it no longer existed in his mind. The classic memory dysfunction. Robertito, at almost six years old, lacked the ability to hold things in his mind, a function usually developed in a six-month-old infant. He lacked an ability to catalogue, process and remember information. Everything existed only in the present. His mind was like a huge warehouse of data and complex files, all without indexes and a reference system. No categories. No folders for animals, buildings, toys and people. Each item remained separate, hardly traceable through the maze of his cerebral cortex.

Like an infant, Robertito remained right brain oriented rather than utilizing and developing his left brain capability. Children moving through the earliest developmental and maturation stages, utilize the right hemisphere of their brain. The world is digested as a series of pictures and images, not very sophisticated, but usable on a crude and primitive level. As the child matures, he begins to learn gestures, expressions and words as symbols. The activity moves to the left side of the brain, the seat of thinking, communication and cognition.

The reticular formation, at the base of the brain, acts as the coding computer. Like the monitor in a vast railroad system, it routes information for identification and storage as well as future withdrawal . . . a complex process that functions with ease in most of us. A car is a car. We can easily think of several different types, sizes and makes without their being within visual range. Our mother's face is easy to remember. We never confuse her with our neighbor or the smiling matronly face on a cereal box. When we become hungry, we think of food immediately, oftentimes contemplating specific delicacies to suit the whim of our appetite.

For Robertito Soto, hunger was not connected to food. Each time he saw his mother's face, it was as if it was for the first time. He was not unattached to the woman who bore him; he simply didn't know her and didn't know how to know her. People were fleeting images which passed before his lenses. On occasion, he made picture associations for concrete things before his eyes. But more often, he could not make sense of what he saw and heard. His perceptive apparatus was normal. The nerves appeared to be intact. Yet the information from outside never seemed to make a clear and coherent picture. The world remained a confusing, useless muddle.

The process of observing became difficult and unrewarding for this little boy. Therefore, he stopped observing and stopped learning. He remained in a primitive state of readiness; lost, disconnected, adrift, except for the soothing motions and self-stimulating games he played with himself on a closed circuit. He was the entertainer as well as the entertained.

So when other children made the transition to the left

hemisphere, Robertito remained stuck. Cells have developed and grown for the past five and a half years without any exercise. If I tied a child's legs together for the first five years of his life, the muscles and nerves would shrivel from lack of use. Even when freed to walk, the child might remain crippled or only learn to hobble on limbs which had disintegrated. I kept imagining the cells in Robertito's left hemisphere. Unoccupied. Without the gift of calisthenics. A literal ghost town in his mind.

Although he flapped with his right hand, he manipulated objects with his left. He tilted his head, illustrating a reliance on his left ear to ingest sounds. His left foot appeared a touch more under control than his right foot. Since body functions are controlled by the opposite side of the brain, his increased skill with the left side of his body would support his greater dependence on the right side of his brain. And what about the encephalograms? Soft and intermittent activity in the left frontal lobes. The physician diagnosed brain damage. Could it have been the result of lack of use? Wouldn't the children whose legs have been bound show concrete signs of damaged muscles and nerves? The enormity of the passage of time struck me. All those years in disuse. Somehow, Robertito would have to be motivated to jump the circuits and travel into unchartered territory within his brain, to walk the ghost town, to climb a mountain so high, so difficult, so untenable that logic defied making such a journey. This special little boy did not suffer while running back and forth across the living room floor. He did not appear depressed due to any deprivation or neglect. His clear face and blissful expression mirrored the Tibetan monk, who, after years of intense study and discipline, found his oneness with the universe through traveling within. And so Robertito Soto had traveled within, and in spite of the urine and defecation which could barely be contained with his diaper and in spite of the sounds and bizarre antics which frightened the uninitiated observer, this little boy had found his own way to make sense out of the world.

His "isms," those repetitive motions and ritualistic rocking, twisting and twirling had become more than just self-stimulating behaviors. They had built-in rewards and reinforcements. No different from the hypnotic chants of an Eastern master of the Gregorian chorus in a Western monastery, Robertito's movements and sounds flooded his brain with alpha waves, soothing him with a hypnotic calm and peace
120

barely achievable by most of us. Then why intrude? For Francisca? For Roby? For Robertito?

I heard no call for help from the little boy. No scream of abandonment. We had wanted to contact him, but still allow him all the choices. Unlike others, we could not condemn him or his sisters or brothers around the world. He did the only things he knew how to do in order to take care of himself. As we had learned to respect ourselves and our own energy, we wanted to respect him and his energies. We would not force him like the behaviorist who would tie a child's hands or enclose him in a portable closet. Robertito Soto had to regenerate areas of his brain and make new pathways. Like the man downed by a stroke, he had to find an incredible source of motivation to facilitate his own rebirth. We had to create a world so comfortable, so stimulating, so non-threatening that he might choose the more difficult path as Raun had three years before. But it would be Robertito's choice...not mine, not Suzi's, not Francisca's and not Roby's.

During the second day of observations, we explored his reactions to outside sensations. Suzi banged a drum with a rubber mallet. No response. I dropped a book on the wooden floor behind him. Again, no response. Yet later, when I jingled the keys in my pocket, he turned and looked exactly at the point where the noise originated. He appeared blind to some things, yet visually alert to others. Robertito exhibited another classic characteristic of autism; selective attending to perceptual and auditory stimulus. He could, in fact, shut off his vision or hearing so completely that nothing could penetrate. In quick succession, he would shut off one sense, then another, selectively focusing on a single stimulus at a time. While Francisca spoke to her son, he stared hypnotically at his paper. I remembered a doctor criticizing an autistic child for turning off the world. My awareness indicated that the opposite might have taken place; the child might have *turned on* a specific part of the world. This little boy had not tuned out his mother; he had simply focused on seeing instead of listening...so the input never reached him. When Roby tried to attract his son with a colorful plastic doll, again the boy was not distractable. The two-note chant emanating from his larynx captured his attention, blinding his eyes while he focused on his hearing. Robertito did not move away from his father; he moved toward one of his many fascinations. I sensed a profound intelligence locked behind the awesome calm on his face.

Perhaps, as a supersensitive child, the trauma of birth resulted in an overbombardment of sensations. If a pin being dropped sounded like a firecracker and a door being shut sounded like thunder, then, in self-defense against an acutely sensitized system, he might have closed down. In doing so, he could have severed connections that he could no longer easily re-establish, leaving the world of perceptions dangling in disarray. Perhaps, the opposite possibility could also be accurate. Robertito, responding to a low-volume intake system, had heightened his perceptions by learning to cut off one sense in order to focus on another. Or was there a wonderful, internal movie screen playing before his mind's eye, continually distracting him from attending to the world around him? The reasons were less important than the awareness to deal with the sense to which he attended, by following his lead and his cues. If we could build bridges to his world, it could only be along the roads he made available to us.

Robertito Soto, a classically autistic child, suffered from a basic and profound disorder of cognition and language as well as neurological dysfunction; autism, from the Greek word "autos," which meant self. More than just an enigma, it set him adrift in another dimension. But why? An act of fate? A microscopic physical mishap in his brain that nobody could detect? Or had he been, in fact, that rare hypersensitive human being who had to cut his own wires in a desperate act of self-protection at birth . . . or even before that while in the womb?

As we observed Robertito for the third day, we became aware of the absence of anger and discomfort usually apparent with these children. We knew the reason for their absence. Though Francisca and Roby felt incapable of maintaining their own program, and sat in judgment of themselves, they had maintained the Option attitude of love and acceptance toward their son. He remained untouched by all the friction and discomfort that might confront most children. A father may scold or pull his child physically in order to make his point. Most youngsters would not be scared or disoriented by such a gesture. Yet the same energy expended toward an autistic child, who cannot understand or make sense of such actions, becomes a frightening act of hostility from which he withdraws or reacts with his own hostility in his own defense. A child's anger and discomfort are not the cause of the problem, but can often be two of many possible results.

At this time, Robertito mirrored the peacefulness of many

very young autistic children we had seen and worked with. Before the scolding, before the programs which pushed and pulled them, before the disapprovals, these children did not act aggressively or self-destructively. A special child required a special world...not one born out of hardship, despair or sacrifice, but one which began with a journey through ourselves in order to find our most loving parts and understand how really to accept and embrace another human being.

I recalled a definition I had read recently in a bulletin from the National Society for Autistic Children. It defined autism as "a severely incapacitating lifelong developmental disability which appears during the first three years of life." The word "lifelong" jabbed at me. A judgment. A belief. Since the problem had been more clearly defined in recent years as physiologically based, they envisioned that as hopeless, unchangeable and irreversible...no different from the prognosis made by many professionals over the last fifty years. Rather than question the techniques for treatment, they pointed to the child as immovable. Rather than review their own attitudes and disappointments, they searched for a magical solution while thousands of these children were being discarded behind the walls of custodial institutions. Did we see Robertito as suffering from a lifelong problem? Defying all predictions of doom, Raun had become a "once-autistic child," bearing no traces of his early dysfunction. But that was Raun. We started working with him when he was one and a half. Robertito was almost six. The passage of time oftentimes haunted me, but I refused to give it credence. Everything was within the realm of possibility, otherwise why had we chosen this path?

*　*　*

The late afternoon sun bathed my little, one-room, hilltop house with an amber light. Set in a small patch of woods behind our home, the vaulted ceiling and clear expanse of glass allowed me to view treetops and open sky. Forty minutes from midtown Manhattan, yet amid the squirrels, the birds and an occasional rabbit, the setting suggested the seclusion of Vermont. Only the distant roar from a nearby highway during rush hour fractured the spell.

Francisca played with my pen as she sat erect on the couch. Her long fingers, though shapely and tapered, oozed with certain power. The soft light, which punctuated her dark eyes

123

and highlighted her clear skin, did not compromise the physical power evident in her squared shoulders. The side of her lips curled downward under the pressure of a tight seal. Roby sat beside his wife, holding her hand. He leaned on his arm, slouching slightly into the pillow which conformed to his body. A smile radiated from his face. His softness and shyness neither embarrassed him nor diminished his strength.

Charlotte crossed her legs in the chair beside the Sotos. Her leg vibrated impatiently while she waited to interpret.

Francisca began the Option session. "Bears, I feel so much better now that we have come here. Maybe you could tell us how you think we should begin with Robertito."

"Okay, I understand your concern, but let's talk about why we're here. This is a very special time, not for me to talk, but if you want, a time for either of you to explore, uncover and, perhaps, discard any unhappiness, confusions or doubts. What we do with Robertito will gradually fall into place. But as you learned back in Mexico, the single most important part of the program is our own personal comfort and attitude...not simply what we do, but how we do it." I watched their faces closely and continued.

"As long as we're uncomfortable, even to the smallest extent, we're distracted. If, for example, Charlotte had a fight with her mother and while she worked with Robertito she kept thinking about the disagreement, feeling angry, then her whole demeanor would change. Her body language would be stiff. Her facial expressions would be strained. All kinds of things would change in her body, hormone and enzyme secretions...even the odor from her skin. Since Robertito doesn't utilize words and other signs to ingest the outside world, he would probably be even more sensitive than most children to the subtle changes in our attitude. Even though the anger and discomfort might have nothing to do with him, he doesn't know that. All he knows is that the environment we created is not all-loving, all-accepting, all-inviting. Animals often interpret our fears as hostility. Robertito might do the same."

As Charlotte finished translating my words, Francisca and Roby nodded emphatically.

"I understand completely what you say," Roby began. "I considered that to be a major problem for us in Mexico. We were confused and worried, especially near the end. During those times, Robertito was the least responsive and the hardest to handle."

"Roby, that's why this time is so important." I wanted to crawl inside their heads and help them see it. "That's why we've set aside many evenings to talk about observations and share ideas. Everyone will be trained and then observed several times each week...and here, too, we will have feedback sessions. Those are, well, program discussions. Here we try to do something far less predictable, but, perhaps, far more crucial to helping us be good teachers. Somehow, before we can be absolutely comfortable and loving with Robertito or anyone for that matter, we have to first become more comfortable and loving with ourselves." I touched their hands for a second. "So this is your time. There's no place to go except where you want to go."

Roby squinted, then peered thoughtfully out the window. Francisca shared with me one of the softest, most open smiles I had ever seen on her face. Then, almost self-consciously, she withdrew the expression and folded her arms in front of her. Back to business...as if those gentle, naked emotions were separate and distinct rather than an integral part of her search for her son.

"Maybe my being here inhibits them," Charlotte said softly.

"Perhaps, you could ask them," I suggested. She questioned the Sotos, but each responded with assurances they felt free to express anything that came into their minds. Two minutes of silence passed.

"Two weeks ago I could have talked about many things," Francisca began again. "But since I've come here, I feel more confident about everything. Oh, I know there is much for me to learn, but we are here to do that, aren't we?" She nodded in response to her own question, rocking her head enthusiastically. "There is something, Bears, that I do think about. I don't know if I'm unhappy about it, but I worry about it."

"What do you worry about?"

"You know we really tried for Robertito. We did everything we could. Maybe we...we should have come before." She eyed her husband, squeezed his hand and then inhaled a deep breath. "Bears, do you think it's too late?"

"Too late for what?"

"Too late to help him."

"If I answered the question, I'd only be telling you about my beliefs. What might be more helpful to you is learning about what you believe. Do you believe it's too late?"

Francisca bit on the top of the pen. Twice she positioned her mouth to speak. Twice she withheld her words.

"Go ahead, Mommy," Roby prodded softly, tapping her hand supportively.

Francisca grinned mechanically. Her eyes wanted to cry as her mouth smiled. "I don't know if it's too late," she answered. "I truly don't know." Tears filled her eyes. "I want to believe we can still help him. I want to!" The pattern of her breathing became erratic. Roby turned to his wife, then looked at me.

"Francisca, what about this disturbs you so much?" I asked, responding to the physical signs of her discomfort.

She hunched her shoulders uncharacteristically over her chest. Charlotte stared at her, poised to participate. "I know all we can do is try," Francisca continued. "Remember how you used to ask me how I would feel if Robertito never changed, never progressed. Well, I kept hearing the question over and over again in Mexico. Bears, my answer remained the same. I want him to understand more, but I don't want to force him to do what he can't or doesn't want to do. I learned to accept him, at least most of the time." She glanced at her husband, searching his eyes for confirmation. Her own exposed vulnerability surprised her. "But you see," she said, "this is different. Maybe while I waited almost two years...two years to admit that I couldn't do it...maybe, uh, I..." Francisca fought her impulse to cry. "Maybe...maybe." She squeezed her husband's hand, then pulled away and hid her face. Charlotte wiped a tear from her own eye as she translated the choked words. Francisca hid her face for almost a minute, then looked at me with blood-shot eyes. "Maybe, he, he missed his chance because of me!" She hit her chest accusingly.

"No, Mommy, no," Roby said, grabbing her arm.

"Francisca, what do you mean that he missed his chance because of you?" I asked in a soft voice.

"I see the difference in him. I do! Sometimes, I tell myself he's only being stubborn today and he's very preoccupied, but I know. It's harder now. He's old, maybe too old. One of the doctors warned us that if Robertito hadn't talked by five, he would never talk. Never."

"Do you believe that?"

"I don't know. I don't know what to believe." She banged the table several times with her open palm.

"What are you angry about?"

126

"I'm sorry." She snapped her body erect again like a football lineman bracing himself for a scrimmage.

"Sorry about what?" I asked.

"Acting silly, stupid. What's done is done," she declared.

"Although that might be so, what is still relevant is how you feel about it. If you are disturbed about what's done, you can ask yourself why."

Roby put his hand forward. "I think I feel some of what my wife feels. We tried to consider everything." His voice was barely audible. "Now that we're here, it becomes clear we should have come back much, much sooner."

"What do you mean when you say 'should have'?"

"I keep thinking...had I only realized this six months ago, a year ago," he said.

"But if you didn't, why do you believe you should have?"

Charlotte translated each word carefully, her voice beginning to mirror the tone and texture of my mood. She smiled at me. I touched her shoulder, then returned my concentration to Roby.

He rubbed his chin. "If I had realized it then, we would have called you much sooner...much, much sooner. We did it only when it became obvious we were lost and we wanted your help."

"Then if you called as soon as you realized you wanted more help, why do you believe you 'should have' called before you had that realization?"

Roby let his lips curl upward and gave an awkward shrug. "It almost felt like we didn't do everything, but...I guess we did." Roby threw his head back and exhaled loudly.

Francisca leaned forward again. "But suppose Robertito is too old."

"Let's go with that fear. Francisca, how would you feel if Robertito is somehow too old to learn and grow...that somehow, and I'm not suggesting this is so, but let's suppose somehow he had passed the age of being reached."

Her face flushed. "I don't want to think about such a thing." She looked away. Roby rubbed her arm.

"Francisca, what's so disturbing about such a thought?"

She cleared her throat and stared at me. "I want him to have more. I want him to be able to play and take care of himself. Not for me, Bears, really. I've never regretted one minute with him. I want that for him."

"I know you want that for him," I replied. "But wanting something is different than being unhappy about not getting

127

it. Why would you be unhappy if Robertito didn't learn to do those things?"

Francisca shook her head. She twirled the pencil between her fingers. "I wouldn't be unhappy about it, not like before." She swallowed noisily. "I want to accept him the way he is. I really do. I guess what hurts is that, maybe, if we waited too long, we're responsible. We've ruined his chances."

"Do you believe that?"

"What about what the doctor said?"

"What the doctor said tells you about his belief. What I'm asking you is what you believe."

A sliver of a smile curled the edges of her lips. She closed her eyes. "We're here because we know we can do something or, at least, we can try. No, I don't believe the doctor. But, you know, I still feel guilty."

"About what?"

"About being responsible."

"What do you mean?" I asked.

"It's back to the situation about coming here, asking for more help. I understand about what Roby said. We came now because we just realized it now. But that doesn't change the fact we could have done it sooner."

"Okay," I said, "knowing what you know right now, right this minute, could you, in fact, have known to come sooner than you did?"

She thought for several moments, then shook her head. "No. We kept trying to work with him. We built the special compartment in the bathroom. We tried to teach volunteers." She sighed. "We even went to that hospital in the Southwest." Francisca relaxed her face. "I guess we did the best we could. I've read that in all your books, Bears, but I have to keep reminding myself it's true. Only when we go over things, like now, does it become clear." She sighed again. "*Gracias.*"

"You can thank me for anything you want to," I said, "but not for good feelings you're experiencing inside. I only asked questions. You supplied the answers. You freed yourself."

"It seems so easy," Charlotte voiced skeptically. "How do you know what questions to ask?"

"Ah," I smiled. "When you learn to listen without judgments, you begin to hear the questions in other people's statements. In effect, you follow them. They become your guide and their own guide simultaneously. On another level, that's exactly what we're going to do with our little friend Robertito."

"But what does that have to do with being accepting and loving, the words you guys talk about all the time." She translated her question quickly for the Sotos.

"If we discard the beliefs and fears we trip over, like Roby and Francisca have done in some measure right here, we begin to suspend judgments, become more accepting, loving and trusting of ourselves. Once we do, our attitude toward others changes as well."

I turned to the Sotos. "Francisca, Roby . . . what else do you want to work on?"

The exchanges flowed more freely. Roby discussed his concern about asking relatives to help in the store during his absence. He never wanted to use people as his father once had. As he explored his discomfort, he reaffirmed his own intent and willingness to trade so that all parties got something of value. Francisca, still slightly hesitant, treaded softly into the area of her limited teaching skill. She had expected, when she returned to Mexico, to be capable of doing Option with others and guiding them. In some way, it was that very expectation that had blinded her. She thought she was supposed to have known everything. During the next hour, Francisca confronted a major source of her unhappiness: expectations. Often she created images in her mind about people and future events and if reality did not mirror her fantasy, she experienced disappointment, sometimes even great sadness. Francisca began to see how she created improbable, if not impossible, visions to fulfill continually.

Chapter 8

The package remained unopened, though a student had sent it to me over a week ago. I carried it every place I went. Each time I entered the car, I placed it conspicuously on the seat beside me. Before I went to bed each night, I stared at it on my bureau, but the weights of my eyelids always managed to close me down. The inevitable juggling between the Soto house and my own, intermixed with the very small group of students I wanted to maintain, combined with my intermittent attempts to write, resulted in a twenty-hour work day. The backlog from setting up the Robertito program had many reverberations. Suzi and I had to set aside special times each day to be with our children, not wanting any lapse in their access to us or our joy in being with each other.

The soft cushions of the Sotos' couch cuddled my body like a womb. When I broke the seal on the manila envelope, a London psychiatrist's notes and transcribed dialogues fell into my lap. He had studied with me several months before, trying to modify his classically Freudian background with a more loving and non-judgmental style of therapy. He joined a parade of Europeans who visited with us recently in New

York. Although I had worked with groups of professionals, as well as non-professionals, in the States, these individuals' passionate wanting and openness gave our teaching sessions a tremendous thrust. Since my commitment to supervise their sessions with clients predated our involvement with the Sotos, I promised myself to deliver a complete commentary on this man's transcripts.

The clock on the wall reminded me of my two o'clock appointment. The Soto house was quiet as I waited for the man who was to do Robertito's first New York psychiatric evaluation. Roby constructed shelves for toys in the basement. Francisca stayed with her son in the special room set aside on the second floor. Each time Robertito made a noise, I heard his mother imitate him. We had all agreed not to begin the program until all the psychological and psychiatric work-ups had been completed, but I found myself laughing, fully aware that "Mama" was cheating. She couldn't wait the two more days. Each morning she requested another dialogue session, wanting to move herself as fast as possible. Her tension had subsided, partly because she had worked through some unhappiness and partly because she felt sheltered by our input.

The accepting attitude presented in the house had already affected Robertito. Although he remained totally encapsulated in his world, he appeared more relaxed and happier. Even Charlotte seemed more comfortable, though she fenced during our first session rather than confronting her own problems.

Returning to the material from England, I moved quickly through the first section of our dialogue. He had really understood. With the exception of one attempt to manipulate and direct his patient, his questions came from a clear and nonjudgmental place. The slam of a car door jarred my entrance into the second section. I leaned over the back of the couch and watched a very specific human being walk up the driveway. A thick, ten-inch long, red beard meshed with a full head of red hair. Everything about this man, from his medium frame to his single-breasted suit, seemed dwarfed compared to the impact of his redness. His face appeared lost like a rubber mask set too deeply behind brighter accessories. The Rip van Winkle of psychiatry. "I love it," I said to myself, admiring his peculiar presence.

Just as he was about to knock, I opened the door.

"Paul Goodman," I said, extending my hand. "We really appreciate your being here."

131

He looked up at me, shook my hand rather studiously, then entered the room. His eyebrows lifted; his forehead furrowed. For a moment, he reminded me of a hairy Woody Allen doing a Bogart routine. But then a special softness penetrated Dr. Goodman's serious visage. "It's a real opportunity to see your work first hand," he continued. "Rita talks about Option with the staff at the clinic, but we, er, use rather more orthodox methods with our cases." He flashed a polite smile. "Child psychiatry is not quite an exacting science."

We discussed the general form of his psychiatric evaluation and our need for precise base lines and details. I offered to pay him, but again he refused. "No," he insisted. "If you can do all this, I'd like to do something too."

Paul Goodman made the primary diagnosis of early infantile autism. "Robertito had not progressed beyond the autistic phase of development of the first few months of life. A secondary diagnosis of mental retardation cannot be ruled out." He considered the lack of language to be a "poor prognostic sign." In each area, his analysis concurred with the endless stream of reports from other physicians.

He summarized his views of Robertito's parents after interviews and lengthy observations. "Mrs. Soto presents as a warm, nurturing mother whose relationship to her son seems to have in no way given rise to his difficulties. Mr. Soto, as well, had always been and still is concerned and involved with his son."

Later that evening, after Paul left, Laura arrived, bringing Bryn, Thea and Raun. With Francisca and Roby joining, we held a surprise birthday party for Charlotte. The cake and candles had an emphatic effect on her, but the special gifts from the children overwhelmed her. Bryn presented her with a small pennant on which she had stenciled Charlotte's name. Thea painted a series of dancing figures on cloth. When assembled in a row, they spelled out the letters of New York. Raun dropped a huge card into her lap, which he had painstakingly signed.

Charlotte looked at these people, these strangers whom she had known for less than one week. It didn't make any sense. Why had they gone to so much trouble . . . for her? Charlotte believed she had to grab everything she wanted. Take or be taken. There's a winner and a loser. Charlotte wanted to give, but within specific limits. She had also come to New York to avoid the surveillance of all those eyes guarding her like a school girl in silent tribute to her patriotic husband, a soldier stationed in the Pacific.

Raun jumped into her lap, sensing her ambivalence. "Charlotte, aren't you happy?" he asked, his dark-eyed, penetrating glance riveted to hers.

"Of course I am," she answered. Raun twisted his mouth into his cheek. He knew she had not delivered the complete truth.

Thea slid off the couch and walked slowly toward her. She approached shyly. Then in an uncanny, intuitive gesture, she stroked Charlotte's arm. The young woman gaped at Thea, who smiled self-consciously but continued to express her tenderness. The exchange caught everyone's attention. Conversation ebbed and died. In the silence, Charlotte Medina grabbed Thea, pulled Raun tightly to her and began to cry.

Several hours after the party, in a telephone conversation with Laura, she complained that no one really cared about her.

* * *

On Friday, we had a complete neuro-psychological examination done on Robertito. The following day, we delivered him to the offices of Dr. Carl Yorke for a complete developmental battery, perhaps the most significant external reference point for our program. Charlotte accompanied us, alleviating the need for another translator to work with the doctor. After a preliminary observation period, Carl eyed the little boy with great interest and compassion.

"He's very low functioning, amazingly low functioning. Of course I haven't worked him up against the scales and developmental graphs, but..." He stopped and shook his head. "Very low functioning. Tell me again, what do you hope to accomplish with this little boy?"

"We want to see if we can help him come to our world, but first we go to his," I said.

He had not heard my last words. "He's an amazingly beautiful child. You know, I've seen hundreds of autistic children. He's a bit different. Some of them are really abrasive, aggressive, hard to like. Something about Robertito. He's very likable. Kind of gets to you." He leafed through the packages of forms on his desk. "Look, I'm going to have to use even more infantile tests than I anticipated. But I'll still give you a whole series. You'll have a lot of different, comparable base lines."

For the next several hours, he put Robertito through an intricate series of tests. The child fascinated him, but his testing scores distressed him. "What you did with your son Raun was a miracle," he blurted out after the examination, "but if you do anything, and I mean anything with this boy, there won't be words to describe it. It would be beyond miracles." He ran his fingers across the numbers and check marks written at the side of the charts and graphs.

"Have any rough figures?" I asked.

"I'll have exact figures for you over the next few days. I have to compute all the reference points to give you a comprehensive profile, but..." Again, he stopped. He scratched his head and moved his chair closer to me. He muted his voice. "It's almost an embarrassment to put down an I.Q. It will probably fall between 7 to 14." He shook his head. "Barry, I have been testing children all my life and this is the lowest functioning child I've ever seen. Here, look," he said, pointing to the figures on two developmental scales, "the boy's over five and a half, yet his receptive and expressive language development is at a two-month level. His lag in social development is just as astonishing." The doctor scanned two graphs again as if searching for some noted accomplishment he might have overlooked. "It's very sad because he's really a nice boy."

Yorke's formal report was thorough and detailed. His scoring and psychological evaluation had been based on six major standardized screening tests for young children at various developmental stages. He also wrote a concise needle-point log of Robertito's behavior with descriptions devoid of the usual psycho-medical vocabulary.

"Throughout the testing, Robertito never uttered a word. He spent a great deal of time on the psychologist's desk, either sitting or standing. He would wander around the room. He would put his hands over his ears or his mouth or he would run in circles. Occasionally, he made random sounds. He would rock on the floor. Occasionally, he jumped up and down. Sometimes he would just spin around.

"Personality characteristics: Robertito is pretty obviously an autistic child and it was noted that there was no indication that he would listen to most commands. He barely ever responded to auditory or visual stimuli. He did not and does not relate much to anybody and, at present, is not saying any recognizable words. He does not seem to either look or listen to people or touch them. As a matter of fact, when he is hugged, he pushes people away. He certainly is much more occupied with objects than with people. He is excessively motoric, but on the positive side it was noted that he never made any strident sounds and there was something likable about the boy. Although he was active, he was not annoying. He was very energetic and most of the time was quite restless. Never once, during all the testing, did he make any specific, recognizable sounds in either Spanish or English. He did not echo any sounds and spent a great deal of his time spinning around. In general, he did not seem to have any particular orientation.

"He is most impaired in his language development. His receptive-expressive language was on about a one- or two-month level. It was noted that his activity did not stop when he heard sounds. It was noted also that he did not give direct attention to other voices or appear to be listening to a speaker. He very infrequently ever looked at anybody's face or looked into the speaker's eyes or looked at his lips. He did not turn deliberately toward the sound of a voice or look out in search of a speaker. He did not become frightened or disturbed by angry voices.

"In terms of his expressive language, it was noted that he did not respond to bell ringing, did not laugh, turn his head or say any two-syllable sounds. He does not imitate any speech sounds either. Occasionally, he coos or babbles or laughs to himself, but he doesn't laugh while playing with an object.

"In terms of his intellectual ability, he is currently functioning on about a nine-month-old level. He passed all tests on a seven-month level, but failed all on a ten-month level. The kind of tasks he did accomplish were motoric tasks such as pulling strings, playing with a string or securing a peller. He could not ring a bell by copying someone's actions. He could not adjust to gesture or words. While playing with cubes, he could not take three cubes. He could not do any tasks requiring him to imitate anybody's behavior.

"From a social point of view, it was noted that he does not ask to go to the toilet, he does not initiate any play activity, he cannot take off his coat or pants and he cannot get a drink of water. The boy is not toilet trained, he cannot dry his own hands, but he does seem to avoid simple hazards, i.e., a pile of blocks in the middle of the room. He cannot relate experiences. Obviously, he cannot play with other children.

"In terms of gross motor coordination, it was noted that he can broad jump, that he can jump in place and he could walk up steps. He cannot pedal a tricycle, balance on one foot for one second or kick a ball or throw a ball. He seems, also, unable to walk backwards.

"In terms of his fine motor coordination, it was noted that he can scribble, that he can build a tower of about eight cubes, but he cannot imitate a vertical line or dump a raisin from a bottle spontaneously or even after it had been demonstrated. He cannot copy a circle or make a bridge of three blocks."

Chapter 9

The six of us became more than a core group. Suzi, Laura, Francisca, Roby, Charlotte and myself, with the support of Bryn, Thea and Raun, gathered not as teachers, therapists or scientists, but as members of an instant extended family. Though we had not shared long and entwined histories like brothers or sisters, we knew each other.

Our marathon observations, the tests, a video session and several individual Option dialogue sessions had been completed. Suzi and I waited a week for this night. Laura had waited for over a year. Francisca and Roby had waited almost two years. Robertito had waited all his life.

We reviewed the premises of our approach, "to trust ourselves as well as Robertito." We reaffirmed the enveloping attitude of "to love is to be happy with," which would become the walls of our teaching womb. Since Robertito could not make sense of our world, we would go to him in his world. We would imitate his activities not only to make us easy to digest, but also as a concrete way to express our acceptance of him. Show him we care. Make our love more than a verbal commitment, but a working reality with this dysfunctioning child. We would not judge him, call his behaviors good or bad. There would be no conditions and no expectations. He did not have to perform or achieve any goals in order to maintain our caring and involvement.

First, we would try to make contact. Then, if he opened a door and allowed us access, we would try to help him find his own motivation to be with us. Finally, all activities would be broken into small, simple components to make them more digestible.

Each person received a special check list we devised in order to chart Robertito's behaviors and responses each week. How frequent were his repetitious behaviors or "isms"? And for what duration? Did he give spontaneous and requested eye contact? What have been his facial and emotional expressions? What were his reactions to familiar and new people? To familiar and new objects? Has he indicated any wants by pushing, pulling, pointing, crying or making sounds? Did his food intake influence his interaction? Did he initiate any contact? What language (words, phrases, motions, signs) did he understand? What about physical contact and physical skills? Any movement toward self-help capabilities like dressing and toilet training? The list swelled to three pages. Each notation helped us see our special friend more clearly.

I wanted everyone to know, including Raun, that each of us had something special to contribute. Though Suzi and I would train everyone, we did not seek to create replicas of ourselves. In fact, that would diminish each person's value. We would create general thrusts, but each person would teach on his or her own terms. Francisca had already displayed a special ease with movement and dance. Roby presented a more athletic, tumbling form. Laura brought with her the gift of music, articulated through voice and instruments. We wanted each person to be himself; to utilize his talents and interests as functional elements of the teaching situation.

We talked about being enthusiastic and physically affectionate when Robertito permitted. Establish any kind of human contact, whether it be facilitated by a ball, a musical instrument, a puzzle, a crayon or a dance routine. We noted the importance of attending to every cue the child made . . . for in the course of an entire day, we might only have one or two opportunities to make connections.

A medium-sized bedroom provided the setting for our work. Its location on the second floor sheltered us from any activity or noise emanating from other parts of the house.

We left the walls bare for the least amount of distractions. A single table and two chairs had been placed in one corner. Pillows and a backrest were stacked by the door.

Language presented no barriers for Suzi. Even Bryn experienced a certain ease. For our other children, for Laura and for me, we had to rely on our studies and the sheets of paper tacked on the walls which contained the most common Spanish idioms and words. Yet, ironically, our simplistic verbal statements became more ideal than the fluency of the Sotos or Charlotte. In a continued effort to simplify the input into Robertito's world, we wanted to limit the intricacy of language, using simple one- and two-word sentences...even using a single syllable for the most important words. But if the Sotos, Charlotte, or any of us wanted to express our excitement and love in long Spanish, or even English sentences, that could be done...for the sentiment communicated beneath the words might touch Robertito more directly than the meaning of our specific vocabulary. The limit on language would apply to a teaching premise. Rather than ask: "Robertito, would you like some milk this morning?" a simple substitute would be, "Robertito, want milk?" or just simply, "Milk?"

The Sotos had brought a carton of toys with them from Mexico. We integrated our own collection of tools with theirs. Laura donated some items, including several musical instruments and art materials. Other friends, who knew of our involvement with Robertito, gave us boxes of used playthings. But our needs, in fact, were quite simple. We brought only the most elemental, infantile toys into the room; blocks, insertion boxes, stacking cups and circles, oversized beads and a string, several simple puzzles, a pegboard and some musical instruments.

The primary focus would be to establish eye contact. Robertito would no longer be left to eat alone. We would feed him at eye level, creating additional opportunities for him to see us. Perhaps, he might glance past a spoonful of food and catch a smile or a playful wink.

"There's so much to remember," Francisca blurted from her squatted position on the floor. She tapped Charlotte, who translated her words immediately. Laura nodded her head sympathetically. She, too, shared the same concern.

"There's nothing to remember," I explained. "You really can't rehearse or memorize techniques if we're going to follow a child, go with him and trust that at any given time, he's

139

doing the best he can. That's why we talk about working on ourselves first, to stay open. We're dealing with a human being and a situation which is not static."

"Francisca, Rha," Suzi interjected, "what I always do is review my notes before a work session with any child...kind of a reminder. Then, I put my notes away and let myself be free, as loving, accepting and clear as I can possibly be."

"Far-out," Laura whispered. "Now if I could only do that."

"Do you want to?" I asked.

"You know I do," she responded. To camouflage her self-consciousness, she flashed a ghoulish, distorted Halloween face. Francisca and Roby gaped at her. Charlotte giggled sardonically.

"Rha, just be you," I said.

She leaned over and tapped my hand. "Thanks, Papa Bear," she replied.

The schedule of sessions for Robertito spanned a period of at least twelve hours each day, seven days a week. We would utilize his every waking hour. We had three months... hopefully. We wanted to use every day, every hour, every second. But the intensity of contact and our responses to his sporadic cues did not override the significance of our attitude. Time was not the teacher. A wise old man doesn't become wise simply by becoming old.

*   *   *

Like the sad face of an old clown, the Victorian porch sagged by the front entrance of the house. Peels of yellow paint, faded by a decade of sun and rain, hung from window sills and gothic arches. Nevertheless, this aged structure retained a charm that time could not erode.

The building attracted Suzi as she admired the gabled roof. "Perfect," she mused, "perfect for Laura." She ducked under the hammock which had been strung across the front steps. Her head hit the plastic bowl of a spider plant hanging precariously in front of the door. Suzi laughed. Two broken chairs, their backs temporarily supported by clothesline rope, had been set neatly around a small table which contained two crystal wineglasses and a bottle of Beaujolais.

"Rha," Suzi called. "Hi, Rha." She entered the apartment with the same ease with which she would enter her own home. The obstacle course combined with the decrepit exterior always created the illusion of arriving at "the promised
140

land." Inside, antique furniture had been offset by a blue oriental rug. Laura's own paintings hung beside ancient musical instruments displayed on the walls. Suzi heard soft flute music emanating from the kitchen. The grace with which Laura moved from saxophone to clarinet to piano to flute to guitar dazzled her.

She recognized the combination of notes instantly. "'Claire de lune,'" she marveled. The memories bombarded her like old movies. Before children, before Option, before marriage, before acting, she had had a seven-year love affair with the piano. She had perfected this piece more than any other. "Claire de lune" promised romance and deliverance during a time in her life when the fabric of her family stretched and ripped. Oftentimes, Suzi, ten years old, arrived home from school only to find the doors locked and no one home. One afternoon, she waited three hours in the freezing rain, huddled in the archway by the front entrance, her dress soaked by the rainwater. She played "Claire de lune" over and over again in her head, clutching her sides to stop herself from shivering. She held onto the inspiration of the music even as she began to cry, no longer able to fight the pressure of her bladder; embarrassed by the warm flood oozing between her legs. The image dimmed.

Laura's flute music filled her once again. She listened attentively until the last lyrical note faded.

"Wonderful," Suzi shouted, clapping enthusiastically.

Laura stuck her head through the doorway and smiled. "You sneak." She bounced into the room and embraced Suzi tightly.

"I noticed your special table setting on the porch. Are we celebrating?" Suzi asked.

"Sort of...I mean, I'm celebrating. You know what this means to me—you and Bears wanting me to be part of the Robertito program. I always remember you training me to work with Raun. Wow, what a crazy lady, I kept thinking. She's going to trust 'me' with her son." Laura smiled in a motherly way. "Now Raun's partly mine, too." She cleared her throat, stalling, searching for words. "Anyway, I wrote a song for you...kind of for you and Robertito. So that's the mystery behind my invitation."

Suzi hugged her friend. "You really did that?"

"Uh-huh," Laura mumbled. "Now don't go humble on me."

"Listen, knuckle-head," Suzi held her friend's hands and

squeezed tightly, "I feel very, very...honored. And I know Robertito, in his way, will be too. Really!"

Laura lit a candle to set the stage. She whipped out her soprano saxophone from its case and tuned it against the piano. Though she had performed in clubs and recitals, she felt the heat rising in her face. She would use any association to tap the softness which often eluded her. She tensed her jaw, manipulating her lips on the reed so that each note had the rounded quality of vintage wine, full-bodied and pure. Laura wanted her love for Suzi and for her horn to move her closer to Robertito, and ultimately, to herself.

Later, as they sipped wine on the porch, Laura became very quiet when Suzi talked about the program for Robertito.

"Rha, anything going on?"

Laura shrugged her shoulders and sighed. "How come I'm such an easy read for you?"

"'Cause you look like uncle Charlie!" They both laughed. "Do you want to talk about it?" Suzi asked.

"I'm getting nervous. I know you guys think of me as trained, but...Robertito's a whole different thing."

"What do you mean?" Suzi asked.

"He's so big and so old. Jesus, then there's the whole language mess. I'm a cripple when it comes to learning a foreign language. I got a 'D' in German...and that was a favor. Look, I'll talk to Bears about it in my session. I don't want to bother you with my shit."

Suzi turned Laura's face with her hand. "Hey, if you want to talk about it now, I'm here."

She looked at Suzi expectantly. "Just tell me. Do you think I'll still be a good teacher?" She held back on the more central question which disturbed her.

"Rha, I could think you would make the greatest teacher, but so what. That doesn't help you. What do you think?"

"I know I'm good with my music students. I felt so clear when I worked with Raun. But that's two years ago." She sighed. "Every once in a while I lose it; then I feel okay, even real confident. I go back and forth."

"Even if you're nervous, tongue-tied; even if your mind goes blank and you forget all your Spanish, all you have to do is follow him and you'll give him a gift."

Laura nodded and smiled. "One more silly thing." She put her hands up. "Okay, okay, don't say it. If it's on my mind, then it's not silly. You see, I'm learning." She tilted her head. "Roby and Francisca are beautiful people, but they're so, so, ah, straight...you know, like formal stiff, always so serious. I don't feel I can really be myself áround them." She began to giggle. "I mean take something dumb. Remember how long our last meeting was? Well, I held in a fart all night." Suzi laughed. "You know what this is for me? On my diet of rice and beans. Could you imagine?" Laura and Suzi became hysterical. "Suppose right in the middle of some detailed discussion of right and left brain function, I just leaned to the side, teacup in hand, and blasted a big one into the living room."

"That's a real problem," Suzi said with mock seriousness. "I'd say either change your diet or get a muffler."

*   *   *

"Eee-ooo, eee-ooo, eee-ooo," Robertito bellowed as he scooted across the room, his right hand flapping energetically beside his head. He side-glanced at his shaking limb. At a first superficial glance, his expression appeared smug and aloof. But, then, after a more careful scrutiny, the incredible softness, the hypnotic peacefulness, the unearthly internal calm of this child infected my every fiber leaving no doubts about the power and the enigmatic beauty of his self-absorption. Watching him drew me out of myself, beyond all familiar points of reference.

Francisca chased merrily after her son, finally duplicating his pace and maintaining a parallel movement. "Eee-ooo, eee-ooo, eee-ooo," she sang, submerging her echo into a musical context. He increased his speed. Francisca escalated her own steps. Against the harmony of cooing and strange babble, they passed before my eyes like dancers inaugurating a new ballet.

After twenty more minutes of fast-paced circling of the room, Robertito dropped to the floor like a sack of potatoes. He giggled, then curled his double-jointed, tension-free body into an embryonic ball. Francisca looked to me for direction. I smiled affectionately at her and maintained my silence, wanting to give her the space to search within herself for guidance. A feed-back discussion had been scheduled for later in the day. We had all agreed, except in emergencies of special situations, conversation between myself and Robertito's mentors during the work time would break the flow. A self-conscious smile gripped Francisca's face. She turned away from my glance and peered thoughtfully at her son. She wanted

143

to be perfect. The best! This was her child, her only child! Then, leaning over his body, she sang him a Spanish lullaby, caressing him with each word and soothing him with ancient lyrics. He remained absolutely still during the entire song.

He moved me, even in his inertia. I had this intense impulse to hug him, to cradle him in my arms, to "mother" him across the abyss with affection and a tight embrace. More than a random thought, I felt a definite jolt, almost electrical, vibrate through my arms and legs, connecting me in some elemental, yet unknowable, way to the biological presence of this little boy. A burst of sentences from Francisca, which followed her musical interlude, fractured the mood, severing the almost "out-of-body" bond I experienced with her son.

Robertito crawled several feet, tumbled over onto his side and rocked energetically. Francisca laughed as she swung her body like his, but her position slightly behind him made it difficult for eye contact. In addition, we had discussed, at great length, the necessity to talk continuously to him in order to share our caring and stimulate audio receptivity to speech; yet Francisca remained silent for the next fifteen minutes.

Each time I made an entry into my book, I felt her awareness of my movement. Just as her son side-glanced, ingesting the external environment through his peripheral vision, she, too, utilized that perceptivity to maintain her surveillance of me. Her nervousness became apparent. In less than three months, she would return to Mexico. This time, she told herself, she had to learn everything about her son, about herself, about Option before she left. The enormous pressure diverted her attention from the session, at times sabotaging her ability to relax. Nevertheless, her sustained input and enormous enthusiasm with Robertito would excite even the most casual observer.

When Robertito let his tongue hang out of his mouth, she mimicked him. He began jumping in place. "*Brinca. Brinca. Sí,* Robertito, *brinca!*" she shouted, joining him. As he jumped with his mother, I noticed he watched her mid-section, more aware of her harmony with his motion. Before we began, he appeared completely oblivious to our presence. Now, after only three days into the program, I knew Robertito, somewhere deep inside, found us more digestible. Though incapable of participating, he had, at least, increased his attentiveness to our existence.

Roby entered with some food, gave it to his wife and settled into a corner of the room. He noticed an increase in his wife's expertise, resulting, he assumed, from the nightly Option sessions and demonstrations. She seemed smoother, more patient, more relaxed. The growing mellowness of his son mesmerized him. The extended periods of crying and frequent tantrums, so common in Mexico, had almost disappeared.

Suddenly aware of the food, Robertito became more alert. His mother faced him with a cup of cereal. He glanced directly at her for a second, then looked away, his mouth slightly ajar. She used that second of contact to smile at him and say: "*¡Hola!*, Robertito."

While Francisca mixed the grains and fruits together, the little boy remained in a state of readiness. "Do you want to eat? I know you do. Shake your head so Mama can know what you want." He neither answered her nor acknowledged her statement. "Well, your mouth is open, so that must be your answer. You're such a smart boy." She filled the spoon and held it directly between her eyes as I had demonstrated during one of the group meetings. "*Comida*," she said, pronouncing each syllable slowly. "*Comida*, Robertito. *Co-mi-da*." When she brought the food toward him, he stopped flapping his hand. Robertito did not look in her direction, yet his mouth opened as if on cue, anticipating the exact moment when the spoon would reach his lips. He gurgled and murmured as he ate. His hands continued their flapping activity. He even twirled his fingers simultaneously. During the meal, little Robertito Soto glanced past the spoon two times and looked at his mother's face. Each time this occurred, Francisca exploded with enthusiasm in response to those one-second gifts. I found myself clapping and cheering. In some visceral way, Robertito was my son too.

After the meal, the little boy rolled on the floor. His mother rolled with him, touching him several times. Only once did he pull away. Francisca placed two cups between their faces as they laid side by side on the floor. Robertito watched her fingers manipulate the yellow and red cups, then he grabbed the yellow one briskly and flapped it in his right hand. His right foot mimicked the motion of his hand. The intensity of the "ism" increased rapidly. He pushed himself faster and faster and faster until a thin lather of perspiration veiled his forehead. Finally, he jerked himself almost harshly, his body pulsating with the self-induced rhythm. Francisca watched him compulsively, trying to block her awareness that her son had galloped into a state akin to orgasm.

Seconds later, he bounced to his feet, ran to the table and climbed on top of it. His tongue hung out of his mouth again. Setting herself in a position directly in front of him, Francisca mimicked his clown-like expression. Again, she remained silent even though her son did not make any sounds to imitate. I continued to log the session and make elaborate notes for our feed-back conferences.

Francisca noticed a wet spot on his pants. She grabbed a diaper from the shelf. Quickly, she unbuckled his belt and pulled down his pants. The urine had seeped through the diaper and plastic pants. As I watched her change him, the realization that Robertito was almost six years old rather than six months old became vividly apparent. Francisca did not notice the incongruity for she had been changing his pants since the day he was born.

When Robertito tried to get up before she had zipped and snapped his jeans, Francisca grabbed his arm. They struggled for several moments before she completed her chore forcefully. His big dark eyes clouded, obviously disoriented or disturbed by the use of physical exertion against him. I starred my entry. Unless questions of safety were involved, there would be no physical manipulation of Robertito. Although our motives might be clear and sensible to us, his lack of ability to interpret our acts might leave him with the unproductive impression that, somehow, we moved hostilely against him, invading his body, the only kingdom in which he could seek secure sanctuary.

With her thumb, Francisca flipped on the tape recorder. He swayed back and forth in perfect time to the beat. "Ah, you love music, don't you? Here I come," she said in Spanish, crawling on her hands and knees until she faced him. Very precisely, she said, "*Música. Esta es música. Mú-si-ca.*" Francisca tried to take his hands several times. Finally, he permitted her to hold his left one as he "ismed" his right.

A mother and child together. For another woman, this might be just a passing moment among many others. For most, touching a child and talking to a child were simple, uncomplicated, everyday acts. For Francisca Soto, these were minor miracles seldom experienced with her son. She stamped these seconds indelibly into her mind. They would become beacons to help light her path.

While he relaxed to the music and let his mother touch him, he kept jerking his hand...his right hand. He rubbed his right foot against the floor with considerable pressure.

146

Something about his movements seemed incredibly familiar. I felt a sense of *déjà vu* all day while watching him. Comparisons to Raun and the other children we had worked with yielded no insights.

"My God," I heard myself exclaim. I remembered! I jumped to my feet abruptly, startling both Francisca and Roby. I delayed my exit for seconds in order to reassure them.

My legs lunged forward down the hallway. I had increased my gait to a near run by the time I flew over the top step. "Charlotte! Charlotte!"

"I'm busy now," a sluggish voice answered.

My charge into the kitchen was aborted by the comical impact of her inert form. She sat with her feet up on the table, a phone tucked between her shoulder and her head, one hand busily applying nail polish to the other. Charlotte gaped at me. "What a lunatic!" she mused silently, her eyes riveted to my heaving chest.

Knowing her thought, I began to laugh. "I guess I do look like a lunatic." She gasped and overturned her bottle. "Really," I said, "I don't mean to interrupt you, but do you or Francisca have a sewing kit?"

"Now?" she questioned.

Pointing to her obvious involvement in her phone conversation, I said: "It's too long to explain, but I really need it."

She mumbled something into the receiver, then strolled out of the room. When she returned, she deposited a portable sewing kit into my hands.

I thanked her as I rummaged through the spools and pin compartments. Once I secured the largest needle, I placed the box on the table and raced back up the stairs three at a time. I entered Robertito's room on tiptoes, then quietly said several words in Spanish and interrupted the session. All the while, I could feel my pulse in my chest and my hands.

Slowly, I guided that sweet-faced little person into the center of the room and coaxed him to lay on his back. I stripped his shoes and socks off, then rolled up his shirt sleeves. Oddly, he did not resist me in any way. His co-operation startled me. It was almost as if he knew.

I stroked his soft, yielding hands. I watched those large apple eyes move in their sockets until they fixed on a light bulb. A very peaceful expression enveloped his face. Robertito lay there like a baby, open and trusting.

"Bears?" Francisca blurted when she saw me produce the needle from my breast pocket. I reassured her with isolated

147

Spanish words, sign language and the softest expression I could plaster on my face.

"Hey, little boy, I'm not going to hurt you," I said to my young friend in English. I held his left hand in mine. "Tito, it might sting, but no one will hurt you. Okay? Get ready. I'm going to do it now. Right now." I picked the soft part of his hand with the metal point. He pulled away immediately and stared directly into my eyes. I smiled at him and stroked his shoulder. He returned his concentration to the light bulb. Trying to telegraph my every move, hoping something, anything would penetrate, I did the same thing to his left foot. Again, he jumped. He bent his knee, tucking his limb underneath him. "It's okay, sweet boy. It's okay."

I felt a momentary sense of relief which dissipated when I scanned the right side of his body. "We all love you. *Yo te quiero*, Robertito. *Bien. Bien, mi amigo*." This time I held my breath as I lifted his right hand. I slid my fingers across his smooth skin, then pricked him with the needle. No response. Absolutely no response. "Maybe I didn't hit it right," I muttered aloud. "It's okay, little fellow. I'm going to do it again. Somewhere, Robertito, hear me." I pushed the tip into his skin. This time there could be no doubt. He did not respond. Neither his face nor his eyes nor his body conveyed any reaction to the pin prick. I tested his fingers and the back of his hand. Only when I pushed heavily did he seem to have some feeling. Francisca sighed nervously, confused by my discovery. Roby knelt beside me and watched in disbelief.

When I had observed Robertito earlier in the session, I noticed he self-stimulated his right hand more often and quite differently from his left. Rather than merely doing a repetitive motion, he shook his hand insistently, with a definite fury and intensity which mirrored what I recalled doing when my own hand "fell asleep." Sometimes, if I slept hunched over myself, I would have to shake or bang my arm trying to revive it in a crude effort to stimulate the nerves and increase the circulation. Perhaps Robertito was attempting to do the very same thing.

Each time we had gently touched this little boy's hand, he pulled away. Yet, sometimes, when we gripped him more forcefully, he permitted the contact. Though I might pound my hand on a table if I had slept on it, I, too, could not tolerate light stroking.

Placing Robertito's right hand in mine, I massaged it as deeply and thoroughly as I could. He did not pull away. I stretched his arm out on the floor and hit it gently with my open hand palm. Robertito smiled. He actually smiled. His head whipped from side to side as he giggled, responding like a child being tickled. Hearty little-boy chuckles filled the room. Francisca covered her wet eyes and laughed. Roby grabbed his son's right leg and followed my procedure. We had found a channel, primitive and crude, but, nevertheless, a channel through which we could share and communicate on a physical level.

The striking image of a ghost town in the left side of his brain reoccurred to me. Perhaps the inactivity not only affected his communication and cognitive center, but had secondary ramifications with motoric activities on the right side of his body, which correlated body function with the opposite side of the brain.

More significant, the neurological pathways carried impulses both ways along the same tracks. In the typical circumstance, the hand feels hot, communicates the heat pain to the brain and, in a seemingly instantaneous response, the brain instructs the hand to move. We had chosen to try to activate Robertito's mind with loving, stimulating parallel play combined with volumes of verbal input. But now, if we helped him "wake up" his right hand, we would, at the same time, massage the brain through his sense of touch. By pounding and rubbing his hand, we would send impulses back along the tracks to the inscrutable throne in his head. The answer? No. But we had definitely discovered a new roadway, a bridge from our world back to his.

As I left the house that evening, I couldn't help but review the mound of reports and tests issued by neurologists, neuropsychologists and other highly trained professionals. Not one had noticed this serious sensory deprivation. Not one had administered this simple test during their entire evaluations.

On the sixth day, after completing her own four-hour session with Robertito, Suzi taught in tandem with Laura, who moved stiffly in the room. As she interacted and imitated the child, an old tape played in her head. "Do I love him? Can I feel anything? He's beautiful! He's weird! He's definitely not Raun! What do I feel? Nothing. Oh, God, nothing. It can't be. I want to love him." Athough diverted by the desperation of her questions and doubts, a natural warmth began to surface, one which Laura herself would probably have denied.

My notes for her feed-back session had exceeded five pages. Laura had fed him when he cried, reinforcing his old tendency

149

toward tantrums. Games had not been attempted at eye level. Her imitation was not enthusiastic; oftentimes, she appeared confused. When Robertito picked up a block by himself, she persisted in trying to introduce a ball instead of following his cue even if he just wanted to flap the wood form. Yet amid all the stops and starts of the session, Laura had been gentle, particularly radiant when she lost herself in her enthusiasm for Robertito's obvious connection with music. She played the marimba, recorder and Japanese wood flute for him. His "isms" decreased. In this quiet, soothing and non-distracting environment, he focused on sounds outside of himself. We had opened another avenue through which we could talk...music!

I remembered the comments of the directors at two separate psychiatric facilities. Both agreed that music should be eliminated from the autistic child's world because it promoted the child's "spacing out" and performing inappropriate behaviors such as rocking, spinning and flapping. Rather than using the child's own preferences as a natural way to communicate and express caring, they opted for their own set of inflexible procedures, often restraining and punishing a child for such actions. The very behaviors which provided us with some hope of making contact, no matter how slim, were the behaviors these people condemned.

Suddenly, I envisioned thousands of Lauras and Robertitos at a concert. They would not be distinguishable from anyone else in the audience. No one would prevent them from rocking or swaying to the music. And what about the people who tap their fingers, or whistle to themselves or sway gently in their grandmothers' rocking chairs? Since they, too, participate in their own self-stimulating rituals, would we want to tie their fingers, tape their mouths and nail their chairs to the floor?

Having completed the musical episode, Laura's participation diminished. She wanted more input from Suzi, who again took a more prominent role. Her soft, playful voice hummed its own private melody as she flapped with Robertito. The rapid improvement in Robertito's eye contact was astounding. Though he still didn't glance at anyone for more than one or two seconds at a time, within twenty minutes, he looked at Suzi three times. Memories of Raun.

Precise, yet unpredictable, in her movements, Suzi experimented with her actions and her words. She further simplified language as we had discussed. She said "*co*" instead of "*comida*" when feeding him. When she gave him freshly made vegetable juice, she did not say "*jugo*." She said "*ju*." At times, she also used the food to trade.

Robertito sat on the floor babbling and rocking. Suzi mimicked him, laughing at the peculiar changes in his facial expressions. His internal calm relaxed his face to such an extent that his features seemed rubbery. "Silly, wonderful boy," she said, poking her fingers softly into his armpits in an endeavor to tickle him. Robertito leaned against the wall without moving. Suzi scooted in front of him, began to whistle the Jiminy Cricket song from *Pinocchio* and deftly folded his legs Indian-style. "Now that's better. You look more balanced." She then assumed the same position herself. Without changing her focus, Suzi pulled out a puzzle from behind her and showed it to Robertito at face level. "Okay, my sweet boy, we're going to remove one piece...that's all, remove one piece." She demonstrated several times with her own hand, then took his and pantomimed the action. Her impeccable Spanish accent compensated for her occasional misuse of words. "Will you let me guide your hand? Wonderful." She kissed him. He backed away and crinkled his face. "I don't blame you," she laughed. "Okay, now let's try again. You can do it, big boy. C'mon, I know you can." Very gently, she demonstrated by modeling his hand movements. He looked at her lethargically, his eyes suddenly at half-mast. "Okay, time for something else."

Putting the puzzle aside, she lifted the insertion box and placed it between their faces. She peered at me with great excitement, awed at his sitting in one position for such a sustained period of time. "Here we go, Charlie Brown. Circle. See. Circle! This is a circle. It goes here." When she gave him the form, he flapped it for several seconds, then dropped it. His hand "isms" had decreased since our intensive massages. Suzi grabbed the circular form off the floor, demonstrated the task and placed the piece back in his hand. His eyes stared blankly at it. Then, quite casually, he pushed it against the side of the box at least two inches away from the appropriate pile. She manipulated the box slyly and matched the space with the circle. The piece fell into the hole.

"Wow," she bantered, clapping and laughing at her own antics as well as his. "Yeah, Robertito Soto! You did it! Yeah! With a little help from your friend, of course." She removed the circle again and pantomimed the entire procedure, overacting each step in wild, amusing gestures. "Here you go," she said, giving him the piece. The boy held the plastic form,

151

surveyed it out of the corner of his eye and then pushed it against the box again. I watched him ease the piece upward, coming closer and closer to the hole. Then, suddenly, he pushed it inside. Suzi, Laura and I shouted simultaneously. We all patted him, stroked him and cheered. Our vocal outburst brought Francisca and Roby into the room. They, too, delighted in their son's achievement. During the next hour, Suzi got him to repeat his accomplishment three times.

My hand ached from writing as I rose, completing my observations for the day. I walked into the center of the room and kissed both Suzi and Laura. "Look, look," Suzi shouted as Robertito slid his hands under my shoes. "Go ahead. He wants the pressure. Oh, my God, I don't believe it. We're getting through, Bears. Look. We must be." His hands! He had actually moved toward us with extended hands. If we can make ourselves loving and useful, then he'll seek more of us, despite the short-circuits and the mountains he has to climb.

* * *

Charlotte arrived for her session late that evening. We faced each other in my hilltop house.

"I don't want to sound ignorant, you know," she began, adjusting her blouse as she sat on the couch, "but with all the cheering you'd think Robertito learned to read this week. He's still the same. Maybe he looked at you more often. I'd give him a half point on a scale of ten. I, personally, haven't seen him put any forms into the insertion box. I mean, he certainly doesn't do that for me." Charlotte scratched her nose, then stopped herself self-consciously. "Why do you have that shit-eating grin on your face?"

"Oh, I don't know," I said. "I guess I enjoy listening to what people say."

"Good. Always aim to please, you know," she quipped. Charlotte removed a cigarette from her case, hung it out of the side of her mouth, then eyed me combatively. "Any objection?" I shook my head. She allowed herself one quick grin and lit a cigarette.

"Anything you want to work on?" I asked.

"Yeah, I guess so. Haven't been very co-operative in my last two sessions, have I? You have to understand, I'm not used to this. In fact, I didn't know this was part of the program
152

until you told me. Roby and Francisca never mentioned it. Figures!"

"How do you feel about that?"

"I guess it doesn't matter." She paused, looking suddenly vulnerable. Then she talked about her desire to date despite her marriage, but her awareness of Francisca's possible disapproval bothered her.

"Why?" I asked.

"Well, I'm sure you heard about her dainty, premarital courtship. Never with Roby alone, always chaperoned, a virgin right up till the end." Charlotte paused. "I know. I'm being catty. But I can't live only for her son. I need a break; but what upsets me is that she'll think I'm cheap if I see other guys."

"And if Francisca thinks you're cheap, just like you imagine, why would that disturb you?"

She avoided my eyes. "Do we have to talk about this?"

"It's your session. You introduced the subject. There's nothing we 'have to' talk about."

"Good," Charlotte asserted. "Then I'm going to change the subject. I want to talk about not feeling comfortable when I'm with Robertito. You see, actually, I do feel comfortable, except when he doesn't listen." She began to laugh. "Which is just about all the time."

"Why do you feel uncomfortable when he doesn't listen?"

"I mean, Jesus," she said, pausing to suck noisily on her cigarette, "I race around the room with him like a fool. The least he could do is sit still when I change him or feed him."

"And if he doesn't, Charlotte, why does that make you uncomfortable?"

"How could I be doing good at teaching if I don't see any results?"

"Why do you have to see results in order to know what you're doing is good?"

Charlotte smiled. "I know. The poor kid can't even understand which side is up. I see that. Sometimes when I'm just nice to him, playing in his crazy little universe, I feel on target. You know what I mean...it does feel good without any results. It's just sometimes I get frustrated...maybe a little more than just sometimes."

"What do you find frustrating about working with Robertito?"

"We do the same thing every day and, to a great extent, so does he. What's frustrating is that he doesn't seem inter-

153

ested. Wait...before you ask another question. What's frustrating is that I want him to do something big, something concrete, something measurable."

"Wanting him to do something, Charlotte, is very different from being frustrated if he doesn't," I said. "Why exactly do you feel frustrated if he doesn't do what you want?"

"I guess I'm back to me. It kind of like means I'm no good."

"Do you believe that?"

"Well, when I hear myself say it, I don't. But before, when I was in the room with him, that's what went through my head."

"And now?"

She threw her head back and sighed. "You know, when I watch Suzi or Francisca work with him, I think they're super. I can't believe their patience. Funny thing is lots of times Robertito doesn't respond much to them either. Yet, I know they're really good. I don't put them down when he doesn't respond. How come I put myself down?"

"Why do you think you do that?"

"It doesn't make any sense, I guess. I can't judge myself against his abilities. I do what I do and he does what he can do. You know, I've heard you say that many times already...somehow it never clicked until now."

"Maybe that's because our lessons don't really come from others. It depends on what we come to know from ourselves. Today, you heard Charlotte speaking to Charlotte."

She began to laugh. "You know, I could get to like this."

As we talked further, she spoke about her marriage briefly, but, again, aborted the dialogue. Though she expressed her amazement at her openness with me, I still sensed her withholding; perhaps frightened to reveal her inner thoughts fully, even to herself.

Chapter 10

Our pattern of living and working together meshed more organically during the second and third weeks. Suzi and I introduced our children as observers in Robertito's sessions, orienting them as helpers and teachers. We took the Sotos to the health food store, the local fruit stand, the bank, the drugstore and dairy market, often sharing our car with them so they could move independently. Laura traded saxophone lessons for Spanish lessons with Charlotte. Francisca registered for a course in conversational English at a local high school. Roby constructed a balancing stand, an incline board and other accessories to help his son. And Robertito, in spite of our willingness to accept the status quo, continued to progress, not in big leaps, but in small steps.

As the child permitted more physical contact, Roby escalated the light gymnastic segments of his work sessions. He held his son upside down while carrying him back and forth across the room. With the help of Francisca, they placed Robertito on his father's back for some age-old horseback rides. Although he made no effort to hold on, frequently falling when Roby turned, the little boy seemed contented to remain on top of his father's body. They jumped together on a mattress we had placed on the floor. Roby wrapped his arms around his son's chest and twirled him in playful circles.

Robertito appeared quite happy and, even with only fleeting eye contact, his awareness of us had dramatically increased. Rather than remain curled inside of his own protective shell, he allowed himself to be passively manipulated by us, occasionally showing passing signs of involvement.

Early on Thursday morning, when the sun sprayed the room with its sharp light, Robertito pulled away from his father and paced while flapping both hands. "Okay, you want a massage?" Roby said with outstretched arms. "Come, I will help you." But when he tried to secure his son's hand, the little boy twisted his body sharply to avoid contact. He raced around the room, gliding along each wall. Then he stopped abruptly, stared at the wall and touched it with his nose. Robertito moved the upper portion of his body to the left, then to the right; his face always in physical contact with the wall. Finally, he pulled himself twelve inches away and proceeded to walk alongside the yellow plasterboard barrier, tracking an invisible course with his index finger. At the corner, he made a half-turn and continued along the next wall. The windows confused him. He floundered, impatiently walking in a wide circle until he connected with one of the other walls.

Roby tried to follow his son and mimic him, but his child's behavior differed so dramatically from previous patterns that he simply watched spellbound. Robertito stopped on the opposite side of the room from his father and began tapping within a limited area on the wall. Suddenly, Roby gasped. His son had tapped the exact outline of his shadow. "You've done it, Robertito. You've discovered your shadow." He cheered the little boy and stroked his back as the child remained absorbed in tracking the dark form.

Putting his hand next to his son's, he, too, tapped the wall. Robertito stopped again and traced the exact outline of his shadow once more. Before completing the exterior line, he dropped his hand. Roby continued along the outside border. His son cocked his head and watched his father's hand, not from the corner of his eyes, but directly confronting the object of his vision. Robertito moved, traced part of his shadow, then allowed his father to complete the form. They continued their game for almost two hours. When Robertito looked into his father's eyes and put his arms around his father's legs, big Roberto Soto began to cry.

156

By the third week, Suzi had our little friend not only inserting forms into the insertion box, but putting rings on large dowels. Of course, his participation usually accounted for only about ten minutes of a three-hour session; yet we had gained some firm ground. She still labored at teaching him to withdraw wooden puzzle forms. Finally, after the eight-hundredth attempt, he sloppily pulled one piece from its place.

After massaging Robertito's hands for almost twenty minutes at the beginning of her session, Francisca sat opposite her son and tried to teach him the parts of his face. Nose. Mouth. Tongue. Eyes. Ears. Over and over, she touched and called out each name, identifying each feature as she recited the lesson. He appeared attentive to her touching, then he flapped and babbled, interrupting her focus. She pursued her activity rather than conform to his. After a lengthy feed-back discussion and dialogue sessions, she finally became more willing to put aside her goals and follow her son if he pointed in a new direction.

Toward the end of her next encounter with her child, she switched on a tape recording. Robertito began to do his ritualistic two-step dance by himself. His mother joined him. He watched her feet carefully, then glanced back at his own. When she took his hands, he permitted the touch, leaving his limp fingers firmly in her grip. Ever so slowly, she began to widen the distance between her feet. Almost imperceptibly her son began to widen the distance between his feet. "It can't be," she mumbled to herself. But as she spread her feet further apart, he matched the pattern. Francisca bent her knees. Robertito bent his. Then, jerking his body, he dropped his hands and raced across the room. He angled his head to the side, staring hypnotically at the light bulb.

Francisca bit her bottom lip. The momentary event was awesome to her. For a few seconds they had reversed roles. He had followed her instead of her following him. No one pushed her son or prodded him. He had dared to take one small step across a very tenuous and unfamiliar bridge.

Laura's concerts for Robertito had a definite effect, yet I sensed her preoccupation, at times, in the sessions. Nevertheless, the little boy's attention to music expanded appreciably in response to her efforts. He used his body more easily as an instrument to echo rhythms. Laura also worked intensively on his body. Her deep massages of his hands had such

157

impact that often Robertito did not flap at all for the following fifteen minutes.

After her session, instead of giving her feed-back, I asked her how she saw herself in the teaching situation. Laura laughed. She knew I knew. "When I'm screwed-up, I always know." As we walked together in the park, she avoided my eyes, feeling transparent. My initial observations about her growing effectiveness as a mentor fell on deaf ears. Every time she looked for proof of her inability to be loving, she found it and ignored everything which suggested the contrary. But then, during the next two hours, she confronted, more directly and more openly than before, her fears about being hard and unmotherly. The expectation of having immediate affection for Robertito traumatized her initial contact when she felt uninvolved, more like an observer than a participant. What had she believed? If she didn't love him now, she would never love him. Why did she believe that? Laura had no reasons, no answers except her fears. "If I don't push myself now, it will never happen!" In further exploration, she realized those very demands intruded in her flow with Robertito. Every time she judged herself in a session with him, she altered her focus, withdrew and, in effect, cut herself off from the very things she wanted . . . to be present and loving. When our session ended, Laura admitted to feeling more relaxed, but not totally absolved from her self-criticism. But in the course of the dialogue, she did liberate herself from the need to fall in love instantly with Robertito . . . for the moment, being an accepting and effective teacher would suffice.

Some pronounced revelations surfaced during Charlotte's contact with Robertito. Sometimes, when a warm smile decorated her face, she displayed a wonderful, intuitive ability to move him. But more often, the impatience and discomfort which curled her lips downward blocked her ability to function sincerely in our teaching environment. Even though she imitated him, the rigidity of her body language betrayed an inner annoyance.

As I watched the young woman with my little friend, I noticed several things which amazed me. He made the least amount of contact with her in comparison to the others in the program. He whined and cried in Charlotte's presence while maintaining a more mellow mood during his sessions with others. Robertito locked himself into his "isms," running and murmuring nonsense syllables with marked intensity, almost as if he responded directly to her attitude and discomforts by further trying to insulate himself. Somehow he knew. Somewhere in that little brain a very important radar system remained operative. He adjusted intuitively to the tone and texture of any environment he entered without ever having to look at anyone or hear anything. He simply knew.

At the beginning of the fourth week, I checked his hands. His right side appeared slightly more sensitive to the pin pricks, though his sensory intake was still severely deficient. Nevertheless, we celebrated every sign. I experimented with a series of instrumental and vocal sounds, finally determining that Robertito exhibited more susceptibility to high sounds and whispers. We adjusted our conversations and teaching patterns accordingly. The lack of strength in his hands still concerned me. When I tried to lift him as he held onto a pole, he dropped off immediately. He lived in a tensionless body with little muscle control, the legacy of his own inertia. We designed a series of tug-of-war and push-pull games with him in order to strengthen all his extremities.

On a Friday night after a seven-hour stretch of observing and participating, I rose to my feet, kissed Francisca and then tapped Robertito on the arm. To my amazement, he tapped me back without ever looking at me. His eyes stared out the window. I tapped him again. He returned the touch. We continued for fourteen consecutive times until he babbled "eee-o" and curled into a circle on the floor.

*   *   *

"C'mon, we're late," I chimed, tugging on Suzi's arm as we half-jogged down the long green corridor. We negotiated several quick turns, avoiding people entering and exiting the hall.

"One day we're going to cut our schedule in half," Suzi said. She ducked her head as a messenger whizzed by with a carton on his shoulder. "How come I'm always breathless?"

"Not enough exercise, Suz," I grinned.

We jumped onto the elevator just as the door whipped closed. "Let's see," I mumbled, searching the buttons. "There it is . . . twenty-seven."

"How'd the conference go this morning?" Suzi asked.

"Good. A lot of students were very receptive. Things are changing." I kissed her on the nose.

After making several stops for other passengers, the elevator thumped to a halt on the twenty-seventh floor. We bolted into the hallway, read directions to locate the rooms by number, then turned left down another green corridor.

We pushed open the dark wood doors, entering the small lobby rather abruptly. Soiled reprints of cityscapes, fixed in metal frames, decorated the walls. Blank-faced people sat stoically on wood benches. An old man leaned against one wall and coughed uncomfortably.

The woman behind the reception desk never looked up once. She leafed through a newspaper with one hand while she fluffed out her hair with the other.

"Hello," I said. No response. No eye contact. "Classically autistic," I diagnosed silently. Her "isms": page-turning and hair-fixing. I imagined a room filled with newspapers and hair spray. We would squat, face each other and do her self-stimulating rituals together. Perhaps, one day, she would look at me.

Suzi nudged my arm.

"Oh yes," I murmured, then addressed the receptionist again. "We're here to see Joan Easter, please."

The woman retained her downward posture, still avoiding direct eye contact. "Do you have an appointment?"

"Yes," Suzi answered. "Could you inform Ms. Easter that Barry and Suzi Kaufman are here."

A grunt served as the reply. She waved to Suzi and me in crude sign language and directed us to an empty couch. We had waited three weeks. Everyone had expressed optimism about our grant proposal. Although we had received many rejections in response to our grant applications from a host of other public and private organizations, we had a certain alliance with Joan Easter. Her department had known about us even before we had applied for funding. Their persistent encouragement and aid in writing the proposal supplied us with a new impetus. And this attempt for funding was more personal. Perhaps that's what we lacked on previous occasions. The money would not only enable us to work with more children, but it would ensure the continuity of the Soto program. Without it, we would have to turn away once we depleted our own rapidly diminishing funds.

A woman called our name, ushered us down another corridor, then deposited us into the large, windowed office of Joan Easter. A print of a Modigliani painting dominated the room. Color photographs of children decorated the walls. A

Chinese urn occupied the top of one file cabinet. Piles of grant proposals were stacked on top of one another.

"I like it," Suzi acknowledged enthusiastically as we both waited for Ms. Easter's arrival. The handmade pottery and other personal objects on display captivated Suzi. She searched for the match, wanting to find a bond between this woman and us; a bond less verbal and more binding than the actual grant proposal.

"So we finally meet," Joan Easter declared, entering the room with definite authority. Her handshake had a specific power. Her grip lingered longer than the traditional time. She wore clothes which did not conform to her body. They accented the business atmosphere. And yet, an inescapable femininity remained. "I feel I know you both already." She smiled warmly.

"You've been fantastic in helping us prepare the forms," Suzi said.

At that moment, a dark-suited man entered the room. "Oh, let me introduce James Blackwell," Joan Easter declared. "He's the attorney for our group and I asked him to join us." We exchanged greetings. Blackwell pulled our proposal from his case and detached his notes which had been pinned to the top. He adjusted his cuffs as he prepared to speak. Only his small mustache seemed incongruous with his Ivy League demeanor.

"I want both of you to know how much I, personally, admire your work," he began.

"Yes, we all do," Ms. Easter assured us.

"We've seen many proposals over the years," he continued. "Yours was unusual. That's why Joan brought me in on this one early. 'Something special here,' she said." Joan concurred with an automatic smile, delivered on cue. "Now the problem is how we can modify this description to conform more to our committee's perspective."

"And just what perspective is that?" I asked, eying Suzi. The glow disappeared from her face.

"You have to understand, Mr. Kaufman," Joan Easter replied. "We get forty to fifty proposals for every grant. Many come from the finest and most renowned medical institutions and schools around the country. Inevitably, you are going to be compared with them."

"For example," Blackwell interjected, "on your proposal, you talked about working with three or four children. To be frank, I thought you people had made a typing error . . . maybe

161

you had meant thirteen or twenty-three. But then Joan informed me, after talking with Mrs. Kaufman, that no typing error had occurred. That's our first problem. The other candidates are willing to work with twenty to thirty youngsters for the same amount of money."

"Mr. Blackwell," I said, "our numbers are different for very special reasons. Most of those large institutions will do a teaching program with autistic, brain-damaged and neurologically impaired children for periods of four or five hours per day. There will be five or six students to each teacher. Perhaps, input from a speech pathologist or psychologist will provide each child with one or two hours of individual contact each week. Those programs operate five days a week ... thus, each child receives, at best, twenty hours a week in a group situation. We're not talking about twenty hours a week in a group, but eighty hours a week on a one-to-one basis. We're not talking only weekdays; we're proposing seven days a week. We also want to train the mother and father, the sisters or brothers, the grandmother, the neighbor next door, so that if she enters the home, the environment will remain consistent. These are very special little human beings. You can't hope to reach them in a behavioral group situation, especially on four hours a day. We've seen what's done. Those children will probably require care for the rest of their lives. We're suggesting a whole different alternative with a different potential."

"Even so, Mr. Kaufman, the net cost per child per year in your proposal far exceeds your competition," the lawyer noted like an efficient scorekeeper at a tennis match.

"What it would cost us to work with a child is less than this state pays to keep one child institutionalized for a year ... and that's a child drugged on Thorazine with little or no input. Over a lifetime care for that person will cost many millions. What we have proposed is, in fact, much more economical, where a child might not need lifetime institutionalization." I paused.

"Well, yes, I can see your point, truly," Blackwell admitted. He adjusted his cuffs again. "That, unfortunately, doesn't alter the fact that the board will see your proposal with three or four children against a prestigious facility offering to work with a population of twenty or thirty youngsters."

"Perhaps," Ms. Easter suggested, "you could increase the numbers on the grant proposal itself to say ... fifteen. Then, just begin with three or four."

"Would we have to work up to the number indicated?" Suzi asked.

"Yes and no," Joan Easter replied. "We'd expect you to try."

It would be easy, I thought, to say fifteen or twenty. Why not? Satisfy their prejudice and begin. We already had Robertito. There were other children we had seen who we could now work with on a more intense basis. Maybe five at the same time. Maybe.

"What do you say?" Ms. Easter said, smiling.

"I'd like to say yes. You have no idea how much I'd like to say yes," I admitted. "But, by diluting the contact, by trying to work with fifteen or even ten, we'd destroy each child's chance. We would have worked with many and, perhaps, helped none."

"Well, at least you do understand the dilemma. We're on your side." James Blackwell grinned ceremoniously.

"Well, let's see how we can do on some of these other points." He turned to page forty-seven in the proposal. "You have no provisions for a speech pathologist, a psychologist, or any psychiatric input. In fact, you suggest you would train high school and college students." He smiled. "I think at one point you said if the dysfunctioning child is seven, you would actually try to train another seven-year-old to work with him."

"Sure," I said. "Children have special connections with other children...and children can be wonderful teachers. High school students and college students have been instrumental for us."

"We know that," he said. "That's been part of your style when you worked with your son and other children. But, you have to understand, in a funded program, you must have qualified personnel."

"I had a friend, Mr. Blackwell, who majored in psychology at college and did his post-graduate work in clinical psychology. He spent eight years reading all the appropriate books, worked extensively with laboratory rats and did a thesis on electro-convulsive therapy. When he received his license as a psychologist, he had never worked with one live human being." Joan Easter nodded her agreement, having reviewed thousands of graduate applications.

"And even if he had worked with people using behavior modification or a Freudian orientation, we would have to untrain all that training, all those beliefs. And I'm not sure

163

how easily I could get a trained psychologist or psychiatrist to crawl around on the floor with a little boy or girl and quack like a duck."

Joan Easter put her hand over her mouth trying to suppress a smile. James Blackwell adjusted himself in his seat. "I understand," he said, "but many of those on the board and consultants to the board are medical people. To put it bluntly, they want to see their own kind participating in order to support such a proposal."

"We're not disagreeing with what you want to do," Ms. Easter said. "But somehow, in written form, your ideas seemed quite...unusual to our people."

"Are you trying to let us down easy?" I asked.

"We're trying to work something out," she insisted.

"But you encouraged us," Suzi added, a slight strain in her voice. "You mentioned that many people here felt a tremendous enthusiasm for how we worked."

"That's absolutely true," she responded, "but..."

"What Joan wants to say," the lawyer interrupted, "is that when the committee saw the same ideas in a formal proposal, suddenly they came to terms with the realities of your ideas and methods...no longer simply focused on a pretty story."

"I hear you loud and clear," I said. "Could you be direct and tell us exactly what you want us to do with the proposal."

Blackwell pulled on his cuff, cleared his throat and began: "First, you have to include more children. Secondly, to satisfy members of the board, you will have to include more traditional personnel. I'm afraid the idea of having children work with children, even high school kids, won't wash."

"And that's it?" I asked.

"At least on the major points," James Blackwell admitted.

Suzi and I looked at each other.

"And if we made those adjustments, what do you think our chances are for getting the grant?" I questioned.

"Good. Better than good," Joan said, dropping her shoulders in relief. "The first installment of the money could be processed in a matter of a month."

I kept thinking of that little Mexican face, the perfect porcelain features and the gentle hands as Suzi and I rose to our feet. "I think we'll have to pass," I said.

"I really don't think we could make such amendments," Suzi added.

Joan Easter also rose. "Suzi, things move slowly. I'm sorry about this. Everything can't change overnight."

"I don't believe that," Suzi insisted. "If we did what you suggested, we'd have the exact kind of program we thought grossly inadequate for our own child."

"It's not a matter of compromise or morals," I interjected. "If it would make them happy, I'd put a hundred and fifty down. But if we strip out the elements which gave us the opportunity to reach a child, then we have nothing left...but custodial care."

"I don't think that's necessarily so," Blackwell countered. "We all have the child's welfare in mind."

"I never questioned that," I said.

"Those changes would not inhibit the child's progress," the lawyer insisted.

"Mr. Blackwell, have you ever worked with an autistic child?" I asked.

"No."

"Have you ever seen one?"

"I'm afraid not," he responded.

The room fell to silence. "We'd like to leave the proposal the way it is and let them decide on what we've presented," I said.

Blackwell and Ms. Easter exchanged an uncomfortable glance. "Well, in that case," Joan Easter said, "I guess I should tell you they've already rejected your proposal."

Chapter 11

As we entered the fifth week in our program, Robertito not only permitted more physical contact but initiated play with blocks and puzzles as well as indicated, in a primitive fashion, a desire for tumbling with his father. He still viewed the world from the corners of his eyes. He still hand-flapped, finger-twirled, babbled and paced the room. While I plotted his growth, I knew he felt no rush to learn, no temporal deadline to meet. This child moved through a time zone few of us ever experienced. Even his face displayed an ageless quality. He had all the time in the world, but we didn't.

"Here, Robertito," Francisca said, putting the block in his hand, during a late afternoon session with her son. "Put it on top of this one here," she said, pointing. He watched her hand, then turned away. He rubbed his fingers against the side of his face, bent his head downward and smiled to himself.

"You can do it. Here, Robertito. Put it here." Slowly, he moved his hand and placed the block on top of the other. Francisca burst into applause and shouts, then lavished him with stroking. She trusted herself more now, giving him another block. Robertito looked at the wood cube and flapped it only for a few seconds. Since the intensive daily massages, his hand "isms" had decreased noticeably. Moving at a snail's pace, the little boy put the third block on top of the small pile. Francisca dared the procedure again. They continued working together until the tower had grown to the height of eighteen blocks.

After this massive concentration, Robertito jumped in place, flapped his hand and laughed. Francisca mimicked him and also laughed. Later, he ambled over to the radiator, grabbed a drumstick, hit one of the keys on the xylophone. Laura and Suzi had worked weeks with him without results. Now, somewhere in the privacy of his own mind, he plugged a circuit together and made a connection in an act self-motivated and self-directed.

When she finished feeding him dinner, Francisca placed the remaining food behind her. Robertito darted for it. She grabbed for the glass but missed it as her son squeezed a handful of lettuce and tomatoes between his fingers. She removed the food from his tight grip. He threw himself toward the glass again. This time, anticipating his action, she swooped it off the floor and put it outside the room. Robertito Soto began to cry. His face cringed, his larynx wailed a noisy protest...yet his eyes remained oddly passive.

Francisca bit her lip and ground her teeth. Although she had realized that her actions often supported and encouraged his crying, she found it difficult to be loving and neutral at the same time. "If you want to cry, that's okay," she said. "When you're finished, we can play again. I'll be here."

She contemplated imitating his cry, but short-circuited the impulse. She repeated a scenario in her head. "He's trying to get what he wants. If he decides to cry, that's his choice." When she touched him, he pulled away. "If you want food, say 'co.' Or point your finger like this." She demonstrated, but her son seemed oblivious to her commentary. "Okay, my love. I'll be here."

The screeching bellowed in her ears. She wished for some of her son's skills, envying his ability to shut off his sensory intake at will. She tapped her fingers together and tried to concentrate on the movement. Then Francisca looked up at her son and gasped. A single tear dripped down Robertito's cheek, then a second one and a third one until a small river ran along the bridge of his nose and down the sides of his chin. In all the tantrums in Mexico, he always cried a dry cry. She watched her son cry real tears for the very first time. A battle ensued within her. He had to be unhappy. The other times didn't count. How could she just sit by? He was unhappy, genuinely unhappy and she wanted to comfort him. When she embraced her son, he pulled away and screamed angrily. Disoriented, Francisca propped herself against the wall. "Okay, Mama will wait." Robertito continued crying real tears for the next forty-five minutes. Finally Francisca scrambled out the door and returned with the food. Robertito stopped immediately upon seeing the glass in his mother's hand. His smooth, wet face seemed curiously devoid of any expression of sadness.

Before putting him to bed, Francisca decided to give her son a bath. Once completely nude, Robertito pulled away from his mother and ran through the halls. He laughed, giggled and cooed. He touched himself freely, exploring with his fingers. Francisca watched her son, awed and slightly embarrassed by his apparent pleasure. For his entire life, major portions of his body had been unavailable to him, wrapped in the seclusion of diapers and pins. As he became more willing to pause from his "isms" and explore, he found himself in a way that he had never done before. Even as she lowered him into the warm bath, he still smiled enthusiastically, kicking his feet in the water and exploring his hidden parts.

He climbed out of the tub very relaxed. Francisca wiped him as he collapsed into a heap on the floor. She dried his arms and legs carefully, having made an art of the few motherly duties he permitted her to perform. Then, quite suddenly, Robertito sat up, looked at his mother and, in a gesture so natural yet unfamiliar, he rested his head on her lap. Although Francisca was filled with emotion, she didn't let herself cry as she gently stroked her son's back.

She had had more concrete opportunities to love her child during the past five weeks than during the previous five years of his life.

*　　*　　*

Each moment brought a special pleasure to Suzi, nurturing Robertito as she had once nurtured her own son. After she guided him to his chair, he waited impatiently, alert to her movements. He had seen the cereal. A moment before, even as his stomach gurgled, the idea of eating never occurred to him. Most of his pursuits resulted only after something concrete stimulated his eyes or ears.

Food no longer came to Robertito as a disconnected item amid a jungle of noise and activity surrounding him. Food no longer suddenly appeared in a cup or bowl sitting solo on a table. People gave him food. Suzi gave him food. She circled her student like a matador. He turned in his chair, not wanting to lose visual contact with the item she carried. Suzi positioned herself on the floor in front of him so their eyes met on the same level. She dug deep into the cup, filled the spoon, brought it up to a point right between her eyes and said "*co*" three times. Then, she lowered the spoon into his opened mouth. "The best," she said each time those big brown eyes met hers. "Yes. It's me, Suzi. Here you go again. *Co. Co.* This is *co*." He did not flap once. Although he made infant sounds as he chewed, Robertito appeared almost normal to her. She noted sixteen different incidents of eye contact.

For the remainder of the session, his interest waned. He began to rock. She joined him, but he did not appear attentive to her parallel motion. He slid within himself. She had lost him in a matter of minutes. As she followed Robertito across the room, flapping and babbling with him, she couldn't help but wonder what she had done. Did she miss a cue? Was she pushing too much? Had she been insensitive to his fatigue?

The session lingered with her. She kept thinking about Robertito all through the rest of the day. In the evening, we talked about her questions. But even as she settled back into bed, our little Mexican friend haunted her.

Exhaustion enveloped her quickly as she fell asleep. Within seconds, she experienced herself airborne. The buoyancy allowed her to float to the ceiling. A warm sensation enshrouded her body. When she looked down, she was no longer in our bedroom. She watched Francisca work with Robertito in his room. The little boy followed directions quite well, surprisingly more efficient than her memory of him that afternoon. She loved to watch Francisca teach him, tickle him, caress him. Though she loved to work with Robertito, she knew, from her own past, the special exhilaration for a mother helping her own child. In the midst of completing an unusually complex puzzle, Robertito tapped Francisca's shoulder and asked for food. He didn't say "*co*." He didn't say *comida*. He spoke clearly, using a very simple, short sentence. Suzi gasped. Francisca gave her son a spoonful of shrimp and rice without any particular expression of surprise. Robertito
169

then asked her to massage his hand. "He's talking," Suzi screamed. "He's talking, Francisca. Don't you know how fantastic this is? Robertito is talking." She heard her own voice as she jumped up in the bed. Her face felt flushed. "It was real," she whispered in the darkness as she grabbed my arm and related the dream. She exhaled deeply, then fell back against the pillow. Suzi remembered Nancy's dreams about Raun...all of which, ultimately, came true. If it could only be, she murmured to herself as her eyelids closed. If it could only be. Sleep grabbed her and another door opened.

Robertito stood in the kitchen by the sink. Suzi greeted him with surprise.

"Why aren't you in your room?" she said, then chuckled to herself. Very gently, she took his hand and led him back to the staircase. At the first step, he bolted and ran back into the kitchen. Suzi called to Francisca and Roby. No one answered. She called to Charlotte, then Laura. Still no reply. How could it be possible? Who's working with him? Then she realized it had been her turn.

"Let's go, Robertito," she said in Spanish.

The little boy looked directly at her and said: "I want some food, please."

Suzi gasped. "Did you talk, Robertito?"

He smiled at her and repeated his sentence. She swung the door open and let him take whatever he wanted. Rather than charge for the food, he removed some bread and butter. Using a knife expertly, he spread the soft creamy substance. "Can I please have some juice?" he said casually. She started to cheer and woke herself up. Suzi stared at the ceiling, confused by the bombardment of dreams. "Wow," she said to herself as she performed a circular breathing exercise. The darkness enveloped her again.

The noise in the room created a strange cacophony of sound. A group of well-dressed men and women conversed in Spanish. Two guitarists played subdued flamenco music. Five animated teen-agers talked together near the couch. One voice sounded familiar. As Suzi side-stepped closer to the cluster of children, she recognized the back of Robertito's head. She pushed a small table aside in order to improve her view. She gasped when she positively identified him. Words tumbled from his mouth. Although she listened carefully, the sophistication of his language exceeded her knowledge. "He talks better than me," she mumbled. "Robertito," she called. He turned toward her, but did not seem to recognize her.

"Wait, don't look away. It's me. Suzi. You remember. You must remember." Her eyes burst open. The voices had disappeared. Her pulse thumped in her throat. She rolled out of bed and reviewed each dream. She loved them, but she wanted to stop them. Again, the thought of Nancy. But Raun was different, she argued to herself. Raun had been one and a half. Robertito was almost six. She placed an image of Robertito pacing and flapping before her mind's eye and then smiled. Suzi did not want to create fantasies which might never be fulfilled. "One day at a time," she whispered to the night.

* * *

Robertito sat by himself against the wall. Though he flapped, he watched Raun out of the corner of his eye. His immediate awareness of Raun's presence had been enhanced by Raun's performance. Suzi observed from the side of the room. Under her direction, our son jumped on the mattress, did somersaults and played flamboyantly with the blocks and pegboard.

"Okay, sweet boy, I want you to be with him," she said. "Do what he does like we showed you."

Raun grinned from ear to ear. He squatted in front of Robertito enthusiastically and flapped his hands. After several seconds, he laughed. Each time he tried to stop himself, he giggled more. "This is funny," he whispered, not wanting to insult his companion. The two children moved as one for several minutes. Then Robertito paced the room. Raun followed. Robertito grunted sounds. Raun imitated him.

"Mommy, can I squeeze his cheeks? You think he'd like that?"

"I don't know, Raunchy," she answered. "Why don't we wait till later. Right now, concentrate on being with him."

As they walked beside one another, Robertito watched Raun's feet carefully, though he did not look directly at him. From time to time, Raun giggled, excited to participate a second time and thoroughly amused by his friend's antics.

When the boys sat together in the center of the room, Suzi supplied them with cardboard blocks decorated with cartoons. Raun began building a bridge. Robertito babbled. With a natural ease, Raun repeated the exact sound and cadence. He turned to Suzi. "I'm talking to him in autistic talk." He thought a moment. "It's different than Spanish."

171

Suzi was amazed at the frequency of Robertito's smiles during Raun's sessions with him.

Robertito put his hand over his mouth. Each time Raun mimicked him, he pulled it off. Then he peered at Raun's hands assembling the blocks. Robertito picked up one cube and turned it around in front of his eyes. Although he had been presented with them many times, for the first time, he noticed the cartoons.

"You see them, don't you?" Suzi bubbled in Spanish. "That's Daffy Duck. And Pluto." She squished her nose, chuckling several oink-oink sounds. "Of course, that's my friend Porky Pig." She laughed at the facial contortions on Robertito's face. "You're a wonderful boy."

Then Suzi turned and smiled at our son. She spoke in English. "You're a wonderful boy, too." She stared at Raun and remembered vividly when he, too, lived in a world dominated by self-stimulating behaviors...when he, too, was mute and unresponsive. The eyes of both children had a strikingly similar intensity. Although Robertito was large and slightly plump while Raun was petite and delicate, the two shared a certain brotherhood.

As they faced each other, Raun touched Robertito's cheeks. Suzi guided Robertito's limp hands along Raun's face. He allowed the contact, giving Raun several quick glances. Then, on his own initiative, the little boy stroked our son's face. Raun's eyes enlarged. "Look. He's doing it by himself. Isn't that great?" He also pushed his fingers into Raun's mouth and played with his tongue.

Later, Suzi invited Francisca to participate. She put the tape recorder on and had Francisca dance with Raun. Robertito watched intently, still relying on his peripheral vision. He began to rock to the rhythm on his own. Suzi took his hands and followed his lead. When the music stopped, Robertito continued his surveillance of Raun and his mother. Suzi asked Francisca to solo. She moved across the room using the loose two-step she had taught her son. He watched her for five minutes and then broke away from the wall in order to approach her. Suzi felt her pulse rate jump. Very slowly, Robertito began the two-step and extended his hands until they touched his mother's waist. I cheered from the sidelines. Francisca poked her chin out, her every movement oozing with pride. She straightened her hair.

After Francisca left, Suzi continued following the cues of her student as well as trying to stimulate his interest in
172

stringing beads. When Robertito began scratching his pants near his genitals, Suzi whisked him toward the bathroom. We had noticed that he touched himself either just after or when he was about to urinate. After Suzi removed his diapers, she stood him at the toilet bowl.

"Raun. Show Robertito how you go to the bathroom," she suggested.

Our son giggled. "Hey, look at me, Robertito."

"*Mira,* Robertito, *mira,*" Suzi said, pointing to the stream of liquid. Robertito focused on the point where the stream hit the water rather than at the point of origin. Suzi modeled him in the same position as her son. Robertito looked down at the water, then made a repetitious sucking sound with his mouth. Suzi waited several minutes before seating him on the toilet. He jumped up several times, but then returned to the seat. Ten more minutes passed. Robertito never utilized the bowl for its intended function. She diapered him again. Before she left the room, she placed his right hand on the faucet. He turned the knob slowly, demonstrating growing strength in his limbs, especially on his right side. The week before, he could not turn it.

Back in the room, Raun leaned over and kissed his young friend. Suzi felt the unstated communion. The energy between them devastated her.

As they left the Soto house, she questioned Raun. "Did you have fun?"

"It was great," Raun declared, rubbing his stomach as if that had been where he felt it. "He was so good that I thought he was about to talk...you know, in English." He smiled to himself. "I like rocking with him and dancing. I like everything else, but I like that part the best."

"Raunchy, were you happy when you were autistic?" Suzi asked.

He thought for a moment. "Yes," he answered, "but I like it better now."

Chapter 12

Roby sipped on the camomile tea he had just expertly brewed. His eyebrows lifted comically, giving further evidence of his increased skill. Before coming to New York, he had never heard of herbal teas, nor had he ever imagined himself taking pride in developing domestic capabilities. Despite a lifetime characterized by serious concerns, none more serious than the plight of his young son, Roby began to break his own tradition of somber expressions, allowing the flesh around his eyes and mouth to wrinkle more freely with smiles. Slowly, as he watched others clown and giggle without being self-conscious and without compromising the intent of the program, he experimented. During the previous Wednesday night conference, Roby related an incident about Robertito. His face contorted in perfect imitation of his son's bizarre and often funny facial gestures. Everyone laughed. Startled, he looked around at his audience. Laura begged him to repeat the story. When he did, the room became engulfed in hysterics. Rather than subdue his pantomime, Roby increased his contortion to his and our delight.

"Bears, I am ready to continue," he said as he folded a

page carefully in his notebook. Charlotte, seemingly distracted, translated his words abruptly. Bryn, who had worked an earlier session with me and Robertito, curled her body comfortably into the corner of the couch and listened.

"I noticed you tend to work with toys on the floor," I began. "Let's see ... you did it with the puzzles, the insertion box and the colored blocks. I think if you could remember to lift everything up to eye level or use the table as a work area, you'll increase your chance for more spontaneous eye contact." He nodded and made notations.

The phone rang. Charlotte bolted from her chair and flew into the kitchen. When she returned, she appeared even more distracted than before.

"Ready?" I asked her. She flashed a curt grin. "Okay. Once, during yesterday morning's session, Robertito touched the xylophone and another time he picked up the drum. Those are great opportunities to follow his cue, to let him see that he can control his environment and use us. Part of the key is to continually show him how we can help him."

Roby's eyes clouded. "I do not know how I missed that. I remember him with the drum. It didn't register." He turned away from my eyes.

"You do so many wonderful things for your son, Roby. The idea is not to be concerned with what you missed or we missed, but to use the awareness to help us focus even more sharply. They become opportunities for us to learn ... opportunities— that's all."

His forehead ruffled with deep creases. "I have much to learn."

"We all do," I said as I squeezed his arm gently. He suppressed a little-boy smile. For a moment, I imagined Roby as a child in the fields with his bull. Determined, yet vulnerable. This time, I wanted to be sure he knew he was not alone. I tightened my grip on his arm a second time. He riveted his eyes on mine and nodded.

"Okay," I said. "Next subject. Let's talk about Robertito's hands. I want to not only increase the stimulation, but diversify it. In addition to massaging, tomorrow we introduce sandpaper, brushes, feathers, velvet and a vibrator. Perhaps we can start expanding the dimensions of his sensory intake with his hands. Hot water. Cold water. Mud. Clay. Ice cubes. Maybe you can come up with additional ideas. I somehow know that as his mind initiates more activities, his hands improve. It's like a complete circle and there are many points of entry. We want to take advantage of all of them."

"Suppose he doesn't want to take advantage of them," Charlotte interjected.

"Then we wait and try again. He has to open the channel if he can and if he wants to," I replied.

"And if he doesn't?" Charlotte probed.

"He doesn't," I answered directly. "Please translate that for Roby." I watched his face as he listened to each word. My answer did not startle him. He smiled a warm, rich, wonderful smile.

"I have learned to love my son for who he is," he said. "Not for what we can teach him to do." Charlotte shrugged her shoulders.

Bryn touched Roby's arm. "Isn't he wonderful, Daddy?"

When Charlotte interpreted Bryn's words, Roby dipped his chin self-consciously. Bryn shook her head emphatically, grinning confidently, refusing to accept his modesty. She never felt embarrassed in expressing her protests or her caring. We never held discussions in our home where she, Thea or Raun would be excluded. Whether we spoke about love, hate, death or sex, we never modified our words or camouflaged our ideas in their presence. We never asked them to leave the room. As we had learned to trust ourselves, we had learned to trust the little people who shared our lives. Often their questions and pristine insights enriched our perspective. At twelve years old, Bryn conversed comfortably with five-year-olds and fifty-year-olds. She loved people and ideas, though her outspokenness sometimes alienated her from her friends.

The thud of footsteps lumbering down the stairs attracted everyone's attention. Rita had observed Laura initially, then stayed to watch Francisca work with Robertito. Her wrists ached from writing continuously. The process more than simply intrigued her. Rita Corwin had taught Option at several universities, had developed her own practice and counseled at a child guidance center. She suspected something crucial might happen here, further validating a vision which encompassed all her activities. Refusing to remain separate, an observer at the sidelines, as she had been with the journey of Raun, she pushed for more. She volunteered to come each month and catalogue her impressions, footnoting them with contrasting data accumulated from her more traditional clinical experiences.

176

The first visit, more than a month ago, registered ground zero. Robertito's infantile manners and extreme dysfunctions startled her, for she, too, had never encountered such a low functioning child. He appeared so inaccessible. As she watched him now, during her second visit, the staggering changes during the first six weeks defied her wildest fantasies. Tears streamed down her face as she witnessed eye contact, participation in simple tasks, as well as a real exchange of affection.

When she entered the living room, she stretched her arms out with her palms facing the ceiling. "I'm...I'm speechless." Suddenly, a loud, jolly, three-second laugh burst from her throat. Rita hugged me, then Roby, Bryn and Charlotte.

"Well?" I asked of the breathless figure.

"Have you any idea what has happened?" She picked up a piece of my carob danish from the coffee table and stuffed it mechanically into her mouth. "I know, in some ways, it's going slower than the first time when the Sotos were here...but from where you began this time, it's unbelievable." She laughed again. "That's it, you know, nobody will believe this. Do you know what I saw Robertito do with Francisca? When he began to do his hand-over-mouth "ism," he side-glanced at her, waiting for her to imitate him. When she took too long, he seized her hand and placed it over her mouth, indicating that she mimic him. Someone else might consider that lunacy, but he's more in touch. I noticed he searched for food on the window sill with his fingers...food he couldn't see. That's a giant step from before. He's made memory connections." Rita sipped some of my tea, then downed another pastry. "I guess you don't want to hear all this. I'm just repeating what you already know."

"When you see it on a day-to-day basis, the changes are inch by inch...no, maybe only a quarter of an inch at a time. Rita, you offer us a different perspective, not to mention forty gallons of enthusiasm." I asked Charlotte to translate, then I added, "I'm glad for the comfort I see in our little friend as well as for his increased abilities."

"Increased abilities?" Rita blurted. She shook her head and consulted her list. "He made a twenty-five block tower, used the insertion box with four different shapes, put in eight puzzle pieces instead of just removing them and watched himself in the mirror. He hugged Laura twice, his mother once. He put his head in Francisca's lap three times. Robertito even gave me a couple of looks."

"How'd you feel about that?" I asked.

Her eyes filled with tears. "Very, very humble."

She hugged me again.

"Thanks for letting us peak through your eyes," I said. "And thanks for recruiting Paul Goodman for us."

"I can't wait to tell Paul," Rita exclaimed.

"I'd rather you didn't talk with him about Robertito," I cautioned. "I want him completely external to the program so that his psychiatric reports remain unbiased."

She put her arm around Bryn and nodded her agreement.

After Rita left, Bryn and I observed Francisca for the next hour. In the midst of the session, Robertito strolled over to me and played with my hair. Then he collapsed into my lap and stayed there while I rubbed his back. Bryn crawled next to me and stroked his legs. Later, I tried to lift him up with the pole. Though he gripped the bar tightly, he continually opened his hands when I pulled upward. But on the fifth try, with great difficulty and determination, he held on for several seconds. His feet cleared the ground by six inches before his fingers opened. Robertito Soto had supported his own weight.

During the same session, he turned the knob of an infant's music box without assistance. Francisca still worked on teaching him parts of his face. He almost touched his nose two times on request. He put his hand up to his face, then stopped as if confused about what to do next. I also noted his level of attention elevated dramatically in the presence of food.

Bryn tucked her arm around my waist as we walked toward the truck. I put my hand on her shoulder and tugged her close to me.

"Daddy, the way you guys are isn't like the real world," she stated matter-of-factly.

"What do you mean?" I asked, withholding a smile.

She pushed her long, dark brown hair behind her head and rubbed her index finger between her lips. Her eyes twinkled as she processed my question. "Well, you know we talk about being open and trusting. Last week my friend Cynthia got mad at me for some crazy reason and told all my friends the secrets I told her. Now about six people are mad at me."

"How do you feel about that?"

"Not too good. I didn't mean to do anything to hurt anybody. And when I apologized, they all called me names. How do you love somebody that's busy calling you names?"

"You know, Bryn, I once worked with a man who beat his

178

wife and children. Now you'd think he was an awful person...this big man hitting a woman and little kids, even to the point of sending his daughter to the hospital with a broken leg. Yet, when he talked during one of our sessions and I asked him questions without judging him, he cried and explained how he was trying to control his family, to make them be good. From his point of view, he thought he had lots of good reasons for his actions, but his unhappiness and fears had blinded him. Whether you love your friends or not when they call you names is your decision, but you certainly don't have to hate them. Cynthia and the others, like the man who hit his wife and children, are telling you how unhappy they are by their actions."

"Yeah, when I see it that way, I don't feel mad at anybody...only sometimes, I forget they're unhappy." She smiled. "Well, I'll work on it."

"Any time you want, we can work on it, together."

"I think I have your phone number," she replied, feigning an imperfect English accent.

As I drove toward our home, Bryn flipped through her schoolbooks before piling them on the seat beside her.

"Bears," she said, tapping my arm, "could I take tennis lessons with Jerri?"

"I don't think so, butch." I scanned her expectant face. "We're a little tight for money right now."

Bryn scratched her head. "Maybe I could get a job after school."

"No," I said abruptly, feeling a touch self-conscious about Bryn's offer. "You sound like your brother. The other day Raun asked me to buy him a cello. Could you imagine...not a guitar, not a piano, not a set of drums. He chooses the cello. I thought his choice was fabulous, but I asked him why. Would you believe that little guy wanted to be a street musician and use one of my hats to collect money so he could help us."

"Oh, Daddy," Bryn sighed. Like Thea, she would always be motherly to Raun. A deep caring and appreciation for him had blossomed during the three years that she worked with us in facilitating his rebirth.

"We'll do all right," I said. "And if we don't that'll be a sign for us to do something else. I spent all my life, Bryn, learning to hold on real tight. Now, I'm learning how to let go."

"Suppose..." She stopped herself.

"Suppose what?"

"Suppose it doesn't work out."

"Then we all sit down together and talk about it. We didn't choose to do this forever. We only chose it for now. We can always make a different choice." I felt clearer, having again put the old money demon to rest.

"Brynny-babes...thanks."

She peered at me quizzically. "I didn't do anything, Daddy."

"Yes you did. You gave me the gift of your questions."

* * *

During the next three days, Robertito withdrew or, perhaps, more accurately, returned to the home inside of himself. His "isms" escalated. As his rituals intensified, the rhythms frantically peaked, forcing his body to stiffen. He banged his chest in a style reminiscent of his earlier days in Mexico. Eye contact diminished. With the exception of a growing fascination with himself in the mirror, his behavior duplicated that of the first week of his arrival. Like the hiker who paused many times on his journey up the mountain, perhaps Robertito found the only way he knew to rest. The energy, the push and the tremendous concentration required to overcome his dysfunctions taxed every last resource in himself. Unlike most children, who would find building with blocks or playing with a puzzle to be an easy affair, Robertito had to move along unplowed roads to do the simplest task. The psychic fatigue involved had to be enormous.

For no apparent reason, on the fourth day, the little boy resumed climbing the mountain.

My brother, Steve, a psychologist, and his wife, Laurie, visited us on the following weekend. We took them to meet the Sotos. We let them observe Robertito separately. Steve found himself fascinated with the insistent repetitive motions and internalized focus of the little boy. "The intensity of the one-to-one format is mind-boggling," he said pensively as he stroked his beard.

The highly charged energy mixed with periods of intense calm left Laurie drained. The beauty of this child combined with his bizarre motions created an incomprehensible portrait. In one respect, he reminded her of her own sons. In another way, he scared her as Raun had scared her years before. "I'm not used to this," she mumbled to herself. The stark reality threatened her equilibrium. Images of a young

180

Raun haunted her. The door opened to an era she had left behind. Initially, her nephew's problem had seemed so insurmountable that whenever she would see him, she viewed him through a soft lens, in her attempt to see him as a healthy child. It will go away. It will disappear and he'll be all right. As she watched Robertito, old questions flooded her mind. What would she have done? What would she do? She knew she did not have to answer either question. Her children had been born fully equipped.

Suddenly, she felt relieved and incredibly blessed by so many things she had experienced as casual, everyday occurrences. Laurie wanted to run home and hug her children. When she kissed Francisca good-by, she squeezed her tightly and avoided her eyes. She wanted to leave only her love, not her fear, with this lady. Deep within, she heard herself say: "If there were miracles, Francisca Soto, I'd give them to you."

When Suzi and I later returned to the Soto house, Francisca was standing alone on the front steps. Her hands covered her face.

"Francisca," Suzi shouted, "are you okay?"

Francisca walked briskly away from us down the driveway.

"C'mon," I said to Suzi as we pursued her. By the time we came alongside of Francisca, she had wiped her tearstained face, straightened her blouse and jerked her head in that funny way, throwing her hair off her forehead.

"Do you want to talk?" Suzi asked in perfect Spanish. Francisca shook her head.

"Okay," I said, "then we'll stay with you. We don't have to talk."

Francisca avoided our eyes. The muscles around her mouth quivered as she tried desperately to control herself, to be dignified, to fulfill the expectation of her upbringing. At the same time, she choked on her impulse to fight herself.

I wanted to hug her, but stopped myself. Like her son, she, too, had to find her way. "Francisca, there's nothing wrong with being unhappy." She pressed her hands against her mouth.

"It's okay to cry, my girl friend," Suzi whispered.

Francisca turned away, held her chest as if it were going to burst and coughed uncontrollably, finally giving in to her body and sobbing heavily. When we tried to touch her, she moved away. We stood there, apart, but together, for almost

181

five minutes until she finished and her breathing returned to a more normal rhythm.

"How about a walk?" I suggested.

The three of us moved slowly down Thelma Street. This time, Francisca did not hide her tears. She did not fix her hair or her rumpled blouse. At the end of the block, we turned around and retraced our steps.

"I feel stupid," she said.

"Why?" I asked.

"Well, look at me! I should be stronger."

"You're allowed to cry. And crying doesn't mean you're weak," Suzi countered. "You have to see me when I cry... much more dramatic than you."

Francisca managed a smile. She related her growing discomfort with Charlotte. The young woman's recent preoccupation with dating dominated her to such an extent that Francisca felt it affected her sessions with Robertito. He's lethargic with her. But all this did not have the impact of her most recent experience.

Since the house had been heated through a forced hot-air system, ducts connected room to room. Francisca's bedroom duct fastened into the same pathway as the kitchen duct. When Charlotte spoke boisterously on the phone with one of her men friends, Francisca heard every word.

"What did she say that's so upsetting?" I asked, fumbling in Spanish.

Tears cascaded down her face again. "Charlotte cursed all of us, called me and Roby all kinds of names. I didn't understand them all, but I knew she used bad words." When I asked her to recall some of the words, she rattled off several unmistakable phrases. "I don't understand. We treat her like part of the family," Francisca said. "Yesterday, she told me I was a tyrant because I asked her not to stop working with Robertito if the phone rang." She paused. "We need her."

"We don't need anyone," Suzi asserted. "A translator is important, but Charlotte's not the only bilingual person in the world. And I'm getting pretty good at Spanish."

"I know that... but the others need a translator. Suzi, where do we find someone else?" Francisca asked.

"New York has a huge Hispanic community," I assured her. "We can call schools, churches, community centers."

"Maybe we should wait," Francisca said.

"Why?" Suzi asked.

"It's very important to have someone here who can inter-pret for us. I don't know about somebody new," she said.

"Francisca, you can't give Charlotte what she doesn't want. If she wants to go out, if she feels annoyed with you and us, then all that will, unfortunately, affect Robertito. He knows. From what you described, you know that he knows." She nodded her head. "She's not a bad person," I continued. "She's simply not ready to do this. We'll be okay for a couple of days or, if need be, a couple of weeks, without a translator."

"I have to be able to communicate for my son's sake. We have to keep her. Maybe we could look; then if we find some-body, we can ask her to leave."

"Does that really feel right to you, Francisca?" Suzi asked.

She never answered the question.

* * *

Roby followed his son around the room, tapping the wall in the same cadence as Robertito. They jumped together. They danced together. Each move brought father and child into a closer harmony. When Roby introduced the insertion box, his son took the red cube and turned the box until he located the correct slot. He repeated this minor miracle with a triangle shape and a star shape. Then he laid his head into his father's lap. Roby stroked his son's back and arms. He walked his fingers like little feet to the underside of Robertito's body and tickled his abdomen. The little boy giggled and hunched him-self into a ball.

The reinforcement of contact became most pronounced during meals. Robertito watched his father's mouth chew in the same cadence as his own. Yet he still maintained side-glancing as his format for visually ingesting his environment. After finishing the last morsel of food, Robertito climbed on his father and flopped over his shoulder. Roby stood up and spun him around. Robertito did not grab onto his father's body. He did not support himself or secure his own safety. But he laughed...not the self-stimulating laughter often seen in sessions, but a deep and hearty cackle. Each time his father embraced him, he pulled him close, then pushed him away...somehow trying to decide. Roby molded to his son's cues. He knew, though the touching might be pleasurable and alluring, it could not be as safe for Robertito as his in-ternal world. He did not want to scare him. Sensing Rober-

183

tito's alternate relaxing and tightening, he backed off and lessened the bombardment of activity.

"*Bien, papito,*" he said softly, often calling him "the little papa" in Spanish. He stood up and surveyed the room. Just as he turned toward the tape recorder, he felt a tugging on his loose shirt. Roby looked at his son's little hand. Awed and flattered in the most profound way, Roberto Soto sat by his son. When the boy began to rock, he let his body trust his child's rhythm.

*   *   *

At the same time that Roberto Soto worked with his son, John Stringer, according to newspaper reports, paced the rain-swept street of another American city. His sandy blond hair darkened from the little pellets of rain. He dug his right hand deeply into his raincoat pocket and fondled the metal instrument which had been a gift from his father. As he dodged puddles in crossing the street, he gawked enviously at a young family exiting their parked station wagon. A little boy accompanied by his sister waited politely on the sidewalk until their parents ushered them into a nearby store.

"So simple," John Stringer muttered to himself. "A family...it was supposed to be so simple."

His car waited in the parking lot, but instead of driving home, he trudged four miles in the rain, having left his office at precisely five o'clock. He could always change his mind. Stringer thought about his wife. It wasn't her fault. It wasn't! Yet the doctors had inferred that their child's withdrawal was caused by a cold and hostile environment. They had leveled their sights on both parents, placing the blame squarely on their shoulders.

He remembered his son's first birthday vividly. His wife, Sally, had invited all their relatives and half the neighborhood. Toys, music, laughter and love cluttered every room in the house, landmarks of a happy, thriving young family. Two months later, Tommy started to act very peculiar. He ignored his parents and developed a complex repertoire of rocking and spinning motions. At first the word autism meant nothing to him. Except for cancer, he thought most diseases could be cured. Even when he heard the prognosis, he would not believe it. "What do they know?" he argued with himself. "They sit in their offices with secretaries and assistants, tell-

184

ing you your son won't get better and you're responsible. What do they know? We love our son...more than most."

After a second and third consultation, his optimism faded. Institutionalize him, one physician suggested with considerable pathos. "Frankly, Mr. Stringer, if Tommy was mine, that's what I would do." How could he institutionalize his son, his own flesh and blood? The Stringers requested assistance from the social services department, but the social workers refused to deal with their dilemma. No existing programs suited their son's profound dysfunction. All the doors closed. Finally, one clinic offered to incorporate them into a therapy series which provided thirty minutes of service per week. Tommy drifted further away.

Two years later, Jamie was born. She didn't become autistic, didn't reject the supposedly cold and hostile environment. John wanted to love his daughter more, but his son demanded increased attention as he became increasingly unmanageable. He never wanted to hit the boy, but he lost his patience when Tommy destroyed all their dishes.

John Stringer saw himself as a decent human being with all the normal sensibilities. Now, in a less than normal situation, his ability to cope and survive became threatened. Anger polluted the love. Self-pity compromised the confidence. The confusion of dealing with his son kept his life buried under a dark cloud. He hated going home after work. He hated listening to his wife cry on the phone every day. He hated the alarm clock beside his bed. The dreams had crumbled. No more vacations. No more weekend trips into the mountains. Their life revolved around Tommy, because Tommy rampaged through the house on a daily basis. They had tried to love him, but did not know how.

The large elms guarding the entrance to his street no longer generated a sense of comfort in him. Sally would barely greet him. At twenty-seven, she looked like a forty-year-old woman, her face lined, her eyes puffed, her lips shriveled from the insidious tension. He did not blame her, though some others viewed them accusingly. John Stringer couldn't stand it any more, not for himself, not for his wife, not for his daughter, not for Tommy. His son's staring eyes frightened him. What demon possessed this child? What happened to his brain to have made him so crazy? Yes, he could admit to himself. His son, named after his favorite grandfather, was mentally disturbed without any hope for a cure. He felt profoundly sorry for the little boy who could not talk or dress

185

himself or keep his pants clean. What a miserable life his son had been cursed with...miserable! The word echoed in his brain as he stopped at the stoop in front of his house. He could change his mind. He could.

John Stringer entered nervously.

"What happened to you?" Sally asked, putting her hands on her hips. "My God, Johnny, you're a sight."

"The car," he mumbled. "The car wouldn't start so I had to walk home." She snapped her head back and marched off to the kitchen. Though they had been married for less than eight years, she no longer greeted him with a kiss or even a light embrace. She wanted to be affectionate, but his escape to the office each morning annoyed her. She had to be the jailer. Sally tried to help her son for years, finally giving up, locking him in his room for short periods in an effort to maintain her own sanity. He had been put in his room today, especially today, after he rubbed his feces all over the living room wall. It had not always been like this. Once, although strange and withdrawn, he exuded an awesome calm. They wanted more co-operation from him so they instituted some standard methods of discipline, sometimes in the form of a reprimand, sometimes in the form of a whack on his hand or buttocks. Tommy changed.

When the doctors hinted at her responsibility for her son's autism, John became the inquisitioner, questioning every move she made with the child every day. He never accused her, but his suspicions became transparent. She would never forgive him...never.

The television blared in his ears. "Damn," he muttered. When he tapped his daughter on the head, she did not even look up. Her eyes remained glued to the action on the set. He meandered through the dining room before entering the short hallway. His feet moved slowly. His hands perspired. He kept reminding himself he could choose differently. He could change his mind.

John Stringer removed the keys off the nail and opened the locked door to his son's bedroom. Tommy lay on the orange carpet, his feet tucked under the bed. He hummed in a high-pitched voice and twirled his fingers in front of his eyes. They had requested a homeworker, but the county said it could not provide one in these types of cases because of a limited budget. John had even tried to hire a babysitter to free his wife at least one afternoon a week. Nobody wanted to say with Tommy Stringer.

"Hello, Tommy," he said in a voice so soft and gentle that he surprised himself. The little boy continued his self-stimulating ritual without interruption. John Stringer knelt down. Water dripped from his hair and coat. He petted his son like he would pet a dog. He began to cry for the first time in four years. He could change his mind. He could.

He removed his coat and put it on the chair. He sat beside Tommy. When you left him alone, he thought to himself, his son always seemed so calm and peaceful. But you couldn't leave him alone.

"C'mon, Tommy, do you want to look at your daddy?" he said in a child-like voice. He no longer knew how to address him. "C'mon, Tommy, look at Daddy." His son stared at his own fingers. John Stringer wanted a sign, any sign. "Damn it, look at me!" The boy held his Buddha-like concentration, never once turning his head.

John scraped his finger along the edge of his teeth until it hurt. He rattled his toes, trying to distract himself. Finally, he dug deep into his raincoat and withdrew the metal instrument, a chrome-plated target pistol. Its menacing barrel loomed at him. John Stringer stared at Tommy. He knew he would never have another son. He wanted to do this for his wife, for his daughter...most of all, for Tommy.

As he lowered the gun toward his son, his hand trembled. The light bouncing off the silver barrel attracted Tommy's attention. The boy looked at the gun the same way he looked at a doorknob. He touched it with his hand and felt its smooth surface. He smiled a peculiar smile, pulling the pistol toward him. John Stringer watched his own hand through a fog. Tommy tried to flap the metal instrument, but his father's grip held it steady.

The gun had been lowered to the side of his son's temple. John Stringer began to talk to God. He would understand. He would know he loved his son. His fingers felt paralyzed. Tommy began humming a tune he heard on the radio. "That's something," a voice inside said. "A tune from the radio. He hummed a tune from the radio." His trembling fingers removed the safety. He could change his mind. He could. John Stringer screamed at the exact moment he pulled the trigger.

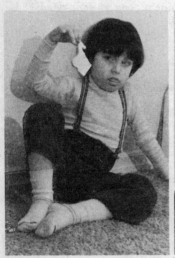 

A typical portrait of Robertito Soto before the initiation of our journey with him. At five and a half, he was adrift in his own world, staring endlessly at inanimate objects such as this puzzle piece which he flapped continuously at the side of his head. Brain-impaired, autistic, retarded, he had created a closed circuit within himself, which excluded the rest of humanity.

A child reborn. After our extended family of twelve people worked together with him intimately, seven days a week, twelve hours a day, for over one and a half years (seven thousand hours on a one-to-one basis), his smile, bright eyes and expression not only reflect the flowering of a little boy that everyone had labeled as hopeless, but illustrate the power and healing of a loving environment.

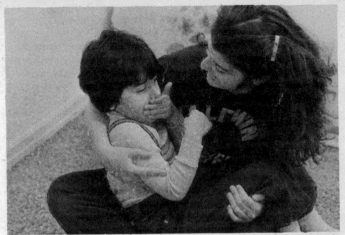

After hundreds of hours of loving, non-judgmental contact in which we followed him into the private womb of his secluded, autistic world, he began to permit physical contact. Laura rocks Robertito in her arms, smiling and talking softly to him as he remains closed within himself.

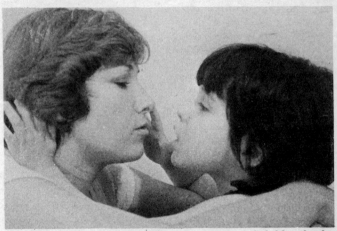

In an all-loving and safe environment, this special child makes his first attempt to touch and explore the human world around him. Despite the confusion of his own perception and dysfunctions, he breaks through old barriers and tries to contact his mother. Francisca had waited almost six long years for this moment.

Robertito's father watches and lovingly encourages his son while he struggles to complete a puzzle that will help him conceptualize shapes and forms.

Once we built bridges from our world to his, we began to slowly introduce the tools of communication. Suzi makes everything exciting—her spirited enthusiasm, throaty voice and animated face capture his attention and interest. Teaching him the letter "a" is secondary to showing him the joy of human contact.

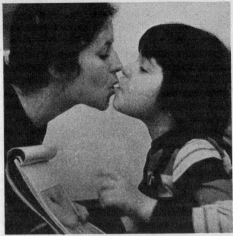

Trying to touch Robertito meant trying first to find the most loving place within ourselves. Carol (Kha) not only shows her young student an enlarged photograph of a mouth, but, in very human terms, demonstrates it as a function of expression and caring.

The simplest games helped Robertito develop and utilize skills which had laid dormant for so many years. He had to climb mountains to do what other children often accomplished with ease. Here Francisca encourages him to insert blocks in squares of the same color, an activity which develops hand-eye co-ordination, figure-ground differentiation, identification of colors and shapes.

Most of the members of our extended "family" staff (left to right).
Top row: Bryn Kaufman, Arcelia (Chella) Granados. *Second row:*
Carol (Kha) Bell, Laura (Rha) Frankfurt, Jeannie Kannengieser.
Botton row: Suzi Lyte Kaufman, Raun Kaufman, Roberto (Roby)
Soto, Thea Kaufman, Barry (Bears) Neil Kaufman, Francisca Soto.

Movements, often to music, mimic many of Robertito's self-stimulating behaviors. Chella rocks him in her arms as he claps and peers
directly into her eyes. Although she had often communicated with
him by using thought patterns instead of words, this time she sings
songs for her audience of one special child.

To really play with a child is to be there as a child. Suzi and Robertito watch each other's cues attentively as they make their own brand of music. She stimulates her little friend to initiate and then follows his lead.

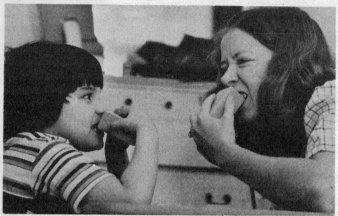

In the midst of building blocks, Robertito picks up one form and explores it with his mouth. As he became immersed in that activity, Jeannie imitates him as an unmasked sign of approval and communion. Robertito responds by looking at her and smiling.

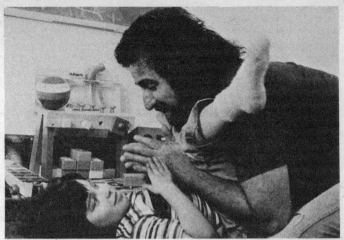

No one specific activity took preference over another. Teaching Robertito how to assemble puzzles or attempt to make sounds had the same value as touching, tickling and smiling. Barry (Bears) reinforces the joy and fun of human interaction by wrestling and clapping hands with Robertito.

Once he became motivated from within, Robertito soared like a bird whose wings had just been freed. Sometimes, in an effort to tickle his curiosity, Angelina, a lifelike doll, was utilized as a competing student. In time, he embraced her as a friend.

Chapter 13

Three young women, dressed in black tights, puckered their ruby-red-lipstick lips while they sang tunes from the thirties and tap-danced on a plywood plank set in the middle of the sidewalk. Across the street, where Seventh Avenue meets West Fourth Street, a sixty-year-old woman sang opera without the benefit of accompaniment. Street vendors hawked "no-nuke" T-shirts, leather belts and African bead necklaces. A couple, complete with green knee guards and headbands, roller-skated around the strollers, expertly avoiding body contact.

Francisca and Roby kept turning their heads, distracted and delighted by the intense activity. They gaped wide-eyed, like infants, at the circus of humanity around them. This marked our fourth stop in a walking excursion through lower Manhattan. Not only did Suzi and I want to share the city with them, we wanted to expose them to other experiences away from the workroom and the house on Thelma Street. This departure from the schedule had the same value and significance as any other ingredient in Robertito's program. We did not want to over-orchestrate their lives; we wanted to love them by helping them understand the importance of their whole universe as a connected circuit, that caring for themselves was a direct and vital way of caring for their son.

We introduced Francisca and Roby to "dun-tahs" in Chinatown, to smooth cappuccinos in Little Italy and to avocado-tofu salads in Soho. After we completed our stroll through the Village, we hailed a taxi to the Whitney Museum on Madison.

In the lobby, Francisca bumped into a guard and quickly excused herself. The man's stone-like disinterest startled her. Francisca stared at him, squinting her eyes and rubbing the back of her head.

"Hey, Bears, what's wrong with him?" she said, speaking very slowly.

"Perhaps, he's sleepy," I responded simplistically, confined by my limited Spanish vocabulary.

"No, Bears," she insisted. "Look, he doesn't move."

Suzi and I trudged over to the officer, who stood sentry in front of a locked door.

"Francisca, at least he breathes," I assured her.

Roby hid his smirk from his wife. Francisca inched closer. Her eyes scrutinized the man's chest. At that moment, a number of people joined her to inspect the guard. They pointed to his mustache, his eyelids and the shadow of stubble just visible on his chin. He held his position in total disregard of the observers. His downcast eyes avoided any direct confrontation. Suddenly, Francisca burst out laughing and hugged her husband in embarrassment. She had been duped by a piece of sculpture, one of many on display in the museum which presented the uncanny illusion of actual biological life.

Our arrival at the Lincoln Center for the Performing Arts highlighted the day. A friend had given me courtesy tickets to the American Ballet Theatre's performance of *Swan Lake* at the Metropolitan Opera House. The complex buildings, with their façades of glass, aluminum and marble, hypnotized the Sotos. Roby gaped at the patterns of floating people visible through three stories of windows as they glided between floors on silver escalators.

Francisca put her hand over her mouth as we entered the opera house. Her eyes could barely absorb the beauty of the endless rows of chandeliers which dotted the interior of the theater. Roby's mouth dropped open unconsciously as he observed the collage of humanity, people draped in tuxedos and gowns standing beside others in jeans and worn overalls.

197

Even as we were ushered to our seats, Roby stretched his neck to view the various balconies which ringed the huge hall. Francisca stared at the diamond-like formation of lights suspended from the ceiling.

The overture filled the darkness. Suzi pulled herself close to me. Francisca and Roby focused on the curtains, waiting to see their first ballet.

"I'm so happy for them," Suzi whispered. We both watched our dear friends, silently sharing their involvement. Panic no longer quivered by their lips. Their son and their situation had become more comprehensible and joyful to them. In their search to touch Robertito, they had begun to touch themselves.

The music swept through the audience like waves of warm water. I had always felt a certain aloofness to ballet. This night, the choreographed allegory swept me beyond the confines of my seat. Maybe the presence of Roby and Francisca had made a difference. Maybe I had opened another doorway and made myself more available to the experience. The dancers' world became my world. Their story became the only story. A complete absorption. The stage floor began to ripple like the surface of a small lake. Had my retina and mind conspired to give me the illusion and added depth of an actual Swan Lake? I closed my eyes and reopened them only to discover the water on the black floor had become even more vivid. I turned away, then looked back. Occasional ripples fluttered beneath the dancer's feet. I closed my eyes once more.

"Anything wrong?" Suzi said in a hushed voice.

"Just experimenting," I said nonchalantly. She smiled at me in the same motherly way she smiled at Raun. Suzi locked her arm tightly around mine and gave her full attention back to the ballet.

The darkness became heavy like thick pea soup. The music and moving figures retreated into the dense fog as my awareness focused solely on the floor of the stage. I did not see water the way I saw the chair or the walls in the theater. I sensed the water so vividly that I experienced its presence without seeing it. No vision. No three-dimensional hallucination. Only the lingering knowledge of water...more dominant in my mind than all the activity in the theater. I negotiated with myself to accept this peculiar distraction.

In the midst of my internal dialogue, I felt the presence of someone else on the stage, someone who did not belong.

I strained my eyes, searching among the dancers. Then, in center stage, away from the activity of the plot which the performers enacted on the left portion of the stage, I sensed the form of a small boy. He was there, yet I knew he was not there. My eyes riveted on his illusive form, too small and too vague to identify. Who was he? What was he doing on stage? No, not on stage...what was he doing in my mind? The ripples marred the flat surface of the dance floor again. The child began to sink...to drown. His arms grabbed wildly for some support. Even as the applause filled the theater and the performers took their bows, I saw only the trauma behind the dancers. Francisca and Roby bubbled with their enthusiasm to Suzi. I remained apart. Though the curtain had fallen, my eyes still perceived the stage, the water and the child, whose form continued to recede beneath the threatening liquid. Then, like a shockwave, my body became rigid in response to a voice, my own voice, which screamed Raun's name somewhere deep inside.

"Wait here!" I said abruptly to Suzi and I bolted from the seat. Adrenalin flooded my arteries, throwing my nervous system into high gear. Everything around me seemed to move in slow motion. Pushing past the people promenading leisurely up the aisle during intermission became a profoundly difficult task. "Excuse me. Excuse me. Thanks. Just let me pass, please; I have to pass," I clamored, weaving through the murky chatter and bulky bodies. Interlocked arms stretched across the entrance to the lobby like a tight scrimmage line. The obstacle course continued even as I approached the escalator and the long column of people poised in front of it. Turning away, I grabbed the railing of a staircase and lunged downward. "Raun. Not Raun. Please, not Raun," I cried breathlessly to myself. The imagery of the stage floor propelled me across the bottom step with such force that I lost my balance in an attempt to avoid a young woman crossing my path. I stumbled, using my hands against the floor to stabilize my body. Eyes peered at me quizzically, curiously, reflecting an ironic tolerance for my irregular behavior.

"Where are the phones?" I asked an usher. Though he stood within two feet of me, the time required for the sound of my voice to reach him felt like a hundred years. His half-smile slowly disappeared from his cheeks. His head dipped in fractional movments, an instant replay energized by fading batteries. I knew to watch his hand, which rose lethargically from his side of his body to a point over the heads of the other patrons. His index finger aimed at a telephone sign on the other side of the corridor. Before his words reached my ears, my legs had lifted me off the carpet into a half-turn and propelled me toward my destination.

An older man collided with me twenty feet from the telephones. We exchanged quick apologies and continued on our separate journeys. All the booths were occupied. I waited two seconds, then tapped insistently on the first window. "An emergency. It's an emergency," I said. The woman shook her finger at me like a scolding mother. She smiled pleasantly, refusing to believe me or separate from her call. The man in the next booth claimed his call also ranked as an emergency.

At the window of the third booth, I displayed a ten-dollar bill. "Ten bucks for the phone this instant."

"Are you kidding, mister?" the young man questioned suspiciously. Our eyes locked. He belched a quick good-by into the receiver, shook his head and departed without taking the money.

I rumbled through my pants' pocket. When I jerked my hand free, a barrage of coins exploded to all parts of the booth. Ten cents. Ten cents. I grabbed the first dime and dumped it into the slot. After depositing an additional twenty-five cents, the line connected.

"Hello," Denise, our baby-sitter, answered in a relaxed voice.

"This is Bears. Don't ask why...just run upstairs right now and check Raun...then check the girls. Now. Hurry. Go." I heard the phone receiver drop against the wall. The sweat poured from my forehead. The wetness under my shirt surfaced near my neck. C'mon, Denise, c'mon, I cheered in my mind. Only the banging earpiece against the wall greeted my urgency. I kept breathing for Raun, filling his lungs with oxygen. Where are you, Denise? I could feel my pulse beat in my gums. Then, I heard footsteps coming toward the other end of the phone. My mind went absolutely blank as if everything I thought or imagined had been completely erased.

"Bears," the breathless voice began, "they're okay. Raun and Thea are playing checkers. And Bryn's reading."

I moaned my release.

"What's going on?" Denise asked. "You scared me half to death."

"I'm sorry," I said. "It's such a strange story. I had this

incredibly, ah, compelling...feeling. I had to make sure Raun and the girls were okay." I sighed. "Thanks, honey."

As I climbed the wide staircase to the second floor, I felt light-headed. People had begun to return to their seats for the next portion of the performance. When I entered the theater, I looked toward the stage. The curtain still appeared transparent; the child still sinking in the water. "Oh no," I groaned aloud. "It's not Raun; it's Robertito. Oh, God, it's Robertito." I turned in my tracks and raced across the second floor lobby, jumped down the stairs and ran for the phones again.

I dialed the Sotos' number quickly and got a busy signal. I redialed it and redialed it and redialed it. How could Charlotte be on the phone when she was supposed to be working with Robertito? After twenty additional attempts, I thought of Laura, who lived nearby.

"Hiya," the voice bellowed into the receiver playfully.

"Rha," I said.

"Hiya, Bears," she replied, instantly recognizing my voice.

"I hate to ask you, but you're the only one who can help."

"Sure, what is it?" Laura said with concern.

"Right now, go over to the Soto house. I can't get through. The phone's busy. Just go there and check everything for me. Okay? Could you do that right now?"

"Yeah, yeah," she said.

"You have to go straight there, okay? No stops. Just straight there. I'll explain everything later. Listen, I may not sound coherent, but I am."

Laura hung up the receiver, ran down the stairs and jumped into her Volkswagen. She drove the bug across part of her lawn and bounced over the curb into the street. The urgency disturbed her. A line-up of cars stalled traffic for almost half a mile. Steering her car on the gravel, she whizzed past the log jam, then re-entered the road. Nervousness merged with embarrassment. She felt uncomfortable intruding on Charlotte, checking on her like a nursemaid. But her fleeting self-consciousness disappeared when she thought about her little enigmatic Mexican friend.

The lock yielded easily to the turn of her key. Laura whistled loudly as she entered.

"Charlotte," she called.

"Who's there?" came the reply.

"It's me. Rha. I, uh, left my box of saxophone reeds here.

I'm just going to look for it." Laura paused, counted to three and said: "Everything okay?"

"Honky-dory," Charlotte sang.

Relieved, Laura began her mock-search in the living room and kitchen. Several seconds later, Charlotte, her hair half-set in curlers, bounced down the stairs.

"I'll help," she said. "It's one of the blue boxes, right?"

Laura nodded sheepishly. "How's it going?" she asked, intending to inquire about Charlotte's session with Robertito.

"Tomorrow morning Brad's taking me to breakfast. Isn't that neat?" she bubbled. "And Sunday night, it's time for other friend."

"You must mean Nick," Laura said. Charlotte winked. Then, as Laura lifted the pillow from the couch, she realized the ramifications of Charlotte's presence. We had all agreed not to break a session unless there was an emergency. Certainly her fictitious box of lost reeds did not qualify as an emergency.

"Where's Robertito?" Laura asked.

"Upstairs," Charlotte chimed.

"Maybe you'd better get back up, okay?" Laura counseled.

Charlotte smiled. "No rush. He was real hyper tonight, so I stuck him in a bath."

Laura whipped around. "A bath! Is he in the bath now?" Charlotte nodded casually. "Jesus," Laura mumbled, pushing past the other woman and running up the stairs.

"What's the big deal?" Charlotte called, shaking her head as she followed.

Frightened by her own imagination, Laura fought an impulse to scream. How long had they been downstairs together? Two minutes? Three? Was that enough time for a life to be extinguished? Laura tripped up the stairs and charged into the bathroom. "Robertito," she hollered, catching her first glimpse of the little boy slouched in the corner of the tub. The water level covered his chin completely and rippled around his lips. He babbled incessantly as his face and hands quivered in the cool water. As she reached for him, he began to sink beneath the water. She grabbed him under his arms and pulled him out. The shiver in her own body mirrored his. Laura hugged his nude, wet form. "It's okay, Tito. You're okay now." A tenderness oozed from her body as she tightened her embrace. She thanked the universe for his life. The dam had burst. She knew she loved him with the same intensity as she loved Raun. Laura felt protective, involved, soft and

202

distinctly feminine. In experiencing her caring for Robertito, she knew clearly, for the first time, that she could love any child and every child.

"See, he's fine!" Charlotte grinned as she casually entered the room.

"What the hell's the matter with you? He's not fine. He's shaking," Laura barked, surprised at her own voice, as she wrapped him in a towel. "The damn water is freezing." She paused and inhaled deeply. "Do you realize how dangerous it is to leave him alone, especially in water? He doesn't have the same responses we do. He could have slid under and drowned."

"Oh, c'mon," Charlotte said, now visibly uncomfortable. "He'd be okay."

"How do you know?" Laura shouted. "He's not an Olympic swimmer or even a normal six-year-old. He can't take care of himself. Besides, Charlotte, you're supposed to be working with him." The insistent ringing of the phone intruded. As Charlotte went downstairs to answer it, Laura gaped at the other woman. "Wait," she ordered. "I'll get it." Still holding the little boy, she went downstairs and picked up the receiver.

"Hello, Rha...is that you?" I asked.

"Oh, Bears, thank God for your strange feelings," Laura said.

"Is he okay?" I asked, having dialed the number over one hundred times before getting through.

"Yes. I'll call you later when you get home," she said. "I'm going to help put him to sleep." Laura hung up the phone and stared at Robertito's trembling lips. He seemed disoriented and lost. His gentle expression matched by his extreme vulnerability overwhelmed her. When she returned to the bathroom, she noticed the hair blower and curlers on the sink. Obviously, with Robertito immersed in the water, Charlotte had decided to set her hair and then apparently abandoned the little boy to go downstairs. In utter disbelief, Laura avoided looking directly at the other woman. She gently wiped the child's body while he flapped with one hand and said: "Eee-o, eee-o."

"I'll do that," Charlotte declared, toweling his back. "I mean you don't have to be so upset," she said, noticing the tension in Laura's face. "Nothing happened. After all, nothing happened."

* * *

Our telephone rang at five in the morning. Laura, relieved and irrevocably changed by the previous night's incident, described in detail her experience with Charlotte. Suzi and I listened intently, trying to extract the lesson from what had occurred.

As we drove to the Soto house the following day, I turned to Suzi. "I know Francisca has known for a long time that Charlotte doesn't belong here. She's been taking care of her fears, not her wants. If she had trusted herself, last night would not have occurred."

"Maybe once she and Roby know about it, they'll decide differently."

"I'm not sure I want to tell them."

"What?" Suzi exclaimed. "Why not?"

"It's important to get Francisca and Roby out of the house once in a while. They have never let that child out of their sight in almost six years. Now, tell them this, and they'll be cemented to him."

When we arrived, Laura had begun her session with Robertito. Roby and Francisca sat at the kitchen table with an unmistakable expression of excitement and fatigue.

"We want to tell you something," Francisca announced, talking in a simplified Spanish. "Come. Sit. Coffee? Tea?" After serving us, she continued. "After you dropped us off last night..."

Roby touched his wife's shoulder. "We want you both to know how grateful we are for everything. We will always remember yesterday. For Robertito, there are no words."

Had Laura told them despite my suggestion to shelve the incident for the moment?

"All aspects of yesterday were important," I said.

"Leaving Robertito for a day," Suzi interjected, "gave you an opportunity to return and see with different eyes."

"In many ways, that's true," Roby concurred. "Mommy, you tell them."

"Roby and I talked till four in the morning," she said proudly. "We did, well, sort of an Option session. We asked each other questions like you do, Bears. We discussed the past weeks with Charlotte. I see my own anger and blindness now. So we have decided to ask her to leave, today, this morning. We are not angry with her. We think it would be best for our son and for her. She's not happy here." Francisca

204

leaned over and hugged her husband. Suzi and I glanced at each other in awe. Laura, in fact, had not spoken to them about the previous night.

"Maybe, one day, Bears, I will teach Option to Spanish people," Roby added.

"Charlotte goes," Francisca reasserted without malice. She and Roby nodded.

"Okay," I said. "Suzi and I will try to locate another interpreter for tomorrow night. We'll try. We'll see." I smiled and touched their hands. "If we don't get one, we'll just keep talking to each other until everyone understands." We need the fluency and the exacting details of language an interpreter could provide, especially during our Wednesday night meetings.

When we left, I turned to Suzi. "Hey, sweet lady, how come you didn't tell them?"

"It didn't seem necessary, at least not now," she replied. "They explored the problem and found their own answer without even knowing about last night. That's really exciting. Really."

Though Francisca and Roby offered Charlotte the opportunity to continue living with them until she found another job or decided to return home, she departed immediately.

Rita, a gatherer of talented and caring volunteers, filled the translator spot within hours. She introduced Amalia, a gentle and elegant woman who had fled Europe with her family before the onset of the Second World War. Unable to obtain visas to enter the United States, they lived for years in Cuba. Amalia's general ease with Spanish and her familiarity with our approach through one of Rita's therapy groups, provided us with a woman who not only translated but further enriched the group with her delicate caring and affection.

The other gap resulting from Charlotte's exit appeared more difficult to bridge. In the interim, her sessions with Robertito had been distributed among all of us. Suzi and I reviewed the recent letters we received from the piles of hundreds mailed to us each month. We had volunteers from San Diego, Chicago, Des Moines, Portland, Washington, D.C., and countless other cities. We separated those from people who lived within the New York area. We reviewed notes from all the recent telephone calls. And then, ignoring hours of research, Suzi jumped to her feet and declared: "I've got it, but it's not in any of these piles. Remember that girl . . . when you spoke at the college?"

"Which college?"

Suzi smiled. "Not only can't I remember her name, but I don't recall the name of the school either." She kissed me on the forehead. "Don't go away. I'll find it."

Then, as I flipped through more letters, I recalled one particular girl. I had been the guest speaker at her college for a special conference. Following the talk, she attached herself to both Suzi and me. In twenty quick minutes, she flooded Suzi with intimate details of her life story. She had read *Son-Rise* for a course she had taken the previous semester. She felt as if she had actually worked with Raun, touched his hands, smiled his smiles. The familiarity of incidents recorded on each page haunted her. A door had opened and she refused to let go. Carol. That's it, I thought. Her name is Carol.

"Here it is," Suzi boasted. "Your Suzi found it."

I put my index finger to the center of my forehead like a fortune-teller. "The person is Carol."

"Hey, that's not fair," Suzi clamored, putting on her sad clown face. "Ah-hah," she beamed. "What you might not know is that the person called me several times since your talk. A super-persistent lady."

"Feels right," I concluded. "You know how people always ask how we decide who to work with. Somehow the most persistent person gives you the clearest message. Well, let's get this Carol person over here."

She entered our home rather formally attired in a skirt and low heels. Carol's long hair covered half her back. Her sharp features, the square chin, the cleft, the dark blue eyes, accented a definite determination. When I hugged her, she stiffened without returning the greeting. Nevertheless, her nervousness did not abort her warmth and intensity.

"I can't tell you what this means to me," Carol said. "I want to learn to work with people the way you do. Here," she declared, showing us a Spanish-English dictionary. "I've already started learning Spanish. I have two other texts and a third on order."

Carol Bell had left college and worked in a bank unhappily for five years full time. When she returned to her studies in order to major in special education, she developed a ferocious appetite to learn. Carol was not just another person completing the expected routine from crib to college. She cared about school with an abiding passion. Every course and every text meant something special...an alternative, an opportunity.

We explained the elements of Robertito's program and the importance of the attitude and our own personal happiness. Her head bobbed up and down excitedly. I purposely described the less attractive details. I gave her a blunt commentary on the experience of changing the diaper of an old boy nearing his sixth birthday. I talked about his possible lack of responsiveness for hours...for days. No matter what I presented, how oddly or graphically I portrayed it, Carol kept her head moving. "Yes, yes," she whispered many times. "If you told me I'd have to assist in open-heart surgery, I'd do it," she insisted.

Her power and her directness supported her intentions. Only her frequent tendency to speak in a monotone voice and her lack of facial expressiveness concerned me. Carol withheld portions of herself.

"One of the most important things with Robertito is expressiveness," Suzi said, mind-reading again. "We really cheer him and smile and laugh and kiss him. I mean like this." Suzi shouted, cheered and applauded an imaginary friend beside her. Then she pantomimed an embrace and finished the monologue with a deep laugh.

Carol smiled easily for the first time. "I'm just a little nervous...but with a kid, it's different. I can do that. I'll be fine."

"Can you start observing right away?" I asked. "I mean like today, this afternoon." She indicated her affirmation with a slight tilt of her head.

Suzi kissed her, though Carol resisted. "I'm glad you're with us," she said. "And one thing we're going to work on is your hug." Carol turned red. "Hey, there's nothing to be embarrassed about. Most of us were taught to hide behind walls all of our lives."

"If you don't want to be hugged, that's not a prerequisite," I added. "That's just the way we tell each other we care." I paused and peered at her eager face. "I think everybody wants to be hugged...including you."

Carol allowed a tiny grin to crease her face. "There's something else you should know. Maybe it will affect your decision." She stared at the table for several seconds, bit her lip, then blurted: "I'm an epileptic."

"And I'm six feet three inches tall," I volunteered.

A second full smile flooded her face. Carol initiated the

hugs this time. Though her body felt tight and her eyelids quivered, she grabbed each of us strongly. "I'll be back at two," she promised, and left.

Carol lingered in the car outside the house for over ten minutes. She did not want to break the spell. Her thoughts drifted inevitably to her father, who had died just after her fifteenth birthday. She did not just remember him; she pulled his presence close to her, back across ten years of time. The memory of his frail and withered form during those last two years receded against the more powerful image of a younger man. The beautiful eyes. The solid, firm body. The strong facial features. The handsome cleft in his chin, which she, too, had inherited. "Frank would approve," she thought, mouthing her father's first name as she turned the ignition and heard his words. "It's beautiful for a man to cry."

Instead of going home, Carol drove to her favorite spot, a narrow, rocky jetty which extended out into the Atlantic. She jumped from boulder to boulder until she arrived at the spot where the ocean dove between and under the rocks. A calmness swept through her.

If Robertito, like Raun, can get better, she thought, then maybe I can. Carol knew she had no logical reason to make such a connection, but she did. Her neurologist, aware of her interview with us, asked her with mild sarcasm why she would choose to work with an autistic child...had she expected to cure the incurable? That very word had also been applied to her illness. Incurable! Robertito had to get better, he had to! She placed the first hope she dared to have for herself in the journey of a little boy she had not yet met.

Carol returned in the afternoon and met Francisca, Roby and Laura. I scheduled a dialogue session for her later in the week. Carol would begin with Carol, exploring her own unhappiness, beliefs and judgments. Observing others would lead to tandem teaching. Finally, when she assessed herself as ready, she would begin solo sessions with our young friend. We discussed these components as Suzi worked with Robertito upstairs.

The little boy grabbed Suzi's hand and placed it in front of her face. They twirled their fingers in front of their eyes simultaneously.

"Can you touch your nose, Robertito?" she asked. "Touch your nose."

Very slowly, he stopped his "ism" and tapped the palm of his hand to the tip of his nose.

"Fantástico," Suzi shouted, lavishing him with hugs and kisses. When his body stiffened, she moved away. She had him locate the other features of his face. He pointed to each one, but seemed confused about the location of his ears. Intermittently, Suzi fed him small portions of food.

They worked with a puzzle together, then the pegboard, then the insertion box. She tried again to teach him how to roll a ball. He pushed it awkwardly with the front of his hand, the back of his hand and his wrist. When he paced in a circle, Suzi followed him, babbling as he babbled. Then, experimenting, she turned around and went in the opposite direction. To her surprise, Robertito stopped, sideglanced at her and finally turned around and followed her. She laughed and sang her support as she led the activity.

Later, Robertito sat by himself in the middle of the room while Suzi massaged his hands. Instead of his traditional "eee-o" or "boy-o," Suzi heard a different combination of sounds. "Ca-a-o," he said. "Ca-a-o. Ca-a-o." He slurred the letters into each other, but Suzi tried to decipher them. Then it struck her. "It can't be," she blurted in English.

"*Caballo?* Is that what you're saying?" she said. "*Caballo.*" Without delay, she assumed the horseback-ride position. Robertito flopped immediately onto her back. She made some appropriate sounds and then crawled around the room with her rider. "*Caballo,*" she repeated every couple of seconds. Roby had often used the word horse to describe the rides he gave his son. As she worked with him, hitting the xylophone, he mumbled those same letters again. Suzi called to Francisca to listen. For the next hour Robertito remained characteristically mute. Only the babbling and cooing broke the silence.

Carol replaced Francisca on the sidelines and watched the continuing session. When the little boy held Suzi's thighs and danced with her, Carol fought back the tears which filled her eyes. She turned away to hide her face, but changed her mind, allowing more of who she was to penetrate the outer walls; for she, too, felt the same comfort and security in the room that she imagined this wonderful, alluring child felt.

After Carol's departure, I returned home to pick up both Thea and Raun for their sessions with Robertito. "I've been thinking," Raun said in the truck. "Robertito is going to get bigger than me faster than he's going to get older than me. That's because he can't have a birthday every day, but he sure can eat every day."

"Oh, Raunchy," Thea giggled, patting her brother on the head.

At the Soto house, Roby played catch with Raun while Thea taught in tandem with her mother. They ran and jumped and danced together. Though Thea was three years older than Robertito, her thin and delicate figure appeared miniaturized against his soft yet solid hulk. She laughed in a tiny, high voice each time he imitated her, although the majority of the action followed his lead. Thea tried to teach Robertito how to sniff with his nose, scratching the indicated areas of a "Smell" book filled with the scents of chocolate, rose, banana, lilac, lemon and orange.

Suzi and I accompanied Raun during his portion of the session. The four of us clapped and rocked together. Then we presented Raun with his first opportunity to feed Robertito.

"Really? Can I?" He shook the upper portion of his torso in delight. With the expertise of a seasoned teacher, he delivered spoonful after spoonful. He stroked his friend gently under the chin as he chewed. After the meal, Robertito kept touching Raun. At one point, feeling the larger boy's pressure, Raun faked a fall and whispered: "I did it so Robertito would feel strong."

Our little friend did his whole repertoire of "isms." He watched Raun carefully from the corner of his eye in order to, perhaps, monitor Raun's responses. Sometimes, Robertito peered directly into our son's face, but only for seconds at a time. When Robertito rolled on the floor, Raun followed. Then Raun put his arm around his friend, spontaneously expressing his affection. To our surprise, Robertito responded in kind by placing his arm limply on Raun's shoulder. When Suzi asked "Where's Raun?" the child pointed to our son. We clapped and shouted our excitement. Robertito smiled at the wall. I turned the music on and guided the two children in a dance together. With their arms around each other, they rocked in a simple side-to-side two-step. Finally, Robertito broke away and began to increase his focus on his self-stimulating rituals.

"Go ahead, Raunchy, sit in front of him in the exact position he's in," I counseled.

"Okay," he replied, half-skipping across the room and assuming the same Buddha-like pose as his friend. Robertito hand-flapped. Our son stared at him curiously.

"You remember, sweet boy, do what he does," Suzi said.

Raun flapped his hand in perfect cadence. Robertito

stopped abruptly. Raun stopped. Robertito turned his head and faced his young mentor. Very purposefully, he stared directly into Raun's eyes. Our son smiled several times. Four seconds became ten seconds. Robertito did not turn away. Twenty incredible seconds had elapsed with their eyes locked together. Astounded, I clocked the first half a minute of sustained, direct eye contact Robertito had ever bestowed on anyone without interruption. Suzi and I held our breath. We dared not move. We had never seen Robertito do this before. Never!

As the two boys explored each other visually, Raun angled his head toward us. A huge, old-man smile embraced his face. In a soft and rich voice, Raun said: "We're telling the truth to each other...we do it with our eyes."

Chapter 14

Despite the imperfections of this turn-of-the-century brownstone on the fashionable upper East side of Manhattan, the
walls of this ancient relic remained reasonably upright. And,
yet, the interior hung over me like the inside sloping bulk-
head of a racing sloop. The high ceilings and huge archways
fell victim to the dark maroon paint which appeared black
during this last hour of daylight. As I waited, quiet and alone,
my eyes rested on the rather bizarre, provocative painting
of an attractive young man displaying his lean crop of chest
hairs through an opened, black leather jacket. Two art-deco
rams, sculpted in the early thirties, guarded the fireplace.
Lavish floral prints covered the peculiar low-back chairs and
odd-shaped divan, all art deco, all salvaged from the early
part of the century; old enough to qualify as valued antiques,
yet too spiffy, too born-again to suggest another time.

Every aspect of Jane's brownstone as well as her business,
a literary agency, reflected her careful preplanning and her
preoccupation with detail. An incisive young woman. Clear.
A workaholic. Only recently had she departed from her single

focus, allowing Carol, a young actor, and Herman, an ever-present basset hound, to share portions of her life.

When I met Jane, she occupied a seedy, cluttered version of her present surroundings. Her former apartment could have been rented as a grade B movie set in an old Boris Karloff film. At that time, she draped her body in basic black. Her decisive hand movements, direct eye contact and commanding voice completely overwhelmed any awareness of her femininity.

The drone of Jane's voice filtered into the room. I listened with obvious enjoyment as she soothed one of her other authors skillfully. More than my agent, she had become my friend.

"Hi, Baa," Jane sang as she entered the room theatrically. She wore a light tan dress without a bra. The curve of her hips was apparent, in contrast to her former attire.

"You always startle me when you dress like that," I said. "Somehow, I think of you more like a lean bulldozer than a person with particular sexual attributes."

She stopped short in the middle of the room and grinned cautiously. "From you, I'm sure it's a compliment." Jane extended her chin and pushed her cheek into my face. I kissed her lightly.

"Only two other people I know express their affection like that," I commented. "The Queen of England and my aunt Gloria...and my aunt Gloria is dead."

"How nice," Jane chimed. She tossed a package into my lap. "These are the galleys from *Giant Steps*."

As I opened the package, Herman romped into the room, barking as he jumped on my legs. "Herman, get down," Jane counseled. "C'mon, Herm, down, boy, down." She laughed. "Hey, Baa, you see what happened. The first Option dog. I tell him one thing and he decided to trust himself instead. I always ask him why he's unhappy. We have to let him work it out...of course." She glanced at her barking, jumping dog. "Okay! Down, Herm, down." Inevitably, the hound became part of the meeting.

"I'll work through the galleys during the next couple of weeks. We're pretty jammed."

"You know," Jane said, getting right to the point, "I still don't quite think you made the best move. Now is the perfect time to write another book. An interruption in your career is not good, not good at all. Besides, if you keep doing things

213

like Robertito, you'll end up on welfare. I don't think that suits your style."

"We're afloat," I said, smiling.

"Hey, Suzi told me about the grant, I'm sorry it didn't come through. I hope it doesn't bring this project to a premature end."

I sighed, then smiled. "One day at a time."

"Uh-huh," she grimaced, avoiding direct expression of sentiment. "Okay, tell me what's happening with him."

"Who's him?" I asked.

"The interruption, of course. The little boy who pulled you away from the typewriter and everything else you were doing."

After my lengthy description of the incidents and movements involving Robertito and those who worked with him, Jane pointed her finger at me. "Could you send me a page or two on it? I want to have it. Okay?" I nodded. Jane dipped her head, anticipating my response to her next comment. "If you could only guarantee me the kid will make it, we might have something big here."

"Hey, Jane, the point is not the outcome, but the evolution...for all of us." I paused. "I know it sounds soupy, but it's not."

She stood up and paced the room. "I know you know what you're doing with this boy, but do you think you're taking care of yourself and your family?"

"I think so," I said, aware of the tentative quality of my answer.

"Do I detect a note of doubt in there?" she probed.

"You sound like my kids."

"That's your fault. You have everyone asking questions now," Jane replied.

"Yeah." I nodded. "Did you ever consider doing what felt good to do and trust that everything else will take care of itself?"

"Not on your terms," she replied. "A great aunt of mine, twice removed, used to say, 'Where God guides, God provides.' Well...it's either that or bankruptcy."

"That sounds rather extreme," I countered.

"Perhaps...but did you ever consider that what you're doing is rather extreme?" she replied.

"It's not," I insisted. Even if it was, we'd already made the choice.

"Listen, I have an investment in you to protect," Jane said

straight-faced, then softened her expression. "I guess I'd like it to work out."

"So would I," I said.

* * *

Roby played patty-cake with his son. Since Raun's extended visual encounter with Robertito, our little friend increased his sustained eye contact. He looked at his father directly for ten seconds at a time. On three occasions, he stared into his face for almost half a minute. His co-operation had noticeably improved. Robertito even grabbed the ball spontaneously and threw it on the floor.

"Oh, you want to have a catch with Papa," Roby said, scrambling for the sponge sphere. "Okay, my son, you sit here. Sit here." He guided the little boy gently to a spot near the center of the room. Robertito squatted on the floor, then watched his father from the corner of his eye. Roby raised his arm. In response to the gesture, the little boy faced his father directly. The ball became airborne. Robertito's feeble attempt to catch the ball met with surprising success as it fell, literally, into his hands. Roby cheered and hugged his son. The child returned the ball awkwardly. Between each throw, Robertito grabbed for food, but his father held it above his reach.

"If you want food, say 'co,'" Roby told his son repeatedly.

Carol entered the room to observe. She had been at the Soto house from morning until night since that first day. She wanted to use every minute of her long weekend before classes reconvened on Monday. Her session observing Laura had infused her with impatience to begin herself, yet, somehow, she did not feel ready. As she watched Roby work with his son, she felt awed by his tenderness. Carol viewed him as strong, incredibly strong, but not in the predictable ways. Robertito suddenly noticed her. He walked in front of her and stood absolutely motionless as he side-glanced at her. Carol raised her hand very slowly and touched him. He remained inert. Carol caressed the side of his arm. Robertito crumbled to the floor immediately and slid his hands under her shoes. Roby nodded to Carol. Flattered by the little boy's approach, she rose and rocked back and forth on his hands. He stared at her shoes. Two minutes later, he pulled away and ran in a circle around the room. His father followed.

"I'm going to get you," Roby shouted. The little boy side-glanced, a smile enveloping his face. "I'm going to get you,"

215

his father shouted again. Robertito tried to move even faster. Finally, like a lover rather than a football player, Roby tackled his son and tickled him gently. Little boy laughter filled the room. Carol shook her head. In the short four days she had been watching, she catalogued changes in the child. Each step this little boy made weakened the foreboding words of her neurologist about autism and, equally as important, weakened his words about her. But he's the expert, she thought, suddenly distrusting her own thoughts, her own dreams.

When Roby introduced a puzzle, Robertito quickly withdrew all nine separate pieces. "Good, *papito*," Roby whispered, his grin overwhelming his face as he replaced the first piece. The boy watched. "You do it. Go ahead. Put the puzzle piece here. Here." He handed him the cow form. Robertito fumbled with it, flapped it, then put it on the puzzle board. "Find the place. Go ahead, find the place." Giving his son a hint with his finger, he coaxed the little boy into action. Within seconds, Robertito had replaced the form. To celebrate, Roby gave his son food. When he went back to the puzzle, Robertito remained focused on the cup. He stretched his lips in several peculiar directions. Then, a very strange unintelligible sound thumped from Robertito's throat as he stared at the food.

"Do you want food?" Roby asked. "Just say '*co*.'" No response. They worked with the other puzzle forms. Then, Robertito made the same peculiar circle shape with his lips. Another crude sound bellowed from his larynx. He repeated the grunt a third time. Finally, in a loud voice, Robertito Soto said "*co*."

"Oh my God," Carol gasped as Roby whipped out a spoonful of tuna and delivered it to his son. He kept feeding the little boy as he wiped the tears from his face. Carol thought of her father and his comment about the beauty of a man crying.

Robertito made the "*co*" sound again. His face seemed as placid and inscrutable as ever, even while he crossed over; from him to us, from the right side of his brain to his left, from being mute to the very first step in verbal communication.

Carol ran from the room to fetch Francisca. When the two women returned, Roby and his son had begun the long process of stringing beads. In an effort to have him murmur "*co*," Roby showed his son the tuna many times. The little boy babbled, whined and hummed, but he didn't repeat his accomplishment. After an additional two hours passed, Fran-

216

cisca squeezed Carol's arm and rose to her feet. At the moment the door touched its frame, a noise filled the room. Robertito said the word "*co*" again more clearly than ever before. Francisca screamed. She grabbed her bewildered son and hugged him ferociously. She screeched upon embracing her husband and Carol. Francisca knew her son had just moved through what she feared had been an impenetrable barrier.

*   *   *

The wind blew her hair to the side as she walked beside me. We strolled along the path next to the duck pond. Carol smiled, locked her face sternly, then smiled again. "After what happened yesterday, all my stuff seems unimportant."

"What do you mean?" I asked.

"Yesterday, we talked about my problem at home, living with my mother. Seems so trivial compared to an almost six-year-old boy saying his first word."

"But it's not. You mentioned this morning how everyone is so loving and so attentive to his every cue. I guess that's because they're reasonably clear when they're with him...and that's because they first work on becoming clear with themselves."

She held her hand up like a traffic cop, then touched her chest. "I guess it begins here. You said that the first day we talked about the Sotos." She paused and rubbed the bump on her nose. "Laura told me she was a wreck for the first couple of weeks. It's hard to believe when I watch her now." Her eyes shifted to the leaves above us. "They're so pretty." She laughed. "I'm looking for my subject. There's so many things to talk about."

"Just pick one," I suggested. A group of sea gulls hovered above us in their quest for food. One dove in front of me, hawked a strange cry and flew away.

After a short monologue revealing her intense feelings about Robertito, Carol talked more about wanting her mother to accept her as Suzi and I had. But as she explored, she realized her own intolerance.

"Remember when we talked about a nurturing environment for Robertito...well, this might sound silly, but maybe I could do that for my mother. I guess I've been pushy and who wants to open up to someone like that," Carol said. "I've always wanted her to take the first step, but maybe I could, maybe."

We sat down on a grassy slope together. Carol lay back and searched the tops of the trees with her blue eyes. She wanted to tell me about the connection she made between Robertito's autism and her epilepsy; but she censored herself. She winced, then flexed her jaw to divert her attention.

"How do you feel right now?" I asked, responding to the discomfort surfacing on her face.

"Not too good," she answered. "Remember I told you I have epilepsy."

"Yes," I replied.

"Well, I am anything but comfortable about it," she said.

"What about it disturbs you?" I asked.

"I've had the seizures since I was fourteen, but I wasn't diagnosed until later. I went through the whole scene with the neurologist, the EEG and all the other tests. They put me on Dilantin, which is supposed to control it...but it doesn't. When I told the doctor I didn't feel well with the drug, he told me to keep taking it. I ended up in the hospital because the amount the doctor had prescribed for me was an overdose. Even now with a lower dosage, I still get blurred vision sometimes or my balance goes off from the side effects. My speech gets slurred once in a while. I know I'm going on and on, but it's not simple to answer what specifically disturbs me. The seizures scare me and so does the medication."

"Why do the seizures scare you?"

"I feel out of control. I'm afraid I'm going to get hurt. I get this aura and then it starts."

"What starts?"

"The seizure. I feel these weird sensations: heat, a *déjà vu*-type feeling, a tingling all over my body. It begins in my stomach, right here, down low, and then it spreads out. When I passed out in school, I banged my head against one of the desks." She paused uncomfortably. "It's kind of like being a freak."

"What do you mean?"

"Once it begins, I can't do anything about it. I get so scared."

"Scared about what, Carol?"

"That I won't come through it."

"What do you mean?"

"I don't know." Her eyelids fluttered nervously. Despite the cool breeze in the park, a line of perspiration dotted her hairline. "I don't know why I said that. I don't think I'm going

218

to die. It's that terrible feeling that I can't do anything about them...out of control."

"Why is having a seizure being out of control?"

"Isn't it?"

"What do you think?" I asked.

"That's the wildest question. I've never thought about it before." She paused and exhaled forcefully. "I remember in a health ed. course, there was a whole discussion on the common cold, how the body and the nose runs as a way of expelling mucus and germs. Like somehow, a runny nose was a good sign, not a bad sign. The body was healing itself. You think that could be with my seizures?" She glanced at me and nodded. "I know. I'll answer it." She sat up and watched the sea gulls. The cadence of her speech slowed. "Maybe. That's the best I can do...a maybe. You know that's what always bothered me about taking anti-convulsant drugs. Why not find out the cause of the seizures and deal with that instead of just trying to sedate it? It makes more sense, but it's still scary."

"How?" I questioned.

"The doctors say I'll have to take the drug the rest of my life. Even with it, I still have seizures...just not as many. I guess what scares me is the feeling I get when I have one."

"What are the feelings you get which frighten you?"

"This warm feeling in my stomach, then all over my body."

"Okay," I acknowledged. "What is scary about a warm feeling?"

Carol stared at me dumbfounded. "I don't know. As I think of it, the feeling doesn't scare me—if I was in a warm bath, that would feel good—it's what it means!"

"And what's that?"

"I'm back to my earlier answer again. It means I'm out of control."

"Do you believe that?" I asked.

"Till today, yes, definitely, absolutely. Now...I'm not sure. I've never tried to control a seizure. I get so scared it never occurs to me there might be something I could do. One thing which is funny—the doctor asked me if I had a job with pressure. I said no, but when I worked in the bank, I was miserable." She smiled. "And I had more seizures during that time than ever before. Do you think there could be a connection?"

"What do you think? Carol, I'm not avoiding answering you, but your response to your question could be more productive for you than my response. What do you think? Do you see a connection? You'd know better than anybody else."

"Maybe. I'm pretty 'maybe' today. I never took it apart before. It was the black area that I wanted to avoid. It's hard to let go of the fear. I've lived with it over ten years."

"Well, what are you afraid would happen if you weren't afraid of the seizure?"

"It would get worse."

"Do you believe that?"

"Yes, yes...until I just said it." Her forehead furrowed. "The opposite is actually true. The more frightened I am, the more paralyzed I get. If I had relaxed that time in school, I would have sat down instead of waiting until I fell down. I never picked it apart before, Bears."

She placed her hands over her mouth and shook her head. "I can't believe what I'm saying." A sigh whistled through her throat. "I feel...less, less locked up about it."

"Do you still feel frightened about your seizures?"

"Not right now, but, well, what happens when I get one?"

"What do you mean?" I asked.

"Maybe I'll forget this entire dialogue and be scared all over again."

"Why would you do that?"

"I don't know. I wouldn't want to; really, I wouldn't!" she asserted.

"Then if you don't want to forget what you've come to understand, why do you believe you would?"

She patted the top of the grass with her palms. "I don't believe I would. I guess I just scared myself again."

"Why?"

She grinned sheepishly. "So I'd remember."

"Do you believe you have to scare yourself in order to remember?"

"No, no..." She threw her head back and gazed at the sky. "That's what I usually do. And it never works anyway. I'll remember and if, by chance, I don't..." She aborted her sentence.

"And if you don't, how will you feel?"

"Like a human being." Carol held her hands together in front of her chin and tipped her head. "A human being, not perfect, but trying."

Laura hung her leg over the arm of the couch as she leaned against Suzi's arm. Her patched dungarees formed to the

220

shape of her athletic legs. The embroidered shirt hung lazily over her upper torso. Carol squatted on the floor opposite my chair. Her eyes squinted repeatedly, then stopped abruptly. Roby's relaxed posture suggested a certain dignity as he waited for the meeting to begin. Francisca, seated on the floor beside her husband's chair, busied herself with her pad and pencil. Amalia, already a regular at our Wednesday night sessions, crossed her legs as she angled her alert body forward. A touch of nervousness fluttered at the corners of her lips.

Bending over her knees, Suzi removed her sandals and placed her feet discreetly on the coffee table. Her red, white and purple argyle socks attracted everyone's attention.

"I lov'em," Laura gushed, pinching Suzi's big toe.

Suzi withdrew her feet, curled them underneath her legs and did an "I-am-embarrassed-little-girl routine." A deep baritone cackle erupted from her throat when she put her feet back on the table and modeled the socks by twisting her ankles and toes.

"I like them. I like them," Francisca insisted supportively in Spanish. Amalia laughed as she translated her comments.

Suzi waved at me, obviously enjoying the attention from her sock fetish.

"Are we ready?" I asked. Amalia translated my question.

"*Sí*, Bears," Francisca snapped immediately, her intense eyes and waiting pencil poised for a fast beginning.

"I'm ready," Amalia volunteered, shifting her weight further forward to balance on the edge of the chair.

"Wait, wait . . . before we begin," Francisca chimed. By the time Amalia translated the short burst of words from Spanish to English, Francisca had already bolted out of the room. Moments later, she returned with a freshly heated organic banana cake and Haägen-Dazs ice cream.

"Hurray for Francisca," Laura shouted. Carol and Suzi applauded. Roby smiled broadly.

"What's the matter, Bears?" Francisca asked.

I shrugged my shoulders and laughed. "You turn every session into a minor eating orgy." She smiled mischievously. "Hey, just look at this," I said, pointing to my stomach.

"I love it, Bears," Suzi assured me.

"Me too," Laura said.

"Hey, Bears," Roby said softly, "maybe if you eat enough, you will one day look like Buddha." Everyone laughed at Roby's rare display of humor.

Francisca suddenly looked dejected. "I'm sorry," she whispered.

"No apologies necessary. You have not done me a disservice," I explained. "Only I can do that. When you notice me eating this wonderful food in two minutes, just remember I decided to eat it; you merely presented it to me."

Carol applauded quietly as she scrutinized her own figure.

"While we do our little ice cream orgy, let's begin with some general observations," I said, switching on the tape recorder. "I noticed Robertito was distant today. Everyone seemed surprised and a little off-centered with his increased 'isms' and diminished eye contact. I think we're spoiled. Perhaps, since he's moved so rapidly, we kind of expect to see it continue day after day. And if so, then we have implicit goals and a timetable irrelevant to our little friend."

"He turned the key and used the phone dial on the activity board on Monday," Laura said. "Yesterday...zero. But I know he can do it."

"We don't know that," I replied. "A doorway that was opened yesterday might be closed today. Sheer psychic exhaustion could sedate his whole system. For example, he said '*co*' many times for three straight days. Then...nothing. Maybe some of us were disappointed." I paused. "Rather than continuing to celebrate what he did and can do, we mourned, just a little, what he couldn't do." Francisca nodded her head in recognition of her own sentiments.

"Can we still keep trying even if he seems not to understand?" Carol asked.

"Sure," I answered. "But first we go with him, than we can introduce whatever we want in the moments between his 'isms' or activities. We can never know when he'll make a connection, be able to do something today that was impossible last week. It's not only what we do, but what we have in mind when we do it."

"When I worked with Robertito using the cloth book with pockets," Suzi interjected. "I watched him open the snap, the self-stick pocket and the zipper. The next day he acted like he'd never seen the book before. At first I kept saying, not out loud, but in my mind—'C'mon, Robertito. Do it! You did it yesterday. Do it again!' Then I heard myself. When I backed off, I saw a difference. He still couldn't do the pockets, but he made several attempts. Somehow, we have to always remember to let it come from him."

"Yeah," Laura echoed. Amalia tipped her head in agreement as she translated Suzi's words into Spanish.

"It's his motivation that we want to stimulate," Suzi added.

I scooped some ice cream into my mouth. Suzi stared right into my eyes and smirked. Laura, noting her glance, pushed her over on the couch and sat on her legs. Carol tickled Laura's foot, dethroning her from Suzi's body.

"C'mon," Francisca said, wanting to hear every word as soon as possible. During our first meetings, she interpreted laughter and jostling as an affront to the seriousness of the program and her son's situation. She had held back her own joy as a statement of caring. Only after working through her beliefs about the reverence of grief and loving could she allow her own smiles. She no longer thought she must withhold happiness until Robertito progressed, understanding she could, indeed, be happy now while on the journey. Nevertheless, her efficient, thirsty mind often clutched for rapid answers.

"Ready?" I asked. Suzi shook her head in defiance. "Excuse me," I said, catapulting myself over the coffee table. Amalia gasped as I grabbed Suzi, threw her over my shoulder and carried her into the empty dining room.

"Bears, I'll be quiet. Bears. Don't." Like a slowly starting machine, I began to twirl in a circle. I could hear Roby laughing. "Bears," Suzi called, "you always tell Raun not to touch other people's bodies against their will, that it's not his property. Well, this body isn't your property, so please put it down."

Although the momentum of my turning had increased appreciably, I stopped abruptly. "Good point," I said, matter-of-factly, and returned her to the couch. Suzi kissed me before I returned to my seat.

"To continue," I said, looking around at this wonderful family. Suddenly, I felt heat in my face. "I'm glad to be here." Laura touched my hand and Suzi's hand. Carol's face flushed. Roby hid his eyes with his hands. Francisca snuggled against her husband's leg and smiled warmly at Amalia. For several minutes, we sat together in silence.

"I want to thank all of you for letting me be a part of your big family," Carol said. Easy smiles greeted her comment.

During the next four hours of our meeting, all of Robertito's other behaviors were itemized and digested carefully. In addition to speaking one word, his greatest advancement appeared to be within the area of receptive language. He

223

could point at different people in the room on request with about 40 percent accuracy. He could pick a circle, square and triangle out of a pile of blocks, although he could not identify objects by color. Twice, responding to our suggestions, he withdrew the horse form and the cow form from the puzzle board. He appeared to know that *música* referred to the tape recorder.

"A very special thing happened only two hours ago," Suzi began. "While I danced with Robertito, I noticed his little fingers scratching at his groin. I hurried him into the bathroom like everyone has a hundred times before. I sat him on the toilet...again, like we've done before. But guess what that cute guy did this time—he urinated in the toilet."

"Far out," Laura shouted, banging the table, as everyone else applauded.

*   *   *

Suzi and I didn't enjoy having to say "no" to people who called for help, but there were no hours left in the day. Because of their month-long campaign, we agreed to see the Gardners. They arrived with their daughter, Joanna, at seven-thirty on a Saturday evening.

Joanna, at four years old, displayed all the autistic patterns. No eye contact. Refusal of physical interaction. Appeared deaf and blind at times. Mute. Twirled herself in circles and rolled her head endlessly like an accomplished yogi. Jack and Meryl Gardner watched their daughter sadly. This pretty, blue-eyed, blond-haired little girl, their first child, their only child, lived in a world they found confusing and frightening. They had attempted several programs, including recent sessions with a pediatric psychiatrist...all to no avail.

Within the first four hours of moving with her, accepting her and loving her, Suzi and I established fleeting eye contact. She even straightened her crossed eyes when she glanced directly at us. Her parents watched, amazed and aghast, at the first genuine, spontaneous responses they saw emanating from their daughter. Jack folded his arms in front of his chest, breaking his pose only to tuck his shirt more neatly into his pants. Meryl leaned against the kitchen cabinet stiffly. She lit one cigarette after another, brushing her ashes into the sink. When I suggested she join us on the floor with her daughter, she refused.

"Uh, you know, I'm, uh, not trained," Meryl said.

224

"Training doesn't matter," I said, trying to reassure her. "Look how she's starting to respond." I faced the little girl. "Joanna, we're talking about you because we care about you." Whether she could understand my words or not, I wanted to communicate, on whatever level possible, that we didn't hold her at a distance. I touched her arm, then smiled up at her mother. "Meryl, nobody can be as effective a teacher as you can for your own daughter."

"Go ahead," Jack said, displaying some discomfort.

"Do you think so?" she asked. Her husband signaled his affirmation with an emphatic frown. Mrs. Gardner took my place and rolled her head, imitating her daughter, as she sat on the floor beside her. Joanna flashed glances alternately at Suzi and her. "Oh, God, Jack, she's lookin' at me. Jack, did you see?"

Jack acknowledged his wife's comments, obviously pleased and confused by what we did with his daughter. Each time she uncrossed her eyes, he pointed at her, but remained silent.

Bryn and Thea took charge of Joanna for the remainder of the evening as Suzi and I spoke to the Gardners.

"Ya see, you people know what you're doing, I guess," Jack Gardner asserted. "But ya see, I'm not very educated. I never finished high school. All this stuff about autism is a bunch of mumbo-jumbo to me. The kid's sick, I mean...you can see that. But we don't know how to get help for her, you know. Mr. Kaufman..."

"Bears...and Suzi," I interrupted.

"Okay, Bears and Mrs. Kaufman, Suzi...um, we come to you 'cause we don't know what to do any more."

"We've been everywhere," Meryl said, her voice quivering. "Absolutely everywhere. My Joanna's not stupid, you know. She's very bright. They all treat her like she's retarded and all that, but nobody knows my Joanna. She knows where everything is in the house, absolutely everything. She walked before she was one. You can't be a dummy and walk before you're one, right?"

"Sometimes," I said, "autistic children learn to do many things, even talk, before they begin to behave differently."

"Yeah," Meryl responded, "that's what one of the doctors told us. But she's bright, isn't she? Do you think she can learn?"

"Meryl," Suzi said softly, "with anyone, whether it's a child or an adult, there's always a possibility, always a real chance."

"But what I mean, ya think she'll be normal?" Meryl asked directly.

"Jesus," Jack sighed, "they're just folks, Meryl, not fortunetellers."

"Maybe I can answer you like this," I replied. "When we worked with our son and with others, we took one day at a time. The past is gone and the future hasn't happened, so our only concern is the now. That helps us focus on what we can really do from this second to the next and to the next."

Jack smiled. "That's kind of how I get through my day at the grinding plant. One rod at a time and before the egg hatches, the day's over." He rubbed his hands together, wiping away the imaginary grime.

"How do you feel about your daughter?" Suzi asked.

They looked at each other for a second. "Me, I'm kinda okay with it," Meryl answered. "She's not like we expected and all, but I love her. Ya know, I'm a very nervous person, but, with me, my kid's okay, if you know what I mean. She's my baby. Jack, well, he's got problems about it." He massaged the area where the abdomen meets the rib cage.

"It kinda began when she was nine months old," Jack said in a thin voice, "about the time she was, uh, called, you know, sick. I got this knot in my stomach, right about here. The doctors gave me all those chalk things to drink and they took a bunch of pictures...uh, X-rays. Said it was nerves. Well, I'll tell you I got angry. I've never had a case of nerves in my life."

"Do you still have that knot now?" I asked.

He acknowledged the pain in his gut, a pain which had plagued him for the past three years. For the next four hours, we concentrated on Jack in a dialogue session. One of the stories he told us in connection with his pain was about the psychiatrist who, just last week, had counseled them about Joanna's bath. The little girl loved the water but she splashed it all over the walls and floor. Meryl viewed the behavior as uncontrollable. The physician labeling the child's antics as inappropriate, explained to them that they must demand that Joanna act in accordance with her age. The fact that this child dysfunctioned to the extent that the world made little or no sense to her seemed irrelevant. He instructed Jack to stand behind his daughter and wrap his arms around her thereby stopping her from playing and splashing in the tub. Since he believed the doctor knew infinitely more than himself, citing the man's education and degrees, he never questioned the directions.

The following evening, Jack held his daughter's arms when she splashed. Joanna began to scream louder and louder and louder. The knot in his stomach tightened. His daughter continued to resist, crying and choking at the same time. Jack felt like he couldn't breathe as a wave of nausea overcame him. He released the child and fled from the room. Why did he feel so uncomfortable? Because what he did felt wrong to him. He knew his daughter did not understand. Restraining her when she merely wanted to play seemed nonsensical and cruel.

After we had worked through some of his fears and discomforts, Jack gave us his first smile of the evening. He touched his stomach, astonished. "It's gone," he exclaimed. "For the first time in years, it's gone." He turned to his wife. "Hey, Mer, it's gone!" She smiled in a motherly fashion at her husband.

"Now that you feel more relaxed, more comfortable, I want you to consider something," I said. "If you were to design a program now, what would you do with your daughter?"

"But how can I, uh, what do I know?" he answered.

"Why don't you try asking yourself and see?" Suzi suggested.

He glanced at his wife, stuck his chest out and began. "First off, I wouldn't hold her in the tub any more. That's for sure. Ya know what I'd do," he said with a sudden burst of conviction. "I'd jump in with her and splash the walls and floors myself." He smiled and slugged his wife in the shoulder. "Ya hear, Mer, right in the tub with her."

For the next forty minutes, Jack Gardner, high school dropout, described in detail a program which in vision and specific techniques mirrored the one we had originally designed for our son. In those moments of comfort and self-confidence, he knew and understood more than any theory or text could teach him.

Chapter 15

As he positioned the lights in different sections of the room, Grattan watched Francisca work with Robertito. The situation had a distinctive make-believe quality. Was this the same child? The body and the face remained unchanged, but the little boy's current repertoire of behaviors differed dramatically from his prior preoccupation which consisted of flapping his hands and pacing across the room. The child's actions had purpose; he played with a puzzle, built a tower of blocks, strung beads, danced in definite rhythms and looked at people in the room. Doesn't make any sense, he thought to himself. For years, he had worked closely with clinics and treatment centers, taping and filming so-called developmentally impaired children in sequential order during therapy programs. Progress was barely visible over periods of months, sometimes years. They'd never believe it at the hospital. Too much. Too fast. He looked at the placid, perfectly formed face. He remembered the director of one program calling autistic children "the hopeless of the hopeless." Grattan did not want to be "done in" by tradition, he reminded himself. Nevertheless, he liked to digest the world in manageable clumps. What he observed this morning could not be catalogued among his previous reference points and he wasn't sure he wanted to throw away his old rule book.

The lights flooded the room with an eerie white glow. As I whispered some suggestions to Grattan, I noticed Robertito's startled response to the dramatic illumination of the room. He made a series of jerking motions with his head, then returned to the cymbals, which he banged together haphazardly. Grattan nestled the cumbersome camera by his head, adjusting the shoulder mount and strapping a leather support around his back. When I tapped him, he pulled the trigger, activating the video apparatus.

Within seconds, Robertito broke from his work with the musical instruments and stared at the ceiling, against which we had aimed the lights in order to achieve a more even light saturation in the room.

"Yes, Robertito," Francisca said. "Lights. See the lights and the wires."

Unlike the first taping session, during which Robertito did not show any awareness of the lights or the cameraman, he responded quite definitely to this intrusion, becoming slightly hyperactive and agitated. Francisca lured him back to the box of instruments. She played the harmonica while Robertito hit the drum limply. He divided his attention between her and the moving figure armed with a large mechanical box from which a strange glass eye projected. The rapidly increasing heat from the lights also seemed to disturb the little boy. He pulled on the collar of his shirt and threw his head from side to side.

I opened the windows and suggested peeling off some of Robertito's garments. Although the room cooled quickly, his behavior became more erratic. He turned over the puzzle board and raced around the perimeter of the room, cooing and twirling his fingers frantically. The lights! Maybe it's the lights. My finger found the switch on one of the lamps, extinguishing its electrical source. Within minutes, Robertito relaxed notably, yet he still exhibited a listlessness I had not seen since his arrival. Grattan tried to keep taping, but finally shrugged his shoulders, unable to manage the correct exposure without a balanced lighting system.

After a twenty-minute break, with Grattan and myself out of the room, our little friend still acted restless and uncooperative. He flapped more and side-glanced rather than confronting people and objects more directly. With Roby joining us, we convened a quick meeting downstairs. They left the decision to me. I decided to try again.

This time, we introduced each piece of equipment to Robertito, encouraging him to touch the lights and the camera. He put his tongue on the lens and smiled. We showed him the switch, the battery pack and the extra reels of tape. Roby installed a portable fan in the window to extract the heat from the room. I asked Grattan to maintain a more unobtrusive posture, reasoning that the accumulation of sensory bombardment had overloaded Robertito, who, obviously, allowed more of the external environment to penetrate.

With the lights on again and the camera rolling, Robertito behaved with only a minimal of concentration. The tape would not be representative of his current status, yet, even with his surprising reaction to the filming, he still demonstrated an awareness and skill which dramatically transcended the scope of his responses and abilities less than two months ago. The tape captured the porcelain-like face and dark sparkling eyes. It recorded his "isms" as well as his understanding and skill with the insertion toys. Suddenly, he threw a cube and triangle against the wall. He banged his foot against the floor. His eyebrows furrowed, locking his face in a grimace. Robertito Soto appeared angry. I halted the taping immediately and rescheduled it for the following week. The bombardment of activity, lights and heat had illicited a reaction we had not witnessed before...at least, not here in New York.

As the day dwindled into evening, Robertito began to increase his self-spinning, rocking and flapping. He no longer displayed an ability to build even the smallest tower. For one hour, he rolled on the floor and laughed hysterically. I found myself chuckling too, charmed by the spell of his joy. Twenty minutes later, he whined and pushed people away. Then, with no apparent provocation, Robertito cried. Love, attention, even food, did not break his commitment to howling and grumbling. When he finished, toward late evening, he remained somber, his eyes glazed...almost the portrait of a junkie after his fix.

The aloof, withdrawn, blank-faced stare persisted the next day. He babbled to himself, smiled fleetingly at the wall and groaned without any visible focus. He did not permit any physical contact. I watched him from morning until night. A hundred, even a thousand, lights would never have disturbed him before. Now, as he began to turn more toward us,
230

three floodlights had overdosed his fragile sensory apparatus. Rather than drown, he pulled back to his own lines of defense. Why not? Wouldn't I have done the same? Yet as I gazed at him, I couldn't help but consider how unimportant the tapes had been. Even in those first moments, I saw the overload, yet I persisted, wanting the video record for later comparison. Was it worth the trade?

"Wow," Laura whispered to me as she left her session with Robertito. Suzi's three hours consisted of little more than flapping, running and jumping. No eye contact. No physical affection. No interaction. In fact, he put more into his "isms" than before, as if he had to try harder to keep the external world out. When Suzi seemed exhausted, I worked with my little friend.

The second and third day after the taping mirrored the first, but now Robertito developed a distinctive Dracula-like style of curling his fingers rigidly in front of his eyes. When a book or puzzle was introduced, despite our attempt to be low-keyed, he whined and moved away.

The week crept by without any visible changes. Francisca and Roby reported some fleeting chest-banging and chin-hitting; old "isms," remnants of an unhappier time in Mexico. Robertito moved his arms and legs mechanically. Awesome. An enigma.

Francisca began her session enthusiastically. She turned on the tape and began to dance. He swayed slightly, but continued twirling his fingers. His mother moved closer and joined him. She took one of his hands and he permitted it. I held my breath. The first real sign of contact in ten days.

The little boy pulled away from his mother, dropped on the floor and made a crying sound with a crunched face...but no tears. "Eee-o, eee-o," he whimpered. Francisca imitated him. He stopped immediately and cried again, louder this time, but still no tears. His eyes swelled with red rims. She tried to touch him, but he pushed her away.

"Okay, okay," she said soothingly.

He fell over into her lap and continued crying. His chest heaved spastically. His shoulders jerked each time he inhaled. Tears streamed down Francisca's face as she stroked his back. They stayed together in that position for almost five minutes; then Robertito crawled to a corner of the room. He stopped crying abruptly, hummed and rocked. When Francisca sat beside him, he moved away. "It's me, it's Mama." He cried again, then paused sharply and grinned at the wall.

She tried to touch him, to comfort him, but he kept moving, listless, agitated and unpredictable.

Robertito cried as a way of taking care of himself. Sometimes, he utilized it as a method to communicate on a primitive level. Other times, he used it as a barrier or a way to soothe himself, no different from the "isms" which he now shared with all of us.

I spent time alone with my little friend, at the end of the day. We tapped the wall together and babbled a thousand times. I kept looking for a key, a hook, but nothing came. Why? Stay in there, I counseled myself, stay in there and trust it. I found myself laughing in the midst of our parallel game. Trust what? Me? Option? You? I wanted to grab him and shake him and shout: "Hey, I love you. We all love you. C'mon, you can do it. You can!"

"Robertito," I said aloud, "I blew it with the lights. I'm sorry. I do the best I can, just like you. You don't have to go that far away to take care of yourself. Trust us. We've trusted you." The little boy never looked at me or acknowledged my talking. He picked up a drumstick and flapped it beside his head. I rummaged through the toys, found the other stick and followed his lead. "What can we do for you? No more video? Okay, no more video. No more games? Okay, no more games. You want to be alone?" I sensed his awareness of me in his peripheral vision. "You were having too much fun before...too many smiles and giggles. Show me! Give me one hint!" His blank face stared at a point a foot below the ceiling. I traced his path with my eyes and saw only the yellow walls. "*Que tu mira?*" I asked in Spanish. "What do you see, Robertito...I want to see too." My words went unheard...but I wanted to stay with it, with him, as we then traveled around the room together, making hundreds of circles. Perhaps a circle would open, just a little.

* * *

The painted horses of the carousel glided up and down like surrealistic phantoms. Their eyes glittered. Whimsical caricatures carved in wood. Red saddles mismatched colorfully with yellow bridles. Green manes topped blue bodies. A little girl laughed and waved to her mother at each passing. Two six-year-old cowboys escaped from a tribe of imaginary Indians. A young man sat expressionless on his mount as he stared at the ceiling. The carousel had revolved on its axis

232

for thirty-five years. An old mechanical No. 150 Band-Organ belted out honky-tonk melodies, a miniature steam engine for its heart. Waltzes. Polkas. Viennese marching tunes from the mid-thirties. The ticket collector, an old man in a solid green uniform, smiled. We watched the horses travel their endless circles... triggering my flashes of Robertito's endless circles.

Bryn, Thea and Raun, firmly atop their mounts, held hands and watched the world whiz by. Suzi and I sat behind them, not as their parents, but as two more children immersed in the innocence of a child's world. Sundays. We had suspended our traditional Sunday family day for almost two months until the Soto program had developed its own momentum. Today, we reinstated it. We had wandered through the galleries in Soho and roller-skated along the avenues in Central Park which had been closed to vehicular traffic. The carousel mesmerized us. We could never leave the park without our ritualistic ride on our wooden friends.

As we strolled leisurely toward Fifty-ninth Street, Raun noticed the tops of the swings visible over the next crest.

"Oh, Daddy, Bears, please, oh, please, could we just stop at the playground?" Raun asked, wide-eyed and hopeful.

"Could we?" Thea said, reinforcing her brother's request.

"Sure," I said, holding Suzi's hand. "How could I deny such a beautifully stated request?"

Within seconds, all three of them burst into a full run.

"Be careful," Suzi shouted, her words melting into the city sounds of Central Park. "They're such great people," she said.

"I missed them," I added. "We've been so jammed. I missed the small talk, the bike rides, our races in the park."

"You said you had some thoughts about Robertito," Suzi said.

"Nope," I replied. "Not today. I consider it therapeutic to leave the program in body and spirit for at least one day."

We entered the playground through one of the open gates. Our children climbed on the wooden towers above the sandpits. Suzi and I sat on a bench close to where Raun did his own brand of five-year-old gymnastics.

"We have to decide about *Son-Rise* soon," I said. "They called me again yesterday and finally agreed to almost all our terms. And yet, I feel hesitant. How about you?"

She laughed. "Declining TV movie offers has become a ritual for us. An 'ism.'" We both laughed. "Sell us your book, then please disappear. But, Bears, this feels different. They

233

want our participation. I don't know if we can get any more guarantees than they've offered."

"Suz, this is not a novel. It will be Raun's life on television...maybe in front of 40 million people in one night. The producer, the director and the sponsor walk away after that night. They go onto the next project. But Raun and all the other autistic children, and that includes Robertito, can't walk away."

"But doesn't our writing the screenplay and consulting during the filming ensure accuracy?" Suzi asked.

"Only to a point."

"If you want to pass on it, I'm with you," she said.

I stood up and looked at my daughters. "I keep thinking about how many people we can reach...it's just that I don't want the story butchered or compromised." I grinned. "I think you were right; we've held back so long it becomes hard to let go. That's my lesson this year...letting go."

"I'm for taking the plunge," Suzi concluded.

"So am I," I concurred. "The first step is giving them the 'option,' which would definitely help us keep afloat next month. And that means at least another guaranteed month with the Sotos." I inhaled deeply. "Come here, midget," I said, gently pulling her to her feet. When I lifted her off the ground and hugged her, she giggled and bit my cheek.

As we lingered together, Raun whizzed by, flapping his fingers in a manner I hadn't seen for over three years. I snapped my head around in disbelief. Impossible! As he came around the far side of the tower, his hand motions were unmistakably autistic.

"Suz," I said. She faced the playground and gaped at her son. Her eyes bulged and her mouth dropped open. Suddenly I noticed another youngster moving in the same pattern as Raun. He, too, had the same peculiar repetitious hand movements. Our son turned away from the other child, waved to us playfully and then continued.

"Oh, wow," Suzi blurted, almost distrusting her eyes.

"Look. Just like Robertito," Raun shouted. "We're doing autistic talk."

"Great, Raunchy," I called. "You stay with him as long as you want."

We walked slowly to the fence, our mouths ajar, gawking at the scene before us. My eyes spotted another autistic child leaning against a wire fence. He flapped his jacket against his chest and rocked his head up and down. A little girl ran in a circle next to him. An older youngster marched in front of us, turned and marched back again. He never broke his pattern or deviated from his hypnotic endeavor.

It couldn't be! It had to be a dream or a joke or maybe both. In a city filled with 8 million people, how could we have taken our Sunday break right in the middle of a group of autistic children?

"It almost doesn't even feel real...but it is," Suzi whispered.

A tall, thin girl started to scream and run out of the fenced area. As she loped across the field like a wounded duck, she banged her shoulders repetitiously. One young man, engrossed in a Frisbee game with two other adults, put his hand up. "I'll get her." He ran after the girl, collared her by the back of her neck and guided her return to a designated area. "Jennifer, you have to stay with the others. You hear!" The girl did not respond. He seated her on a bench next to an older boy whose facial expressions and body movements suggested retardation. "Watch her, Timmy," the young man commanded as he returned to his game.

I counted eight autistic children. The boy that Raun followed began to skip. Our son mimicked him. Another youngster stared at Raun's feet and smiled. "Look at your wonderfully crazy son," I said.

Suzi grinned. "It would be nice if each of these kids had a Raun to play with."

"Uh-huh." Then I thought of Robertito. So many people loved him. I felt a sense of peace knowing he would never be pulled by the neck. I turned to Suzi. "Somehow, in the last two days I've been pulling at Robertito, though it was only in my mind. I never wanted to do that again, not even in my thoughts."

Suzi grabbed my arm. "Don't even start thinking you have to be perfect."

"I'll settle for being reasonably happy."

Bryn took my arm and Thea jumped on my back.

"Give me a ride, Daddy." Suddenly, she stared at the group of children in front of us. Slowly, she slid off my back and walked silently up to the fence.

"Bears!" Bryn said. "Are they..." She never finished her sentence, noticing Raun imitating one of the autistic children.

"Why isn't anybody with them?" Thea asked.

"Those people, playing with the Frisbee...they're with the children," Suzi explained.

"Can't we do anything?" Bryn asked.

"We are," I said. "We're working with Robertito. The only real way to help is by the demonstration of your own life."

Thea tugged on my coat. "What's demonstration mean?"

"It's kind of like sharing with others through your own actions, in your own life."

Thea nodded her head, then watched the slender autistic girl whining on the bench. She ran on the other side of the fence and began to stroke the girl's arm. The youngster bolted from her seat, accidently knocking Thea to the ground. A look of amazement appeared on Thea's face. Her lips quivered and puckered as she began to cry. I picked her off the pavement and held her tightly.

"I...I just," Thea stuttered, "wanted to, to be her friend. I didn't...mean, mean to...scare her. I didn't."

"I know you didn't, Thee-Thee. Maybe she hasn't had very good experiences with people," I offered, "and so she wanted to be left alone."

"It's okay, Thea," Bryn said, taking her sister's hand in a motherly fashion.

"Raun, it's time," Suzi called.

"Five more minutes," he shouted back.

"Now," I answered. He flashed me a silly grin, said goodby to his friend and scooted to our side.

As we began to walk toward the path, a chubby, ten-year-old autistic boy ran along the fence beside us. He stayed within the designated area as he repetitiously sang one stanza from an old popular tune. His hands moved like a conductor's before an imaginary orchestra. When he passed us a second and third time, the words became clearer and clearer. The child kept singing one refrain.

"I can make all your dreams come true. I can make all your dreams come true. I can make all your dreams come true."

*   *   *

Two weeks crawled by. Robertito continued to find solace inside of himself. Refusing to participate, he paced and "ismed" all day, each day. Although we paralleled his motions and stayed with him, we could not break the veneer. The irritability and shrieking, which erupted immediately after the video session, persisted.

However, when Laura arrived to take the session after

236

Roby, she noted, with surprise, Robertito's peaceful expression. No crying. No whining. No listlessness. "Now don't get too excited, Rha-Rha. You never know. Just let it happen." Since the night she pulled Robertito from the bath, her ease and caring for the child had flowered. The softness which blossomed in this workroom began to extend into every area of her life.

"Here we go, Robertito," she said, presenting a puzzle board to her student. At that instant, he climbed sluggishly to his feet and stared at a point on the wall near the ceiling. "Still out to lunch, huh?" she whispered. She stood up beside him. "You see something there? Huh? Tell Rha-Rha." Robertito ran to the window, looked outside, then turned and jumped. Laura imitated him for over five minutes. "I know what you're doing, my love. You don't want me to have to go to the gym. That's it, isn't it?"

The little boy flopped to the floor. He retrieved a puzzle piece without any direction or encouragement. Very softly, Laura clapped, maintaining the more sedate posture we had all assumed during the last two weeks. She stroked his arm and he did not pull away. As she moved her fingers along his skin, she realized the implication of his acceptance. He had not allowed affection in weeks. "Oh, shit," she shouted, trying to contain her excitement. "You're ready . . . so am I. Let's see now. Give me the pig. Oink. Oink. The pig. Give me the pig."

Very slowly, his hand glided over the board, back and forth four times. Finally he lowered his fingers, grabbed the pig form and dropped it on the rug. "Oh, that's wonderful. I mean, Robertito, you did it." Though he had previously, weeks ago, been able to locate the horse and cow form, never had he been able to identify the pig form on request. He retrieved the chicken, the duck, and the dog forms. "You're a genius," she hooted.

"Now let's see," she mumbled aloud, extracting the tool bench from its carton. "We'll try something new. Right, Robertito. We can at least try." She demonstrated the use of the hammer. He banged the plastic nails easily through their respective holes. She illustrated the use of the oversized screwdriver. He had extreme difficulty controlling the tool, but made several strong attempts to use it properly.

Suzi arrived next. She found Robertito's return awesome. She thought about the children in the park as she massaged his hands. Together, they played the marimba, the chimes, the drums, the xylophone and the battery-operated toy piano.

Occasionally, he "ismed" or paced across the room, but, most of the time, he worked with the insertion box, the beads and the tool bench. Suzi brought him into the bathroom, where they played in the sink with soap, small boats and bubbles.

Since he had asked for "*co*" four times during her session, she decided to try to teach him other sounds. She held a three-dimensional replica of a cow in her hand and said "moo." She repeated the demonstration with the cow puzzle piece and the cow picture in the book.

"Hey, sweet boy. Mooo," she droned, bouncing the plastic animal along the rug as if it walked. "Moo. Moo."

Robertito grabbed for the form, stared at it directly, then flapped it. Two seconds later he put the piece in his mouth. He grimaced.

"Not to eat, silly boy. It's a cow. Moo."

Robertito squinted his eyes peculiarly. The muscles in his face contorted as he belched out his first "oo" sound.

Suzi cheered and hollered. By the end of the hour, he had added, in rough form, the "m" sound in front of the "oo" sound, making a noise distinctly like a cow. Two hours later, she had him approximate a dog's bark. "Robertito, I can't believe you. Full of surprises, aren't you, sweet fellow." She kissed him enthusiastically, a gesture from which he withdrew. "Sorry for the assault, I just get carried away." He rocked gently and side-glanced at her. Suzi thought of how lucky she was to be sharing these special moments and feelings with Robertito as she had with Raun in the bathroom.

Carol began her first solo session with Robertito on this very special day. I had to force myself to concentrate on her, for this little boy's return triggered an avalanche of thoughts. Because we had let him leave, he felt free to return. That incredible awesome calm had returned. Because we had loved him without conditions, he found comfort in our extended hand. I knew he didn't have to make that choice. He could have remained in the secure womb of his inner universe. I wanted to thank him, to shout hurrah. Robertito had become more than Francisca's and Roby's son, he had become everyone's child . . . mine, Suzi's, Laura's and now Carol's. I felt this incredible pulling, almost craving, to leave my position at the side of the room and hug and squeeze my little friend.

Refocusing my attention, I watched Carol dance lovingly with him. I detected a certain nervousness in Carol's actions. Though she followed his "isms" and worked smoothly with various toys, at times, her manner of speaking dulled, becoming monotone. Carol held back. Her mimicking did not match Robertito's intensity. Her applause and facial expression needed more animation. Perhaps my presence diverted her...perhaps she still had to integrate her evolving awareness with her body language.

In each instance, when Robertito changed direction or refused her initiative, she followed his cue. The beauty and softness of her accepting attitude was evident throughout the session. Yet, I suspected, her willingness to suspend all judgments with Robertito had not been equally extended to herself. But Carol felt right in this room and, like all of us, she struggled to find the Spanish words to express herself. Although Robertito did not respond to her as much as to Francisca or Suzi, he glanced at Carol with surprising regularity and smiled easily three or four times during the session.

Before he went to sleep, I tried to teach him how to assemble the facial features of the potato-head toy; first the eyebrows, then the nose, the lips, the ears, the eyes and, finally, the hat. I tried six different times. On the seventh attempt, he put the nose and hat in place by himself. I cheered and tickled him. He giggled, then rolled into my lap. His little hand stroked my leg.

Seconds later, he sat upright. I held the potato-head and pointed at the nose.

"Here we go, Robertito. What's this?"

He peered at the goofy brown form curiously, then said "moo."

Chapter 16

The pressure of the plane speeding down the runway riveted Roby to the back of his seat. The stress in his stomach increased as the huge, mechanical bird lifted off the pavement. His eyes snapped frozen pictures of a late afternoon sun descending behind the towering skyline of New York City. The people on the ground were no longer visible. Cars and trucks had the appearance of match-book miniatures. As he thought about his wife and child, his conviction about returning alone to Mexico weakened.

His business had declined to such an extent that its very existence was threatened. His cousin, lacking Roby's expertise, sent out a loud cry for help. Roby would have let it all go for the sake of his son, sacrificing the little shoe store he had spent most of his adult life building. But he knew they needed more time in New York, even more than their original commitment of three to four months. Their savings had almost been exhausted. He needed the support of his business in order to sustain a further stay in New York. Roby wanted that time desperately...for Robertito, for Francisca and, if possible, for himself.

The evolution of his son dazzled him. Although Robertito had only begun to learn the most primitive responses and functioned at a fraction of his chronological age, the pattern of growth defied the fruitless and often brutal alternatives they had encountered during those years of searching. But he wanted more time for another reason which he had difficulty admitting to himself. Francisca and he, too, had found something special for themselves during the past two and a half months. His wife smiled and laughed and displayed a confidence he had never witnessed before. The years of tears had ended.

The concept of family haunted him. He could not love his wife or son any more than he did, but he had found, within the context of his new family in New York, a more profound and fulfilling way to express his love and caring. Roby smiled as he remembered the few jokes he had told over the past weeks. He had never played the comic, leaving that role to others more gregarious than himself. His father had called laughter a frivolous whorehouse diversion. Even the smile had been banished from his early childhood. But here, in New York, the old taboos no longer appeared valid. Laughter and smiling had become part of the loving. Everything had developed so naturally, so easily, that the process of exploring and discarding his fears and doubts almost receded into a secondary position, although he knew that very process had given him the key to open so many locked doors. He wanted more, much more! And Robertito needed more, Roby thought, supporting his desire to extend their stay. Francisca had begun to find the first glimmer of joy and comfort since the diagnosis of their son. He did not trust her euphoria. She could slip back. She could! He had to bolster his business. If it meant standing in the street like a circus barker, he would.

The nose of the plane dipped as it reached its proper cruising altitude. Roby reassured himself he had made the right decision despite this separation from his family. He calculated each possible step, hoping to return in less than a month. The flight attendant fractured the internal conversation. She offered him a beverage, which he declined. He stared at the blanket of clouds beneath him. He imagined endless white pillows and quilts covering the earth. "Co...Co..." His son's little voice danced in his ears. "Moo..." Roby hummed to himself. "Moo..." Against the teal-blue sky above a golden horizon, he watched a faint image of Robertito's lips pucker and curl as the child blurted the sound of a cow.

"I will take care of everything," Francisca had assured him bravely at the airport. Not one tear escaped from her eyes. She had locked everything in, refusing to let her husband know how sad she felt about his departure. They had never been separated before. Earlier that morning, alone in the kitchen, she cried more for Roby than herself. But she promised to leave him with a smile, the very one she practiced when she fixed her hair and make-up in the airport bathroom. "I love you, Roby," she shouted as he passed through the gate. "I love you, Mommy," he called for the last time as he turned the corner and joined the river of people moving down the ramp. He fought the vertigo which threatened to envelop him. But now, thirty-thousand feet above the ground, he stabilized that uncomfortable floating feeling. He trusted his new family in New York even more, perhaps, than himself. He smiled. "Bears," he whispered, "I'm learning. One day I will trust me more than you. One day." Within seconds, Roberto Soto drifted into a deep sleep.

Suddenly, he found himself transported to the town of his birth. Small, white buildings clustered around one central street. An open market and a hardware store with two gas pumps provided the village with its most notable landmarks. The remainder of the small town stretched to the west toward the desert. Roby felt peculiar driving his old Thunderbird through these streets. The donkeys, cows and goats, which had once accompanied the residents across the dirt and gravel roads, had disappeared. Black macadam covered the three-block distance from the store to the wind-swept square in front of the church. Old buses, dusty trucks and vintage American cars lined the three-inch clay curbs. Everything appeared incredibly familiar and unfamiliar at the same time. The left turn into his street startled him. The old sheds were gone. The stone walls of his house had been painted brown. Anemic shrubs softened the presence of the building against an arid landscape. In the distance, he saw Francisca carrying a basket through the front door. And then he knew. This was no longer the house of his parents, but his own home. Roby felt disoriented as he left the car and walked along the neatly set cobblestones to the front door. He drew a set of keys from his pocket mechanically. To his amazement, he selected the correct one and opened the door as if he had done it a thousand times. He stepped forward hesitantly and almost tripped over the basket, the same one his wife had carried into the house. Annoyed, he searched for Francisca.

"Francisca," he said in a loud voice when he entered the kitchen and noticed her motionless figure by the rear window. Her shoulders looked broader than he had recalled. Her arms and hands were bruised and calloused from excessive physical work. Dusty strands of hair lay lifelessly on her shoulders. "Francisca!" he called a second time, betraying his growing impatience. She did not respond. She stood there like the statue he had seen in the museum. "Aren't you going to greet me?"

His wife turned around slowly; her body pivoted on her toes like a ballet dancer. She cocked her head and side-glanced at him peculiarly. Her glazed eyes did not blink, though she smiled momentarily. Her nostrils flared while her lips moved spastically. Finally, in a deep, choked voice, she bellowed: "*Co.*" Her body became rigid. She twisted her face, breaking her own inertia. Then Francisca twirled around in circles and flapped her hands beside her head.

Roby hunched over and held his chest as he stared at his wife. He could not distinguish her actions from those of his son. "Francisca, for God's sake, please," he begged. But the woman did not seem to hear him as she repeated the mono-syllabic word "*co*" many times. And then he knew, irrevocably, without any doubts. She, too, had become autistic like his son. How could he have been annoyed with her? How could he ever have considered scolding her? He noticed a puzzle board on the table. He picked out the duck form and held it up. Francisca peered at it from the corner of her eyes. "Quack. Quack, quack," she shouted. Roby looked up stunned. He couldn't breathe any more.

The hum of the engines buzzed in his ears as he opened his eyes. A chill rippled down his spine. The sweat lay caked on his face. A dream! Only a dream! He bent his head and peered out the window, trying to eradicate those disturbing images of his wife. He pulled the flight magazine from the seat back in front of him and tried to lose himself in the articles and advertisements. Seconds later he turned to the window again. Portions of the dream repeated themselves. Perhaps, he reasoned, he had not been so good in his past. Perhaps he had not been as supportive as necessary. Perhaps he should not have left Francisca in New York. Roby tried to stop accusing himself. He closed his eyes and forced his mind to go blank.

"Hello," a little voice chimed.

Roby opened his eyes and stared at the blue-eyed little

243

girl standing in the seat directly in front of him. She flapped her fingers at the side of her head, waving to him. He smiled and returned the gesture. In his peripheral vision, he observed the motion of his own hand. He recalled the rhythmic flapping gestures of a flamenco dancer in Mexico City. He saw Francisca in the dream. Everywhere he looked, he saw signs of Robertito.

"Hello," the youngster said again, her face radiating with a warm smile.

"Hello," Roby answered in heavily accented English. The child grabbed his hand playfully. He tapped her palms and clapped, as he had done hundreds of times with his own son.

She followed his lead instinctively and sang: "Patty-cake, patty-cake, baker's man, make me a cake as fast as you can."

Less than a week after Roby left, I found myself on a plane headed west. I had been asked to attend a two-day series of meetings in Los Angeles to discuss the possible writing of a treatment for the proposed "Son-Rise" television special. The producers had not exercised any further commitment beyond the initial option. All projects pending. Even the Soto program hung in the balance. Suzi and I had anticipated Francisca and Roby's asking for more time—another three months, another six months, or perhaps, a year. We had decided to try to give them whatever they asked for. And yet, how could we possibly make it through a year or even two more months without additional funds? The involvement with Robertito consumed a mammoth amount of our time, sprinkled over six, sometimes seven, days a week. What would be right for Francisca and Roby had to be right for us as well. It had to be!

The California conference with the producers had a certain tone, respectful, yet patronizing. Everyone had an opinion. They subdued their own conflicts and fenced politely in my presence. Their response to my specific ideas for the film as well as individual scenes was enthusiastic.

When I returned to my hotel on the second night, I found a telegram slipped under my door. As I ripped open the envelope, I noted the name and address of the sender. Jane had written the wire. Good ol' Jane. The master hand-holder. She had probably wanted to give me additional support, having warned me against the tinsel madness of Hollywood and false gaiety.

I walked onto the balcony and flopped into a chair. The lights of the city glittered before me, obscuring the shroud of brown smog which had encased the buildings and landscape since my arrival. I pulled the telegram from its enclosure. A pep talk. Yes, I would welcome that. But instead, the telegram contained a very different message.

"SIT DOWN! STOP HAVE SECURED THREE OFFERS FOR BOOK ON ROBERTITO PROJECT STOP ONE OFFER VERY SPECIAL STOP THEY VALUE JOURNEY AS YOU DO STOP ADVANCE WILL FINANCE YOU WHILE YOU WORK STOP YOU ARE MAKING A BELIEVER OUT OF ME. SIGNED: RED ROSES."

* * *

Breakfast had been awkward for her. Suzi delighted in the cards and handmade gifts from our children in celebration of Mother's Day, but my empty seat unsettled her. Although I had been scheduled to return the following day, she wanted a closeness she could touch and she wanted that closeness now.

A visit from my father and his wife, Roz, gave her a more enriched sense of family. Abe, tall, thin, sporting a dapper mustache, kissed Suzi and greeted the children with his usual understatement, yet his eyes radiated an abiding warmth.

Raun jumped into his grandfather's arms and turned his face by pushing on the man's nose. "Grandpa, how come you have a big nose like Daddy?"

My father laughed. "I don't have a big nose like your daddy; he has a big nose like me ... because he's my son. And you are his son. So one day you will probably have a nose just like us."

"Oh no, no I won't. I like my nose the way it is. You guys have the biggest noses I've ever seen. Honest!" he said.

"Raunchy," Suzi interjected. "I think Grandpa and Daddy have wonderful noses."

"Well, I'm not saying they're bad or anything," Raun insisted. "I just don't want one."

Thea hugged Roz and laughed at her brother's commentary. "Raunch, you'll have to concentrate on keeping your nose small."

"Since I'm neutral," Roz said, patting her own small nose, "I'd say a nose gives character. A strong nose for a strong face."

"Here, here," Abe said happily, until Bryn jumped into his arms without warning. He groaned.

"Oh, Grandpa," she said, disappointed.

Suzi laughed. "Brynny, maybe you haven't noticed, but you've grown in the last few years. You're almost as tall as me."

"That's only because you're a shrimp, Mommy," Bryn commented matter-of-factly.

"Oh yeah," Suzi said, eying her daughter. Bryn, sensing an impending assault, ran into the living room. Suzi trapped her on the couch and tickled her into a minor fit of hysterics.

"Okay, okay. You're not a shrimp," she pleaded. "You're not."

Later that afternoon, Suzi took Abe and Roz to meet Francisca. Despite the fact that this was Mother's Day, Suzi had a work session scheduled.

Suzi entered the workroom quietly. She guided Abe and Roz to positions along the wall. "Oh, look, Robertito," Francisca said, in Spanish. "We have guests. Do you want to say hello?" Robertito stood on the top of a low bureau, a favorite place he had learned to mount. He side-glanced at the new arrivals, then he faced Roz directly.

"Come," Suzi said softly, walking up to her student, "¡Hola!, Robertito." She caressed him and kissed him. He accepted her affection, but his smiling eyes were drawn to Roz. "Go ahead," Suzi encouraged her visitors. "You can say hello to him."

Abe found the child's face hypnotic. Something about his dark, penetrating eyes reminded him of Raun. He approached slowly. "¡Hola!, Robertito," he said, affectionately, taking the little boy's hand.

When Roz approached, Robertito put his head against her chest and stroked her with his soft fingers. He smiled. Suzi and Francisca gasped. He had never been affectionate to strangers before. Roz rubbed his back while he leaned against her. After several minutes, he stood upright and flapped his hands vigorously. Suzi mimicked him, as did Francisca. Abe and Roz watched, bewildered and slightly uncomfortable with the pantomime. Robertito bent forward toward Roz and twirled his fingers in front of his face and hers. She watched the others, then, she, too, imitated him. In abandoning familiar rules, Abe and Roz entered into a world which, in these moments, no longer appeared strange.

It seemed impossible, but during my four-day absence, Robertito had matured noticeably: happier, more receptive, longer periods of concentration, less "isms," more vocalizing. During the next few weeks, his attempts to duplicate sounds increased dramatically. He began to imitate songs in a mumbled fashion. We taught him the vowels. We would say words and letters and put his hand on our throats so he could feel the vibrations. Many times, he mimicked our lip and mouth formations, but could not drive the air through his larynx to make the sound. But after days of practice and abortive attempts, he slowly gained control over the apparatus he had not used in a purposeful manner for the majority of his life.

Robertito learned how to make the simple sounds of most of the animals. Though he learned very slowly the words "*ju*" for *jugo* (juice) and "*sí*" for yes, he said "*agua*" immediately instead of the shortened form for water. His Gargantuan leap in receptive language during the period astounded us. He understood where is, more, pull, push, close, hit, touch, kiss, hug, jump, sit, turn, put, lie down, look, look at it, look at me, come, run, walk, bathroom, music, dance, stand up, give me, circle, triangle, square, dog, cat, duck, chicken, cow, horse, bird, book. With apparent difficulty, he learned the meaning of red, blue, yellow, green, black and white. Often, upon entering his workroom, he indicated by touch or body position a preference for a game or activity. The use of books allowed us to expand his visual and language-recognition skills. The "isms" persisted, but our interaction now competed seriously for his time and concentration.

Variation in moods became more apparent. In seconds, he could switch from laughing to crying. In general, he exuded an incredible sense of calm and inner well-being. His fixation on food had also escalated, although the focus of our support came from our overarticulated enthusiasm, love and affection. Though the rate of his development soared, he still spent the majority of his time within himself. We had managed, by using all those fleeting moments of contact, to help him exercise and fill some of those empty file cabinets in his mind.

Since he appeared more willing to imitate us, we developed an elaborate program of physical exercise for Robertito. Running, skipping, jumping and tumbling because part of the curriculum. We also had him lift small weights, trying to strengthen his arms and hands, especially his right arm and right hand. We worked his fingers with smaller objects which required more skill, trying to increase his hand-eye co-ordination as well as his small motor dexterity.

247

We had a blood and hair analysis performed. Though his diet had been all organic and vegetarian, marked by the absence of sugar, salt, artificial preservatives, colors and flavors, we refined his intake further based on our increased data.

By touching his groin, he indicated not only when he wet himself more often, but he used that gesture before he voided. Toilet training now became a possibility and Robertito seemed willing to use the bathroom facilities.

Yet in the midst of all this growth and movement, our young friend rode a roller coaster of contact and withdrawal. For two days during this period, he stopped participating completely. He "ismed" to the life-sized, air-filled Popeye in his room. He flapped at Angelina, the little infant-sized doll we introduced to him. His autistic behavior no longer secluded him totally from his surroundings. In his ironic and humorous manner, he used those rituals as a tangential way to touch the world. We noted short periods of hyperactivity as well as unpredictable withdrawals for two and three hours at a time. The sessions took on a seesaw quality, touching the extremes of non-distractable self-stimulating behaviors to needle-point relatedness. The gap widened as if he kept one foot firmly planted in his autistic world while making bold and adventurous thrusts outside with the other.

In Roby's absence, Bryn, Thea and Raun took turns sleeping at the Soto house. Their presence gave Francisca a sense of security and a bond to us. Bryn conversed with her on a basic level, relying on her textbook Spanish to help. Thea tried sign language and pointed to make her wishes and thoughts known. Raun babbled incessantly in English. At times, he stopped himself, recognizing Francisca's inability to understand him, but then, two minutes later, he would continue his happy barrage of verbiage. The two little boys slept together. Often, Raun fell asleep with his arms tucked securely around his friend.

*   *   *

Amalia positioned her chair equidistant from Francisca's seat, Suzi's and mine.

Having sprinted up the path to our house, Francisca panted conspicuously. An awkward smile fluttered across her face, then disappeared. "I am late again," she began, "and I have so much to discuss." Amalia translated her words into

248

English, preserving most of the inflections and idiosyncratic qualities of Francisca's speech.

"If we can give you extra time, we will," I said. "Two people are coming from Boston later this afternoon. Ironically, this is the first time I've scheduled anyone outside of the program in three weeks."

"Don't worry," Suzi assured her, "if we don't finish now, we'll do it tomorrow. But before we talk, I want my hug."

Suddenly aware of her omission, Francisca seized Suzi vigorously. "My girl friend," she announced proudly. She followed her embrace of me with the words "*grande oso,*" which meant big bear. Amalia received an enthusiastic hug as well. Francisca had converted the simple greeting into a formal ceremony. Even the act of seating herself seemed a touch rehearsed. She leaned forward as she talked. She relayed the news about Roby's business steadily improving since his return to Mexico. They could stay longer. Despite the fact that our previous commitment for six weeks in England had finally solidified, she wanted to stay through the summer and into the fall...at least for an additional six months, maybe more. "Robertito is doing wonderfully here. There's so much we still have to learn."

Suzi and I had anticipated their request and our own response even before the book commitment. Somehow our affirmative answer had a special sweetness now, knowing that, indeed, only beautiful and realistic things came from our socalled unrealistic decision to work with the Sotos. We celebrated that gift. Nevertheless, we found ourselves cautioning Francisca again. The bond between all of us and her son was embryonic and fragile. Anything, from the lights of a video session to a loud noise, could shatter the connection. Even Robertito, by his actions, had demonstrated his unswerving, hypnotic attraction for the autistic womb.

Francisca said her awareness mirrored ours and for that reason she wanted to talk about the summer. "Everything is so delicate; that's why I'm not sure about the summer. I am sure about staying here, but, who will direct the program?"

"Who would you want to direct it?" Suzi asked, deciding to transfer some of the initiative to Francisca.

"Either of you," she affirmed.

"And in our absence?" I questioned.

Francisca straightened her back and gestured authoritatively, like a princess holding court. "I think maybe me and

Roby..." A little girl grimace surfaced on her face as she abandoned her studied pose. For the first time, as a conscious decision, she freed her body to relax and be spontaneous, a physical state of being she had previously reserved only for her son. "I said me and Roby, but I'm not sure."

"What aren't you sure about?" I asked.

"Us. We have much to learn," she said, doodling on a pad. Her hair fell over her forehead, but she didn't seem to notice.

"Even if you have much to learn, Francisca, why do you question directing the program for a six-week period?"

Her face tightened. She licked her lips. "We love our son very much. And even with Laura and Carol...I mean, they could help make decisions, we can all do it together...even so, maybe, well, it's scary."

Suzi bent forward and touched the other woman's hand. "Francisca, what's scary about it?" she asked.

"Suppose we make a mistake. Suppose we decide something very stupid. When I listen to both of your suggestions on Wednesday nights, I think to myself—hey, Francisca, how come you did not think of that? Now I would have to."

"Perhaps you never asked yourself that question on Wednesday night," Suzi said. "I used to do that all the time, let somebody else do it instead of me. If you did do it, if you made the list each week on what the group would concentrate on, how would you feel?"

"Scared," she snapped. "Really scared!" A peculiar grin quivered on the lower portion of her face. The area above her high cheekbones remained fixed.

"Why would you be scared?" I asked in a voice barely above a whisper.

"It's that thing about making a mistake." Francisca clasped her hands together.

"What do you mean by making a mistake?"

"Suppose, uh, just suppose," she began. "Well, let's say I decided we would take Robertito to the park one hour each day. Okay?" Suzi and I nodded. "And let's say when he is outside, he withdraws. That would be terrible."

"Why?"

"Don't you think it would be, Bears?"

"Maybe the important thing here is what you think, Francisca?"

"It would be, uh, terrible because he'd stop learning. I mean that's okay," she asserted, "as long as it's not my fault."

250

"Francisca," Suzi interjected, "if you take Robertito out and he withdraws, how is that your fault?"

"Well, maybe he did not like to be outside. Maybe the noise and wind, the cars were too much. So he withdraws—I know it's to take care of himself—but he withdraws."

"How is it your fault if he does?" Suzi asked again.

Francisca stared at her curiously and shrugged her shoulders.

"Do you make him withdraw?" I questioned.

She paused for a moment. "No."

"Then if you didn't make him withdraw," I said, "how are you responsible for his withdrawal?"

"I don't know." She stared at the window, smiled fleetingly at Amalia and said: "He withdraws because he doesn't like the outside or it is too difficult for him." She stared at the ceiling again. "But I should have known it would be too much for him...that's why it is my fault!"

"Why should you have known?" I inquired.

A disturbed expression rippled across her face. "I don't know, Bears. I should have...that's all. I should have known."

"Francisca, why do you believe you should have known?"

She tapped her fingers together nervously. "First, I would have thought he needed a break from the room. If his contact improved, even more than now, he might be able to relate to things outside. I'd ask Roby and Carol and Laura what they thought. I guess, if no one objected, I'd try it."

"Okay," Suzi acknowledged, shifting her position on the couch by crossing her legs beneath her. "And suppose you did all those things, gathered as much information as you could, and still Robertito withdrew—then, how would you feel?"

"I know I can't decide for him how to be, Suzi, you know, he's so unpredictable. Sometimes he deals with us wonderfully; other times he stays by himself." Francisca smiled thinly. "It doesn't look the same now, not after talking about it. I wouldn't be responsible for what he does, only what I do."

"If you're not responsible for what he does and you did the best you could, how would you feel about that?" I asked.

"Well, if I did the best I could, then...that would be okay."

A smile adorned Suzi's face. She could feel Francisca's movement and wanted her to go the whole distance. "And, my girl friend," she said, spoofing Francisca's favorite idiom, "if you looked at the situation, and considered all the alter-

251

natives, then made a decision, would you be doing the best you could?"

Francisca glanced back and forth between Suzi and myself. "Yes," she declared. "Of course I would." A hint of a smile creased the skin around her eyes. "If taking him outside is the only thing I can think of, then I'm doing the best I can do at the time." She allowed a full smile and crumpled into the chair, uncharacteristically, like a little girl. Francisca laughed, closed her eyes and whispered: "It's like learning to forgive yourself."

* * *

After a nineteen-day absence, Roby returned to New York. Instead of eating or resting upon his arrival, he volunteered to take Francisca's next session with Robertito. I sat on the side of the room after Suzi left. The little boy jerked his head upward and looked directly at his father.

"My son. How is my son?" He knelt down and embraced the child. The little boy rested his head on his father's shoulder and ran his little fingers up and down his arm. Roby lived for this moment. They held their easy embrace for almost four minutes until Robertito turned around and held his arms up. "You remembered," Roby shouted. "My boy!" He locked his hands under his son's arms and swung him in giant circles around the room. The little boy laughed.

Spontaneously, Robertito said: "*Co.*" Roby gaped at the child, then glanced wide-eyed at me. I smiled and pointed to the food on the shelf. He grabbed the cup quickly and gave his son an ample portion. Robertito jumped while he chewed. His father imitated him. Robertito twirled his fingers. His father repeated the same motions. When the child sat down with a book, his father nestled close to him. Roby asked his son to locate the cow. Without the slightest hesitation, he pointed to the spotted animal.

"Where's the duck?" he asked. The boy touched the fluffy white form depicted in the book. Roby looked up at me aghast. I pointed to my mouth and pantomimed the duck's cry. "What does the duck say, *papito?*" No response. "What does the duck say?"

Robertito touched the drawing in the book, his small fingers caressing the yellow beak. "Quack, quack," he barked. "Quack, quack!"

His father applauded, cheered and hugged his son. They

252

rolled together like wrestlers on the floor. Roby's awe led him to extract the cardboard basketball unit from the closet and demonstrate throwing the ball into the hoop. When he gave the huge foam replica of a basketball to Robertito, he dropped it. But on the second deliverance, the little boy made an energetic attempt to toss the ball. Though he missed the backboard completely, Roby jumped and shouted. "You threw the basketball! Didn't you?" Roberto Soto sank to the floor and laughed. His son picked up the ball again, this time hitting the backboard and almost sinking his first basket. Robertito dropped to the floor beside his father and like the older man, he, too, laughed.

Time had stopped for the two of them, a father and a son, both of whom had defied every prediction and found each other. I lost it in that moment, the tears blurring my vision as I rose to my feet. I felt like an intruder witnessing the most intimate scene. What a wonderful gift this child had given his father on the first day of his return. Rather than disrupt them with my good-by, I slipped out of the room unobtrusively.

In the kitchen, I hugged Francisca and Laura, told them about what I had just observed, then turned to leave.

"Wait," Laura said, fumbling through her pocketbook as she followed me into the living room. "I want you to read something my mother clipped out of the newspaper." She extracted the piece and held it poised in the air. Her fingers twisted the corner of the page angrily. "I . . . I, well, here, you read it."

I recognized the article immediately as duplicating other copies which had been sent to me in the last two days from people in various parts of the country. Until this moment, I had not taken time to read it.

"Thanks, Rha."

"I don't know if you'll thank me after you read it," she declared.

"Things come our way for a reason," I said, smiling and tapping the newspaper.

"Okay, Papa Bear. Anything for your enrichment." Laura winked, hugged me and returned to the kitchen.

The floor of the porch was unyielding as I sat against the wall outside of the front door. Roby and Robertito's animal sounds and intermittent laughter filtered into the yard through an opened window.

The story about a treatment center in the Southwest had

whipped through the wire services and appeared in newspapers throughout the country. The reporter had watched and recorded his findings with unswerving fascination. I gave myself to his printed words.

At ten years old, a little girl named Lisa, dressed cheerfully in an orange polka-dotted dress, leaned against the side of the building. Her eyes gazed at the trees towering above her. Her expressionless face suggested a child lost in a daydream. But Lisa's stare could not be distracted. Locked in a world without emotion, she never giggled or smiled. She never cried.

Lisa was not retarded. Diagnosed autistic, she exhibited the usual constellation of severe learning disabilities and bizarre behavioral problems. When she arrived at the clinic, her only expression response was to throw every object she could find. At that time, her inability to communicate made her indistinguishable from a deaf mute. Recently, she had begun to learn to speak in sign language on a primitive level. On command, she had even hugged her mother.

Progress with Lisa and other autistic children was attributed to treatment which included pinchings, slappings, the placement of children in dark closets and, in some cases, the administering of electric shocks with a cattle prod.

After two years in the program, Lisa uttered five recognizable sounds and demonstrated a significantly larger sign language capability. When instructed, she touched her nose; after a teacher's elaborate illustration, the little girl put her hands over her head.

"We can teach them," said Dr. Whitney Denton. "We can make them manageable. We can train them, but the question is whether we can make them normal. Many of these kids become self-destructive. They bang their heads against the wall hard enough to crack their skulls. They claw the flesh off their faces or try to put out their eyes. Some of them bite themselves—take chunks of flesh out of their arms and shoulders."

Preventing the children's deviant behavior, whether self-destructive or not, became what the doctor and his staff envisioned as their first responsibility. The exploration of why the behaviors might have begun or what reorientation could help the children express themselves in other fashions had not been considered relevant.

"We punish them to reduce the rate of response we're trying to eliminate," Dr. Denton explained. "Then we go in and try to teach them something else. An alternative to the inappropriate behavior."

The doctor profiled a description of the "normal" child who might, he suggested, explore various methods to secure attention and affection, including self-destructive behavior. That child might strike his body, but after a period of time, the parent will get impatient and angry, commanding the child to stop. Since the hitting does not get the child what he wants, the "normal" child will stop and choose another behavior in order to get a favorable response from his parents.

"But the autistic child," according to Dr. Denton, "can't do that. 'It' doesn't know an alternative. So 'it' will just keep hitting harder and harder until physically restrained."

No one, not the doctors or the staff members or even the reporter, had realized the distinctive use of pronouns in Dr. Denton's commentary. The autistic child was no longer a boy or a girl, but, matter-of-factly, an "it."

And so the physician continued, "It could literally beat itself to death."

"In milder circumstances," added Dr. Elber, an associate director, "we punish merely with a slap on the arm or a simple 'time out' procedure; that is, placement in a dark closet."

"If the behavior continues," Dr. Denton said. "its arm or hand may be slapped hard enough and often enough to get it to stop. Hopefully, after a significant period of time, the child will associate the slap with the behavior and will often stop. Sometimes, the dark closet has the same effect."

In many cases, Dr. Denton and his staff used cattle prods to deliver a painful electric jolt to stop undesirable behaviors. Despite the center's successful record within its limited boundaries, the doctor still wondered if the other problem could be treated—the absence of emotion.

At that moment, I stopped reading and listened to the little-boy giggles of Robertito Soto and friend; then I pushed myself to finish the article.

The staff members of the clinic recounted more details of Lisa Carey's story. Initially, the young girl recognized her mother but showed no emotion, no affection and no love. Now, "for some reason," she will greet her mother with a kiss and even hug an instructor, although those gestures have a certain mechanical quality.

"We can teach them almost anything," Dr. Denton commented, "but we can't make them human."

I dropped the paper on the floor. What if that had been

255

me? What if I had difficulty understanding and assimilating my environment? What if I had severe learning and behavioral disabilities and then someone subjected me first to the ritual of pinching, slapping, then confinement in a locked, dark closet and, finally, painful electric shocks with a cattle prod? Would I want to deal with this world and those in it? Would I want to hug my "instructors"? And if I didn't, would they, too, point their accusing fingers and call me something less than human?

Chapter 17

We moved through the next three weeks in high gear. The producers, in conjunction with the sponsor and the network, decided to move forward with the "Son-Rise" television special. Each night, after observation and dialogue sessions, I withdrew to my one-room retreat and wrote sections of the treatment, which, ultimately, would become the blueprint of a screenplay. Suzi and I had to compress our schedules since a scant three weeks had been allotted for the development of this detailed outline.

Each morning, at about six o'clock, before the children awakened for school, we discussed scenes and dialogue. We ran through the corridors of old memories, discovering turns and twists which I had not included in the book. The startling parallels and obvious differences between Raun and Robertito became even more apparent. Each child required a very different journey, hand-tailored to his individual needs. But the foundation of an accepting and non-judgmental attitude toward ourselves and the child we attempted to reach remained identical.

Concurrent with our other responsibilities, we instituted

the first stage of our quest for a new house for the Sotos, having rented the one they lived in for only three and a half months. This time we omitted all references to Mexico, the Spanish language and autistic children. Francisca and Roberto became Fran and Bob, Robertito became Bob, Jr. The place of their residence became the "West Coast." Their reason for a limited relocation to New York, we explained, centered on their desire to secure help for their child, who had certain developmental and language delays. In effect, all the facts were true, but composed in a way so as not to incite the fears and prejudices of the people we contacted. Nevertheless, Suzi's daily visits to available apartments and houses did not meet with success. The combination of privacy, lack of noise and a layout conducive to working with Robertito could not be easily located.

The frenzy to handle all those responsibilities intensified when Roby announced, with significant satisfaction, the impending arrival of a replacement for Charlotte. During his recent stay in Mexico, he had interviewed many young women, hoping to find someone who would help them. Both he and Francisca wanted a person to translate on a daily basis so the flow of communication would continue uninterrupted, especially on matters requiring needle-point discussions on Robertito's behavior. Amalia's availability was limited essentially to Wednesday nights.

Less than three days after his announcement, a young Mexican woman, armed with copies of *Son-Rise* and *To Love Is to Be Happy With,* burst into our midst. "I'm ready. Definitely. I am here to serve you all." She wanted an Option session the day of her arrival. Unlike her predecessor, Patti's total focus and energy fixed on the unknown child she had traveled three thousand miles to help. We did not have to stir her enthusiasm; we had to channel it.

Resourceful and independent, Patti Vega had once considered becoming a nun and founding an orphanage for homeless children. When she quit her clerical job to come to New York, which she envisioned as a preparation for more spiritual calling, her mother branded her idealistic. But Patti persisted, wanting to confront her dreams rather than hold them at arm's distance.

I observed her in that first encounter with Robertito. Though willing and able, she could not hide her shocked expression. The words never quite matched the description. The hand-flapping and head-shaking seemed more bizarre

258

and unfamiliar than the image of her fantasy. Within seconds, her expectation crumbled. I watched her muscles tense in her arms and face. Yet, despite the jolt, she lusted to learn to be useful, helpful and more humane. Though stiff and confused in her meeting with Robertito, Patti lived in a perpetual euphoria which surrounded her like a force field. She felt at home immediately. Finally, she had found a place where people did not judge her, where sharing and loving were not irrelevant themes, a dramatic contrast to her previous employment situations. "I don't have to say my wants and ideals here, because you are already the way I want," she shared before her first dialogue session. "Can it be, Bears, that I am changed already...on the first day?"

Patti studied and observed from early morning until Robertito's bedtime. The milestones of Tito's movement astounded her as well as all of us in the program. His growth was rivaled only by Carol's progress during her first weeks as teacher and mentor. In one session, I watched Carol exercise a special inner authority with our little friend. He watched her continually for twenty to forty seconds at a time with no visible stimulus to do so. Her eyes compelled him, drawing him close. He touched various parts of her body spontaneously and on request. Although Robertito flapped his hands and paced the room in wide circles, he spent a significant amount of time with her engaged in playing such games as ring-around-a-rosy and London Bridge.

Carol's face moved like Silly-Putty: expressive and lavish in its display of joy. Her voice no longer sank into the monotonous drone of a monotone, though outside of the workroom the remnants of her past still infiltrated her speech.

With exaggerated animation, Carol pronounced each vowel. Robertito watched her mouth attentively and repeated each sound. When she attempted a sequence of sounds, he slurred the letters together. Carol laughed. "Oh, so you want to get through it quickly, do you? Slowly, Robertito, slowly!" She began the exercise over again. This time the little boy said each letter perfectly. Though wonderfully accepting and responsive to his "isms," she drew a special hope for herself in his accomplishments. "You and me, Tito, we'll make a pact. We'll both get better together." But often, her joy and growing love for this child obliterated thoughts of her private goal.

She ran through the alphabet. Robertito's verbal ability to mimic sounds had increased significantly, but he had difficulty pronouncing consonants like t, n, s, l and f. On request, he repeated such words or sounds as *pan* (bread), *i-ya* (for cereal), *ooon* (for *atún* or tuna), *agua* (water), *ca-ca* (for bowel movement), *ojo* (eye), *boca* (mouth) and Tito (for himself).

Carol's accomplishments with his toilet training impressed all of us in the group to such an extent that one Wednesday night meeting we nicknamed her ca-ca. Unable to escape the comical and endearing reference, she aggressively individualized the name, spelling it "Kha-Kha" or "Kha" on all her sheets and forms.

Robertito's obvious sensitivity toward music and rhythms led to Suzi's suggestion not only to teach him more songs, but to sing our requests instead of merely saying them. Noting that he hummed tunes spontaneously, she taught him to sing "Old MacDonald Had a Farm" by letting him do the "e-i-e-i-o" refrains and all the animal sounds. Often, she set her directions to old thirties' tunes. Suzi taught Robertito how to say everyone's name perfectly, but ironically, his best articulation of her name sounded like the Japanese dish sushi.

His increased skill with more sophisticated puzzles intrigued her. Somehow, she always asked him for the impossible, which, he, at times, delivered. He learned to retrieve many objects from a box on request, but his ability to distinguish colors seemed amiss.

One morning as I observed, Suzi stared at Robertito with intense determination. "This time, here and now, you are going to identify each color. Not just one. Not just red or blue or green, but all of them. You're going to do it because you want to and because we love you. Now, my sweet fellow, can you find the blue block? Blue. Robertito, blue!"

He rummaged through the mixed pile of blocks, animal forms and letter shapes. He lifted the cow and peered over it diligently before returning it to the mound. His eyes gawked at the letter "s." Then, to her amazement and mine, Robertito grabbed the blue block and delivered it into her hands.

"Wow," she exclaimed, applauding and kissing her student. When he crawled over and sat in my lap, Suzi pushed all her tools next to me.

"Ah, so you want something soft to sit on. Can't blame you." She kissed him on the forehead. "You're such an intelligent boy. Sushi's proud of you," she said, spoofing his pronunciation of her name. "Now, Robertito, fantastic boy, find the green blocks. C'mon. Green! Green!"

Again, he sifted through the pile of toys with no apparent

aim. But then, he lifted the green form and deposited it in my crotch.

"Perfect aim," Suzi laughed, rewarding Robertito this time with food and affection. We did our hysterical clapping and cheers. Though he seemed pleased, his casual attitude had comic overtones; bright eyes in the limp body of a contented cow. Later, Suzi had him identify a red block, a red car and a red shirt. His towering concentration and Suzi's conviction moved him to another plateau. He had learned to generalize.

Attentive to the toll of psychic fatigue, Suzi nestled him into a corner and produced her bag of hand puppets. With her fingers secure in the mouth and eye mechanism of one cloth mannequin, she brought Foggie Froggie to life. "Glup. Glup," she giggled, simultaneously the performer and audience. "Hello, Francisca. Nope. Are you Rha-Rha? Pretty fat face for Rha-Rha. No, of course not. Glup! Glup! I know, you're the one and only Robertito Soto." The little boy watched the puppet, then grabbed its nose. "Jumpin' Jennifer, ah, I mean Holy Frog, you got my schnoz. And where's your schnoz...point to your nose." In an aside to me, she feigned a stuffy British accent. "A very civilized request, you know." Robertito touched his own nose while still in physical possession of the puppet's foam nostril.

"Ra, ra, sis, boom, ba; Tito, Tito, the Option bandito," she cheered, rolling her eyes.

Skillfully, in a display of increasing enthusiasm, Suzi whizzed through mindless skits with each puppet. She changed her voice, vocabulary and personality for each character. If Robertito "ismed," the puppet "ismed" with him. Sometimes, he ignored Suzi's hand people, but, often, he smiled in their presence.

Laura worked him intensely during her evening shift. He disassembled and reassembled a five-piece puzzle quickly. The knobs helped him manipulate the forms since his hands still lacked a more sophisticated dexterity. She set out a row of colored cups and asked him for the black one. He handed her the white one. She requested the green cup and he gave her the orange one.

"Have you forgotten, or do you want to do something else?" she asked. He stared at her blankly. "Oh, I see, your gig is reading." As she pulled the dictionary picture book from the shelf, Robertito spilled over the case of pegs and counting blocks.

"The book...no. Pegs and blocks...yes. Of course." Laura

261

stroked his arms and I laughed. She displayed a long row of pegs. "Here we go. Now get your act together. Can you give me two pegs? Two pegs?"

Robertito looked up at her, touched her cheek and said: "*Co*."

"You want '*co*.' Rha-Rha will give you '*co*' right after this little game of ours." She jabbed him gently in the side.

"'Be,'" he blurted, our monosyllabic designation for vitamin.

"Holy shit!" she muttered in awe of the little boy's accomplishment. "It's coming, Robertito. Right here."

Over the next two hours, he demonstrated his awareness of number concepts by putting groups of two, three and four pegs in the board as requested. The accuracy of his responses punctuated the growth of his developing intellect.

Francisca arrived in the room, carrying her son's dinner. She offered to replace Laura while she answered an urgent telephone call. Five minutes later, the young woman returned with a downcast expression. Laura took charge of the session again, continuing the number games, but her enthusiasm waned. Francisca watched. Her hawk eyes catalogued every gesture, every disguised grimace. She knew Laura's attention had drifted to other places as a result of that phone conversation. Her son's interest diminished as well. She could finish the remainder of Laura's session, she postulated, but let her thought go immediately, not wanting to insult the other woman in any way. Laura's skills amazed her. Music. Art. Athletics. Teaching. A Renaissance person. When she compared her abilities to the younger woman's talents, Francisca could not balance the scale. Her two notable skills of mother and wife dominated an otherwise empty list. She had never questioned the meaning or value of her life and actions until Robertito arrived. But what about teacher? She considered that a skill in the process of being acquired. In detecting Laura's mood change and hypothesizing about its genesis, she reaffirmed her own growing awareness. "Maybe, I could direct the program this summer." She smiled, more confident of subduing her demons. Even as she watched Laura stumble and show fleeting signs of impatience, she loved her without judging her actions and without fear for her son. She knew they would both survive and, perhaps, flourish.

Robertito peered at his mother often, rather than maintaining his traditional focus on food. As she exited, he rose to his feet. His face contorted peculiarly, his lips slopping together. Francisca gazed at her son and waved, not wanting to divert his attention from the session. He struggled to control his mouth. She waved a last time and started to close the door.

"Mama," a throaty voice bellowed.

Francisca threw the door open and gaped at her child. "Yes. Yes. Oh, God, yes," she said. She knelt down and hugged her son tenderly. Her hands trembled. Robertito's little fingers made a gentle scratching motion along her back. For almost six years, Francisca had tried to identify herself to her son. For almost six years, he chose people indiscriminately, never showing a discernible preference or attachment to anyone. She had waited alone, as only a mother could wait, often filled with anger and fear. But for Francisca, today was her first Mother's Day.

* * *

I arrived at the Sotos' during Carol's session and found Robertito sitting on the toilet. He leaned against Carol and played with her hair. He stared at me often while I watched from the doorway.

"¡Hola!, mi amor," I said, responding to the unspoken language of his eyes.

"Who's that?" Carol asked, pointing to me. Robertito stared at the tips of her fingers. "Not my finger. Look, that big hairy bear." The child eyed my form curiously, then grunted a muddled sound. "Say it again. Louder."

He shouted in a throaty voice, "Bears."

Francisca arrived noisily to take the next session. During the changing of the guard, I hugged each of them, including my little friend, and then left.

At the bottom of the staircase, I paused, searching for my pen. My notorious habit for losing pens, keys, wallets and phone numbers plagued me once again. Suzi said my mind rejected the existence of what it deemed as minor details. And yet, throughout my adult life, my body spent countless hours trying to relocate what my mind refused to register. Rather than go back for the pen and intrude on the next session with Robertito, I accepted my loss and continued my exit. At that moment, in a voice neither loud nor soft, Carol called my name. The undercurrent of intensity and desperation in her voice rammed my system. I twirled around and catapulted myself up half the staircase. At the first landing,

I caught a glimpse of her backed against the wall at the far end of the hall. As I jumped up the remaining steps, she began to slide downward, her feet crumbling under her. The white pallor of her skin highlighted her blue eyes. She stared at an indeterminate point on the opposite wall. Her eyelids froze open. When I reached her, I helped guide her body to the floor.

"Are you having a seizure?" No response. Her face appeared paralyzed. The muscles in her cheeks fluttered.

"Carol, can you hear me?"

She dipped her head fractionally.

"Okay. I'm going to take your hands. I'll stay with you." Her fingers laid limp in mine. The sweat oozed from her forehead and around her mouth.

"Are you scared?"

She moaned in a weird, barely audible voice.

I felt a tremor through her body. "Kha, try to follow my voice. As long as you do, you will keep your options open. Can you hold on to me with your hands?" Her fingers wrapped around mine. "You did it. Wonderful. Tell me what you feel. Try to talk." She shook her head. "I know it feels like you can't, but try. Describe what you feel."

Her words were garbled, as if compressed and submerged under water.

"Burning. Tingling. Stomach. Hot."

"What else?" I asked. "What else, Kha? Tell me what else you feel."

"Not here." Her voice had dropped an octave. It resonated around her as if coming through a speaker rather than originating in her throat.

"I don't understand! What do you mean by 'not here'?"

"Not in body," she answered. "Hot."

"Does it feel good?"

"Making it."

"Are you making it feel good? Is that it?" No response. "Kha, are you making the hot feel good?"

She nodded slightly.

"Can you hold me tighter?" Her hands squeezed me again, then she went limp. The last ounce of color drained from her skin. I pressed my fingers into her palms. "I'm still here with you," I said. "I'm still here." The tension returned to her hands. "Great. I feel you. Are you frightened?"

"No," she grunted.

264

I waved my hand in front of her eyes. No response. No reflexive defense. During the seizure, she had turned inward.

"Do you see my hand?" I asked, still waving it.

"No."

I pulled it around to the side of her head. She dipped her chin. Carol could not see frontally; she only had visual intake through her peripheral vision. I thought of Robertito.

"Do you want to stop those feelings and come back? You don't have to, but do you want to?"

"Yes," she muttered as if her tongue had been paralyzed.

"Then c'mon back. Let the heat go. Let the tingling sensations go. Squeeze me tighter if you can." I felt no response in her hands. "Kha, you can do it. Try. Like you try every day for Robertito, try this time for Carol." Her thumb pressed the back of my hand. Her eyelids closed. Suddenly, she inhaled deeply. At that moment, I realized I had had no sense of her breathing during the seizure.

She opened her eyes, which were bloodshot and glazed. "Hi," she said weakly. "They're getting lighter . . . ever since our talks. Usually I pass out. This time, I made the heat go away. I can't believe it." She giggled abruptly. "Me. Laughing about my own seizure. What would my mother say? What would my doctor say?" Carol laughed again. She tried to get up, but fell against the wall. I steadied her, helping her to her feet.

Carol lay on the couch, pale, exhausted, but strangely cheerful. "You know, there's such a thing as a reformed alcoholic, but I'll bet you've never heard of a reformed epileptic?" She giggled again in a high, thin voice as if slightly drunk. "If I have to live with this the rest of my life, at least it won't scare the shit out of me any more."

"Do you have to live with it the rest of your life?" I asked.

She wanted to say "no," but short-circuited her thoughts. Every time Robertito learned something new, she felt a touch more liberated from her illness. "What are you saying, Bears?"

"I didn't make a statement, Kha. I asked a question . . . whether, in fact, you had to live with it the rest of your life?"

"I don't have an answer," she mumbled.

"That's okay. All questions don't have to be answered."

Chapter 18

Less than four weeks remained until our departure for England. That commitment, predating the Sotos' re-emergence in our lives, created a gnawing sense of urgency, further complicated by a series of unforeseen events which played havoc with our schedules. It began with Patti, who received an impassioned plea from her father to return to Mexico for two or three days so that her family, as a group, could complete the necessary papers and interviews for their planned immigration to the United States. But a senseless maze of complications arose which blocked her re-entry into this country. "Somehow, I'll get back here," she promised. It would be almost a year later, when Roby searched for yet another translator, that Patti would reappear and return to New York. But for now, our problems were immediate. We no longer had a translator and teacher-in-training. Amalia rejoined our family on Wednesday nights. Roby compaigned through his family and friends to find a replacement. Though everyone had learned some Spanish, our ability to converse remained primitive and inadequate in view of the detailed exchanges and dialogue sessions necessary to maintain our program with Robertito.

Concurrent with this upset and our continued search for new living quarters for the Sotos, we began training a summer replacement for Suzi, who would work her scheduled session with Robertito until we returned. Lisa had made her appearance over a month ago. She had fallen in love with Raun, Bryn and Thea during one of their rare visits to a local pool. When we realized we needed another mentor during our absence, she came to mind immediately.

"I'd like to work with Robertito more than anything in the world," Lisa replied to our solicitation.

Rather than yield to the limitations of time, Suzi and I expanded our work load. We maximized Lisa's exposure through sessions and observing. The language barrier became her Mount Everest. Each night, after extensive observation periods, she studied with Suzi, Laura, Carol, or Francisca, trying desperately to master pronunciation. Bryn played teacher gladly and administered tests to check Lisa's memory and increase her fluency in "thinking" Spanish. Since Robertito's receptive vocabulary had blossomed and his expressive utterances had begun to develop, our endeavor to stay ahead of him required a more conscientious effort. All of us had to expand our vocabulary and comprehension of idiomatic expressions. Lisa attempted to absorb in two or three weeks the language capability we had gained over a period of almost three months. We tacked huge lists of words on the walls in Robertito's room for her.

When she worked in tandem with us for the first time, Robertito's immediate affection surprised her. Short and attractively chubby, Lisa looked more like our little friend's playmate than teacher. And in some respects, he related to her in a way akin to his responses to Bryn, Thea and Raun. I fantasized him thinking... "Ah, she's one of us." Though her ability to work puzzles, books, number and word games was limited due to her initial difficulties with language, her contact with him dramatized the very essential non-verbal components of our program. They jumped, danced, ran, skipped, exercised and wrestled together. Although she sang and played simple games with him, the physical aspect of their relationship dominated her session.

One afternoon, following my observation session with Francisca and Lisa, Roby stopped me in the hall. Three minutes later, after an exchange of Spanish words, English words, hand gestures and pantomime, the message penetrated my spongy brain. They had located a replacement for Patti. This young woman would arrive about a week before we left for Europe. "How can we train her? Even if Suzi and I worked with her day and night, a week is simply not enough!" I laughed. No, I would not train her. Suzi would not train her. But Francisca and Roby would. And since this girl was bilingual, Laura and Carol could help. Although I had put extra time into teaching Francisca and Roby how to observe and facilitate awareness in feed-back sessions, I doubled my commitment to provide them with a more solid base and trust in themselves. One day the Sotos would return to Mexico. If they hoped to continue the program, they would have to live and share an accepting attitude, train others, assess behavior and guide the direction of input. The summer would provide them with an essential and unique opportunity to flex their wings.

At the moment we felt reasonably assured of fulfilling our commitments, I received an urgent call from the West Coast. My treatment for the "Son-Rise" movie had been endorsed enthusiastically by all involved, and now, in order to make a projected air date the following spring, they wanted to commission me to write the screenplay immediately. My efforts to delay were aborted by Jane's counsel, which reminded me that if I could not deliver under their timetable, the producers did, contractually, have the right to seek the talents of another writer. In order to make the impossible possible, I turned to the person who had become my mentor, my first editor and my alter-ego during the preparation of my books...Suzi. Rather than review my writing after I committed it to paper, I asked her to co-write the screenplay with me. Her extensive background is acting and her natural ear for dialogue made her a perfect partner for this project. A silly, little-girl expression dominated her face as she blurted: "Really?" Two days later, I accepted the assignment for both of us and had her name placed beside mine on the contract.

We had less than two months to deliver. This meant writing during our last weeks in New York and continuing while in England. We substituted script meetings starting at 5 A.M. in place of our morning jogging sessions so we could be available during the day for the Soto program. After lengthy dinners with our children, Suzi and I retreated to the den, barricading ourselves until long after midnight. Although we wrote scenes independently, often, we role-played the various characters and tape-recorded the exchanges. They became the nucleus of many sequences later incorporated into the final script. Despite the profound seriousness of the project, on occasion, we found ourselves consumed with laughter. Perhaps, after eighteen hours of sessions and writing, we had tipped the scale and, like Robertito Soto, we, too, found our very existence a source of incredible humor.

* * *

My concern about the early hour proved unfounded as I maneuvered through traffic. This would be Robertito's second developmental work-up since his return. Although we had awakened him, instead of allowing him to rise on his own impulse, he appeared content, sitting quietly in the back seat with his mother. I exchanged sleepy smiles with Suzi, who, during the testing, would serve as translator.

This was Robertito's first real excursion out of his room in three months. His world had existed within the four walls of our protected womb. Unlike his behavior during the ride from the airport, during which time he flapped his hands, twirled his fingers, shook his head from side to side, whined, babbled and cooed, he now leaned against the door and let his eyes follow the path of passing cars. When Francisca asked for his hand, he put his into hers with an easy, natural movement. When I told Robertito that I loved him, he looked directly at me for the few seconds I talked, then turned back to the activity visible out the window. Never before had he displayed interest in his environment and, despite the bombardment of motion and noises, he demonstrated an exceedingly greater capability and strength in absorbing a variety of sensory input.

At Dr. Yorke's office, Robertito scurried into the room following Suzi's invitation. The little boy eyed the doctor intensely and then, without any direction, he hugged the man as he had once hugged my father and his wife spontaneously. Suzi and I could barely believe our eyes and the dramatic and wonderful statement Robertito had made about his joy and growing trust in people. Visibly moved, Carl Yorke sat in his chair and extended his hand. Robertito took it. When the psychologist shook his hand, the child imitated the gesture. They both smiled, though, perhaps, not for the same reasons. Also spontaneously, Robertito grabbed a ball beside

269

the wall and threw it to Suzi. When she rolled it back to him, he caught it and returned it again.

"*Comida,*" Robertito said, asking for food and, unknowingly, demonstrating his recently acquired skill to use a limited number of full words instead of the simpler monosyllabic words we had introduced originally.

Carl's mouth dropped open. In addition to the volume of first testing data he reviewed prior to our arrival, he recalled a vivid portrait of a totally withdrawn, mute youngster who flapped, ran in circles, babbled, did not respond to people or words, appeared fleetingly deaf and blind, lost behind that enigmatic wall of autism.

"If I hadn't seen it myself, I wouldn't believe it!" he blurted. "How could this be the same child?"

"He is...and he isn't," Suzi said, grinning.

"I have never seen anything like this in my life...and in only three months," he declared, shaking his head as he admired the child.

"You've probably never seen this in three years," she countered.

"You're right." Carl bent forward as if to get closer. He found Robertito's happiness and calm hypnotic.

"I think he wants to go to the bathroom," I interjected, noting Robertito scratch his groin.

"That's okay," Carl replied, putting his hand up. "I just can't get over it. Let him wander around a bit. You can take him in a minute." Robertito tapped his groin a second time. "I see, I see," the psychologist said, obviously impressed. He smiled at the child. "*Ven,* Robertito," he called, using his minimal vocabulary to see if he could establish contact.

In a flash, our little friend walked over to this relative stranger and stood in front of him without, even momentarily, sliding back into one of his self-stimulating rituals.

"You're quite a young man," Yorke said softly, unconsciously slipping back into English.

As the doctor spoke, Robertito watched attentively. "*Boca,*" he declared clearly, his little fingers touching the man's mouth.

"Did he say mouth? Another word! He talks?" Carl whispered.

At that moment, as if on cue, as if he knew the purpose of our visit, Robertito Soto put his index finger in Yorke's eye and said: "*Ojo.*"

270

"And where're your eyes, Robertito?" Suzi asked. The little boy touched his own eyes.

Dr. Carl Yorke shook his head again. "If there's a heaven, there's going to be a place reserved for you people."

In the silence that followed his remark, everyone became aware of the distinctive odor filling the room. Suzi smiled comically, shrugged her shoulders and led Robertito to the bathroom. He had given us ample warning.

Without further delay, Carl aborted his awe and delight in order to administer the same battery and sequence of tests he had used three months ago. The initial statistics defied his previous experiences in recording change and growth, especially in such a so-called low functioning child. Robertito's I.Q., which had floated between a 7 and 14, had now jumped to 30. His receptive and expressive language, which was on about a one- or two-month level, had leaped to over a twenty-month level. In this area alone, Robertito had exhibited a developmental surge of almost nineteen months in a scant three-month period. More impressive to Yorke was the obvious fact that the child had pierced through the walls of a seemingly hopeless dilemma and had evolved from a vegetative-like state into one of a functioning human being. In addition to scoring the developmental test data and scales, his summary report reflected his many observations.

"Personality Characteristics: The most impressive change that has come about in the last three months in Robertito Soto is the fact that he is now attentive; he looked at the psychologist most of the time; he did not tear up any paper to flap; he did not sit on the psychologist's desk. His behavior was much more conventional. He sat quietly most of the time. He did not spin around and he was certainly not as active and self-stimulating as he was the previous time he was seen. His hands were not flapping. He did not wander around the room restlessly. He attended to Suzi Kaufman and to what she did. She demonstrated most of the tests the psychologist wanted the boy to take and maintained excellent rapport with him.

"Robertito would imitate sounds purposely; he would listen; he would attend and did not stare out the window or stand on the table. He still needs a tremendous amount of attention and direction, but he was co-operative, followed instructions much better and his attention span, in general, was much better. He uttered words; he can now make random sounds and he did not run around in the room in a mean-

271

ingless fashion. What was most impressive was the fact that when he made sounds, he was always trying to either imitate Suzi, sing songs or speak. He listened and responded during the entire test period. Most important was the fact that he attended to what was going on in the room. His actions were conventional. He sat quietly and he wanted to please and be involved.

"Language Development: The most impressive evolution has been in the area of receptive and expressive language. In terms of receptive language, it was noted that he localized the source of the voice, recognized his name, understood nuances and words, knows the names of objects, stopped when the word 'no' was said and recognized the names of family members. He is attentive to music and singing and listens to conversations between adults. He understands simple verbal requests and will give objects or toys to a parent figure upon verbal request. Not only does he follow simple directions, but he demonstrates an understanding by making appropriate verbal responses to some requests; for example, saying 'bye bye.' He certainly recognizes and identifies various parts of his body and can comprehend simple questions and carry out consecutive directions.

"In terms of expressive language, it was noted that he can use at least ten true words with some consistency and can say: horse, mouth, eyes, egg, food, juice, cereal, cow, sheep and dog." Of course, he says these words in Spanish, but the psychologist, who understands some Spanish, was able to understand the boy. Robertito now uses gesture language, such as shaking his head 'yes' and 'no,' he mimicks the sounds of other people and uses some exclamations. He tries to imitate new words and he 'talks' to toy animals that he plays with. He points to a doll's clothes, he scribbles, identifies pictures and uses words on a 20 and 22 month level.

"From a social point of view, he functions somewhere between an 18 to 24 month old level. He now asks to go to the toilet by gesturing and tapping his genital area. He initiates his own play activities and plays with simple toys. He now can remove his coat and get a drink unassisted. He avoids hazards, which he did not do before. He uses the names of familiar objects.

"Notably in terms of fine motor ability, he can imitate a vertical line, build a tower of eight cubes and play with blocks.

"In terms of gross coordination, at present, he can kick a

272

ball forward, can jump in place, but cannot yet pedal a tricycle. He still does not throw a ball overhand.

"This boy has made fantastic progress in the last three months considering his low level of achievement when he first started out. He is being given intensive training by Mr. and Mrs. Kaufman and their staff and is now verbal, social, more interested and less self-preoccupied than three months ago.

"The change is dramatic, gratifying and most unusual."

*   *   *

One week prior to the expiration of the current lease and two weeks prior to our departure, we located another house for the Sotos. Suzi and I arranged for some painting and repairs as well as a mover to transport the larger pieces of furniture.

In an effort to see Robertito again before any change in his environment, Rita visited the day before the move. She reviewed her notes, climbed the staircase and entered the room. As she seated herself against the wall, Robertito walked up to her and said, "¡Hola!" She gasped and smiled at the same time. We had not told her that our little friend had begun to talk. He hugged her and kissed her spontaneously and then returned to Laura, who contined the session. Over the next two hours, Rita watched, aghast, as Robertito completed complex ten-piece house and bus puzzles, as he pointed to an endless stream of people, objects and activities displayed in two books, as he indicated and utilized the toilet correctly, as he initiated physical contact and affection, as he played the harmonica, marimba and drums and as he sang along with "Mary Had a Little Lamb" and "London Bridge," often completing sections by himself. His "isms," which Laura still imitated with unending enthusiasm, accounted for less than 15 percent of his behavior. He had, without coercion or threat of punishment, chosen to participate and, in that choice, he found less interest and time for his self-contained autistic rituals. Rita catalogued over thirty words which he had initiated with decent accuracy: dog, cat, donkey, hair, goat, pig, sheep, cow, horse, duck, mouse, wolf, mouth, eye, ear, nose, care, neck, elbow, thank you, yes, Robertito, okay, Bears, Mama, Papa, Suzi, Carol, Rha-Rha, bear (animal), more, music, jump, dance, food, juice, water. She watched Laura teach him numbers, number concepts and numbering sequences including counting of fingers, eyes, pegs and blocks.

The notebook closed under the weight of her hand. Everything she observed was simple, direct, loving and yet, she had the same sensation as her last visit. This room did not exist in the same time and space as the other events of her life. It was, at once, permanent and unreal. Leaving, for Rita, meant forcing her awareness back into her body, lifting herself off the floor and moving toward the door. When she felt the knob in her hand, she heard Laura asking Robertito to say good-by. Her eyes met his the moment she turned.

"By-by," Robertito said softly as he waved his little hand. He cocked his head slightly, rippling the smooth skin of his forehead. The little boy remained enveloped in his own silence, his tenderness and unearthly calm leaving the last imprint in Rita's mind. She found herself feeling alarmingly sentimental.

The psychiatric follow-up occurred on the same day as the move to the new house. Dr. Goodman had been anxious, like Rita, to examine the child while still in familiar surroundings, voicing his concern that a dramatic environmental change might trigger a withdrawal. During the hours he observed and examined Robertito, the movers began stripping the house. When Paul returned to the first floor, he looked around amazed. The completely furnished living room was now empty. Only the bare walls faced his wide-eyed grin."

"Paul, in here," I said, motioning from the kitchen. "We have camomile or lemon grass."

He smiled tentatively. "What's that?"

"Tea. Herbal tea. Wonderful for your digestive tract, among other things."

"What are you having?" he asked.

"Lemon grass," I answered.

"Me too." He sat at the opposite side of the table as I poured the tea. "It's remarkable. You should have the whole medical profession behind you."

I smiled. "Paul, you are the medical profession."

He forced a laugh and pulled at the tip of his long red beard. "The changes are uncanny. It makes little sense according to the prognosis. And... in three months. Is what I saw upstairs typical of the therapeutic input most of the time?"

274

"Not most of the time... all of the time, every day of the week, at least twelve hours a day, more if he gets up early."

He sipped the tea cautiously and rolled the liquid around in his mouth. "A three-month miracle. I mean he's far from being a six-year-old and the autistic syndrome is still in evidence, but... well, he's functioning. In this case, that's quite an achievement. I am also impressed with how happy and affectionate he is."

At the same instant, both of us became aware of the three husky men looming over us.

"Excuse me," one of them said, "but this is the only room left."

As Paul and I rose to our feet, the movers scooped the chairs from beneath us and carried the table from the room. We continued our conversation standing, our voices reverberating off the walls of the now empty room. I could hear Carol and Robertito upstairs, working diligently in a house that had been evacuated.

At the door, Paul shook my hand and said in a low voice: "Hummm. Lemon grass. Very interesting."

His report, consistent with his manner, highlighted various notations.

"In a general way," the physician wrote, "Robertito shows a strikingly greater degree of relatedness and responsiveness to people than was the case when he was initially observed three months ago.

"For the initial forty-five minutes, he sat still and paid good attention to various tasks such as learning colors, learning names of objects and animals, being read to, doing puzzles and manipulating other educational materials. Towards the end of the session, he became somewhat restless but still could have his attention focused by the therapist. Robertito made frequent eye contact with the therapist, smiled a lot and enjoyed hugging and kissing her. He also responded to offerings of food. He followed simple instructions, is in the process of being toilet trained and has acquired a small vocabulary. His expressive language consists of one word utterances at this point.

"When not stimulated by the therapist, Robertito becomes relatively unrelated and re-engages in autistic mannerisms such as hand-flapping, lying on his back, rocking and jumping up and down repetitiously. However, he was able to stop this type of activity and spontaneously re-establish contact with the therapist somewhat similarly to the way that a toddler

275

will go off on his own and then return to his mother. There is the suggestion of the beginning of a symbiotic attachment to his care-takers."

Two hours after the completion of the psychiatric evaluation, Suzi, Carol and I transferred Robertito and his boxes filled with toys to the new house. Laura volunteered to take Francisca's session so that she and Roby could work at putting the new house in order. As I watched Robertito resume participation with the same consistency despite the unfamiliar surroundings, it occurred to me that he would probably not have any adverse reaction if we reconvened our teaching sessions in a crater on the moon. Our environment was not a place, but people.

The very next morning, after I did a triple session with Francisca and joined Suzi in giving Carol and Lisa additional pointers, the new translator arrived. The frenetic activity ceased momentarily we gathered in the hallway, sat on top of unopened cartons and introduced ourselves.

Arcelia, or Chella as we came to call her, viewed us with a *déjà vu* sense of recognition. Had she been here before? Why were these faces familiar? In coming to New York, she had pushed aside her traditional cautiousness. At twenty years old, Chella had left school, her family and friends in order to join us. She had spent most of her life trying to suppress what she termed her "sixth sense"; but this time, she followed a path which seemed scripted in advance.

Exactly two weeks ago, she drifted off to sleep after several listless hours in bed. She found herself strolling along huge cement sidewalks crowded with people. Buses, cars, horns and sirens bombarded her. Usually, Chella paid little attention to her diminutive size, but the gigantic scale of the surrounding environment accented her petite body. She weighed little more than one hundred pounds. Yet Cella had no fear. Rivers of cars rushed frantically across twenty-foot distances only to bump and grind in abrupt stops. Straight-faced and self-absorbed pedestrians, their heads bent, scurried busily across cluttered streets. Nevertheless, Chella maintained a slower pace, which allowed her to be simultaneously within the activity but apart from it. She watched the panorama and hustle with the sheer delight of an infant. Suddenly, she felt compelled to look up. Skyscrapers! Endless rows of huge glass buildings lined every street. New York! Chella knew immediately she stood in the center of New York City. Though she had never strayed far from the suburb in San Diego where she lived, she recognized that towering skyline from the hundreds of pictures she had seen.

When she awoke in the morning, she reviewed her dream. She had never thought about New York. Why had it appeared in her dream so vividly? A day later, she answered a public service announcement on a local Spanish radio station. A man solicited for help with his autistic child. Only after she arrived did she learn that the program was not in southern California or Mexico, as she had assumed, but in the metropolitan New York area.

During the interview in Mexico, Chella remembered *Son-Rise*, a book she had read for a college course which had left an indelible mark. For her, it presented a compassionate and loving alternative to deal with a special person. She thought of her mentally retarded sister, Martha, who had been forcibly placed in a residential facility. Not only had Chella wanted to work with special children and adults, but submerged in her goal was the passionate desire to be of greater assistance to her own sister. The book. Martha. The dream. Everything pointed to New York. Twelve days later, she arrived in the city she had previously visited in her dream.

She felt comfortable with everyone, except Francisca, whose rather powerful and authoritative manner intimidated her. In the crunch to train Chella, she had bombarded her with volumes of information on the first night. A loving and accepting attitude suddenly sounded like a regulation rather than something which flowed freely from each person. After Chella and I had several talks and sessions, she shared with me her responses to some of Francisca's guidance. Though she saw her as an amazing therapist, she questioned the other woman's perspective of an accepting attitude. I tried to explain the kind of pressure Francisca might feel since Chella would become her first pupil. In less than one week, Suzi and I would be gone, a fact which laid heavily on Francisca's mind as well as in the thoughts of the other members of the group. Although I would have preferred Chella to work through her own feelings, beliefs and judgments about Francisca, we had to be content with the limited impact of discussions and pep talks.

In response to Chella's observation, I set aside even more time for Francisca, sharing with her my own observations and Chella's. We worked through her burgeoning fears with regard to asserting autonomy over the program. Despite the support of Roby, Laura and Carol, Francisca felt inwardly

277

alone, hypothesizing problems and their solutions. But here again, she dispelled some of her beliefs about the permanency of decisions and responses. As time passed, I sensed a mild discomfort in Carol as well. Suzi and I both knew they had the capacity to handle the program, individually and collectively...but did they know it? We asked Rita to be available for Option sessions should anyone feel the need. We asked her, in addition, to give the group input if difficulties arose with Robertito. My brother Steve, whose college Spanish allowed him to converse reasonably well with the Sotos, volunteered to call and visit several times each week so that they would have his support during our absence.

We gathered for our last Wednesday night meeting two days before our departure. Laura, Carol and Suzi sat together on the couch, legs entwined, leaning bodily against each other not only for physical support but to solidify further the bonds between them and us. Lisa cuddled her compact form against the side of my chair. Roby occupied the love seat by himself; Francisca squatted on the floor in front of him, using the coffee table as her desk again. Chella, whose long, jet-black hair and impenetrable black eyes matched Robertito's, sat near Mercedes, a woman who volunteered to be a back-up translator in case of some unforeseen event during the summer. Rita, our reserve Option therapist, joined us this evening. She listened attentively, making notes and jotting down ideas. Amalia, sitting with her legs crossed, surveyed the group nostalgically, aware that her role as translator expired that very night.

Suzi and I had developed a list of critical considerations. No physical manipulation. Stimulate his hands, rather than compete with his "isms." Allow him to cry, without necessarily feeling the need to respond. Work on pronouns. If Robertito becomes restless, break the session with physical activity. Ease off if he displays constant resistance to participation. Ask for what you want without being overbearing. At all times, follow his cues; imitate him. If he becomes more consistent in toilet training, space out scheduled visits. Be flexible. Try to remember to keep language simple. No fast or abrupt physical movements, which apparently frighten him. Help him develop more self-help skills: washing, dressing, brushing his teeth...except feeding, which could remain as a joint activity and an arena for eye contact. The point of all the games is not to teach him specifics as

278

much as to give us vehicles for more contact, hopefully to stimulate his motivation to learn even more.

"But the most important item on this list is the last one and that's...trust yourselves. As soon as we leave, everything we've said tonight or any other night no longer counts if you think differently." I peered into each person's eyes. Francisca and Carol looked surprised. Laura grinned and rocked her head up and down. Rita eyed me curiously, as did Roby and Lisa. "In effect, this is what we think and know now, but the world for Robertito might change next Monday; therefore, this list or portions of it would no longer be applicable. These are not rules, only guides. If there's anything we could leave you with, it's that you will know better on Monday than we could ever know now."

"I know we've gone the circle a thousand times," Suzi said, "but this is a very special opportunity for all of you." She paused, allowing Amalia to translate. "For Francisca and Roby, it's a practice run. One day they'll return to Mexico and be on their own."

"Laura's the old-timer of the group," Suzi said, "so we've asked her, with Francisca, to define areas of concentration each week."

"What happens if we have questions about where to go next, say with one of the items you just discussed?" Carol asked.

"Let's go back to the question of attitude and trust," I suggested. "If you act out of fear or discomfort or if you think about what Bears or Suzi might have done, then in all those instances, you won't be there to see what you can do."

"If you're not," Rita interjected, "and you want a session or some input...anything, you call me. Okay?" Amalia translated her words into Spanish. Everyone nodded.

"*Gracias. Muchas gracias,*" Francisca said, genuinely touched by the offer.

"Nothing matters but being there with him from moment to moment, being happy and deciding for yourselves," I continued. "And I mean that to an extreme. For example, if we suggest not to respond to his crying, especially since he's developing effective language, but you decide, for reasons we can't foresee now, that it would be more productive to respond to crying, then do it. We talked about no fast, startling movements around Robertito so we don't scare him. But if all of you decided it would be good to frighten him"—I smiled mischievously—"then do it!"

Laura screamed her delight as everyone became consumed with laughter. Suzi's deep, bellowing cackle dwarfed the hysterics. Even Francisca and Roby, who at one time maintained only the most serious attitude during our meetings, allowed a loose response to the humor.

"Bears," Roby said, "maybe we frighten him all the time." More laughter.

"Far out," Laura chimed, admiring Roby's infectious comfort with his son's autism.

"Laura would remember," Suzi volunteered. "When we worked with Raun, we would get together each night with Nancy, Maire and the others to discuss the work sessions...only, sometimes, we'd have contests. Who would give the most convincing portrait of Raun? We'd all imitate him and laugh at our impersonations...kind of a release, a freedom, a special way to love him. And nothing was more important in the world to me than helping my son. Bears and I used to talk about the silliness. We thought other people wouldn't understand. I've seen teachers and therapists mimic their clients and students as a way to belittle them and give vent to their contempt. We love Robertito. Our spoofs and laughter could never diminish that."

Carol pointed at Roby. "Perfect," she whispered. Everyone turned to see Robertito's father side-glancing and twirling his fingers beside his head. Applause and cheers greeted his momentary performance. Roby blushed. Only Francisca appeared a bit reserved at his action.

"What do we do about his increasing echolalia?" Francisca asked next.

"Yeah," Laura said, "he repeats everything now. Every time I ask him something, he repeats most of my question...to the letter, including the way I say it."

"Usually, people see echolalia as one of the gruesome symptoms of autism," I noted. "But I think it's wonderful. We've arrived at another plateau and not a strange one at that. We've all been echolalic at times. In how many instances have I repeated a question, saying it to make it clearer in my mind? In some cases, trying to determine what to do about the question."

"One thing you might try, which we've found effective," Suzi interjected, "is to say the question and if he repeats it, then give him the answer. After all, right now, he's doing what he learned to do...imitate. Now we have to teach him

280

there's an answer to our questions." She demonstrated with diverse examples.

"How does everyone feel about guiding the program yourselves?" I asked.

Francisca's face quivered. If we could have left clones of ourselves with her, we would have. She was trying so hard. "I feel...uh, more sure of myself now than when we tried to do it two years ago in Mexico."

"Here! Here!" Laura shouted, whistling as if at a rock concert, her two fingers shoved between her lips. Carol, following her cue, clapped.

Francisca's face flushed as she acknowledged their support. "I am more relaxed, also. I hope I make less judgments." She glanced at me, then looked at each person gathered in the room. Her eyes filled with tears. Nervously, she flattened her hair against her head. "I can't begin to tell you what this has meant to me and Roby." A hushed quiet blanketed the room for almost a full minute. Suzi took Francisca's hands; Roby stroked her back.

"I'll go next," Carol finally offered. "I feel strong in myself. We'll do it, I know we will. Only I'm going to miss my sessions. That's a very special time for me each week."

"The same for me," Roby said.

"Me, too," Francisca concurred.

Laura stretched her body across the floor and assumed a yoga cobra position. "Me. I feel perfect." Using my bare foot, I pushed her over. She giggled mischievously. "Seriously, I feel more me than ever before in my life. We'll make it. We'll do just fine."

"And I have all of them," Lisa added, spreading her arms like an evangelist, "all these teachers."

"You're doing beautifully," Francisca said, smiling at Lisa and trying heroically to regain her composure. "I can't believe how fast Robertito has taken to you." Lisa smiled self-consciously.

"And don't be afraid to say what you see and feel," I said. "The gift is sharing with someone else what you think is the truth, whether it is or not. In either case, someone learns."

"Feed-back is crucial," Suzi added, "especially notes on attitudes."

"Bears, I really don't want to work with Robertito until I've finished reading the other Option books and observe a lot," Chella said, adjusting her body position.

"When you think you're ready, you can start. It's up to you

to decide," I replied. "The most important aspect is your attitude toward yourself as you enter the room. If you're loving and accepting, then what you do will come naturally...it won't be something you had to rehearse."

"If anyone feels he or she has personal things which might be getting in the way of working with Robertito," Suzi commented, "talk to someone in the group...or to Rita, of course."

"Don't be afraid to ask questions," I added, corralling the hundreds of last-minute thoughts circulating in my head. "If you're not judgmental when you're asking the questions, they become acts of love." I paused. "And speaking of an act of love. Amalia, tell Roby if he has an accident with our Jeep over the summer, we'll break his legs." Everyone laughed. "Any more questions before we review this week's observations?"

Carol raised her hand and smirked, camouflaging a genuine concern. "Yep, I have a question. Do you have to go away?"

Chapter 19

They all cared just as intensely during the summer as during the previous months in which Suzi and I participated. Everyone still wanted the best for Robertito Soto. They still wanted the best for themselves. And yet, almost without anyone noticing at first, the euphoria of the first week deflated. The program tottered on good will until good will was simply not enough. The mechanics remained intact, but something less visible and more insidious eventually contaminated the program. The slide engulfed everyone; most of all our little friend and his parents, who, instead of embracing more of their dreams, found themselves witnessing the birth of a nightmare.

Notes, letters and progress sheets revealed pieces of a jagged puzzle, but the most telling commentaries came from the tapes of the Wednesday night sessions. As planned, Carol and Laura shared our home, enabling them to be within a five-minute drive of the Soto house. Everyone helped in the continued training of Lisa as well as the more intense orientation of Chella, with whom Francisca assumed the dominant role as instructor and mentor. My brother and Rita called and visited periodically.

Francisca directed the flow of the first Wednesday night conference, using weekly data sheets as her guide for listening and discussing the specifics of her son's behavior and progress. Although she learned to temper her comments with a smile, her loud and authoritative voice rippled across the tape with unabashed regularity. Laura counterbalanced the dominance of facts. She exerted a significant teaching influence by asking questions and relating symbolic examples. Carol resisted a major role initially, though she expressed her ideas confidently to the group. Her input increased from week to week. Chella added her own comments frequently to those she translated. And Lisa, Suzi's summer replacement, sometimes expressed herself in a surprisingly incisive, yet wispy and meek, voice. Although people crisscrossed their comments and interrupted each other, everyone became quiet when Roby Soto talked. His soft energy and infrequent statements always commanded attention.

Robertito's excellent eye contact during the week excited everyone. Nevertheless, Laura suggested the introduction of a table and chairs to further his visual participation. Referring to her work with Raun, she illustrated the dynamics of having the student on the chair and the teacher-therapist on the floor, enabling faces and eyes to be on the same level. The group agreed immediately to implement the suggestion.

Francisca and Carol noted Robertito's deepened concentration on watching their lips as they talked. They would mouth the first letter of a word silently and Robertito would complete it. Inattentiveness, not lack of memory, compromised his ability to expand his vocabulary, Laura observed. "But that's not typical. I can't begin to tell you guys how far out it was for me to observe this week. Wow, does that little fat-cheeked boy want to be here with us and does he want to talk! He looks right into everyone's eyes and watches. God, how he tries to talk!" She whistled as the best expression of her own amazement.

Chella, after sharing her experience about Robertito lying in her lap spontaneously, translated the Sotos' joint observation of their son's more consistent verbal indications to use the toilet.

Each time someone raised a question, Francisca repeated it. Roby eyed his wife curiously, finally announcing to the group that she might be exhibiting the first signs of echolalia.

Everyone laughed. Francisca hugged her husband and snickered.

The introduction of the next subject came hesitantly. Lisa noticed that toward the end of the week, her little student made noiseless cryfaces and pulled her hair in response to his own hunger. "I think he's experimenting," she giggled. Everyone mentioned experiencing the same phenomenon, but no one corrected Robertito or demonstrated to him a more effective way to express his wants. Only Francisca had dared to explore an alternative by pulling his hair gently in return. At first, Robertito appeared surprised, but then he grabbed her hair again and tugged on it. Embarrassed by her own actions, she laughed at her son's retaliation.

"I know he doesn't want to hurt anyone," Laura insisted, questioning whether laughter and/or no response was being supportive of his behavior.

Lisa raised her hand. "Um, sometimes I get a little lost as to what to do next."

"It's funny," Laura responded eagerly. "But when I put my trust in Robertito and know he's going to lead me, there's none of that. I don't become anxious or say to myself, holy shit, I have four hours—how am I going to keep going and know what to do? When I just go with him, I never get anxious or confused."

"*Exactamente,*" Francisca concurred, her eyes aimed unflinchingly at Lisa.

Carol coughed before she spoke, trying to ignore her own hidden pressure to see Robertito advance. "Sometimes, I get this feeling like I'd love to be able to turn on the switch in him...like he's standing at the gates, ready to go."

"What am I lacking to turn on that switch?" Francisca blurted.

Both Laura and Carol were surprised by her comment and insisted that she, like all of them, did the best she could.

"It's his choice," Carol affirmed. "He does it, he flips the switch, not us."

"Yes," Laura said, "it's his decision, not ours."

Although the question received a direct and insightful response, no one, in the immediacy of that moment, dealt with the touch of anxiousness in Francisca's voice or the implicit blame she appeared willing to direct at herself. In an effort to neutralize her own mild discomfort, she talked about her son's hugging her. "He doesn't want to work; he wants love!" She nodded her head as the others in the group

285

smiled sympathetically. Francisca was "Mama," a fact everyone always remembered.

The slight escalation of "isms" since our departure tapped everyone's concern. "I was upset for a while about him being so 'ismy' this week," Laura shared. "But then I said, 'Hey, Rha-Rha, do you have expectations?' And I did...a little. I sorta figured he'd keep moving in the same direction...more participation and less 'isms.' Then I remembered what I knew. Robertito's taking care of himself and that's okay with me. Really! It's okay."

"Yeah, right on," Carol cheered. Francisca and Roby listened carefully to Chella's translation, but did not comment.

When the conversation shifted to diet, Francisca cut Lisa off three times in her overanxiousness and trampled one of Roby's thoughts with her own monologue. Francisca talked about the decision to use multiple selection of food, which allowed Robertito to verbalize his preferences. Roby, less enthusiastic, questioned the burgeoning accent on food. "He worked hours with me today without food." What had been originally an intermittent support of some work sessions had become, in the last week, more fundamentally entwined with much of the interaction. Francisca said that although Robertito certainly worked and participated without food, his attentiveness heightened when food was in the room. But in spite of her own observations, she wanted to keep food out of the room so her son would not become dependent on it.

"Keep it out of the room as long as you feel comfortable doing that," Laura suggested. "I agree, let's try to change his focus off eating and back to us."

At the end of the meeting, Laura itemized points to accent for the following week, which included talking slowly, encouraging spontaneous answers, increasing sensitivity to bathroom indications and practicing consonant sounds.

The second Wednesday night session after our departure was more sedate than the group's first solo meeting. Although Laura did not hypothesize a rationale, she noted Robertito's increased crying. She had not responded or supported him, recalling the suggestion Suzi and I offered before the summer. When she turned away, telling him it was okay to cry, he stopped. Each person then related his or her experiences with Robertito's developing tantrums.

To further encourage toilet training, they had instituted a small food reward each time he urinated or defecated in the appropriate place. His indications for the bathroom increased markedly. Robertito no longer wet his pants as he urinated tiny amounts in the toilet, then asked for food abruptly. Either he pushed the last drops out of his bladder or held back in order to increase his frequency. In any case, his ability to understand and anticipate the actions of others had mushroomed.

Francisca focused on his listless pacing, concerned about his increasing desire to stand or sit in the corner, which she labeled as unproductive.

"While he's in the corner, I work with him," Carol volunteered.

"Good. Nothing is really unproductive," Laura said awkwardly, uncomfortable about contradicting Francisca. "We just have to find a way to use it, like Carol did. Also, as you all might have noticed, Robertito is getting more sensuous. Those are real first-class kisses he gives now." Everyone laughed.

Lisa mentioned his decreased hair-pulling since she no longer supported it with laughter and expressed her wants.

"His crying is still of great concern," Roby said, returning to their original discussion. "He cried for one whole hour during a session with me." Unlike Laura's experience, Robertito kept crying when his father had expressed his love, turned his back and offered to wait until he finished. Chella confirmed Roby's experience, which she had observed. She also mentioned that Robertito had asked for "Sushi" several times this week, a fact greeted with "ahs!" He had remembered. Even after two weeks, he retained and withdrew information from his recently awakened mind. Most significantly, our little friend had formed an emotional attachment to another person—an attachment strong enough to trigger his recall.

The behavior of observers became the next central issue at the meeting.

Chella, who had worked in tandem and alone for short periods, felt stifled not only by repeated interruptions but by Francisca's insistence that she pattern her teaching in a certain prescribed cadence. In effect, Francisca's push for uniformity, squashed Chella's freedom to develop her own style and curtailed her initiative. Chella did not talk to Francisca, but, instead, shared her discomfort with Laura and Carol, who had, themselves, experienced the same pressure. Francisca had interrupted their sessions by correcting pronunciations and instructing about the use of some of the teaching tools.

"The observer shouldn't talk," Laura counseled. "I think that distracts and confuses Robertito as well as his teacher." She decided to couch her suggestion in the abstract, discreetly avoiding any criticism or confrontation with Francisca. After all, she's the mother, Laura repeated to herself. And so the concept of mother and the beliefs about the vulnerability of motherhood began slowly to short-circuit the easy, steady flow of communication between members of the group.

"Everyone works differently," Laura continued. "Each of us has to trust the other. We want to share with Robertito, teach him to relate to all different people. We should, really, trust each other. We're here to allow each person his or her own individuality and that's something special we want for Robertito as well."

"I've really learned this week," Lisa interjected. "He, he likes to do different things with different people. It's all okay. I feel like a little kid with him." Lisa looked at Francisca, who had questioned the quality of her participation. "Maybe, because of my size, he sees me as just another kid to play with. We jump, roll and tumble...that's me. After talking to Carol and Laura, I realized it was okay...to be me." She stared down at the floor. "Everyone is different. I don't have to do what someone else does. I just have to be me with a loving and accepting attitude." Everyone agreed.

When Chella's translated Lisa's statement, Francisca concurred enthusiastically. "Yes. Everyone is different. And the most important part is the attitude." Laura listened to her words, dumbfounded.

Carol initiated the next subject; Robertito's decreased participation. "He knows if you want him to do something. You feel it in yourself. Bears always talked about being emphatic about our requests, expressing our wants without pushing. He can always say no or turn away. Maybe, well maybe, we're backing off in some way, like getting into what this means and what that means instead of just being there."

"It's far out," Laura added. "He's a mirror. He hears what you really say. You know, like when you tell someone 'oh no, I'm not angry' when you are. Robertito knows; he hears the real part and he reflects where you're really at. If you don't mean it, he'll know that, too."

A long silence met her remark. Finally, Francisca changed the subject, asking the others not to work her son in the bathroom. "Let's keep him aware of what the bathroom is for."

"That bathroom's no different than any other room," Carol countered. "The problem is the food, feeding him as a reward for making. He's getting mechanized."

The group discussed the point for an extended period without consensus. Finally, Roby suggested limited use of food in the bathroom. Everyone concurred.

Itemizing each of Robertito's accomplishments with pride, Francisca described how her son learned to draw a straight line, a circle, a cross and even erase this week. She had everyone write down the questions he now understood: what is this? where is it? and what do you want? Francisca confined herself to pragmatic and functional concerns. We have to move him along, she kept thinking, wanting to continue the pace of the first three months. She felt a certain pressure to substantiate her ability as a directing force. Slowly, she began to see Robertito's actions as a reflection of her own worth.

Carol reiterated the concept of working for extended periods without food, except for meals. Francisca, skeptical, supported food as another facilitator.

"A lot of time, we do physical play and contact. I love it without food—no bribes," Lisa said.

"Hey," Laura countered, "it's not a bribe. Nobody's pressuring him or coercing him or doing anything to anyone's detriment. Robertito's free to accept our offers or not. That's a trade, just like people who work for a salary. The money is not a bribe; it's what they're willing to work for; it's their trade. I get something. You get something. That's the principle. Hopefully, we both get what we want."

"*Exactamente*," Francisca said emphatically. She then highlighted her son's increased ability with self-help skills— assisting in pulling his shirt down and his pants up. "Don't you get the feeling he's proud, so proud of himself afterwards?" She tossed her hair off her forehead and held her chin out.

Carol tapped her and said: "You have a very sexy son."

Applause greeted her comment. Roby laughed as did Francisca.

The third Wednesday night meeting reflected more than merely the changes in Robertito's behavior; it illuminated each person's response to those changes. The frequency of "isms" escalated, occupying major segments of some days. Robertito no longer slept through the night. Crying became a sustained ritual, fracturing most of his sessions. Was he trying to manipulate them? Had he elevated hysterics to an "ism"? They toyed with the questions, but found no answers. Although they explored what they observed, they did not probe their own actions and responses.

For the first hour, they avoided facing the dilemma.

They discussed the introduction of more difficult puzzles and elementary lotto games, which he mastered easily when attentive. But his participation had ebbed.

With great pride, Francisca talked about how her son rose one morning and said "Pee-pee" spontaneously. But Roby, concerned with the frequency of Robertito's bathroom visits, clocked eighty-eight times in the bathroom. Again, the use of a food reward was questioned, but never resolved.

"Before I took Robertito to the restroom," his father said, "he indicated 'pee-pee' first. When I got up and went to the door, Robertito stopped and watched me. He looked at me and then at the food still on the floor, then back to me again as if to say: 'Hey, why aren't you bringing the food?'" Everyone laughed.

"Ah, he knows," Carol whispered aloud.

"Listen, folks," Laura said, "I use physical play as a trade."

"Perhaps, because of his crying, we should get him out of the room," Francisca said. "Maybe he doesn't want to be there all the time. He wanted to go downstairs on Monday and got very upset and cried when he couldn't."

Laura cautioned about teaching him to manipulate by crying and screaming. "All we have to do is respond. Then, like we taught him to talk, we'll teach him to cry. I observed some of us backing off when he cried and then doing what he wanted. We want to go with him, not only on terms he feels comfortable with, but on terms we feel comfortable with too."

Carol believed the crying had to be supported as an explanation of its very existence. The others agreed, with the exception of Francisca, who listened without betraying her thoughts.

The morale of the group tumbled during the fourth week. Robertito slipped more into himself, crying and screaming much of the time. The resurgence of "eee-o" and "boy-o" vocal "isms" obliterated much of his talking. He wanted to go to the bathroom every two to three minutes, often yelling and banging his foot on the floor if no one responded. Their tactic of telling him "later" did not neutralize the problem. In effect,
290

he wanted the food, often to the exclusion of other supports such as hugging, wrestling and tickling. Francicsa thought his bathroom indication had become an "ism," but Carol insisted her son used it to manipulate for food.

Laura, lacking her usual enthusiasm, shook her head. "At times, I couldn't even reach him...for long periods of time."

Carol, Chella and Lisa had the same experience. Roby nodded his head knowingly. "He's getting hyper," Francisca said, trying not to draw the inevitable parallels between the participants. Laura felt disconnected, annoyed with herself for not participating more in discussions, annoyed with Francisca's excessive talking and annoyed with Robertito for his behavior. Are we losing him? Carol thought to herself. Is it all a mirage? The sardonic, skeptical words of her neurologist echoed in her ears. "Do you expect to cure the incurable?" She also noticed a slight increase in the frequency of her own seizures.

Lisa tried to make the meeting fun. It had always been fun before, but now, with growing difficulties and obvious disagreements, she felt pressed and pushed. Francisca intimidated her even more. Both she and Chella struggled to find their own centers. Though their attitude of acceptance became a major strategy for the work sessions with Robertito, their discomfort in being observed and in dealing with Robertito's crying sabotaged the tactic. The mood even touched Roby, whose optimism faded.

"Most of the days with him this week have been 'bad'!" he said, his head downcast.

"Yes, it is true," Francisca affirmed. "He spends most of the time within himself. This week," she noted sadly from her chart, "Robertito indicated 'pee-pee' one hundred and twenty-three times."

"But he urinates each time," Chella said.

"Then he's not faking," Laura observed.

"Maybe he's holding it in," said Carol.

"Bears and Suzi talked about surprising him if we wanted to use food," Laura said. "Every once in a while and then maybe not at all. Our affection, our clapping, our hugs...that all counts for something. I say no more food in the bathroom."

Francisca spoke in an unusually deep and raspy voice. The muscles in her neck tensed. "Then he won't be toilet trained." Nobody responded. Carol viewed toilet training as secondary to communicating and interaction, but withheld her thought. Francisca's comment annoyed Laura. Who cares whether he

291

shits in the toilet, she mumbled to herself. We're losing him. Can't you see? Whoa, Rha-Rha, let's get your act together. Laura tried to contain her growing resentment by remaining silent.

"If he urinates a lot, then feed him a lot," Francisca bellowed.

"Maybe he has a bladder infection," Roby suggested. No one answered.

"How about only rewarding his big 'pees,'" Carol countered. Everyone agreed easily with the compromise. "Great, now what about the food?" she asked. "He's getting so angry and frustrated. That's all he asks for lately. When I offer something else or say 'later,' he walks away screaming and pounding his hands on the floor and walls. His anger scares me."

For the first time, someone had verbalized what they all secretly dreaded but had not expressed. Our calm, peaceful little friend had begun to act in a manner typical of the anger and aggressiveness documented in some other autistic children. No one wanted to lose him to violence and unhappiness.

"Wait," Roby cautioned. "I don't think it's all bad. Robertito knows what he wants. He just doesn't know an effective way to express it."

"I don't know if that's all of it. Yesterday morning, he cried for hours without asking for food," Chella said.

"Maybe he has a stomach virus?" Francisca suggested.

"Or he's cutting teeth," Lisa observed.

The decision to have Robertito checked by a doctor was made. Nevertheless, even though colds and viruses affected the child, he never exhibited the kinds of responses they had witnessed in the last several weeks.

"He never smiles any more. Always straight-faced and angry," Carol confirmed. "Anybody have any ideas about why?" Silence. She did not want to share her fears with them. Was Robertito rejecting her and the others? Would the anger explode in some unspeakable act? If she dared to verbalize her thoughts, would they suddenly become true?

"Even when he's not crying, he wasn't so good this week," Laura volunteered. "I called him sixteen times one morning and he could care less." Deflated and hardened by his contrariness, she added: "The only thing he was into this week was his penis."

Francisca agreed. Because of the heat, they had him semi-dressed most of the time. Perhaps, she postulated, his nudity added to his "hyper" state.

"If he touches himself so much, maybe it means he has some sort of irritation," Carol said.

"I don't think that's it," Laura countered. "I think it gives him pleasure, pure and simple."

Aware of the cloud which settled over the group, Roby talked about his son's growing ability to imitate sounds and physical movement when he concentrated. Robertito also imitated head gestures and tone when he learned new words. He also used *más* (more) and *sí* (yes) more often, illustrating his increased ability to abstract and generalize concepts on a simple level.

"When he's there," Laura bellowed, "he's amazing. Only now, well, he's out in space most of the time."

"My little space cadet," Carol laughed.

Francisca looked at her sternly, then forced a half-smile. How could they joke? How could anyone joke at a time like this? She used all her power to hold herself together. She loved these people as deeply as she loved her own family in Mexico, yet she found herself confused and distant as she became more anxious.

The gathering on the fifth Wednesday night began like a wake. Greetings were subdued. The stress of the past week had taken its toll in joy and laughter. Roby and Francisca watched their son cross a dreaded line. Carol clutched at the sparse signs of hope amid the jungle of foreboding indicators. The softness eluded Laura once again. The more Robertito removed himself, the more difficulty she had caring. Even Lisa and Chella were overwhelmed by the seemingly inevitable turn of events. Only Rita, whose presence had been requested by the Sotos, seemed unscathed by her observations.

"As a result of less food in the bathroom, he's wetting his pants again," Carol began, refusing to tackle the larger issue.

"I don't think he has to be wearing diapers any more," Rita said. "If he wets training pants, he'll feel it and probably not like it. I think it's time to graduate him from diapers."

Roby agreed. He, too, believed his son did not find wet diapers uncomfortable.

Francisca cut into her husband's last sentence. They must go to the heart of the matter quickly. Robertito had begun to hit and pinch himself. Small welts and black-and-blue marks began to be visible all over his body. Although the chest-banging and chin-hitting recalled old "isms," the intensity spilled the activity into an almost unspeakable category. Francisca and Roby remembered the institutionalized children tied to chairs, wearing football helmets and soft boxing gloves. Vivid portraits of Robertito being restrained haunted them. No. Not Robertito, Francisca pleaded silently. Please, God, not my child. She'd give anything, even her life in trade. A sharp pain whipped from the base of her head down her back, distracting her from her waking nightmare. Her son had begun to exhibit signs professionals might catalogue as self-destructive. She stuttered over the word. It dropped like lead from her mouth. She wanted to scream. What happened? Tell me why? Francisca had watched him soar for over three months, only to witness his dramatic decline during the summer. How cruel the universe, she thought. How cruel! But somewhere, not far beneath the surface of her thoughts, she knew nothing was inevitable, neither his rise nor his fall.

"I think it's self-stimulation," Lisa said innocently.

"Me, too," Laura agreed, not out of conviction, but in an attempt to shelter Francisca and Roby.

"When I asked him to play the number game with me," Francisca said, "he pinched himself immediately, then slammed his chin so hard I thought he'd break his jaw." Chella translated her words meticulously. If it had been her sister, Martha, she couldn't begin to imagine her own response. Despite Francisca's pushing, she found herself admiring this lady's courage and being more accepting of her imperfections.

Rita had observed for the past two days. She found it peculiar and noteworthy that Robertito's actions did not necessarily originate with anger. At times, he participated on a minimal basis while pinching himself or crying.

"Yeah," Laura substantiated. "The crying is weird sometimes. Almost like a call for help. But I don't know what he's saying."

"Maybe he thinks that's what he's supposed to be doing," Carol offered as she shrugged her shoulders. "But you know, when he's into his 'isms,' he's really into it now. It's no longer a game. Like when he paces, you can't reach him. It's so hard to attract him."

Laura laughed uncomfortably and joked. "He hates me."

"Then why does he say Rha-Rha all the time?" Lisa countered.

"Is that the issue?" Rita asked.

"But he's a different person," Laura insisted.

"Even so," Rita replied, "are we seeing Robertito clearly?"

Laura turned away. " I know it's getting to me," she admitted.

"Well, that's a start," Rita said, smiling.

"Me too," Carol confessed. "It's been the longest period he's been like this. He cries two out of three hours with me and then pinches or hits himself. Sometimes I get dizzy watching him. Where'd that soft, gentle human being go?"

"He's still there," Roby declared. The intensity of his voice startled everybody. He would never abandon his child, not even in his thoughts. "I remember reading in *Son-Rise* Bears's comment on how the doctors labeled the children without ever looking at their own methods or attitude. Perhaps that is what we have to do."

"Exactly," Rita agreed. "I observed Francisca, who's a wonderful teacher, offering a choice between milk and cereal. Robertito cried immediately. And she gave him the cereal immediately. In Robertito's eyes, it means, if he cries, he'll get what he wants, possibly faster than if he asks for it. Without being aware of it, parents often teach their children to respond that way. Laura explained to me that you offer him different foods so he can show his preference. That's one way to do it, but I wouldn't use food. I'd use toys or something else."

"Why not food?" Francisca asked.

"Food becomes an issue with children...a bargaining issue. If they stop eating, it's not the same as if they stop playing. It's loaded. Food is always a loaded issue," Rita said. "I work with a child that uses food all the time to control his parents. Now that's not an autistic child, but I think there are parallels. It's a power play. So I'd keep away from the food issue."

"But how do I get him to eat certain foods?" Francisca asked Rita.

"You want to be with him where he is. The whole idea of Option is not to make him do what you want, but to be where he is. And if he's not wanting it, why force him?"

"Then if certain foods upset him, let's get rid of those foods," Carol said. Everyone agreed with the exception of Roby, who questioned the logic.

"Tell Francisca and Roby not to be bothered by the crying and hitting," Laura said to Chella, motioning her to translate her thoughts. "Tell them he's trying to express what he wants."

Rita's presence had sedated the escalating panic, but had not defused it. When Carol suggested increasing the cheering, the hugging, the clapping and the wrestling as supports for his behavior, Francisca voiced her fear that perhaps her son would be disappointed and, therefore, increase his radical behavior.

"Is it okay if he cries or 'isms' if he doesn't get food?" Laura asked.

"Yes," Francisca replied weakly. "If that's what he wants to do."

"Let's stay in touch with having him relate to us," Carol said. "What he does or accomplishes doesn't matter."

"Well," Lisa said, "I laid with him on the pillow and when Francisca walked in, she said 'Ah, no work.'"

Rita addressed the group. "Maybe you want to ease up on the concept of work." Francisca nodded after Chella interpreted her words.

"Bears and Suzi always talk about loving contact and stimulating Robertito's own motivation," Laura recalled. "We've been accenting achievement. Who cares? That's not important. Right?" She looked to Rita for confirmation, which she received.

The suggestion was made to take Robertito outside for periodic breaks.

"Let's not take him outside until Bears gets back," Francisca snapped. Roby agreed.

"Why not?" Rita asked.

"What happens if he gets hyper?" Francisca questioned.

"Well, of course, then take him back to the room," Rita replied.

"Bears and Suzi said he would just get into his own world outside. They said they didn't want him outside," Francisca said.

"But Bears also told us the most important thing," Carol countered, "was to trust ourselves when they were gone." An awkward silence blanketed the room.

"It's up to you," Rita said. "Perhaps breaks from the session would have a positive effect. And I also thought you might want to get him new toys. But above all, don't push him."

"Can he lie on his bed if he wants?" Lisa asked, directing her question to Rita.

"Of course. Yeah!" Laura interjected.

"Well, all I hear about is that he's not working," she retorted, avoiding Francisca's eyes and non-verbally soliciting Rita's support.

"I feel as if I dropped in from another planet," Rita said cautiously. "I don't want to rock the boat."

"You've said a lot of things we haven't been considering," Carol countered.

"We need an outside inspiration," Laura said.

"You're a wonderful person," Francisca affirmed, ever grateful for her presence. "Just having you here has made a difference."

Though the pinching and the hitting had not been directly dealt with, everyone assumed that if Robertito was happier, as before, those behaviors would disappear.

After Rita left, the hard, fact-facing conversations continued until Laura broke the prevailing mood with a story. "Robertito was behind the shower curtain in the bath. I kept calling his name over and over again, but he didn't respond. 'Where's Robertito Soto?' I asked. He didn't answer. Then I said, 'Where's the food?' Bam! He whipped the curtain aside and looked at me expectantly." The laughter which followed gave them their first emotional reprieve of the evening.

The meeting ended without definitive revelations. The confusions and fears remained, but the desperateness evaporated for at least a few days. The last week and a half before our return passed slowly. The pinching persisted, though with less intensity. Robertito still slammed his chest and chin. His fingernails, on one occasion, broke the skin on his face and drew blood. "Oh no," Francisca murmured. She covered his chin with trembling hands. "Please, my love, don't do this." His hitting became more insistent. Finally, she grabbed his hands. Robertito squirmed. His eyes opened wide. He pushed against the physical barrier, throwing his head wildly from side to side. A high-pitched whine bellowed from his larynx. Francisca released him. "I'm sorry, Robertito. I'm sorry." She knew she had violated his universe. But this was her son! How could she watch her son hurt himself? Robertito withdrew to a corner of the room and slammed his chin with the side of his hand while rocking and humming "Old MacDonald Had a Farm." The anger in his face disappeared within seconds. Francisca stared at the blankness in her son's eyes, trying to ignore his swinging arm. "Please come back," she begged him. That very morning, for a fleeting half-hour, he had identified animals in the picture books and had retrieved

297

a series of toys on request. Robertito had left at least one door ajar.

Francisca packed a towel under his shirt and protected his chin with a pile of Band-Aids. He adjusted to the padding by banging other parts of his body. Seemingly angry hands signaled an angry protest. And yet, oftentimes, they moved more abstractly in a mechanical and habitual fashion as if programmed like his other "isms." Francisca considered putting grease on his body to prevent the pinching, but, instead, she increased her massages and requested everyone else to do the same. Some of the apparently self-injurious behaviors declined.

The scheduled breaks in the sessions had a positive effect for the first two or three outings. In the park, Robertito watched other children, stared at airplanes passing overhead and touched the leaves and flowers in his path. He studied his shadow on the ground, ran up and down the parking lot, then lost interest. Those big expressive eyes dulled. He moved mechanically like a toy soldier. He seldom smiled.

The awesome calm had been replaced by a hollowness, an emptiness evident in his glazed eyes. While salvaging the child who particiated on a very limited basis, they had lost the happy, smiling and self-motivated little Buddha that had once greeted us joyfully each morning.

Chapter 20

During the first day of our return, Suzi and I dashed over to the Soto house excited to see where, if anywhere, our small friend had traveled in our absence. But how do we take someone else into the room with us to watch this little boy and see him as we did that day? How do we tell another person the truth of what we felt without being accused of heartlessness? We did not weep for Robertito Soto as he slammed his chest unrelentingly with a stiffened hand. The little fingers that pinched his skin until welts appeared neither offended nor unnerved us. We watched him spellbound, trying to reconcile the idyllic imagery we retained through the summer and the obvious reality before us. Where were the gentle eyes which stared so studiously at our lips? Where were the soft fingers which scratched our arms in tender displays of affection? The happy, peaceful child had disappeared behind blank eyes and a straight-faced veneer. His alert and blossoming mind had closed down the circuitry; perhaps, in order to facilitate a slide inward. But why?

At the very moments he tried to return to the autistic womb, he kept part of himself available to us. He demonstrated some triumphs of the early summer such as counting, piecing three puzzles simultaneously and playing lotto games; but his actions were mechanical. Even his infrequent use of language had a programmed duality as if he had put himself on automatic pilot in order to free himself to search for the path back. The old "isms" no longer worked. He had come out too far, crossed too many bridges. He needed something more dramatic, more overwhelming. The body contact and the pounding on his chest or chin dazzled the whole constellation of his sensory apparatus more emphatically than mere hand-flapping or finger twirling. He saw it; he felt it; he listened to the thuds.

The literature would damn his actions as self-destructive, as if Robertito's intent was to hurt or maim himself. No. Not here, not in this instance...perhaps nowhere does a child mean to hurt himself. More vulnerable than ever before, Robertito Soto had to find a more commanding self-stimulating ritual to re-establish his own equilibrium and protective shield. We also noted a dramatic resurgence of toewalking and an emphasis on balancing himself as if he had lost his sense of comfort and grounding in our environment.

Francisca cringed and Roby winced at their son's behavior. Laura, Carol and the others talked about his sad and disturbing conduct. Somehow, those judgments kept them separate from Robertito. We wanted to bring him closer, to reaffirm our commitment to him, to communicate that all of us still wanted to accept him unconditionally.

"If this is what you want now, Tito, it's okay with us. Just help us understand why." He never acknowledged my words or our presence.

After observing for days, we saw that everyone had seemingly continued within the context of our method. The mechanics or techniques had survived the summer. They still imitated most of his "isms" with the exception of those they judged self-injurious. They still cheered his accomplishments, followed his cues and instructed him in a caring manner. But those were details of a skeleton rather than revelations of the heart. Francisca, obviously shaken by his so-called self-destructive behaviors, fed him when he cried and screamed, supporting the very behavior she dreaded. Chella, who exhibited excellent skills as a teacher, followed her mentor's guidance and delivered food to her student at the onset of a tantrum. Lisa, though loving and sincere, hardly smiled in her sessions...neither did Robertito. He became most hyperactive with Laura, whose body language reflected her impatience with his sluggishness. Roby's own confusion with how to extinguish the hitting resulted in his son's constant drifting and inattentiveness. Carol put him through the paces as he used one hand to stack blocks and the other to pinch himself.

Everyone had clearly set up an invisible barrier which he or she dared not cross. No one followed the cues they assessed as self-abusive or "bad." Their implicit judgments infiltrated their facial expressions and body movements, ultimately creating a passive resistance which Robertito pushed against. What most people would have ignored and others might have dismissed as subtle became significant points for us to note . . . for what we did was less consequential than how we did it. In effect, Suzi and I detected beliefs and fears which had fractured the loving and accepting attitude fundamental to our program.

As we gathered for a group session, an undercurrent surfaced. No one looked at Francisca, who dominated the discussions. The discontentment with themselves and this strong, yet frightened, lady eroded the comradery of our special family. It became apparent during the summer; their input in the sessions with Robertito had reflected that strain. The private, intimate tensions had seeped into the teaching room. When Robertito responded with sluggishness or crying, they became more unsettled, which, in turn, began to splinter the walls of a safe, loving, accepting and non-judgmental environment. The first emergence of hitting or pinching was met with panic, which further subverted their attitude. Those changes could have sent Robertito scurrying back across the bridges to the safety of his own internal Shangri-la. He had committed himself, in part, to exploring our world and found himself standing precariously with one foot on home plate and the other in the bleachers. Any inclination he might have to disconnect and withdraw to his secluded, autistic cocoon required more energy and perseverance than ever before.

As a result of mini-dialogue sessions, each person became more willing to confront the events of the summer, even in the presence of the others. Their scattered conversations created a telling portrait.

"The attitude, the whole feeling, makes it work," Laura said, "so without it during the summer, I just didn't want to be there any more."

"I could never have made it through another week," Francisca shared nervously.

"I know it doesn't matter what you do, but where you're coming from," Lisa said, "and I couldn't have been coming from a wonderful place when I was uptight all the time about Francisca interrupting my sessions with Robertito."

"I love that lady so much," Laura interceded, "but sometimes I wonder if she'll ever make it for herself, if she'll ever be able to inspire people."

"But it's our fault too," Carol admitted. "We didn't talk to her because we wanted to protect her . . . but if you really want to know, that wasn't it at all; we weren't willing to put ourselves on the line and be honest."

"We trusted you and Suzi more than ourselves," Roby stated. "We listened to all your suggestions when you left, except the one you said was most important . . . to trust ourselves."

"It's the attitude," Laura concluded. "I know that so clearly now—clearer than ever before. We had everything in the summer, including the best of intentions . . . but that wasn't enough. The one missing ingredient which would have made the difference was individual Option sessions."

"We never cleared our heads," Carol said, "and boy, can I see it now. There's no way we can really help another person until we help ourselves."

After each person had at least one full session, Suzi and I assembled the group again. This time all the participants shared their discomforts completely, without camouflaging their thoughts or feelings. Carol and Laura apologized to Francisca for their silence. Their fears of giving her honest feed-back had not only perpetuated her behavior, but fueled their own anger and discomfort. Chella took responsibility for her own lack of candidness. Lisa hugged Francisca, who admitted tearfully her own panic and distrust in herself and others when she observed, saying that she wanted the best for Robertito. In exposing her vulnerability to all of us, she took another step toward dealing with her insistence on excellence in herself. Somehow, I knew her new-found strength had been bolstered by our presence. Suzi and I wanted her and Roby to feel free, to no longer need to look back at us for direction and insight. For us, the summer reaffirmed that although these caring and sensitive people understood and used all the techniques we championed, they had little chance of accepting and facilitating the rebirth of another human being without first confronting and accepting themselves.

Our first concentration had to be on re-establishing the attitude and dispelling the most diverting fears. I scheduled multiple sessions with each person, concentrating my initial efforts on Francisca. Suzi observed the teaching sessions with Robertito and gave immediate feed-back, often involving herself in discussions which extended past midnight. An evolution of attitude occurred during the first few days as certain beliefs and judgments were confronted and discarded. Others lingered: "Robertito cried because of hunger," "tears meant unhappiness," "only persistent intrusion kept him in contact with us" and "self-destructive was a polite metaphor for suicide." Although we wanted either to substantiate or dissolve such ideas directly with Robertito, Suzi and I directed our prime burst of energy toward the teachers. Without their internal harmony, we had no program.

By the middle of the week, we felt we could finally turn our focus toward our little friend. We wanted to recapture a feeling, a mood, a joy which no longer emanated from him. We wanted to do it now before he drifted outside our reach.

Everyone registered surprise when I canceled all the teaching sessions for an entire day. Suzi and I arrived as Robertito awoke. We dressed him and guided him into the playroom. He appeared somewhat irritable, but the crying which Francisca reported as occurring each morning had not yet happened. Robertito paced the room listlessly and banged his chin. As planned, Suzi and I stretched out on the floor at the side of the room and pretended to fall asleep. Occasionally, we snorted and sighed, trying to duplicate typical sounds he might have heard in his parents' bedroom. Robertito "ismed," sometimes hand-flapping, sometimes hitting his chest emphatically. The more I observed him, the more convinced I was that what the others identified as self-destructive was an intensified version of a self-stimulating ritual. His eyes had that drugged, almost euphoric, faraway look. When he paused, I saw glimmers of that compelling calm in the spaces between the rituals. A softness enveloped his face, an unearthly luminous quality radiated from his bright eyes. I imagined his brain flooded with alpha waves, lifting him onto a soothing energy plateau which so many masters and meditators seek to reach. I stopped myself from rolling over and hugging him. He continually reinforced the closed-circuit system in which he glided. Hey, Tito, I wanted to shout. My hands trembled as I forced myself to hold my position, denying an impulse to stroke him, to mother him, to provide him with safe quarter in the arms of another human being. Let him go, I counseled myself. Let him be where he feels most comfortable.

Perhaps, in their desperation to maintain contact and a learning process during the summer, Francisca, Roby, Carol and the others had pushed him beyond his tolerable limits. When he turned away, they increased their attempts to foster participation. But was that the only alternative? If we left him alone, here and now, would he, could he come to us? Perhaps he believed he had no choice. Perhaps he had felt the tension of his teachers and perceived himself as being forced.

Suzi recognized Robertito's frantic attempt to secure his universe. She had seen this happen before in other children we had helped and in her own son. But something was different here. The awesome intensity of this child's statement seemed to suggest he broke connections in deciding to return to that safe place within. Suzi didn't want to take that from him or block his path, yet she did not want to lose him. We love you wherever you are, sweet boy, she said silently, trying to cross the expanse of the room to nurture him from a distance. Take your time. You decide. With those words, she confirmed the ultimate acceptance for this child she loved, an acceptance she had learned to lavish on her own son, a willingness to let go and to allow him his choice.

We maintained our bogus sleeping positions for over two hours. He neither cried nor indicated for food. The intensity of his "isms" subsided as if he had become bored with his own rituals. He wandered over to the toys, flapped a puzzle piece, hit the xylophone and turned pages in a large picture book without looking at the content. Then Robertito paced the room over a hundred times before dropping to the floor exhausted. He began to hum. I looked over at Suzi. We smiled at each other, recognizing the tune at the same moment. Despite his withdrawal, his hitting himself and his emotional neutrality, he had taken pieces of our world with him. As he rocked in the sheltered cradle of rhythms and rituals, he hummed "London Bridge's falling down."

Another two hours passed. If his stomach didn't register hunger, mine certainly did. Yet, we still did not see any indication for food. From time to time, he stole a glance at us from the corner of his eyes. I wanted to shout, but squelched my excitement. If, indeed, this tiny gesture represented a connection with us, I did not want to destroy it by bombarding him with any input which might overload his circuits. Despite a leg cramp and growing fatigue, we continued our pretense to be sleeping hulks, as safe, stable and inert as the walls of the room. At one point, Suzi actually dozed, then jerked herself awake.

The morning faded into afternoon, then late afternoon. Perhaps I had overestimated our bond with Robertito. I knew if we had left the room at that moment and stopped the program, it would be as if we had never worked with him. Eyes at half-mast. Rituals abounding. No demonstrative human contact. No real statement of intellect. I felt drained, exhausted, as I lay there immobile, bombarded by one thought after another. I did a breathing exercise to quiet my mind.

In the middle of exhaling noisily, I heard footsteps pass by my head. Through tiny slits, I watched our little friend circle Suzi and me as he twirled his fingers. His eyes fixed on his own hands. Each time he passed, he lowered his head slightly, finally allowing himself to see us through the blur of his moving fingers. "¡Hola!" almost bubbled from my throat, but I aborted the impulse: He closed the gap between his path and our bodies. Robertito dropped on his knees by my head. Rather than allow him to see through the charade, I closed my eyes completely. Only his breathing kept me in touch with his presence. I heard his hand tap his chin several times, then stop. Suddenly, I couldn't hear anything. I strained, but nothing penetrated. Was he holding his breath? Had he moved away? Then I felt something so distinct that I held my breath. Little fingers began to pull on my beard. A thumb touched my lips, then withdrew. Seconds later, he pushed his fingers into my mouth and played with my tongue. Welcome home, Robertito Soto. Welcome home.

I remained very still, allowing him to explore my mouth and beard. Then a little boy voice began to sing "Old MacDonald Had a Farm." Suzi's soft voice joined in. I opened my eyes slowly and encountered those huge, dark brown eyes staring directly at me. My face couldn't contain my smile. I, too, joined the chorus. "And on his farm he had some ducks, eee-i, eee-i, o."

He had come to us, crossed the bridge by himself, by his own choice...without coaxing, without coercion. He sat back on Suzi's legs and smiled at her. She put her hands up and nodded. Robertito tapped her palms. Suzi tapped him back as they began to play "patty-cake" together. When he hit his chin, Suzi hit hers. When he slammed his chest, I slammed mine. My thoughts jumped back to the lecture I gave just before the Sotos came to New York. I remembered his criticism of the psychology chairman and his beliefs about established plans to deal with a child's behavior, especially those labeled self-destructive. We could not have known what we would see or do until this very moment. We mimicked him with an intensity and fury beyond his own. He stopped and started several times as if testing our willingness to follow. Those behaviors increased, until, after an hour, they, too, subsided markedly. Later, he joined us in verbal imitation games and played with the lotto cards.

When Francisca arrived with his meal, he cried immediately. I asked her to leave, wait outside until he finished, then return without the food. Robertito stared at her hands as she made her second entrance. He screamed and banged his head with his fist, yet his eyes remained curiously peaceful. Again, Francisca left. When the crying decreased, I brought the food into the room again and placed it on a high shelf. Robertito watched me and whined, finally resorting to kicking his feet and crying. An expression of hunger? Signs of unhappiness?

"If you want to cry, that's okay with us," Suzi told him. "When you're finished, let us know," she said softly in Spanish.

We sat together, faced away from Robertito and waited. He kept his tantrum going for almost half an hour. I heard a cough from the other side of the door, knowing that Francisca remained in the hall listening, wanting to help but also torn by an impulse to charge into the room and feed her son. All she knew was that her son sounded unhappy. His wanting triggered every motherly instinct in her. I wanted to see him through her eyes, but then he fractured my concentration when he stopped crying completely and looked quizzically and peacefully out the window for several minutes. He started sobbing again and, just as abruptly as before, stopped a second time. He rolled on the floor until he came face to face with Angelina, a small, delicate doll Francisca had brought for him. A smile creased his tearstained face. Suzi giggled with delight. Robertito also laughed. Several seconds later, he stood in front of my wife, played with her lapel and very softly said "*comida*." I watched her beam while she fed him his meal. He often peered past the spoon held in front of her face and watched her eyes.

We worked with him for the remainder of the day. At times, the contact was intense and concentrated. In other instances, he drifted, withdrawing into himself, gliding on the high of his "isms." Rather than directly approach him, we stayed passive, letting him initiate moves in our direction. We wanted him to realize his choice and his own power. More hours were spent waiting and yet, in some profound way, that held more of a promise than simply trying to feed him information and teach him skills. We couldn't heal the damage, connect the circuits; only he could do that.

* * *

I had set aside half the day for Francisca. Chella, acting as interpreter, walked between us as we circled the duck pond near the Soto house. Her dark eyes searched our faces as we talked. She enjoyed her responsibility as translator.

"I let everyone down, Bears, didn't I?" Francisca asked.

"Francisca, you did the best you could," I said. "Nobody could ask for more. I love you even when you're crazy."

She smiled and grabbed my hand. "Perhaps, I am crazy too much of the time."

"Maybe you got scared, Francisca," Chella said supportively, sidestepping her role as interpreter.

"I just can't do it. I can't!" she shouted, attracting the glances of other people in the park. Embarrassed, she focused her eyes on the ground as she walked. "I can't," Francisca whispered. She cradled the front of her body with her long arms as if physically chilled in spite of the hot summer sun.

"You can't do what?"

"Imitate him when, when he hits...or pinches."

"Why not?" I asked softly.

"Oh, Bears, you know."

"Maybe not. Why don't you try to explain it?"

"My son," she began, her voice barely audible, "has grown and learned so much in New York. But have I? Maybe I'm still in the same place." She laughed uncomfortably. "Bears, maybe I'm the hopeless one," she said, attempting to hide the seriousness she felt by sounding casual.

"Why do you believe that, Francisca?"

"I should have imitated him when he hit himself. I watched you and Suzi do it and all the things I was scared about never

307

happened. It didn't get worse. You see, I knew what to do, but couldn't."

"What do you mean?"

"The most terrible thing for a child is to be self-destructive. I saw how they treated them in the hospitals...like, like animals. I couldn't stand that for Robertito."

"Are you believing that's going to happen?"

She covered her face with her hands. "Yes, maybe, I guess so."

"Are you going to put him in an institution?"

"No. Never!" she shouted, angry at my question.

"Why are you angry?" I asked.

She straightened her blouse nervously. "How could you think I would ever do that?"

"I didn't say that's what I thought, Francisca. I just asked the question. And now that you've reaffirmed the answer, why do you see Robertito being treated like the children in the hospitals?"

"I'm sorry, Bears," she said, looking surprisingly young and vulnerable. We exchanged smiles. "Nobody would treat him that way. Now I know that, but two minutes ago I didn't! Do you see? It's so hard for me to face things when I don't have the answers. What's going to happen when we go back to Mexico?"

"Why do you believe you don't have the answers?"

"Look what happened this summer. I drove everyone crazy. Worst of all, I panicked." She stopped and stared at the sky.

"And why does that mean you don't have the answers?" I asked.

"When it counted, Bears, I didn't," she declared. "That's what the summer proved."

"Is that what it proved?"

She shook her head as if trying to free herself. "No," she said tentatively. "I guess not." She stared off in silence. "I learned that when I get scared, I don't know what to do."

"Okay. And if you got scared this summer, why does that mean you'll get scared when you return to Mexico?"

"It doesn't mean that," she asserted. "Bears, I really missed these sessions."

"Still feel hopeless?" I asked.

"It really makes a difference when we talk."

We strolled across a wooden bridge together and continued our dialogue, exploring her feelings of rigidity and stiffness in the face of change. She realized her discomfort germinated from the belief that others knew better than she did. Why did she believe that? That was the premise of her indoctrination and schooling as a child. Did she still believe it now? No, not really. She had watched Suzi and me do everything in the past few days that she had thought to do with her son during the summer, but hadn't. Francisca always relied on what she considered to be an expert; first the doctors, then us. She had yet to learn that, in some real way, we all share the same knowledge. But now, more than ever before, she recognized she had to focus more on herself to be effective in helping her son.

As we climbed the steps to her house, we hugged each other. Chella looked away politely.

"Hey, get over here," I said, pulling her into our huddle. "Thanks for helping us talk." She nodded.

"I understand much more after today," Chella said. "Francisca and the others have been wonderful teachers, even with the confusions, but I wanted to know more about the philosophy behind what we did. Now I'm learning that, too."

"Chella, have you ever told Francisca you thought she was a wonderful teacher?"

"No," she replied.

"Maybe that would be a nice thing to share with her," I said.

She turned to Francisca, smiled and translated the essence of our conversation, telling her that she thought she had been an amazing teacher, that watching her work with her son was one of the most beautiful things she had ever witnessed in her life.

"If I can only give half of what you give to your son to my sister when I go home, I will feel fulfilled," Chella concluded.

Francisca hid her eyes with her hands as her face flushed. She turned away from us. Being a loving and effective teacher with her son meant everything to her. To hear Chella's compliment dared her to contemplate what she had always considered beyond her grasp. She wanted desperately to be more open and loving. In an abrupt move, she faced us again, exposing her blood-shot eyes and quivering mouth. She messed her hair purposely and began to laugh, then locked her face into a serious, almost tormented expression.

"I will keep trying," she said as she clutched my shirt. "Please keep helping me."

* * *

The old exuberance returned as all of the members of our special family confronted their demons and discarded their discomforts. By the end of the second week after our return, our little friend was moving again. The crying had almost totally subsided. The hitting and pinching had completely disappeared. Smiles, hugs of affection, laughter and giggling bubbled from Robertito once again. We reintegrated Raun, Bryn and Thea into the program. They loved to watch Lisa work since she mirrored their childlike relationship with Robertito. Her special gift enriched our perspective on just how different and just how useful each person's unique input could be. She smiled brightly on that last day before she left for college, saying she felt more open now to hold and touch those she loved. She said she had survived the passing difficulties of the summer because she remembered something Raun had once told her when he saw her crying. "Everything happens for a reason."

For Roby, his growing awareness of the subordinate role he assumed during the summer motivated him to question his own trust in himself. In day-to-day situations with his son, he relied on his wife as if her motherly instinct far exceeded the understanding of his fatherly instinct. He laughed when he finally articulated his belief. "Maybe, Bears, I am prejudiced against myself," he said with a mock-serious expression. We laughed together. Then I asked him whether a mother was more capable than a father at parenting because of her sex. He grappled with old myths. "If I believe I am not as good, then I won't be," he admitted. He delivered his final authoritative statement on male-female roles by making cheese tacos and enchiladas for Suzi and me.

Laura had suppressed her anger toward Francisca and hated herself for it. She faced her inability to take risks and explored her chronic need to be liked by others...almost at any cost. Did she want their affection for what she was or for what they wanted her to be? After several dialogue sessions, she concluded that she had remained silent in order not to risk her ralationship with Francisca and yet it had deteriorated as a direct result of that silence. Laura came to understand the harvest of fear. With that revelation, she faced another impulse which she had refused to entertain previously. Her commitment to our program had no fixed termination date. But as we entered the sixth month, Laura wanted

310

to refocus all her attention back to music and concentrate more on her developing career. "How could I leave," she asked herself, "especially now since you guys returned and it's fun again?" As she attempted to answer her question, she recognized that she had made herself unhappy and hardened herself emotionally during the summer, all to ensure her exit from the program. Did she have to make the experience unpleasant in order to leave? "No," she said, "of course not, but why would I leave something that's good for me?" With that question, she realized she could just "know" to move on, that she now wanted something different or more for herself. Her broad smile confirmed a new decision. She would allow herself to enjoy and love her work fully with Robertito, knowing the time neared for her departure and knowing she could make that decision without using unhappiness to propel her.

Our impending return altered Carol's entire gestalt for the remaining summer weeks. Nothing had changed but her own sense of relief. Slowly, she acknowledged her control over her feelings by recognizing the judgments she made. He's getting better... she's feeling better. He's getting worse... she's feeling worse. What did she mean and fear when she labeled him "worse"? Carol uncovered her expectations about progress for Robertito and for herself. As she gave up some of those beliefs, she doubled her participation and volunteered her opinions more easily in group sessions and conferences. She wanted to talk more about her seizures, but hesitated until what she called the more pertinent concerns about the program had been explored. She knew she had to search further but tried, for the moment, to take care of Robertito as a way of taking care of her own superstitions. Each person had to find his own time.

We had not witnessed the initial evolution of Chella, but, within these few weeks, since our return, she became considerably more daring. She expressed her thoughts more authoritatively and became less secretive about her feelings. In her sessions, she dealt with her awe and discomforts with Francisca. Her concerns about her sister, Martha, preyed heavily on her mind. Why? She wanted to help her more now than ever before, especially since she had acquired a vision and technique which she believed held the answer. But Chella wanted to learn more. "I want to be as clear as you and Suzi," she quipped. I suggested she might want to be as clear as Chella. She smiled. "I'll remember that."

Suzi entered the room quietly and watched Carol and Raun work with Robertito. Playing a verbal "Simon Says," Carol called instructions to her two young friends. Robertito responded accurately, touching his feet, his nose, his hair. Raun struggled with the requests, his knowledge of Spanish still embryonic. When Raun took charge of the session, he pantomimed a "Simon Says" game based on imitation. Both Carol and Robertito became his students.

"Okay, Raunchy," Suzi said softly, "it's time to go." She turned to Robertito and held out her hand. He looked at her for several seconds, then touched her hand.

"By-by, Robertito," she said. He stared at her, a slight smile curling his lips. Suzie pumped his hand briskly and repeated herself.

"By-by," he answered finally.

Carol tapped Suzi's arm. "Who is this, Robertito?" she asked.

He glanced at Carol, who was sitting on the floor, and leaned his head on her shoulder.

"Sushi," he mumbled. Everyone applauded. When Suzi put her hand out a second time, Robertito grasped it and said loudly, "By-by, Sushi."

"He's so smart, Mommy," Raun gushed as they exited the room. "You know, autistic doesn't mean you're dumb."

"Nobody's really dumb," Suzi explained. "It's just that some people allow themselves to know more than others."

"I think that's what Robertito is doing," he said. Suzi nodded. "Mommy, can you teach him in English from now on?"

"Why, Raunch?" she asked.

"I don't like playing 'Simon Says' in Spanish...that's why I always lose."

Chapter 21

The three-by-five-inch portraits of each person in the program had been spread across the table in front of Robertito. The little boy rubbed his nose like an infant, mashing the palm of his hand into his fingers as he pushed haphazardly against his face. A satisfied rumbling gurgled in his throat. He raised his eyebrows and then sighed.

"You are ready now?" Roby asked gently, admiring the chiseled features of his son's face. "Good. Who is this?" he asked, pointing at his wife's photograph. He watched his son, trying to retain each movement, each little facial expression. Roby had tried to wish this day away, but couldn't.

Robertito looked directly at his mother's portrait and touched the surface of the print with his finger tips. "Mama," he blurted.

"Yes. That's perfect. Perfect!" Roby clapped and cheered. He took his child's hand. "Soon you will have your Option degree. Okay, ready? Who is this?"

The little boy identified Lisa quickly, then Laura, Carol, Suzi and me. His recent progress and participation amazed everyone. When Roby introduced a book, his son flipped the pages like a scholar, then tapped the cover with his finger. He cocked his head to the side and listened to the rhythmic sound. A simple gesture became a self-stimulating activity.

"If you want to tap, *papito,* you tap," Roby said, participating and waiting patiently until the boy exhausted his impulse and pointed to an owl. "What's that?" When Robertito did not answer, his father proceeded to make the sound of the animal.

Robertito touched his nose to the picture and said owl. Elated, Roby pointed to the turtle, a difficult word to pronounce in Spanish. Within seconds, Robertito identified it. In addition to the more common farm animals, he named the seal, a beaver, a crab, kangaroo, squirrel and cricket.

"*Música,*" Robertito announced as he left his chair and picked up the tape recorder.

"Yes. Yes," Roby chanted, delighted with his son's continuous contact. He had worked both his and Francisca's session today, insisting on monopolizing his son's time...at least for this day. Father and son danced together for a short period, then Robertito ran over to the life-sized Popeye balloon. He "ismed" at it, almost in the form of a greeting, then hugged it, kissed it and finally dragged it into the center of the room. He initiated a "two-step" and rocked to the music with Popeye as his partner. His father laughed. Despite the "isms," the lack of sophisticated language and the periods of withdrawal, Robertito appeared worldly to him in comparison to his vegetative-like existence only six months before.

Toward the end of the second session, Roby Soto sat opposite his son as he fed him dinner. Each time the child looked beyond the spoon, he tried to engrave the glance in his memory. In a teaching context, he spoke very simply and directly to his son as he had been trained. But since having watched Suzi and me, on occasion, talk to Roberito as a peer, he freed himself to communicate his feelings and thoughts to his child without needing to know if his son understood. He wanted to express himself and risked using speech as one less-than-perfect path through the silence. He knew something of what he felt would touch his son.

"Papa has something to tell you." He delivered a heaping spoonful of fish to Robertito's opened mouth. The boy smiled. "Good, my son. You like it. It's protein. Very good for you, *papito.*" While the youngster ground the food between his teeth, Roby imitated that same chewing motion and made
314

the same purring sounds echoing from his throat. Robertito giggled as he stared at his father's mouth.

"Tomorrow I will have to leave," Roby said. "This time, *papito,* it will be a long time until I return. Many months will pass before I can come back to you and Mommy." He turned away from his son and stared at the floor. He sighed heavily before resuming. "I must help my business so you can stay here to learn and grow. Do you understand?"

Robertito delighted in the meal. He did not respond directly to his father's words or question, but his face reflected a certain attentiveness to the spoken sounds.

"I don't want to leave you or Mommy, but I don't know any other way to help keep you here. I don't want to leave, Robertito." He had to stop talking and fortify himself. He wanted to be clear for his son. Roby knew he would not see Robertito for at least four or five months, maybe half a year. He worried that somewhere in that strange and complex brain, his child might interpret his absence as desertion. "Papa loves you, more than anything in the world; Papa loves you and Mommy and all the nice people who help us." Robertito tried to grab the cup of food. "You don't have to do that. I will give you all you want." As soon as he fed the child another gulp, the boy sat back into the chair and chewed with great concentration and satisfaction.

"You will always be with me in my heart. I will never forget you, not even for a second, *papito.*" He stroked the hair off Robertito's forehead. He thought of his own father, who never touched him except to hit him or hurt him. Hadn't he understood? Couldn't he see? To Roby, nothing was more precious than his own child. He felt himself blessed, not burdened, in the presence of his son. He couldn't imagine striking this little boy. As he touched his son's cheek with the tips of his fingers, he closed his eyes. He wanted the impression to be so intense that he could re-experience it thousands of miles from here and many months from now. He wanted his finger tips to remember in the same fashion that he commanded his mind to retain each image and each sound his son made.

At the airport, Francisca handed her husband a small package wrapped like a gift. He peered at her, surprised and slightly embarrassed. He hesitated, wishing he had something for her.

"Go ahead," Francisca said. "Open it."

Roby removed the tape carefully without destroying the paper. When he uncovered the overalls which his son had worn on their last day together, he pressed his teeth together, trying to be strong, trying to smile. He held the garment in front of his face and inhaled deeply. Then Roberto Soto began to cry. Francisca took his hands and squeezed tightly. They stood alone, facing each other, as people pushed past them in the busy terminal.

"You concentrate on Robertito and yourself," Roby counseled, forcing a tearful half-smile. "Sometimes I am very sentimental, but I will be fine, especially if I know you and our son are happy here in New York." His voice began to crack. Roby inhaled deeply, then hugged his wife. "Mommy, I am very proud of you."

*   *   *

The following week, Laura gave notice, offering her continued support and input until we trained a replacement for her and Roby. Rather than search for two people, we tried to find someone who could give us enough hours to fill all the gaps. Suzi and I began the hunt at local high schools and colleges. Carol, who had been pressed by her fellow students, submitted several names. We tried to prescreen people on the telephone, explaining our perspective and our program. The idea of learning Spanish frightened most people. To our amazement, despite the huge Hispanic population in and around New York City, no bilingual students applied.

Our particular young lady made a very special impression on the phone. She didn't say anything particularly insightful or memorable. She didn't attempt to dazzle us with references or any academic accolades. A special warmth and enthusiasm permeated her every word. She knew Carol, attended the same college and had heard my talk as guest lecturer the preceding year. We decided to schedule her for the first appointment.

Jeannie didn't walk through the door, she bounced into our living room with an amazed smile on her face. She wore a white polo shirt with a funny Snoopy-type character on it. "I'm here. I'm really here," she giggled. She embraced us without hesitation. "I feel I know you and Raun and Robertito. Thanks for seeing me." We smiled at each other and laughed spontaneously. Her vivacious grin displayed her immediate comfort. Suzi and I both knew, in that very instant, that Jeannie would be a wonderful addition to the program. She relaxed her tall, trim form on the couch and listened attentively before responding. "I want to help," she said. "I do very much."

In many ways, her easy smile and open affection reminded me of Suzi. As a special education major, Jeannie had worked with a variety of children with different problems. She had just begun to question techniques and attitudes when a teacher exposed her to *Son-Rise*. The method articulated in the book seemed like a dream, a fantasy rather than fact. And yet, at the same time, she talked about it as being direct, simple and obvious. Her interest in education was based on her attraction to people who were loving, yet she reported finding many harsh professionals working with children.

Jeannie hoped she could add something special to a student's life...like caring and humanity. As we sat together and talked, it seemed as if we had all known each other for years. Even her nervousness in answering some questions could not sedate her vigor and animation.

"You're on," I said to her, acknowledging what Suzi and I already knew.

Jeannie looked at us.

"I think you'd have something special to offer Robertito and all of us," Suzi added.

"You're kidding." She laughed self-consciously this time, then smiled. "You're not kidding." Without saying another word, Jeannie hugged Suzi, then planted an impassioned kiss on my cheek.

"When could you start?" I asked.

"Today. Now. Whenever you want," Jeannie blurted.

"C'mon with me," Suzi said. "I'll bring you over to the Soto house and you can begin by meeting Francisca and Robertito."

For the next two weeks, we concentrated all our energy on Jeannie. In our dialogue sessions, she confronted her doubts about herself willingly, even questioned her talents as a teacher. Her fear of being judged by an observing supervisor plagued her most. I could have assured her she would not be judged in our program, but I chose, instead, to help her deal with the anxiety and underlying beliefs. Since she would tandem teach and participate in feed-back sessions, eventually, I wanted her to find her own strength rather than rely on us for support.

When she arrived for the second teaching session with Suzi, Jeannie brought a huge, stuffed monkey slightly larger than Robertito. The big, blue furry animal wore a Scottish plaid hat

317

with a matching jacket. Together with Suzi, she introduced "Chango" to our little friend. On request, he hugged and kissed the enormous doll. Often, while working puzzles or lottos with Suzi, Robertito glanced at the new figure leaning against the wall. Finally, he broke away from the teaching session to confront Chango directly. He tried unsuccessfully to push his little fingers between the monkey's sealed lips, then he flapped his hands in front of the doll. Suzi half-expected the animal to respond in kind. Thoroughly confused by the doll's inertia, Robertito pushed it several times. Then, he leaned forward and hugged and kissed Chango spontaneously.

"I don't believe you, Robertito Soto," Suzi exclaimed. "You're beginning to make 'friends with the whole world." She cheered the little boy as did Jeannie, who laughed boisterously, flattered by the effect of her gift.

After that session and the others which followed, Jeannie bombarded Suzi with questions in an attempt to understand every aspect of the teaching process. Later, she observed Robertito's other mentors. Carol and Chella spent evenings with her, helping her learn Spanish and perfect her pronunciation. Jeannie Kannengieser gushed with enthusiasm, turning a face full of love toward all of us.

The transition of changing teachers, the initial phasing-out of Laura and the constant monitoring of Robertito consumed a massive portion of our time and energy. Like all the others in the program, Suzi and I sought to keep ourselves clear and vitalized, but our efforts were diverted rudely for several days after the arrival of our "Son-Rise" script, which we had submitted during the summer. Changes, which represented gross inaccuracies, had been implanted throughout the draft. In effect, a Hollywood writer, having no clear awareness of actual situations, worked diligently under the producers' direction and added formula changes which included a bit of violence, a subdued version of a car chase and two token bedroom scenes. Rather than risk trusting the story, violence, action and some sex had been added. The revisions we demanded and ultimately received, resulted in a final script very close to our original. But the battle to force the producers to adhere to the original story required over four months of constant legal skirmishes. Often, in the midst of a Wednesday night meeting or while observing Robertito, an urgent phone call or courier from Los Angeles interrupted. Each time I considered walking away, I thought of Raun's comment to Lisa: "Everything happens for a reason."

318

* * *

The moon illuminated the room with a blue-gray light. I propped my head against the arm of the couch at an angle which afforded me a panoramic view of the sky through the windows of my one-room Option house. I waited alone, silently—my phone unplugged from the jack. The wind whistled through the trees. Clouds, trimmed with white halos, whipped across the horizon at great speed. Then the footsteps intruded. Twigs cracked under the pressure of heavy shoes. A caped figure suddenly appeared outside the sliding glass doors. Bizarre limbs slowly rose from its side, giving the form a bird-like appearance. A groan penetrated the walls of my room. Then two hands separated from the outer garment and hung precariously on either side of the head of this hooded figure. The flapping gestures were oddly familiar, but the hissing sounds were unmistakable.

"Eee-o, eee-o, eee-o," Laura whined, entering the room with a flurry.

I began to applaud as she tackled my legs, dumping me rudely off the couch onto the floor. Carol arrived for her session seconds later.

"I don't want to take Carol's time," Laura said. "I, sorta, you know..." She assumed a boxer's stance and jabbed me several times in the chest and shoulders, then hugged me. "Jeannie took over my sessions with Robertito. I watched her for a while. She's good...real good."

"That's because you helped train her," I said.

She nodded her head, forcing a bright smile. "I won't take up your time with more Rha-Rha crazies. I, a..." Laura touched Carol's hand, hugged me, then scooted to the door. She turned, her face engulfed in another smile. "I thought it would be easy to leave."

"You're not going to get rid of us so quickly," I said.

"I know," she whispered. "Thanks, Papa Bear," she mumbled as she left.

Carol and I sat facing each other without talking for several minutes.

"First Roby and now Laura. I can't imagine the program without them," Carol said. "Every time I arrive for my sessions with Robertito, I think I'm going to get my good morning greeting from Roby. It's hard to believe he's not there."

"Maybe that's because he's still there," I offered. "For the moment, only his body is missing."

Carol grinned. "Well, at least Laura's body will be here." Her expression clouded. A faint rocking motion dominated her body. "Bears, I think I've been pushing Robertito and he knows it. Today, he cried and avoided me for over an hour."

"Why do you think you've been pushing him?" I asked.

"It's something we've never really talked about." She squinted her eyes. "You see, ever since I started, I've had this little arrangement going...sort of an expectation. I thought if Robertito could make it through autism, then, well, I could do it with epilepsy. During the middle of the summer, when he drifted real far away from us, my seizures actually increased. Like I was tied to him."

"Do you believe you are?"

"That's just it. When I realized what was happening, it didn't affect me any more. I kind of pushed away." Her eyes fluttered nervously. "Now that he's on the move again, I hooked myself in all over again. I sort of need him to move."

"Why?" I asked.

"It's going to sound silly, but I'm right back to—if he can make it, so can I."

"Why do you believe his movement has anything to do with yours?"

She laughed self-consciously. "It's ridiculous. I know that. I mean..." Carol aborted the sentence and closed her eyes. When she spoke again, her voice dropped an octave, reflecting the inner strain. "It's kind of like a sign."

"What do you mean?"

"I needed something to believe in. My doctor said both our diseases are incurable. But if Tito could break out of it, then what he said couldn't be true...and if it's not true for Robertito, then it's not true for me."

"Why do you need Robertito's progress to decide whether it's true or not for you?" I asked.

"It sounds dumb, doesn't it?"

"In what way do you see it as dumb?"

"I know better, I do," she answered. "That's what I've really learned from these sessions. Nobody does it for Robertito. We might help, but every time he learns something or builds something, he does it...not us. It's kind of like my wishing him to do it for both of us...like some sort of magic. How could I do that to him?" Carol pressed her hands against her temples and groaned.

"What are you feeling?"

"Guilty. Like I laid my problems on some little kid. This

would be easy if I didn't care about him, but I love him. Sometimes I feel like I'm his mother too." She shook her head. "I've been pressuring him for something that has nothing to do with him." Her face flushed. "I feel terrible."

"Why, Carol?"

"Look what I did."

"Why do you feel terrible about what you did?" I asked.

"Wouldn't you feel the same way, Bears?"

"If I did, I'd have my reasons. What are yours?"

"I don't know," she declared.

"What are you afraid would happen if you didn't feel terrible?"

She slumped into the couch. "Then I guess I might just be stupid enough to do it again."

"Do you believe that?"

"Believe what?"

"Do you believe that if you didn't feel terrible about what you did, you would do it again?"

Carol looked at me quizzically, then exhaled noisily. "No. The more aware I am, the easier it is for me to handle things the way I want. I won't press him any more, I know that now."

The remainder of the session focused on her seizures, which had decreased since she began working with us. She attributed that, in part, to her burgeoning happiness and comfort. The subsequent increase and decrease of the seizures during that short period in the summer furthered her conviction about the impact of her attitude on her illness. It also reinforced her awareness of the separateness between her and Robertito. Even as he had continued to withdraw, she noted a small improvement in her own condition.

"Do you think I could stop them?" she asked, leaning forward.

"What do you think?" I countered.

"C'mon, Bears, I want to know what you think."

"Carol, it doesn't matter what I think. I'm not a doctor giving you medicine or a priest giving you advice. It's your body. It's your illness. Ultimately, it's your decision. Nobody knows more about you than you."

"Okay." She closed her eyes again. "My neurologist said Dilantin would control it, but the drug didn't...not really." She peered at me, locking her eyes into mine. "Even after years on the medication, I have had almost as many seizures. It's only in the past four or five months, since I've been with Tito, that it's decreased. I can't remember feeling generally

321

as happy or clear as I do now. And, you know, I haven't had one seizure in the last two weeks." Suddenly she grimaced. "It gets so damn confusing. What controls it? My body chemistry? The drugs? Or my attitude? The doctor insists it's out of my control, just like the other experts insist brain damage and autism are out of Robertito's control. I wish I was as courageous as . . . as Raun."

"What do you mean?" I asked.

"He went the whole route."

"And why do you think he did it?" I questioned.

"Because he wanted to," she acknowledged. "He did it because he wanted to."

*　　*　　*

Chella sat on the opposite side of the table from Robertito. The morning had been a series of ups and downs for her. First he worked beautifully with the puzzle and pegboard, then he paced and "ismed" for over half an hour. They danced together for ten minutes, then he refused to participate for almost twenty minutes. As part of a new thrust, she asked him to use words as a whole, rather than break them into syllables. He seemed to understand completely for the first hour, but, soon afterward, he broke every word he used into sections again. *Ca-ba-llo* instead of *caballo*. Rober-ti-to instead of Robertito. She didn't want to ask him for more than he could handle. Chella remembered how her sister would often explode into a tantrum when the world became too difficult for her. She felt a protectiveness for Robertito.

"Okay, my silly friend, I'm going to make it easy for you." She set out five blocks on the table, all different sizes and colors. "Can you give me the blue one?" He pushed the blocks off the table. "Well, I can see you want to try something else." She opened the animal book in front of him. "They're a lot more fun to look at, aren't they?" She surveyed the forms depicted on the two opened pages, trying to decide which was the most familiar to her student. Perhaps, she thought, if he could succeed in such an easy exercise, he might be willing to tackle more difficult tasks. The cow. He had been able to identify the cow for many months. Before she could make her request, Robertito picked up his hand and aimed his index finger at the cow.

"How did you know?" she murmured out loud, laughing

322

at his move. As she searched the page, she concluded the duck might be the second-best choice. Easy. Make it easy for him. When Chella turned to address Robertito, she knocked the peg set off the table accidentally. She bent down and retrieved it. Smiling at her own clumsiness, she climbed back into the chair. Robertito's pose startled her. He had his finger pressed against the picture of the duck. Her body stiffened as if shocked electrically. She knew she had not verbalized her request. The child's soft, infantile smile sedated her initial panic. Her eyes drifted across the page one more time. She purposely looked at the ceiling and visualized the spotted dog. Within seconds, Robertito changed his position. Chella hesitated, biting her bottom lip. Finally she forced her eyes to peer at the table. Impossible! Ridiculous and impossible! Robertito touched the spotted dog while watching her, apparently awaiting her next request. She kept mumbling denials of what she saw. The little boy withdrew his hand and started flapping it beside his head. The calm evident in his face fractured as he began to whine.

Chella pulled the book away and closed it. It was the second time in a week that this had happened with Robertito. Though she had begun to trust her dreams, like the one about visiting New York two weeks before she ever knew she would come, this event frightened her. Could he know her thoughts? Could she move him without speaking? Chella mumbled the word "impossible" over and over again, hoping to convince herself by repeatedly denying what she suspected.

"Dance, Robertito. Come, dance with me." She stroked his face with great tenderness as she voiced her suggestion. Chella danced with Robertito, refusing to engage in any complex games. She wanted to strip her mind, to start again. Her increased relaxation in the session and her love for this child had solidified a bond which scared her. Chella tried to lose herself in the music in an effort to diminish her discomfort.

An hour passed. As she sat on the floor feeding Robertito, he pointed to a spot about a foot below the ceiling. This was the same point he stared at often during his work sessions in this room.

"*Mira, mi amor, comida para un niño fantástico,*" she bellowed, drawing his attention momentarily to her. While he chewed, he looked up and pointed again.

Suzi entered the room to take the next session. Initially,

she sat against the wall and watched, thankful for the moment's rest, having worked a four-hour training session with Jeannie earlier in the morning and then spending two hours with me on the phone with our lawyer concerning the "Son-Rise" script dispute. Robertito appeared more attentive than earlier in the day when she, too, had experienced his constant moving toward us and away from us. The sessions had a seesaw quality. "What is he pointing at?" she thought as his arm snapped up four different times. Chella tried to ignore the diversion. When Suzi took charge, Chella kissed her and Robertito. Just as she turned to leave, she heard Suzi ask a question that she herself had suppressed for the last half-hour.

"What do you see, Robertito?" Suzi asked.

The youngster stared into space. Although he had turned away many times, his eyes returned to the exact same spot. "Face," he answered, matter-of-factly. Suzi's mouth dropped open. Chella gasped and left the room immediately.

Alone with Robertito, Suzi wanted to test his response a second time. She asked him to touch his nose, hair and eyes, then she remained silent. The moment he completed the short exercise, Robertito turned and stared at the same spot again.

"What do you see, Robertito?" Suzi questioned.

"Face," he said.

Suzi took a deep breath. "What kind of face?" The child did not respond. "What kind?" Again he did not answer. She rephrased the question. "Is it a happy or sad face? Happy or sad?"

Without hesitation, Robertito said: "Happy."

Suzi laughed, releasing the rush of tension which had just assaulted her body. "Thank God... at least it's a happy face." She did not want to draw any conclusions from what Robertito thought he saw. Just as she would not want to deprive him of his autistic world, she would not want to diminish any other openings he might have discovered in the cracks of the universe.

The scene I encountered upon my arrival defied anything I could have fantasized. Suzi and Robertito faced each other on the floor. They both sat in perfect yoga positions, legs folded in half-lotus, palms upward with the backs of their hands resting on their knees, the index finger and thumb forming perfect circles. They breathed and hummed in unison, keeping their eyes closed. I couldn't decide whether Suzi was serious or whether this was a product of her incorrigible

324

sense of humor. Later, she explained that she used this device successfully to help him relax when he became hyper or listless.

For the next two and a half hours, they worked together on the table. Demonstrating with her hands, eyes and a book, she tried to teach him the concept of open and closed, which he mastered rather rapidly. Teaching him the idea of same and different appeared more difficult. Despite grouping letters and blocks, he floundered with the notion, which, in fact, articulated a very sophisticated concept. Suzi created several intermissions, using dancing and exercises as activities to combat any fatigue. I engaged Robertito in a quick basketball game. He landed three shots out of nine directly into the basket. I wondered if he thought of his father when he aimed the ball, for Roby had been instrumental in teaching his son athletic skills. The session continued in the same spirit for another twenty minutes, then our little friend whined and "ismed." Suzi invited him to the table, but he remained on the floor, rolling his head back and forth. Did he feel pressured again? Was he psychically fatigued? Did he understand, finally and irrevocably, that if he joined us it was his choice?

I jumped to my feet and squatted, as best I could, into Robertito's miniature chair by the table. Suzi looked at me dumbfounded. When I pointed to the book, she understood.

"Okay, Bears," she said loudly. "Where's the red car?" I searched the page with great theatrics, moving my finger through the air like an airplane approaching a runway. My throat rumbled like the exhaust of a jet engine. Robertito side-glanced at us.

"*Aquí,*" I announced, landing my finger on the small painted form.

"*Bueno.* Fantastic," she cheered as she patted my chest and kissed my lips. "Now, Bears, where is the yellow bus...the big, yellow bus?" Again I played the charade of an intense hunt, landing on the proper form. Suzi repeated the applause and affection. By this time, Robertito had turned on his side and stared directly at us. We continued our little interaction for at least fifteen minutes. Then Robertito rose to his feet and circled the table several times. When Suzi fed me some of his food, he came right to my side. He fiddled with my shirt, twisting the material between his fingers.

"*Listo,* Bears?" Suzi asked, signaling the resumption of the lesson.

"*Sí*, Sushi," I said, mispronouncing her name purposely. We both laughed. Robertito stood at my side and watched for several minutes. When I pretended I couldn't locate the school bus, he pointed to it.

"Yes, Robertito," Suzi shouted in disbelief. "Yes, yes, you wonderful person. That's the bus." She kissed him and hugged him, fighting back her own tears as she embraced our little friend.

For the next ten minutes, he actually competed with me, trying to point out the answers before I could. Robertito Soto had taken another giant step. Although he vacillated back and forth and in and out, his grasp of our actions had marked a new level of sophistication. His interest in applause, cheers, hugs and, ultimately, food, motivated him more than the abstract concept of competition, but the introduction of another student had, obviously, reignited his interest. Suzi congratulated both of us with equal intensity. Thus, the notion of a second student as part of the program developed. Often, it became a useful device in rekindling Robertito's interest in learning and participating.

Before I left, Suzi illustrated how Robertito could match numbers of dissimilar objects: the Roman numeral three with the number three with three blocks. Though, here again, he was inconsistent, he did demonstrate a basis of understanding of numbers and the function of counting. Just as I opened the door, Robertito pointed to the top of one wall. Suzi motioned to me to wait.

"Robertito, what do you see?" she asked. He did not respond, but tilted his head and smirked. "Tito, what do you see?"

"*Cara*," he said, again identifying a face.

I looked from him to Suzi several times, then focused my attention at the wall. Nothing. I saw nothing but the flat surface of the wall painted yellow.

"Robertito, what kind of face do you see?" she pursued. Again, he remained silent. "Do you see a happy face or a sad face?"

"*Feliz*," he responded.

"Wow," I muttered, trying to catalogue what I witnessed. Did I believe what he said? Would anybody? In the immediacy of that moment, I decided if something lived for Robertito, then it lived for us in terms of working and helping him. He knew his world and derived comfort from it no matter how different it was from ours. To belittle or deny that would be to move away from him. In accepting him, we also accepted his experiences.

"Bears, I think you should talk to Chella on your way out."

I nodded and left the room. Francisca, Carol and Jeannie greeted me in the kitchen. They worked together in an elementary Spanish book.

"I think we're getting better than you, Bears," Carol boasted, rattling off a quick idiom for my benefit.

I pointed to my ear and bowed slightly. "Tin. It's made of tin. A genetic handicap, if you guys believe in handicaps." We exchanged smiles. Francisca offered food. "Are you playing Mommy again?" She stopped in the midst of a motion. Mommy. She had not heard that word since Roby left. Carol looked up at Francisca, wanting to say something, but finding no words to match her thoughts.

When Francisca offered Jeannie food, she said: "*Graciass.*" Even I could detect the mispronunciation. Carol pounded the table in hysterics, then corrected her. Jeannie still had difficulty reproducing the word correctly.

"You know, Bears, I think it's easier working with Robertito," Carol quipped.

"Hey," Jeannie giggled.

"Where's Chella?" I asked.

"In her room." Jeannie pointed.

"She's been kind of weird today," Carol added.

Chella sat on her bed and stared out the window. She did not acknowledge my presence in the doorway.

"Chella, can I come in?" I asked.

She looked at me and smiled nervously. "Sure, Bears."

"Anything wrong?"

"I'll be okay," she declared, a little too forcefully.

"I know that," I said, "but if something's rattling around in your head, maybe we could talk about it."

"My session's not until tomorrow," she teased.

"Ah, and you only talk on schedule," I said.

"Yep," she smirked.

"How about twenty questions?" I asked.

"Shoot," Chella replied.

"It has something to do with the face Robertito saw."

"Yes. But that's not it, exactly."

"Then what is it?"

She stretched her arms over her head and pulled her knees in toward her stomach. Chella twisted her hands through her legs and rested her head on her knees. She always managed to wrap her small, subtle form in compact, pretzel-like positions. Without looking at me, she talked about her dreams, her tendency toward so-called psychic experiences and the apparent responses of Robertito to her thoughts.

"It scares me," she whispered.

"Why?"

"'Cause I'm manipulating him with my...my ideas, my thoughts. It's like I'm in his head or he's in mine. That's frightening."

"What's frightening about it?"

"It's like controlling somebody. God, I don't want that responsibility. Not now. Not ever!"

"How do you imagine your thoughts control Robertito?"

"Well, maybe they don't always control him. But he did exactly what I wanted him to do in my thoughts. I thought dog and, bingo, he pointed to the dog."

"How does that differ for you when, for example, he does exactly what you want when you ask him?"

She cupped her face in her hands. "He has more of a choice."

"What do you mean?"

"He can still do anything he pleases. It's different when I think it."

"Why?"

"I don't know. Maybe, then, he just does it, like a robot."

"Do you believe that?"

"Well..." she paused. "If that were true, I guess he'd be doing everything I thought all day long. He only did it twice."

"So can he choose, just like he does when you verbalize your requests?"

"Yes, I guess so. Sure." She peered at me intensely. "All I wanted to do before was to stop my thoughts, to cut them off."

"And now?" I asked.

"I don't know. At least I don't feel quite as sinister."

"Chella, if you can reach Robertito on a more direct wave length than the rest of us, that's not sinister...that's a gift."

"How do I remember that next time it happens?"

"If you don't judge it, you'll be clear on the value and meaning of the experience."

"Maybe I'll join the others in the kitchen now." A smile

of relief rippled across her face. "But I want to talk more about this during my session...okay?"

"It's your session."

"Good."

As we walked into the hall, Chella stopped me. "One more thing, Bears. When I heard you in the kitchen, I thought about you coming to talk to me. I imagined you coming into my room and you did." We both laughed.

"I guess the question you could ask yourself is...do you control the universe," I offered, "or are your thoughts in harmony with it?"

"What do you think?" she asked.

"Maybe it's a little bit of both."

* * *

No matter how many times she oiled the hinges, the door creaked when she opened it. Francisca pushed very slowly, not wanting to awaken her son with the noise or the light from the hallway. She slipped through the narrowest opening and shut the door behind her. Once inside, she switched on the flashlight and aimed it at his bed, which had been positioned beside hers. Empty. She rarely found him in the appropriate place when she retired. Francisca shined the beam on her own bed...also empty. Then she scanned the room with the light beginning her ritualistic hunt for her son. She located a head and arm sticking out from beneath one of the beds. Robertito never opened his eyes as she lifted him carefully into her bed and tucked the covers around his body. Francisca sat beside him, stroking his chest.

"We love you very much," she whispered in his ear. *"Papito,"* she said, wanting Robertito to remember always his father's nickname for him. *"Papito,* we accept you as you are. We do. We accept your world. All of us are very happy and we're with you in every way."

Her blossoming comfort gave her a greater ease with herself and her son, even in her husband's absence. Could she run the program with Roby back in Mexico? The sting of the summer was too vivid. No. Not yet. Francisca prayed for more time as she sat next to her son. She brushed the hair from his face as she chanted the names of each person in the program, part of a ritual closing for each day that she had begun at the end of the summer. "Good night from Mama, from Papa, from Suzi and Bears. Good night from Carol, from

329

Chella, Jeannie, Laura, Lisa. And Bryn and Thea and Raunch. We're all with you."

Francisca leaned her head on the mattress and slipped her hand into Robertito's. Her eyelids closed slowly as she visualized Roby beside her and heard him say: "Good night, Mommy."

Chapter 22

I propped myself against the pillow as I watched Jeannie work with Robertito. She had completed almost four weeks with us, marking our entrance into the seventh month of the program. Her responsiveness to an onslaught of dialogue sessions and feed-back discussions propelled her into an immediate and effective use of her teaching talents.

She growled and scratched her hands on the floor like a young lion, then lunged at Robertito, tickling him while trying to wrestle with him as well. He remained gentle, passive and rubbery in her hands. Little-boy giggles filled the room as she rolled him over and over like a limp sack of disconnected limbs. Jeannie played peek-a-boo with him by asking him to hide his face behind his hands. He separated his fingers enough so that he could peek out at her.

"Whoaa," she groaned comically. "You're cheating, Tito. C'mon, I see your eyes." Jeannie pushed his fingers together tenderly. They opened immediately. "Okeydokey. I'm gonna get you." She assaulted him again with her playful fingers, tickling his belly and thighs. He tried to scramble out from beneath her when she tucked her bare feet under his body and shook her sandy-blond hair in his face. I remembered my first impression of Jeannie. I could easily recall the warmth, the caring and the wonderful enthusiasm, but something had changed. She had grown prettier in the past weeks. I noticed that phenomenon after some of our dialogue sessions. After she discarded a problem or fear, her face actually seemed to change, or evolve, as if she felt freer to be and expose more and more of herself.

As we had discussed the night before, everyone began to concentrate more on massaging his hands, particularly the right one. Although we had continued stimulating the right side, the time allotted to that activity had gradually diminished. Our constant vigilance allowed us to keep reassessing all our decisions. I had tested his hands with the needle a week before. His right one had almost as much feeling as his left. As he put the left side of his brain to more and more use, we noticed a dramatic increase in physical sensation. We also noted that the more we stimulated his right side, the more active he tended to be in terms of talking and game-playing for the remainder of the day. When we brought these elements into sharp focus, a renewed effort with tactile sensory input appeared appropriate. In itself, such an accent had little meaning. But in conjunction with our total teaching and therapeutic effort with Robertito, physical stimulation had a significant supportive role.

Jeannie sat him at the table and rubbed his soft, fleshy hands. "They're like little paws," she mumbled, smiling at the child who waited patiently while she worked on his limbs. In conjunction with her physical contact, she tried to create a dialogue of questions and answers.

"What is your name?" she asked.

He watched her mouth studiously, then said: "Robertito."

"Robertito what?"

"Ro-ber-ti-to-So-to." He grunted each syllable separately. His eyebrows arched into his fleshy forehead as he pushed out each breathy sound.

"Wonderful. Fantastic. But how do we say it? Not Ro-ber-ti-to-So-to, but Robertito Soto."

"Robertito Soto," he repeated perfectly.

She hugged him, then gave him a silly high school cheer. "Okeydokey. Ready? Okay, how old are you?"

He looked at his fingers to find the answer. "*Más*, Jeannie," he said.

Flabbergasted by his use of two words together, Jeannie

gaped at him wide-eyed. I couldn't believe it either. He had strung two words together. An image of Raun flashed before me. I still remembered the day, the hour, the instant when he first used more than one word as he sat, smiling, on the bathroom floor.

"More what, Robertito?" she asked, recovering from the shock quickly. He did not answer. "C'mon, we'll try again. How old are you?"

"Six," he replied. When she applauded him, he, too, clapped his hands. But when she finished the accolade, he continued banging one hand against the other. In recent weeks, he had elevated this activity into an "ism."

She looked at me, obviously seeking advice with her confused grimace. Realizing her own responsibility to decide how to respond, she shrugged her shoulders innocently, then smiled and waved at me. Jeannie and Robertito clapped together for over two minutes, then she resumed the massage.

"*Qué es esto?*" she chimed, touching between his lips.

"*Boca,*" he answered correctly.

"And what is this?" she asked, touching his eyes.

He pulled his hand away from her and ran to the window. A plane passed overhead. He followed it until it passed out of view, then, still holding her question in mind, he mumbled, "*Ojo,*" the Spanish word for eye. Jeannie lavished applause and affection on him, ending her celebration of his achievement with some food.

Later, she and Robertito lifted weights. He pushed his hands up together, favoring his left slightly. Two months ago, he could barely get the dumbbell off the floor with his right hand.

"Okay, now let them down slowly...slowly," she counseled. But instead of listening, he let them drop to the floor. She repeated the exercise countless times, yet, no matter how much she asked him and demonstrated how to put the weights down, he still let them drop. I felt he enjoyed the sound of the loud thud against the floor as well as the vibration beside his body. Seven months ago, such a sound might have sent him scurrying from the room.

Jeannie introduced the blocks next. Robertito started to build a tower. He moved his hands mechanically, frequently looking away as he constructed his little building. We made a special effort to vary the games and interaction since Robertito often learned things by rote, repeating exercises and accomplishments as if programmed. We wanted him to flex

333

the membranes of his mind by using them creatively, rather than performing sequences on automatic pilot. Jeannie built the exact same tower as Robertito, allowing him to be teacher. When he put four blocks together, she put four together. He put a block on his head. So did she. Jeannie loved her sessions with Robertito. She used more of herself with him than when in school or student teaching. Aware of the sameness of some of his actions, she reasserted the initiative again in the session. She placed two blocks parallel to each other and a third block on top of them. The design was infinitely more sophisticated than a vertical tower of single blocks on top of each other. Robertito eyed her; then clapped his hands rhythmically. She put a second story on her original form. Robertito threw his head from side to side, then stopped. He looked directly at her structure and, without hearing any request, proceeded to duplicate it on his own.

"Jesus, Mary and Joseph," Jeannie exlaimed. In that instant, Robertito had graduated on to the next level, illustrating his increased ability to understand as well as a dramatic improvement in his small motor dexterity. I found myself clapping and cheering with her. His intensity of concentration continued throughout the remainder of the session. He reassembled three puzzles simultaneously after Jeannie mixed all the pieces together. His ability with the contrasting lotto cards also increased. His receptive vocabulary had grown enormously, but now, as he viewed some of the cards, I noticed him mouthing words before Jeannie even said them, documenting the expansion in expressive language as well.

The final activity of the session had a very special meaning for all of us. Jeannie lifted several big books from the shelf and put them on the table. They contained portraits of animals, household objects, vehicles, tools, people and a host of other diverse elements. Each item had been expertly cut out of magazines or reclaimed from other sources and then glued on a page. The Spanish name was placed below each form. These handmade education books had been fashioned by Roby Soto for his son. Each night, alone in the silence and emptiness of his house, he turned his energy to making these books. He had spent weeks collecting pictures, photographs and magazine illustrations, often securing discarded publications from customers and other store owners. As I watched Jeannie use these hand-crafted tools, I felt the soft, gentle man by my side. Roby remained as much a part of the program as any of us.

I brought Robertito back to my house at the end of the day, enabling Carol, Jeannie and Chella to treat Francisca to dinner and a movie. Suzi and I, with Bryn, Thea and Raun, played with our little friend as we prepared him for bed. Raun made funny faces which Robertito tried to imitate. Thea played patty-cake with him. Bryn experimented with short memory sequence games, saying three dissimilar words in a row and having him repeat them. Initially, his success at it astounded us, but soon he tired and stopped participating.

Despite the fact that he was in unfamiliar surroundings, a strange house, a strange bed and without his mother, he seemed entirely relaxed. We took turns camping outside our bedroom door and waited for him to fall asleep. But for the next several hours, we heard him clap his hands, hum and sing in English a refrain from a Billy Joel song which we often danced to called "I Like You Just the Way You Are." He babbled a host of different words, disconnected and disjointed . . . but words. Perhaps, he verbalized a fantasy in his head. Perhaps, he simply reviewed the file system developing in his brain. In any case, instead of whining or cooing or grunting unintelligible sounds, Robertito now exercised his intellect by taking his own excursions into the left side of his brain. In the darkness of a room and in the privacy of a bed, he chose to play with the language symbols he had learned; symbols which gave him his only chance of ever grasping and utilizing our world.

As I listened, I wondered whether in some intrinsic, cosmic and, perhaps, unknowable way, we had, in fact, done him a favor.

When Suzi and I went to sleep, our little friend was still busy with his movements, words and "isms." We kept him between us in the bed. Within seconds, Suzi fell asleep, exhausted from the rigors of our schedule. Unfortunately, his clapping kept me awake. He lay on his back and, with his arms extended, hit his hands together. Finally, in an attempt to find a creative solution to my dilemma, I tucked one of his arms under my body. Since he did not resist and seemed perfectly content with my solution, I proceeded to try to sleep. The repetitious motion emanating from his body continually distracted me. When I opened my eyes, I saw his single arm still extended, making the same clapping motion but without a companion hand. I couldn't help but consider an old Zen riddle which asked...what was the sound of one hand clapping?

* * *

At the beginning of the following week, Robertito became physically ill, a rarity since his move to New York. Rather than simply rest, he withdrew dramatically, retreating into himself and escalating his "isms," a response typical for a child whose internal systems draw much of his attention. Our little friend became totally unreachable. His only interest focused on food. Jeannie, after working with him for three hours, left the room visibly drained. She smiled at me as I passed her in the hall and said: "I wish I had the charisma of tuna fish and toast." Carol kept calling him her little space cadet. Several times, I heard her say: "Hey, handsome, you're on Mars, aren't you?" Suzi whistled and laughed at him, nicknaming him "mush-face" during this period. Despite his unavailability, Francisca flowed with it, not once exhibiting anxiousness. Slowly, the idea of trusting herself and her son became a working premise. She understood the lack of equilibrium in his body and accepted his response to it. She maintained her conviction even as his withdrawal persisted into the end of the week and through the following one as well.

Unlike the summer, this major "pause" did not evolve into the anger of hitting. After the symptoms of a mild flu passed, Robertito vacillated between lethargy and self-stimulating rituals. Often, he laughed and giggled without any apparent reason. His infectious smile bathed everyone in his strange, timeless and surrealistic mood. He could sit quietly for hours with a soft, blissed-out grin on his face. Although most of us solicited him for more contact, no one panicked or disapproved, even implicity, of Robertito's passivity. An accepting attitude prevailed.

On the thirteenth day since the beginning of his happy inertia, Francisca dressed him and fed him as usual, almost expecting the current state of affairs to continue. Nevertheless, consistent with her attempts to engage her son, she began to build an irregular tower of blocks in front of him on the table. He side-glanced at it, then raced around the room, balancing on his toes. When he touched the wall, he giggled.

"Come, my love. Build a tower like Mommy." Surprisingly, the child turned, walked to the table and sat down attentively. Francisca furrowed her forehead. "Robertito . . . are you ready?" No response. She could feel a wave of excitement bubble within her. His eyes were different. More alert. Less glazed. "Build a tower like Mama." His first effort to lift the block reflected the same lethargy evident all week. But then, he quickened his pace, finally duplicating the exact tower his mother had built.

He learned over, flapped his hands for a moment and said: "*Lo mismo* [the same]."

Francisca could not believe her ears. He had never used that word before and as he said it now, he used it in the correct context. "Yes. The same. Mama and Robertito made the same tower. The same." She showered her child with affection, then fed him some food. "Okay, Robertito Soto," she bellowed, priming herself for the first real teaching session in two weeks. "I think you are wiser than all of us. I think so." She set a small blackboard in front of him and handed him a piece of chalk. Guiding his wrist, she had him draw a circle, a straight line and a cross. Within ten minutes, he made the marks on his own.

"Look at my hand, *papito*. How many fingers on my hand?" she asked.

"Using his index finger, he touched each finger tip and counted. "*Uno. Dos. Tres. Cuatro. Cinco.*"

"*Bueno, mi amor*," she said, beaming at his achievement. She held up her other hand and asked the same question. Again, he counted each finger. Then she raised the first hand again, but this time she pulled her hand away from him, thwarting his attempt to touch and count.

"Look carefully. How many fingers?" she asked.

Robertito made a clicking sound and turned away.

"Ah, my child. You don't have to answer. We will find something else to do." She left the table, crossed the room and rummaged through the piles of toys on the shelves.

Robertito, still sitting in his seat, said: "*Cinco.*"

Francisca whipped around and screamed. "You understood. You did." She grabbed her son out of the chair and hugged him. He continued to perform a series of minor miracles for her. Her attitude and quality of teaching motivated him to try harder and harder for both her and himself. Francisca was wonderful to watch.

When she took him to the toilet, he pulled her close to him as he sat on the bowl. Robertito played with her hair, then he flapped his hands. She admired her son, learning each day from his softness. Robertito flapped his hands even more, but Francisca, so taken by the communion of this day, forgot to imitate him. He finally took her hands and physically motioned for her to join him. They did that for a minute while looking into each other's eyes. He stopped, rested his head on her shoulder and refused to leave that position for over an hour. Francisca took a ride on a cloud with the child who used to frighten and frustrate her.

Carol introduced him to the flannel board and taught him to assemble faces and bodies on it, which he did with a rather lopsided expertise. She built an obstacle course in the room using old cartons, pieces of lumber, the chairs, the table, rubber tubes and a slant board. Once she demonstrated how to move through it, her student followed. She supported his every step. This day proved something special for Carol. Despite Robertito's co-operation and concentration, she loved him no more now than during the past two weeks when he had been distinctly unavailable. She knew she no longer needed him to grow. Robertito worked for Carol. As I watched them together, I suspected he knew and trusted her wanting. For some, she might have seemed like a tough taskmaster, but she remained flexible, loving and acutely responsive to his every cue.

As she left her session, she stopped at my squatted form by the door. Carol flashed a wild grin, bent over and whispered: "Today's my anniversary. One month without any seizures."

"How do you feel about that?" I asked in a hushed voice, not wanting to interrupt Chella, whose session with Robertito had just begun.

She inhaled like an athlete ready to sprint, then hugged me aggressively. "I feel like I just took my first step off the planet."

The implications of Carol's willingness to take responsibility for her illness were awesome. It took me almost a half an hour to focus my attention back into the room after her dramatic exit. Chella worked the lotto cards with Robertito, who not only identified almost all the images she verbalized, but, for the first time, used words like hot, cold, day and night in response to seeing corresponding scenes. Suddenly, Chella put the cards away and did something which surprised me. She threw about twelve different objects into a carton, placed it in front of Robertito and closed her eyes. Ten seconds passed. Robertito dipped into the box, grabbed a tennis ball

338

and handed it to her. As she cheered her student, she turned and looked at me. We both smiled. She repeated the exercise four times with the same results. On the fifth try, Robertito picked something she had not visualized. The spell seemed broken. Chella reverted back to voice requests for a short period, then attempted to use her thought patterns for communication again. This time he completed five out of the next six simple tasks correctly, an average better than his response to verbal cues, yet by no means infallible. As she tried to get him to insert pegs by using an image held in her mind, he left the table and went to the window. I knew Chella was relieved. In effect, Robertito's responses confirmed what she had come to understand in exploring her fears during our dialogue sessions. She didn't control this little boy ... nobody did. She had found another bridge to cross by opening a new route through which they could touch each other.

Though others in the program tried the same technique, only Chella seemed to have the ability to relate to Robertito in this manner. When she thought of a word, he usually never responded. But when she made a picture in her mind, he always reacted in some form, though not necessarily correctly. Again, his dependence on the right side of the brain, the picture-making side, and the probability of his developing an alternative internal radar system during those years of silence and isolation seemed confirmed by his reactions to Chella's picture-thoughts. We tried to maximize his skill by co-ordinating our words with something he could also see.

For the last part of the session, she brought him outside, capitalizing on our recent decision to take short breaks from the ritual of teaching and the sameness of the room. We believed his development had surged ahead to such a point that such sensory bombardment would not overload his circuits. As Chella and her young student walked together on the sidewalk, a man, dressed in a gray sweatsuit, jogged by them. Robertito shouted the word "run" in Spanish, turned and immediately ran behind the jogger. Chella burst into laughter, calling to her little friend. She chased them down the street. Finally, on his own initiative, Robertito stopped. About four minutes later, when the man passed again, Robertito said "run" again. But rather than join in, he watched the man intently, ultimately laughing at him as he passed.

Suzi and I sensed Robertito's readiness to climb to even more sophisticated plateaus. During her session, she taught him spatial concepts, such as over and under, in front of and behind. Slowly, very slowly, he began to grasp each idea as he placed objects on top of the table and under it. Suzi clapped and laughed. "What a smart mush-face," she exclaimed. They danced, lifted weights together and counted birds, flowers and toes. When Robertito disengaged from participating, Suzi placed Angelina in his chair.

"Okay, Angelina, are you ready?"

Robertito walked directly to the table, pushed the doll out of his seat and sat down.

"Ah, my sweet boy, you want to play," she said to him in a low, supportive voice. His moment of lucidity suggested all the untapped intelligence lurking behind those huge, dark brown eyes. In spite of the incredible, mind-boggling progress, he still kept a foot planted in each world...his own and ours. Unlike Raun, who discovered he loved to talk, Robertito had yet to develop a passion which would swing the pendulum to one side.

While I observed, he came over to me often, though I tried to be unobtrusive. One time, he stood in front of me and "ismed" in my face, an action I quickly imitated. In another instance, he stood beside me and leaned on my shoulder in an old Charlie Chaplin pose. I rubbed his arm gently and told him what a special person I thought he was. He pulled on my beard and watched my jaw flex up and down. Finally, he flopped into my lap and buried his head in my chest. I rocked him like an infant, trying to find the most loving part in myself to share with him.

Before I left, I put my hand out to him, which he took. "By-by, Robertito," I said.

"By-by, Bears," he grunted, demonstrating his new proficiency in using two words. Suzi giggled and furrowed her eyebrows. She repeated his good-by in exact tone and quality. I kissed them both and left.

"Okay, big boy," she said, acknowledging his scratching of his genital area. "Off to the bathroom we go." Since the summer, the number of "accidents" in his pants had decreased sharply, making him almost completely toilet trained.

Suzi kissed his nose as he stood in the doorway beside the tub. "Now you know how to do it...at least you can help." Together, they pulled his pants down. Since he had been so willful today, Suzi decided on furthering his ability to take care of himself and get what he wanted. She sat on top of the toilet seat, crossed her arms and waited. Robertito looked at her without moving. She would wait until he pushed her aside as he had done with Angelina. The little boy stared at her, then approached her seated form. She smiled at him. Suzi prided herself in helping Robertito break new ground. When he stood directly in front of her and squinted his eyes, she realized suddenly what he was about to do. Before she could move, Robertito urinated right in her lap.

* * *

As Jeannie pulled the car into the parking space, she marveled at her own ingenuity. She had thought of the idea all by herself. As we began to explore other experiences for Robertito, we now ventured out of the room several times a week for periods of almost an hour. Jeannie wanted that experience with him, so she suggested the local library. She took Robertito's hand and led him through the front entrance. He seemed slightly more agitated than usual, yet he stood quietly, like a gentleman, as they rode the elevator downstairs to the children's section.

Jeannie guided Robertito into a large room occupied by other children and their parents. Taking the initiative, Robertito grabbed a book from the shelf. Jeannie helped him set it on the table. Since she spoke to him in Spanish, she attracted attention immediately. She suspected the other mothers thought she was Robertito's mother, an illusion she enjoyed. Jeannie could not have loved her own son any more than this little boy.

The noise in the room seemed to unnerve Robertito slightly as his attention drifted from the book. He finger-twirled and hand-flapped, but without his usual intensity. Jeannie joined him until he worked through the self-stimulating rituals. When she tried to concentrate on the book again, she felt a heaviness as if the air had become thick and burdensome. As she looked up, a woman holding a baby in her lap turned away. Several other people avoided her glance. Two women, standing by the book shelves, whispered as they stole glances at Robertito. Yet the children in the room didn't seem to notice anything unusual.

Jeannie tried to ignore the obvious sentiment developing in the room. As she flipped a page in the book, Robertito bolted from the chair and circled the tables. He said "blue," indicating the painted walls, and "green," indicating the painted floor. He approached a mother with an infant near the corner. As he watched the child and smiled softly, the

341

woman pressed her baby to her and turned her back to Robertito. Jeannie wanted to confront her, but suppressed her impulse to protest, not wanting to destroy her own calm and connection with her special student. Perhaps, the noise, the light and the people were too much for him. When she tried to take his hand, he moved away. He ran to the desk and "ismed" at the lady on the telephone. She laughed, waved to him and proceeded with her call.

Now the other children began to note the difference between them and this little boy. Taking their cues from the parents, they avoided him when he came near them. Jeannie tried to smile at the mothers, but they turned away from her as well. She felt like she was losing control of the situation. Again, she tried to take Robertito's hand. She could see him withdrawing, the exact impulse she felt herself while in the room with these people. Instead of venting her own feelings, she focused on her little friend. "C'mon, Robertito," she said softly in Spanish. Everyone watched them like they were freaks.

As Robertito jogged around the room, he paused in front of a chubby little girl chewing gum. Her enormous cheeks flopped in and out like a giant expanding and contracting bubble. She smiled at him. He flapped at her as if saying hello. She giggled. Then wonderful, open, silly and loving Robertito Soto hugged the other child spontaneously and kissed her. The mother, who had been one of the women whispering by the bookcases, grabbed her daughter's arm. Frightened by her mother's response, she began to cry. Jeannie wanted to scream as she lifted Robertito off his feet and carried him up a flight of stairs and out the front entrance of the building.

"You're a beautiful boy," she told him as she knelt in front of his small form in the parking lot. She wanted to dispel whatever he might have absorbed in the library. "You did right. You loved that little girl better than anyone else in the room." Robertito threw his head from side to side, inattentive to her words. Jeannie realized that somewhere, somehow, he had felt the assault of their disdain and disapproving glances. She led him back to her car as the tears began to flow. Her initial anger at those people had dissipated, but she wondered how she could ever explain to this child what made absolutely no sense to her.

Robertito recuperated from the experience within the hour and continued his surge forward. The discomfort lingered

342

with Jeannie for the remainder of the week. She asked me for an additional Option session to deal with her unresolved feelings. Eventually, she freed herself from her anger when she realized that by holding those people in contempt, she did to them exactly what they had done to Robertito.

Chapter 23

The slow, even cadence of his respiration filled the room with its rhythmic music. Francisca listened to her son's breathing, embracing and cuddling the sounds like soft, dimensional objects. The blanket of darkness in the room provided her with a different kind of intimacy from the daily sessions. Although Robertito slept in another bed, three feet from her, she experienced an intuitive touching as if the night linked them together as solidly as a chain. They had gone through the "good night" ritual, mentioning everyone's name before separating. Robertito had fallen asleep quickly, but she had remained awake with her thoughts. Roby had been gone almost three months and, although Suzi and I and the others in the program had bolstered her at every turn, she felt incomplete. Despite her desire to have her husband next to her in bed, in this very bed at this very moment, the image most prevalent in her mind was a living portrait of Roby running and laughing with his son. Rather than finding the phone calls and letters unsettling, she held onto those moments tightly, sensing a peace and comfort in her husband as she described each event and milestone in the program. If it had been her, if they had traded places and she had returned to Mexico alone, she didn't think she could have survived with only the mail and a thin telephone wire to connect her with everything she loved. The three thousand miles which separated them seemed unthinkable.

Little-boy laughter interrupted the somber mood of her thoughts and drew her attention. Robertito cackled and giggled in his sleep. Francisca smiled and found herself giggling quietly with him. Her son laughed in his sleep often. When the merry burst of sounds subsided, his breathing dominated. Then the room became quiet. Francisca strained to hear him. Instead, she heard only her own pulse and respiration. She turned toward her son's prostrate form, ready to spring from her bed. At that moment, she heard him whimper. He turned and twisted, pushing himself against his pillow. Francisca speculated that he might be having an unsettling dream, a rarity for Robertito. The restlessness and guttural sounds escalated. Rather than wake him and possibly startle him, as she once had, she decided to let him pass through the dream in his sleep.

Robertito cried out, then bolted upright in the bed. Wide-eyed and panting, he scanned the darkness, alert like a frightened animal, holding himself in a primitive state of readiness. He rolled to the edge of the mattress and dropped his feet to the floor. Robertito crossed the short expanse and climbed into his mother's bed. Francisca heard him inch across the mattress toward her. Did he want her? Her son had never solicited comfort from her or any other person in the face of fear or pain. When his body touched hers, she felt his arm slip around her torso. His breathing relaxed immediately. Within seconds, the child fell asleep. Francisca touched his hand, trying to quiet the trembling in her own body. Was it possible? Robertito, frightened in a dream, had reached through the darkness to find his mother. He had turned to her instead of curling into a fetal position and seeking safety inside of himself. "Yes, I am your mama," she said in a hushed voice to the sleeping form. "I am Mama." This time she had no doubts that he understood their relationship. She had been here for him in this way for over six years and now, for the first time, he latched onto her, squeezing his arm tightly around her body. Francisca continued to pat his hand as her eyelids closed and she settled into a deep sleep, an umbrella under which she took another kind of journey with her young son.

The street glistened. The wetness on the boulevard reflected the lanterns and neon signs of the stores. Francisca walked proudly beside Robertito, holding his hand. Her eyes feasted on the various window displays in her first little excursion in months. As she paused to admire a long dress, Robertito pulled his hand from hers. When she turned to him, he stood on a level about three feet above the sidewalk. He placed one foot in front of the other as if grounded on something solid. He took the initiative, indicating his intention to continue their stroll.

"C'mon, Robertito, walk...ah, walk beside me," she said, awed at her own lack of amazement.

Her son glanced at her, smiled, then proceeded with his elevated promenade. Rather than force him to do something he obviously did not want to do, she tried to maintain a casual attitude as they paraded down the boulevard. The next time she looked away for a fraction of a second, his position changed radically again. Now his portion of the sidewalk appeared recessed. He walked on a level below hers. Robertito laughed as he watched his own feet.

"Robertito," she exclaimed, registering her surprise. "What are you doing?" He peered up at her and said matter-of-factly: "I am walking."

His simple, direct answer forced a smile on her face. Certinly, she had a far more complex, disjointed and confused response to what she witnessed. Okay, she thought, if he's walking, he's walking. On the next street, the levels of cement rejoined, but Robertito now appeared slightly taller than usual. When Francisca scrutinized his body, she realized he glided about five inches off the ground. He seemed to have the ability to choose any path he wanted, no longer confined by the rules and realities which dictated her own limits. As they approached an antique store, with two bureaus and several chairs set in front of the shop, she began to walk to the left, instinctively detouring around the furniture. Robertito paraded straight ahead.

"This way, my love." No response. "Robertito," she bellowed urgently. Francisca tried to grab his hand, but missed it, unable to prevent his collision with the huge oak cabinet. She gasped as her son walked through the structure, his body penetrating one side of the wood and reappearing on the other. What's happening? Is this a dream? Yet her experience seemed solid, reliable, indisputable. They proceeded in silence. She stared at the smooth skin stretched across her son's face. There were no scratches...no bruises. Even the cabinet appeared untouched. Francisca experienced neither fear nor repulsion...only awe. She had learned to trust Robertito, even in her dream. As she watched his small form, she confirmed that awareness.

At the end of the row of shops, they passed an empty lot, then walked in front of a separate building housing a huge hardware store. Robertito made a right turn abruptly. Before Francisca could catch him, he walked into a Gargantuan display window. Instead of breaking it, he walked through it, leaving a distinct imprint of his body in the plate glass. Francisca shouted to her son, but he didn't respond as he disappeared in the darkened store. She ran to the door. Locked. She kept jiggling the handle, hoping to free the latch magically. She had to get her son. Francisca banged heavily on the metal frame. The noise ricocheted through the street. A surly man descended the exterior metal stairs from the apartment above the store.

"Yes, what is it?"

"You have to open the door," she begged him, pointing to the shop. "Please help me. My son's inside. He's only a little boy."

"Listen, lady," the man barked, "I don't know what you're talking about. I locked up over an hour ago and I can assure you, no one, except a very mean dog, is in that store."

The panic made her dizzy. A dog! She hadn't heard a dog. As the man turned from her, Francisca grabbed his sleeve. "Please, señor. You must help me get my son."

He pulled away from her. "Try the police station, lady."

She pursued him halfway up the stairs to the second floor. She cornered him against the railing and clutched his arm. "He's only a child. You can't turn your back on a child."

The man peered into her frantic eyes and, for reasons he himself did not understand, he followed her back down the stairs. As he turned off the alarm and unlatched the locks, he listened for his dog.

"Hurry," Francisca pressed.

"I'm going as fast as I can." He struggled with the last mechanism. "Where's the damn dog?" he muttered.

Once they entered, the owner threw the master switch, illuminating the entire two floors. "Robertito," Francisca called as she raced down the aisles.

"Jesus, lady. Wait for me. You want to get hurt? There's a guard dog in here," he yelled, running after her.

But Francisca ignored the warning. She searched behind every counter before she climbed up a flight of stairs to the balcony. There she saw her son gazing casually at the array of tools. "Oh, Robertito, thank God." She approached him, then stopped short as the low, foreboding rumble of a growling dog reached her ears. Robertito turned to the massive animal innocently and petted it. The dog relaxed immediately. Francisca took another step toward her child. Sensing no opposition, she grabbed his hand and turned to leave. The man watched them from the top of the stairs. He couldn't imagine how the child had gotten into the store. He also could not understand why his guard dog actually appeared docile with this child and, now, with its mother.

Robertito smiled warmly at the shopkeeper. Against every natural impulse to express outrage and anger at the youngster, the storeowner just stared at the little boy. The muscles in his face eased as he, too, smiled.

Francisca ushered her son out the door quickly. When she looked back, she saw the imprint of Robertito's body still molded in the display window. Suddenly, everything, absolutely everything, seemed possible to her. Rather than scold her son, she began to laugh.

The cackling in her throat reached her ears, awakening her. Her son's arm still kept its firm grip around her. A wave of warmth flooded her body as she reviewed her dream, which confirmed her own belief that Robertito, indeed, could do whatever he wanted to do. Yet she still envisioned her own powers as severely limited. Francisca remembered the question I had asked her in a dialogue session earlier in the day. Could she handle the program with Roby? Could she do it without us? Her hesitant response still echoed in her head. "Not yet, Bears, but I'm getting closer to knowing I could." Francisca knew she had been afraid to say yes. But if Robertito could do anything he wanted to do, why couldn't she? She knew she had not been ready before the past summer, but said she was as part of a pose of confidence. This time she wanted to be sure...she had to be sure. No more role playing. To hell with the appearance of strength. The surface of dignity she had valued all her life did not bring her through those frightening weeks. She had lied to herself and, now, she refused to do it again.

Francisca kissed the top of her son's head. "Will I ever be good enough?" she whispered. "Will I ever really know?"

* * *

Suzi held Robertito's hand and I held Raun's as we all crossed the street and entered the park. Over my left shoulder, I carried Robertito's two-wheel bike, equipped with training wheels. As I watched our little friend, he looked like any other six-year-old in the playground. He "ismed" occasionally and for relatively short periods. Today, he had the appearance of having his two feet planted in our world. Rather than this being a reflection of his total presence, it only told us about this moment, here and now.

Robertito still vacillated between his internal universe and the one outside of himself. He responded inconsistently, though his learning process rocketed forward on a steep inclined curve. His comprehension of generalized concepts, such as separate versus apart, yes versus no, opened versus closed, big-small, vertical-horizontal, same-different, was awesome most of the time. Nevertheless, we still came upon isolated hours or days where he had the appearance of not knowing or remembering what we knew he had once learned. Then, during the next session, he would demonstrate a sharp and decisive comprehension of these notions. When Lisa visited after a three-month absence, he called her name, hugged and wrestled with her in the special way which had been a distinct part of their sessions together. In Chella's presence, he chased a fly around the room. Previously, an insect could land on his nose and he would remain passive. We catalogued the growing frequency of two-word answers and responses: "More, Carol," "¡Hola!, Bears," "Want water." As part of an over-all design to elevate his cognitive abilities further, we instituted more sophisticated questions. "What color are your eyes?" "How many chairs in the room?" "What do you do when you're hungry?" His answer to the last question: "I eat." His receptive and expressive language capability soared.

Suzi and I lifted both boys onto the swings. They eyed each other.

"Push, Daddy," Raun instructed. "Robertito, we're going up-up," he said in English. Then he shrugged his shoulders and made a goofy expression, not unlike his mother. I whispered a Spanish equivalent to him. "I mean, uh...*arriba*," he shouted.

349

"*Quiero arriba,*" Robertito grunted, confirming his own desire to go up.

With an even thrust, we sent them both gliding through the air. Raun laughed, shouting, "Higher! Higher!" as he pumped with his legs. Robertito, his feet dangling, stared at the open field in front of him.

"Where's Raun?" Suzi asked her student in Spanish.

Robertito pointed emphatically and said: "*Aquí!*"

"That's right, Robertito. Fantastic. Wonderful. Now, can you look at him?" Robertito's eyes remained fixed.

"Aw, c'mon, Robertito," Raun chimed. "I'm your friend. Look at me."

The little boy turned to his smiling counterpart. He noticed Raun's legs with great interest, then, spontaneously, began the same movement with his own limbs. "Look, look . . ." Raun screamed in delight. "He's doing it . . . see, I told you guys he was smart."

Later, Raun guided Robertito down the slide. He held the other boy's chubby hand with his long, delicate fingers and led him to the monkey bars. Robertito tugged on Raun's arm, pulling him back to the slide. Raun giggled. "Well, why didn't you say so?" Robertito flapped his free hand, almost as if his "ism" was a response to the question. Raun imitated his friend's motion.

Suzi and I maintained a low profile. Our son had become more accomplished as a teacher and therapist. Perhaps, most significantly, we did not want to interfere or divert their attention from each other. We tried not to dilute their special connection with our presence.

They ran together through the fields holding hands until they were exhausted. Raun handed Robertito pieces of bread to feed the ducks, but his little friend shoved the food directly into his own mouth. Raun tapped Robertito. "Watch me," he said, throwing a piece into the water. "Watch me again." After completing his second illustration, Raun handed his young charge another piece. Robertito stuffed it quickly into his mouth. "Hey, that's not fair," Raun protested, then he burst out laughing, patting Robertito on the shoulder as he smiled back at us. "I like feeding him more than the ducks."

Five minutes later, after his own stomach had been adequately filled, Robertito threw his first piece of bread to the ducks. Raun jumped up and down, applauding. Robertito turned to our son and applauded back.

A plane passed overhead. Robertito Soto looked up and said correctly: "*Avión.*"

"Raunch," Suzi called. "Want to try the bicycle?" Our son nodded, took his friend's hand once again and brought him back to us.

"Maybe you can show him first," I said.

"Robertito. Look at me. C'mon, look at me." He hopped onto the bike and rode it in a circle. Robertito watched for several seconds, then looked away, twirling his fingers beside his head. "He's not watching."

"Call him," Suzi suggested, "and say *mira,* which means look. You remember, don't you?"

Raun nodded. "Robertito. *Mira.* Here I am. *Mira,* Robertito." The boy stopped his "ism" and watched again.

When they traded places, Robertito appeared confused on the bicycle. Raun and I pushed him for a while, hoping that the moving pedals would aid him in understanding the process. Each time we stopped, Robertito just sat there, waiting.

"Use your feet," Suzi said. "Like Raunchy did...you can do it, sweet boy."

"Yeah, sweet boy," Raun chimed innocently. "You can do it. I know you can."

We both looked at our son and laughed.

"Maybe you can show him again," I suggested. Raun whizzed around in circles, then made figure eights. When he delivered the bike back to Robertito, he stared into the other child's eyes. I helped our little friend climb back on the seat. Raun held the handle bars tightly and smiled. Robertito watched him, then picked up our son's hand and kissed it. Raun's face registered shock, then surprise. He appeared flattered and bewildered at the same time. Without further hesitation, he picked up Robertito's little hand and kissed him back.

"You're going to do it now, aren't you?" Raun said softly as he began to pull on the handle bars, propelling the bike forward. Still, Robertito did not push on the pedals. Raun persisted, then suddenly let go. The bike kept moving. Raun started to jog backward and Robertito followed, slowly propelling the bicycle forward. After about twenty feet, he put considerably more energy into his effort. As the bike moved faster, Raun turned around and started a slow trot. He waved to his friend, coaxing him to follow. For the next ten minutes, Raun, like the pied piper, ran around the playground with smiling Robertito Soto in hot pursuit on his little bicycle.

*　　*　　*

The old buses, painted in garish greens, yellows and reds, whizzed by. The dust whipped up from the street like miniature tornados and assaulted his nostrils. Motors sputtered; the incomplete combustion belched fumes into the narrow corridors between stores. Roby tried to hold his breath as he zigzagged across a major intersection. Since the sidewalks were cluttered with people marching home at the end of a workday, he walked his own path next to the curb. Roby waved to familiar faces, nodding a soft hello. Instead of his usual stop at a small diner, he decided to go directly home, wanting to be closer to his family.

He swung the door closed briskly behind him, then stopped, closed his eyes and inhaled deeply. In the darkness, Roby fumbled for the light switch, finally flipping it and illuminating both the dining room and the kitchen. He placed his wallet and coins in a small metal dish, a present from Francisca. He checked his watch against the electric clock on the counter. No matter how many times he performed these familiar rituals after work, he always had a three-second fantasy that the house would be filled with people... Francisca, Robertito, Alicia, perhaps Francisca's mother, her cousin José, their little niece Chella. Each face came to him as vividly as if the person stood before him. He reached out to his wife's and son's images, but they disappeared before he could touch them. Roby Soto thanked the universe for the momentary illusion.

He gazed at the photograph of his son centered on the living room wall. He waved to the little face. "¡Hola!, Robertito," he whispered in the empty house. He proceeded to make the same gesture in front of his wife's portrait.

The cold, stagnant air in the house chilled him. He reached for one of Francisca's shawls in the closet. In an effort to economize so that he could send the needed funds to New York, Roby had had the gas line shut off. He had survived the lack of heat since the temperature outside had not dropped below forty-five, but he shivered each night when he forced himself to take a cold shower.

In the kitchen, he scanned the clean counters. Seven months ago, they might have been filled with fruits and vegetables as well as hot dishes awaiting his arrival. When he coughed, he heard his own echo in the room. He opened the refrigerator and surveyed the limited selection of items. Three gallons of mineral water, half a loaf of semi-stale whole wheat bread, a small piece of cheese and a jar of jam occupied the otherwise empty shelves. Since he had to work oftentimes in the days and evenings, he had little opportunity to shop at the market.

Roby removed a glass from the cabinet and filled it with water. He made himself a rather anemic cheese and jam sandwich, then inserted a cassette into a small tape recorder on the table. His teeth chewed mechanically as his eyes fixed on the moving spools in the machine. A smile exploded on his face the moment he heard Francisca's voice. He mouthed every word and knew exactly when to pause.

He had recorded every telephone conversation with his wife in an effort to extend their time together. In order to be close to her and, in turn, his son, he played the tapes back each night, sometimes listening to them three and four times an evening. This particular one contained Robertito answering simple questions and singing a short Spanish lullaby. With his mouth partially filled, Roby stopped chewing and hummed along with his son.

After dinner, he retreated to his workshop behind the garage. To match Robertito's burgeoning vocabulary, Roby fashioned another series of books to supplement our supply in New York. He sat at the workbench for hours, cutting out photographs from the huge pile of magazines in front of him. The tape recorder filled the room with Francisca's voice. Working diligently, Roby pasted the pieces neatly, pressing the edges and holding them until they became fixed. He did not want the corners to lift. This book was for his son, for Robertito.

By eleven o'clock, he had finished ten pages. His eyelids began to fall. Roby rubbed his hands together as he rose from the chair. The cold had begun to settle in his bones. The tiny wall thermometer read fifty-seven degrees. Roby jogged in place for about five minutes until the rush of circulation warmed his hands.

He entered the bedroom hesitantly. For Roby, this was the loneliest room in the house. He lifted his son's overalls from the chair and smelled them. He touched the glass covering his wife's portrait, trying to re-create the sensation of her skin beneath his finger tips. Roby slipped into a pair of jeans and a sweat shirt, shivering from the cold again. Once in bed on his back, he pulled the blankets to his chin. A vivid image of Francisca working with Robertito in that second floor room in New York flashed in front of him. Roby Soto thought he had to be one of the luckiest men in the world.

Chapter 24

Francisca flipped the pages in the magazine for Robertito, who consumed the splashes of colors, shapes and forms with eager eyes. Spontaneously, he pointed to a car and identified it verbally, then he stared at a smiling face and said the word "happy." Both Suzi and I joined Francisca in cheering him as we sat together in the waiting room outside of Carl Yorke's offices. Almost four months had elapsed since the last developmental work-up.

The door to the other office finally opened. Dr. Yorke, sporting a reserved grin, motioned to us. Suzi, who would again act as translator, invited Robertito to follow her into the other room. He trailed after her without hesitation. The doctor asked me to join them so he could review with us certain questions and the battery of tests he planned to administer.

In spite of Robertito's intimacy with both Suzi and me, he approached the psychologist first. Carl, noting our little friend's initiative, tapped his own legs in an affectionate gesture. To his surprise and ours, Robertito jumped into his lap.

"¡Hola!, Robertito," Yorke blurted.

"*¡Hola!*," the child replied. "*Yo quiero agua.*"

"Water?" Carl asked, glancing at us for verification.

"*Sí, sí,*" Suzi nodded. "*Más tarde,* Robertito."

"You people are unbelievable. You mean this boy is not only saying words, but he talks in sentences?"

"Not big ones," I assured him.

Carl smiled. "How do you do it? It's been less than four months. Last time I saw him he could only say the first syllable of a few words." He looked back at the child and smiled.

Robertito took his hand and stared into the man's eyes. "*Café ojos,*" he said, identifying Carl's brown eyes.

"Fantastic," the psychologist said boisterously, registering his own delight as well as responding to his own natural impulse to congratulate the boy. He still found himself amazingly attracted to Robertito. Yorke shook his head, peered at Suzi and me, then pointed skyward. "I'm telling you, they already have your places reserved up there."

After the completed examination and a short conference with us, Carl stood at his door and watched Francisca help her son put his coat on.

"Mrs. Soto's a very lucky lady," he said.

"Lucky?" I questioned. "She helped make this happen... every step of the way."

"We make our own luck," Suzi offered.

The psychologist grinned his affirmation. His attention focused back on Robertito. "I've never seen it before," he said. "Really, folks, if this little boy never learns one more thing, what you've done here is still a miracle."

Francisca sat beside her son in the back seat of the car. Suzi leaned over the front seat and played with Robertito. I rattled off all the quick statistics the psychologist had accumulated during the testing. Her son's I.Q., a factor which supposedly remains fairly constant throughout a person's life, had jumped dramatically again...from 14 to 30 and, now, to over 45. His total language capability, initially on a one- to two-month level, had soared. His expressive vocabulary had reached a three-year-old level and his ability to understand approached a four-year level. Even Carl, in relating the figures before submitting the written report, found the comparisons startling.

As I completed my enthusiastic monologue, I noticed Francisca's rather sedate expression. "Hey, aren't you excited? Listen to the man's findings."

"The doctor's report is not important," she said with unusual calm. "I used to think it meant everything, but not now. I know my son better than anyone. I can see he has changed. I can see how much he has learned. That's what is important."

Suzi and I glanced fleetingly at each other. In that instant as she spoke, in that recognition of what she knew, she had affirmed her own power and her own authority. Although she valued the caring and expertise of Dr. Yorke, she realized that she could correctly assess and understand her own child's ability and situation. She knew the test scores and data gave us an additional way to plot growth, but her excitement and appreciation would no longer be tied to figures or intelligence quotients. Francisca prized, unconditionally, the flesh-and-blood child next to her. I wanted to stop the car, leap over the seat and hug her. I considered shouting as a lesser celebration, but the peacefulness in her face aborted my impulse.

"You are a very special lady, Señora Soto," I said.

Francisca smiled self-consciously. She did not feel special or even different. But then, as she turned to her son, she sensed a new kind of strength, one more secure, more reliable, begin to blossom within her.

Yorke's report confirmed the various areas and stages of Robertito's recent development.

"This boy had been worked with continuously by Mr. and Mrs. Kaufman and their staff since he was last seen about four months ago. He can now say about fifty words in Spanish, can say short sentences, has improved his weight-lifting ability, recalls names of people and says them and apparently he's more socially competent, more socially assertive and more affectionate.

"Robertito was tested while Mr. Kaufman's wife, Suzi, was in the room. Mrs. Kaufman constantly spoke to the boy in Spanish after receiving instructions from the psychologist. She would very frequently hug and kiss the boy if he did things correctly. She encouraged him constantly without giving him answers or leading him. The psychologist is somewhat knowledgeable of Spanish and could readily understand the direction she was giving to him and would stop her if, in any way, she was directing the boy or inadvertently leading him to answer.

"Robertito's behavior during testing can be characterized as much better than it has ever been before. He was more cooperative, he followed instructions better and his attention span had improved. He expressed his ideas more clearly. Most impressive was the fact that he no longer flapped his arms; he no longer ran around the room; he came over to the psychologist and talked to the psychologist. He did not stand on the desk as he had done during the first examination and his ability to focus attention on the tasks at hand was infinitely better than when he had been tested on previous occasions.

"From a social point of view, it was noted that the boy now focuses in, his behavior is more appropriate, he looks at people, talks to them, touches them and listens. He does not withdraw and seems much less restless. He certainly is less autistic than he had been. Occasionally, he will flap his arm around but at no time did he withdraw or spin around or do something that was totally inappropriate; i.e., like standing on a desk. The boy appears more confident of himself, is certainly much more conforming and he relates better. He shows his intelligence more now because he is more interested in the environment. His frustration tolerance has improved and he now attacks tasks more efficiently in a less disorderly way than he had previously.

"In terms of gross motor coordination, it was noted that now the boy can catch a ball, whereas he was unable to do this before. In terms of fine motor coordination, he is now able to copy a circle, imitate a bridge using blocks and hold a pencil more adequately. He can now get a drink by himself, dry himself and he tends to avoid simple hazards. He is now going to the toilet by himself, but is unable to wipe himself.

"It was noted that he now talks in very short phrases of two and three words. He could do such things as tell you his full name, repeat three digits, name colors, respond to simple commands and recognize common objects. It was noted that Robertito is now able to understand prepositions, he can name body parts, he can sing rhymes and songs and is beginning to act more verbally appropriate.

"There has been an infinite improvement in the boy's overall behavior in all areas since he was last seen.

"When Robertito was first seen, seven months ago, he showed symptoms that were rather classical of an autistic child. At that time, during the initial testing, he spent most of his time running around the room, he tore papers, he never said any words, he showed inappropriate behavior and would run around in circles. At that time, he made only random sounds, never looked at the psychologist, would show inappropriate motor behavior such as jumping up and down or running without provocation or would merely spin around. At that time, he did not listen to requests and did not respond to either auditory or visual stimuli. At that time, he did not relate, did not say any recognizable words, look at or listen to people. At that time, he was occupied with objects, was restless and never uttered an understandable word. When first seen, his receptive and expressive language was on about a 1 or 2 month level and his I.Q., at that time, was on about a 7 month level despite his chronological age of over five-and-a-half. He did not show any indications of being able to do anything of a fine or gross motor nature and was socially inept.

"Now, he was able to understand words on a four-year-old level and his expressive vocabulary was on a three-year-old level. His I.Q. had increased from under 14 to over 45. The boy's progress has been remarkable in all areas."

I couldn't help but think about all the hospitals, clinics and physicians that had dismissed this special little boy as hopeless. They assured the Sotos he would not be able to think and talk, that even their "clinical" evidence supported the conclusion that he would live out his life in little more than a vegetative state. When I tried to conjure up the image of that ghost town in the left frontal lobes of his brain, I imagined only activity and sparks of energy. My thoughts drifted to Roby and Francisca. I wondered who, indeed, had learned more...they or their son?

Several days later, the bearded Paul Goodman arrived to do his follow-up psychiatric evaluation. When I offered him herbal tea, he answered affirmatively this time. Francisca, who had become openly skeptical of all tests and evaluations, greeted the psychiatrist enthusiastically. Despite her point of view, she felt indebted to this man. He had offered his time graciously, a fact among many which had helped change her perspective about people since her arrival in New York.

While I waited in the living room of the Soto house, I remained acutely sensitive that today had been the downside swing of the seesaw. Sometimes, the intense energy required by this little boy in order to learn sapped all his reserves. He had to rest, to pause, to regenerate. Robertito balanced himself between our world and his, not as a statement about us, but, perhaps, as a way to ensure his own survival. Every new word, new concept and new activity required more than his utmost attention; he had to push himself to the limits, pulling

359

his cargo along rusty tracks. Yet, despite the inconsistencies and the back-and-forth wavering, the curve of learning still soared upward. We had hooked him with our joy, enthusiasm and love, but I wondered, even now, whether he had found his own compelling reasons to be with us.

After the examination. Dr. Goodman lingered on the staircase.

"So?" I asked.

"Sometimes, he holds onto the autism," Goodman observed.

"We always allow him that," I answered.

"I know you do. And obviously, there's something to it. When I first heard him talk, I couldn't believe my ears. How? In such a short period of time, or in any period of time, how'd you do it?"

"We didn't do it," I assured him. "Robertito did it for himself."

Paul nodded his head and smiled as he began to descend the stairs.

"Robertito has now been worked with on an intensive daily basis for seven months," Dr. Goodman summarized in his report. "He spends virtually all of his waking hours involved in his treatment program. He has continued to make dramatic progress, although presently his behavior is characterized by frequent shifts in levels of functioning. For example, he has periods of seemingly 'almost normal' periods followed by regression to his old state of being very unrelated.

"Toilet training has progressed to a point where Robertito is almost totally bowel trained. He is mostly trained for the bladder during the day, but still wears diapers at night.

"At the onset of the program, it was discovered that Robertito had diminished touch and pain sensation on the right side of his body, especially his right hand. Also at that time, he was unable to support the weight of his body with his hands. Exercises were then developed to strengthen these weaknesses. Robertito is now able to support his weight with his hands and can be lifted up and down while holding onto a bar.

"Language ability has been steadily increasing. In comparison to the total lack of language and pre-linguistic ability at the onset of the program seven months ago and the approximately ten word monosyllabic vocabulary noted four months ago, Robertito's spontaneous vocabulary now is at least fifty words. He is able to form a sentence when he wants
360

something. He is now learning concepts such as 'same-different,' 'up-down,' and other pairs of opposites. He knew the sounds animals make. He sings songs. He is learning to distinguish geometric shapes. He mumbles words to himself even when not being directly stimulated.

"In comparison to the totally unrelated, self-absorbed and self-stimulating activities when seen initially, Robertito's relatedness to other people has not only developed, but continues to expand. He pays more attention to what other people are doing in the room even when they are not trying to involve him. He will approach people spontaneously to join in what they are doing. Robertito will hug and show affection spontaneously.

"Compared to the baseline observation seven months ago, Robertito is now quite a different child. He has lost none of the gains noted at four months into the program and has made substantial progress since then. At present, there is a greater unevenness to his functioning; he can change abruptly from a state of attentive learning to one of autistic withdrawal. When he is paying attention and involved with the therapist, he gives the impression of a neurologically-impaired child who must make a great effort to receive and decode what is being presented to him and then to organize and produce the correct response. Robertito must experience a great deal of fatigue, which I think is one of the reasons for the greater degree of restlessness and more frequent periods of withdrawal. It is tempting also to compare this to the irritability and mildly-regressive behaviors often seen in normal six-year-old boys.

"In contrast to the initial examination, when he did not talk, and to four months ago, by which time he had developed the ability to say the first syllable of approximately eight words, he now demonstrates the ability to communicate and verbalize his wants and interest by spontaneously saying complete words—and, in some instances, short sentences. As a rough approximation, his abilities range to a thirty-six-month level. This is quite a significant and impressive movement from when first observed, just seven months ago, when his general behavior had not developed beyond the first few months of life."

In effect, both the psychological-developmental and psychiatric examinations recorded a developmental surge of three-to-four years in a seven-month time period.

"Why are the walls painted green?" Carol mumbled to herself as she waited in the reception area of the school. They must reserve all the green paint for hospitals, schools and institutions. She wiggled her foot as she itemized the varied achievements with Robertito during the morning session. His ability to cut with the scissors had shown a dramatic improvement. They had played memory games together. Each time she rattled off three or four objects or unrelated words, he would repeat them easily. Once, he actually managed to remember five words in a row. Carol felt a certain pride in having introduced the concept of first, middle and last. In only two days, her young student had mastered the notion with about 80 per cent accuracy. Robertito also demonstrated his ability to count up to twenty. In the month since the tests, he had already outstripped the new base lines.

A man in his early forties, impeccably dressed in a tan suit, appeared at the door and beckoned to her. Mr. Sharp had been assigned by the director to give Carol a brief orientation before introducing her to the other teachers and their program. As part of a seminar course and her student teaching responsibilities, she had to observe and research various special education programs. This particular facility had been noted for its work with all kinds of handicapped and developmentally disabled children, having a section specializing in autistic and autistic-like youngsters. Mr. Sharp queried her about her own experiences. When she talked about our program with Robertito and the previous one with Raun, the man smiled indulgently. He assured her that any child worked twelve hours a day would improve. Carol tried to explain to him about the summer, how they all had worked those same long hours with, unfortunately, unproductive and, potentially, disastrous results. She tried to talk about attitude, but Mr. Sharp discontinued the conversation politely. He directed her down a long corridor and into a huge classroom in which she met three teachers.

Carol spent the remainder of the day observing and, at times, trying to participate. Six teachers worked with a population of thirty-five autistic children, ranging from nine years to fifteen years old. Most of the students had a glazed, drugged appearance, although one of the teachers insisted that despite the fact that some of the children had been placed on medication by their private physicians, the school neither prescribed nor administered any drugs.

"Come with me," Mrs. Doren said, guiding Carol into a second classroom, smaller than the first. The woman smiled. "We call this the wing-ding ward."

A group of students stood in a long line. Some rocked in place, others stared at their hands or the floor, still others made distinctively peculiar gestures, often repetitive in their occurrence. The first child in line, a little boy, walked toward the far wall holding a green hanger out in front of him.

"Jimmy, do we have to do this a thousand times until you'll finally understand? Not against the wall. The hanger goes in the box. In the box! Do you understand?" The teacher, obviously exasperated, crossed his arms in front of his chest. He squinted his disapproval.

The little boy turned to him nervously and grinned in confusion. His feet appeared cemented to the floor.

"We don't have all day," the man barked. "Jimmy, put the damn hanger in the box."

A young woman, perhaps only a few years older than Carol, paraded into the center of the room and knelt in front of the child. "Either you do it on your own steam or I'm going to have to bring you there." Jimmy began to rub his hands and hum. "Okay...have it your way." She grabbed his arm and pulled him away from the wall. At first he resisted, but then he stopped his ten-second tug-of-war. When he arrived at the carton, he dropped the hanger into it.

"Now you can wait at the wall." The boy did not move. The young teacher sighed noisily, took the child's arm and pulled him to the side of the room.

"Next," the man chimed like a drill sergeant. Mrs. Doren excused herself in order to deliver another green plastic hanger to the next child in line. "Okay, Sharon, in the box it goes." She inched toward the carton as if approaching a bomb. Finally, about four feet from it, Sharon tossed the hanger without looking and ran to the wall. It missed its mark. A fourth teacher, who had been sitting at the desk, rose to her feet and promenaded into the center of the room. She flipped the hanger expertly into the box.

Carol couldn't close her mouth, nor could she neutralize the acid taste burning in her throat. The class taskmaster joined her. "My name's Foley, Jack Foley." He eyed her parentally. "Listen, you get used to it. Have you ever seen autistic children before?"

"I work with one," she whispered.

"Ah, then you know," the teacher grinned. "It's sad, but this is a wasteland. You need a firm hand to keep them in line."

She tried to ignore his comment. For a moment, she couldn't believe her own thoughts...she actually considered physically attacking the man. "Why the hangers in the box? What do you hope to teach them?"

"Nothing," he replied casually. "We've long since given up trying to teach them. The goal, young lady, is to keep them busy." He strutted back into the arena, belching out his orders to the inattentive youngsters.

Carol peered at a little boy with sandy brown hair and piercing dark eyes. That could be Raun. She watched another youngster, a beautiful, slighty pudgy child with jet black hair. That could be Robertito. And what about the blond-haired girl with bangs? And the handsome black child twirling his hands gracefully in front of the windows?

She felt lightheaded. For a second, Carol thought she might lose her balance. She refused to recognize these sensations as signs of an oncoming seizure. Almost three whole months had passed since her last one; an amazing record, especially since she had not taken any medication in that time period. They're doing the best they can, she thought to herself. They are! Based on what they know and believe. Stay with it, she counseled herself. Stop judging them...just be here now. The anger dissipated as she refocused on the activity in the room.

Mrs. Doren returned to her side. "There's so much you can do," Carol offered.

The older woman nodded. "That's what I said when I graduated school. But you get used to it. There's really nothing much you can do. Trying to teach these kids is like banging your head against the wall."

"But why do you believe that?" Carol protested. "Have you ever taken one, just one, and tried?"

The woman gaped at her. "What's this...an inquisition? Listen, Carol, you're our guest. If you want to start a crusade, you've got the wrong place."

Carol followed the teachers and the class into the cafeteria. Most of the children seated themselves at four tables, but some were pulled, pushed and, literally, shoved down onto the benches.

One little boy sat on the floor by the side wall and twirled a piece of paper. Relieved to be able to concentrate her attention, Carol slipped between the rows of benches and chairs, pulled a soiled napkin from the garbage pail and sat beside the child. She ripped her paper to duplicate his and imitated his motion. Within seconds, the boy stopped and looked at her. A tiny smile wrinkled his face as he now continued his "ism." Carol followed him, finally feeling connected. "Wow," she said, "you sure are good at it." She touched the little boy's leg with her hand. He stared at her fingers as he twirled the paper.

"Bobby," Jack Foley shouted, "what the hell do you think you're doing?" He directed his question to Carol as much as to the boy. The man slapped Bobby's hand down, then pulled him to his feet. "Let's go. I'm putting you at table four today." As they walked away, the child turned back to steal a glance at Carol. She ground her teeth. Her body felt stiff and brittle.

Later, as she sat at a table, trying to engage some of the children, a boy knocked over a container of milk by accident. The avalanche of white liquid hitting the floor attracted everyone's attention. In a fury, a teacher Carol had not seen before, approached the table. She pulled the child out of his chair. The boy went limp and slid to the floor. Frightened, he tried to curl himself into a ball. The teacher grabbed him by the hair and jerked him off the floor, then forced him to sit in a corner of the cafeteria.

"That kid's always doing things like that," one teacher muttered.

"You can't leave them alone for a minute or all you'll have left is a zoo," another added.

Carol forced herself to approach the other teachers. "Have you ever thought of going with these children, doing what they do, instead of stopping them?"

"Ah ha!" the younger teacher remarked. "I see you've been doing your reading. I've heard about a book, about some family who did that with their own son. If you believe it, then you probably also believe in Santa Claus."

"Have you ever read it?" Carol asked.

"I don't have to," she answered, then turned away.

As she walked through the lunchroom, Carol tried to remember each child's face. She didn't know why it mattered, but it did. Each face was a life...a Raun, a Robertito, maybe even a Francisca, a Roby, a Jeannie, maybe even herself. She knew that what she did with Robertito had been right. Carol also knew that what she had done with herself had also been right. At the door, she paused. She turned and saw a room full of anger, fear and unhappiness. She wanted to do so much, but felt so helpless. And then she remembered a saying she had read on a poster. "If you save one person, one child, it is as if you have saved the whole world."

Carol ran down the empty corridor. She did not go home that night, but returned to the Soto house...to Robertito.

Chapter 25

The snow had been falling since late morning. By dusk, the white powder blanketed the trees, the grass and the pavement. The rush of rubber wheels against macadam was muted. While people huddled in the warmth of their homes, I leaned against the Jeep, lingering in the special silence created by a snowfall. A group of geese, flying in a "V" formation, began their untimely trek south. The months had passed like momentary daydreams. I gathered a bundle of new toys in my arms for my second son. I had come to know Robertito with the same intimacy I knew my own children; perhaps, even more so, since I continually catalogued his every move, his every glance, his every smile. And yet, some inner essence remained illusive. Not I, nor Francisca, nor any of us could ever know the internal universe he visited from time to time. But what he did share with us, the calm, the softness, the lucidity of a developing mind devoid of fear, bonded us together.

After I climbed the steps onto the porch of the Soto house, I stacked the boxes beside the front door and searched for my key. A taxi cab pulled into the driveway behind the Jeep.

The glazed windows and approaching darkness hid the occupants from my view. Had Jeannie's car broken down again? Had Chella returned from an afternoon excursion? A man, in a long dark coat, exited the back door. He paid the driver, who pulled a suitcase from the trunk, and turned toward the house. Our eyes met at the same moment, bridging a gap that spanned five months. Roby Soto stood there, a sad-happy smile on his face. He kept nodding at me, at the house, at the snow. For a moment, the twenty feet between us did not exist. He looked beautiful...my friend, the father of my second son. I stepped off the porch and embraced him. We hugged each other like overgrown bears, patting backs and lifting each other off the ground. And then in a gesture I usually reserve for my father, I kissed him on both cheeks. When we separated, we grinned at each other through wet eyes.

Chella saw him come through the door first. She whizzed across the living room and jumped into his arms. Carol embraced him, then began to cry. Jeannie, whose car had, indeed, not started today, watched from a distance. When I introduced them, Roby hugged her.

"Thank you for helping my son," he said to her, then he turned to me. He tried to say something, to squeeze the words from his throat, but he couldn't. He turned away and held his hands over his eyes. I put my arm around him. We all stood, together, in that room, touching each other through the silence.

His expected arrival had been four days off, but his passion to return drove him to the airport earlier. Carol and Jeannie pointed upstairs simultaneously. Roby nodded again. As he reached the second landing, he paused, fortifying himself. The door to the bathroom opened. Francisca, kneeling on the floor, had just completed helping Robertito buckle his pants. When the little boy spotted Roby in the hallway, he cocked his head and peered at the man curiously. Then his eyes glistened. He pulled away from his mother, ran down the hall and jumped into his father's arms. "Papa, Papa," he said. Francisca screamed, then put the brakes on her emotions. She didn't want to interrupt this moment between Roby and his son. As he stroked his little boy, holding back the flood of tears, this soft and gentle man stared at his wife kneeling on the bathroom floor. He kissed her with his eyes.

As I might have anticipated, Roby insisted on taking the very next session with his son. Suzi joined me at the side of the room. Though I wanted to record Robertito's initial responses to his father, I knew, like Suzi, I was there for another reason. This little boy had already defied his past. Today, he demolished old horizons by recognizing his father after five months, by running to him and displaying, in a very ordinary way, the natural warmth and affection of a child. Suzi and I were not only there as therapists, therapists and family members, we were there for the joy in Roby's eyes, in Francisca's expression, in Robertito's quizzical smile.

Robertito kept jumping on his father. They wrestled together on the floor, laughing and giggling. Roby tickled his son's feet and thighs.

"I want the ball," Robertito said in Spanish, pointing to the basketball net on the wall. He had remembered their favorite game together, one which Roby taught to him, a discipline which had required weeks of practice and concentration.

Roby gaped at his son, then looked at us and his wife, who sat beside the wall on the other side of the room. "*Sí, Sí,*" she whispered enthusiastically. Indeed, he had remembered! As Roby reached for the ball, he had difficulty absorbing what he heard. When he left, his son could say only single words, often poorly pronounced. Now, he not only knew what he wanted, thought about it in his mind, but could express that desire in a sentence. A sentence! How could he be so fortunate, he thought, to have such an amazing son? The fact that Robertito had now passed his seventh birthday was of little consequence to his father. The fact that Robertito could look at him and say anything was the gift.

He threw the ball to the little player, who caught it expertly. When Francisca clapped, he threw it to her. She, in turn, threw it to Suzi. Not once did Robertito lose track of the ball. After Suzi dumped it into my lap, I threw it back to him. Robertito ran toward the basket, stopped at a distance of five feet from it and then, in a calculated, one-handed throw, he tossed the ball through the loop. The cheering and applause stimulated Robertito to grab the ball again and sink yet another basket.

Unable to contain herself any longer, Francisca crawled into the center of the room. Her eyes bulged as she nodded at Roby, then turned to her son.

"Robertito, *mira,*" she said, pointing at his father. "What is Papa? What kind of person?" she asked, enunciating each word clearly in her native tongue.

He stared at his father without answering.

"Wait," Francisca shouted, holding her hand in the air for everyone's benefit. Thirty thoughts bombarded her. She pointed at me and asked the same question. "What is Bears?"

"Bears is a man," he answered without hesitation, having composed a perfect sentence in Spanish.

Roby gasped, dumbfounded by the sophistication of Robertito's awareness. Francisca screeched like a little girl as she watched her husband. She shifted her focus again and pointed at Suzi. "What is Suzi? What kind of person?"

Robertito touched his mother's sleeve, glanced at his father, then said: "Sushi is a woman." Everyone celebrated his response, especially Suzi, who had refused adamantly to correct his pronunciation of her name.

"And Mama? What is Mama?"

"A woman," he answered.

She now directed her son's attention back to his father. "What is Papa? What kind of person is your papa?"

The child stared at his father. His forehead furrowed and his eyes danced in their sockets, external hints of his thought process. "Papa...Papa is a man."

Roby grabbed his son and threw him in the air. He twirled him around until they were both dizzy, then he collapsed on the floor breathless.

"There's so much to show you," Francisca bellowed, "so much." She sat beside her son and husband on the floor. Roby rubbed his wife's back as she directed herself toward Robertito. For the first time in five long months, he felt complete.

"What is this?" Francisca asked, accenting each syllable of every Spanish word she spoke, while pulling on Roby's pants.

Her son watched her hand touch the material, then answered. "It is pants." Francisca looked again to her husband for his response. His amazement glittered in his eyes.

She put her hand up in the air and spread her fingers. "Now, Robertito, think carefully. How many fingers do I have?"

When he put his index finger up to count, she withdrew her hand. "Without counting my fingers...how many do I have?"

He stared at her hand for several seconds. "*Cinco*," he replied. For the next two minutes following his response, Robertito flapped his hands. His parents imitated him. Not once did the child lose eye contact with their faces or limbs.

They became a trio of dancers and mimes sharing their expression through movement.

As the session continued, we noted a slight increase in "isms." Robertito had been engaged for twelve hours already and, perhaps that, in addition to his father's arrival, had drained him. Yet, despite any fatigue, he remained lively and attentive. For Roby Soto, this was not the same child he had left. The depth of Robertito's contact had intensified. His verbal ability had blossomed into completed thoughts and sentences. He demonstrated a capacity to think beyond anything he had ever dreamed possible for his son. Even the boy's general demeanor reflected his burgeoning maturity. For the first six years of life, Robertito's face never reflected expressions beyond the primitive ones usually displayed by infants. Now, the energy of his developing intelligence creased it with distinctive character. In effect, his face had come to life.

During the next hour, Roby played a whole series of games with his son based on those either Suzi, Francisca or I demonstrated. The man sat there, awed, as he helped his child do three puzzles simultaneously, identify a whole series of diverse items, build small bridges and answer a battery of rather sophisticated questions. He laughed each time Robertito pulled a toy from the shelf and initiated the interaction.

Although Roby knew he could not stay more than one month, he wanted to be reintegrated into the program immediately.

"And my sessions, Bears. Will we have them too?" he asked as we gathered in the living room that evening.

"You will have it all, my friend," I answered.

He bowed his head slightly and put out his hand to us. When Roby lifted his head and turned his blood-shot eyes toward us, he moved his lips without uttering a sound. Francisca nestled close to him, wrapping her arms around his waist. "You have given us our son," he said.

"Not us alone," Suzi countered, grabbing my hand. "We've all done that together."

Roby looked at his wife. "In six days, Mommy, it will be Christmas. Always, I have said, since Robertito couldn't appreciate it, we would not celebrate a Christmas. I think, now, it's time."

Six days later, Francisca, Roby, Robertito, Suzi, Bryn, Thea, Raun, Carol, Jeannie, Chella, Laura and I gathered together around a very large, very well-decorated tree. Carol, with the help of some friends, had gone to the mountains and cut the tree down herself. Bryn, Thea, and Raun made decorations for it as did Robertito, who used his scissors and thick crayons. With Francisca's and Suzi's guidance, he made circles, lines and crosses all over the paper he cut.

That evening, during dinner, Bryn, who had recently joined the program as a full teacher, tapped her glass with a fork theatrically. "Listen, listen, everyone," she shouted. "Robertito is going to sing for you...in English." Everyone cheered. Under Bryn's guidance, he stood at the front of the table. He watched her hand, which she raised like a conductor.

"I wait by the window," he sang, "with my only dream." He stopped, looking at Bryn, who had memorized the "Son-Rise" television special theme song and, in turn, taught it to our special friend. Tears came to her eyes as she looked at her little student proudly and remembered the time she had once worked with her own brother. Bryn moved her arms again, signaling him to continue. "And long for the day there will be," Robertito intoned, "the sound of your laughter, the gift of your touch, oh I love you so much...is there room in your world for me?"

* * *

The time with Roby and his son passed. In his subsequent absence, Bryn, now thirteen, assumed an even greater role as a therapist, working with Tito three days a week. Like Lisa, her smaller size accentuated the childlike energy she shared with her young friend. When Raun realized that his sister also had separate Option sessions on the hill as part of the program, he demanded equal treatment. Doing dialogue sessions with them reminded me of the sessions Suzi and I had with Bryn and Thea when they worked with Raun. The evolution astounded me. Raun himself had now become the teacher.

Chella, whose support of Francisca and work with Robertito enriched our extended family, left several months later, confident and hopeful of her ability to help her sister and others. The reappearance of Patti in New York, after her abrupt exit almost a year before, caused a celebration. Her exuberance and love injected the program with new sparks. Concurrent with her arrival, we began to train Ginny Lea, who, initially, had been Thea's flute teacher. She was not a stranger to different people and different children. Her own brother had become a paraplegic as the result of an accident as a teen-ager. As he had turned his energy toward helping others, she, too, wanted to find a way to share and participate. Music became her metaphor. In the context of the program, Ginny infused the sessions with waves of rhythms and melodies. She taught Robertito many chants and songs. To everyone's amazement, she showed Robertito how to play the xylophone with startling expertise. In his first tiny recital, which she engineered, he played "Mary Had a Little Lamb" expertly on the instrument.

Our group underwent continual changes, yet we were tied together, not only by a very special child, but by an attitude and approach to living that we had come to share. Lisa visited on her vacations from school. Laura came often to express her affection. And Robertito kept us alert with his ability to grasp new things. Sometimes, when we became beguiled by his development and skill, I had to reaffirm that all his accomplishments were secondary to his general contact. Inconsistencies remained. I reminded myself that we had only worked with him for fifteen months since his return to New York. Suzi and I, with another extended family, had worked with Raun for over three years. Our son was then one and a half. Robertito was now past his seventh birthday. We couldn't measure the time...we had only to value the moment.

When spring arrived, we used the park and other outdoor facilities more often, although most of our teaching took place in the yellow room. I continued the weekly sessions and feedback conferences. Suzi, in addition to observing, maintained her role, innovating new steps through experiments in her own sessions with Robertito. But both of us began purposely to recede in terms of directing the program. Francisca assumed more responsibility over the Wednesday night meetings. She highlighted areas of concentration and decided on the basic teaching focus each week. Carol also became more instrumental in guiding the program as I began to teach her how to do dialogues with others. A very special incident reinforced her confidence.

As part of a maintenance and check-up program for her epilepsy, Carol went for a biannual check-up which included an EEG. The neurologist was amazed that the read-outs approached an almost normal configuration. Carol had not had a single seizure in almost six months, a record which defied dramatically her previous history. In celebration, she increased her time commitment to the program. Carol wanted to share everything for she believed, in some profound way, she had received much more than she had given.

By late spring, our special little friend began to absorb the initial concepts of mathematics. His ability to conceptualize and generalize stimulated an even further sophistication of interaction and verbal exchanges. After they taught him how to pronounce the alphabet in Spanish, Francisca suggested they teach him how to spell the most simple words. We all concurred.

Jeannie had the first session the next morning. After Robertito worked with more advanced lotto cards, she presented him with a pad and crayon. He scribbled over the surface of the paper, humming while he worked.

"A masterpiece. Picasso Soto," she giggled. "How about some spelling?" She wrote the letter "R" on the page. Robertito pronounced it. "Good boy. That's the first letter of your name. 'R' in Robertito." She drew a large "O." He pronounced it. "A boy-genius. Those are the first two letters of your name. Now say them with me."

Following her cue, Robertito pronounced each of the two letters written on the drawing paper. Just as Jeannie was about to write a "B," the child continued on his own. "B-E-R-T-I-T-O." Jeannie gaped at him. Impossible! How could he know? Before she had a chance to applaud or acknowledge his feat, he spelled: "S-O-T-O." He looked into her face. The soft, calm expression melted her panic.

That afternoon, Jeannie queried every member of the program. No one had taught him to spell his name. Other than having learned the alphabet as letters written in a certain order, he had had no instruction in spelling, even for the most simple words. He also had very little opportunity to see his name written out. Had Tito, in the quiet of his pauses, passed us in some way? Had he synthesized combinations of what he had already learned? No easy answers presented themselves. For the next several weeks, he did not demonstrate other unexplained knowledge. Even his ability to spell his own name faded until he relearned it as part of a general spelling curriculum. Nevertheless, everything about Robertito's regeneration, even the pauses, was awesome.

For two weeks in May, Suzi and I had to withdraw from active participation in the program. The private screenings of the upcoming network production of "Son-Rise" had generated such enthusiasm that we were invited to speak before

374

the Congress. Acutely aware of the thoughts and feelings of other parents and professionals who might see the film, I wrote the following disclaimer, which appeared on screen as the film began. "The story you are about to see is true...it concerns an alternative created and chosen by one family which in no way is meant to be a commentary on others who may have found themselves in similar circumstances. We each do the best we can and with that awareness, this experience is an expression of hope and possibility." The National Education Association endorsed the film as "highly recommended" as did reviewers around the country. But one organization, the National Society for Autistic Children, publicly attacked the film and suggested in an information packet sent to major newspapers and networks that viewers send protests to Suzi and to me. Without having ever witnessed our work with either adults or children and without having ever made any request to do so, they condemned and belittled the notion of acceptance, dismissing the basis of our work with Raun and, by inference, our work with other children. Noting the first air date for the story, one official of that organization wrote: "It was originally scheduled to be shown on Mother's Day—God Help Us." Francisca cried when she read the newspaper quote. She wanted to know how an act of love could generate so much fear and anger.

During our short absence, Francisca directed the program, observed and gave the others feed-back. No panics materialized. No need to see her son surge ahead or even remain in the same position possessed her. Francisca embraced her child in the way she had come to embrace herself...without judgments, without conditions. In love, she found joy. In acceptance, she found clarity. She even began to understand how Robertito himself could be her teacher. One afternoon, while working with him, she asked: "How can I help you more?"

Robertito cocked his head in that silly, beguiling, innocent way. "I want a lot of love," he answered.

"Yes, I know, *papito*," she said, hugging her child. "We all do."

Francisca, with Roby, who had returned for a two-month stay, assumed greater responsibility for the program during that summer. Unlike the previous one, the attitude not only survived, but flourished...as did our special little friend. There were many signs of Robertito's growing awareness and verbal initiations. One morning, as his father entered the room, he said spontaneously in Spanish: "Hello, Papa, how are you?" As he ran through the park with Jeannie, he said: "I am running. I am smiling. I am happy." When Carol extended her arms, holding him at a distance in a swimming pool, Robertito exclaimed: "Carol, help me." Suzi challenged him to a very abstract game, asking him to name words that began with a certain letter. Often, he could list three to five words. Patti increased his skill with simple addition. During a session, when I asked him if he wanted help pulling up his pants, Robertito replied: "You do it, Bears."

In early fall, Francisca took on sole responsibility for the program for a short period while Suzi and I went to South America to adopt an abandoned child. We worked with the staff at the orphanage, made a presentation at a major psychiatric clinic and trained members of individual families who wanted to work with their special children. We returned with Tayo Lukanus, a smiling survivor, a gift for everyone in our family. This tiny ten-month-old orphan had suffered from the severest form of malnutrition as a result of poverty and neglect and had to be fed intravenously in the neck in order to be kept alive. He could barely hold his head up and he could not crawl. We instituted a stimulation and exercise program immediately for our new son, a program not dissimilar in attitude from the one we had created for Robertito and other children. Within weeks, little Tayo began to sit, stand and crawl thirty paces at a time. Francisca cuddled him possessively, chattering away in Spanish. Since we had worked with her son, she wanted to work with ours. She even argued, in a comic dissertation, that she knew Tayo's language better than any of us. We declined her offer, counseling her to focus on her expanding responsibilities in her own child's program.

One unforgettable morning in early fall, Francisca and Robertito marched into the living room. As she prepared food for him, he sat himself in a chair. Patti, Suzi and I tried to engage him, but he appeared distant, preoccupied. Then, quite suddenly, while staring at the wall, he said a Spanish sentence which required a vocabulary and knowledge of grammar far exceeding his.

"I don't know," he said, "but somebody else will know soon."

Patti gawked at him. Francisca peeked through the doorway and eyed her son. She did not believe her ears.

"What did you say, Robertito? Repeat it."

He looked at her with an incredibly vulnerable and soulful

376

expression. "I don't know," he repeated, "but somebody else will know soon."

Two weeks later, at the end of a joint session with Francisca and Roby, I asked Francisca a question which I had posed many times. "If you went back to Mexico, do you think you and Roby could handle the program with Robertito?"

She glanced at her husband seated beside her. "Yes, Bears," she said. Francisca did not stick her chin out. She did not throw the hair off her forehead or adjust her blouse. Her answer originated in a very deep and quiet spot within her. "Yes, Bears," she said again. "I can do it." She kissed her husband and corrected her statement. "No...not I...we can do it." Roby nodded his aggreement.

With that clear response, Francisca Soto signaled the conclusion of our journey together. Suzi and I had waited patiently until they had come to know, in a deep and quiet place, that they no longer needed us to continue.

The only difference between a teacher and a student, both of whom draw from the same well, is that the teacher knows he knows, while the student has that to discover.

My feet did not seem to touch the ground, but I knew I was there, alternately holding and embracing Suzi, kissing and hugging Francisca, smiling to Jeannie, then Carol, tapping Patti on her shoulder, touching Thea and Raun, watching Bryn with her new brother sheltered in her arms, then finally fixing my attention on Roby Soto, who walked hand in hand with his son.

Although we had been in the airport for almost an hour, Robertito never once displayed a self-stimulating ritual, as if he wanted to leave all of us with a special gift, as if he knew this was the last good-by. He pointed to items he had never seen before and said something about each: "It's a triangle," "The light is red," "Big airplane." At the ticket counter, he stood quietly, like a little gentleman, beside his father. Those huge, dark eyes followed the dancing fingers of the airline attendant punching the keys of her computer. He laughed as the lights flashed on and off. The memory of his arrival haunted me. He had crossed the threshold into this very terminal building in little more than a vegetative state; mute, blank-faced, staring, self-stimulating and "hopelessly" withdrawn. And now, though not abreast with other seven-year-olds, he could talk, love his parents, share his

377

affection, even play basketball...a responsive, participating and loving human being.

Raun kept looking at his special friend. He knew we had come to say good-by, but didn't quite know how to express it. In a playful gesture, he grabbed Robertito's hand and guided him to a quiet corner by the window. Silhouetted against a bright sky, the two boys stared at each other.

"We will always be friends," Raun said in English, trusting something other than his words. When Robertito smiled, Raun giggled. "When you do that, your cheeks look like suitcases." He proceeded to touch his friend's face. Robertito, in turn, lifted his hands and placed them on Raun's cheeks. As I watched the two boys staring at each other, I wondered what their eyes were communicating. Though they originated from different families, in some way, I knew they were brothers.

The hugging, which followed, seemed to continue forever. Arms, lips, bodies all touching. How do you say good-by to your family? How do you end a journey which we all lived, every hour of every day, for a year and seven months? In the end, we formed a giant huddle, holding each other arm in arm. All the tears came with smiles.

"I can't believe it," Francisca said, stroking Suzi's arms as she cried.

Roby watched Jeannie and Carol say good-by to his son. He rubbed his wet eyes with his hands, still holding on. And yet he knew they had all worked for this day. He and Francisca had come to New York in the hope of finding their son...and they had. Now they were taking him home.

I knelt down beside Robertito and whispered into his ear. "Your mama and papa love you just as we all do. If you can, help them help you. There's more, Robertito, if you want it." I pulled him close to me. He put his arm over my shoulder and stroked my back gently. "Oh, Tito, how do I tell you so you know? We won't be here with you tomorrow. But we still care, we'll always care." I put his hand in mine and shook it. "By-by, Robertito Soto...my friend," I said.

"By-by, Bears Kaufman," he replied.

When Bryn burst into tears, Suzi took Tayo, then hugged her.

"I'm sorry, Mommy," Bryn said.

"There's nothing to be sorry about," Suzi reassured her.

"I'm happy they're going home, I really am," she said.

"It's...it's just...just that, well, we won't see each other any more."

"Letting go is part of loving somebody," Suzi said. "And you can see them anytime you want to...you have all the pictures you need in your head."

Bryn nodded and grinned.

Roby gathered his family around him as they prepared to enter the boarding area. I put my hand out to him. He grabbed it and held tightly. We shared a smile and looked at his son.

Suzi bent down to say one last good-by. The tears cascaded down her face. Robertito cocked his head to the side, put his finger into the stream below her eye and said in a soft and soothing voice: "Don't cry, Sushi...don't cry."

"Even if this little boy never learns another thing," the developmental psychologist had said, "what you have done here is a miracle."

If the rebirth of a child and the rebirth of those who loved, accepted and worked with him is called a miracle...then miracles will happen only to those who believe in them.

ABOUT THE AUTHOR

Barry Neil Kaufman, born and raised in New York City, teaches a uniquely loving lifestyle and vision called the Option Process, which has both educational and therapeutic applications. He is a mentor and teacher to individuals and groups (Option Living, P.O. Box 388, Roslyn, New York 11576) and lectures in universities and hospitals, and has appeared often in mass media throughout the country.

With his wife, Suzi, he developed an innovative and successful "Option" program for their once-autistic child and other children; together, they assist parents and professionals with special children.

As a writer, Mr. Kaufman has written five books, co-authored two screenplays with his wife (winning the coveted Christopher award and also the Humanitas award) and has had articles featured in major publications. His first book, SON-RISE, which details his family's inspiring journey with their special child, was dramatized as an NBC-TV special network presentation. His second book, TO LOVE IS TO BE HAPPY WITH, shares the specific application of his non-judgmental learning process as it applies to all different life situations. In

GIANT STEPS, he details very caring, intimate and uplifting portraits of other young people he has worked with and touched during times of extreme crisis. Loving a child back to life is the subject of A MIRACLE TO BELIEVE IN.

In this latest book, A LAND BEYOND TEARS, co-authored with his wife, he uses a real-life situation to present a new and liberating approach to death and dying.

CLASSIC BESTSELLERS
from FAWCETT BOOKS

☐ THE LIVELY LADY	24482	$2.95
by Kenneth Roberts		
☐ THE LAST ENCHANTMENT	24207	$2.95
by Mary Stewart		
☐ SELECTED SHORT STORIES OF		
NATHANIEL HAWTHORNE	30846	$2.25
Edited by Alfred Kazin		
☐ MAGGIE: A GIRL OF THE STREETS	30854	$2.25
by Stephen Crane		
☐ SATAN IN GORAY	24326	$2.50
by Isaac Bashevis Singer		
☐ THE RISE AND FALL OF THE		
THIRD REICH	23442	$3.95
by William Shirer		
☐ ALL QUIET ON THE WESTERN FRONT	23808	$2.95
by Erich Maria Remarque		
☐ TO KILL A MOCKINGBIRD	08376	$2.75
by Harper Lee		
☐ THE FLOUNDER	24180	$2.95
by Gunter Grass		
☐ THE CHOSEN	24200	$2.95
by Chaim Potok		
☐ THE SOURCE	23859	$3.95
by James A. Michener		

Buy them at your local bookstore or use this handy coupon for ordering.

COLUMBIA BOOK SERVICE, CBS Inc.
32275 Mally Road, P.O. Box FB, Madison Heights, MI 48071

Please send me the books I have checked above. Orders for less than 5 books must include 75¢ for the first book and 25¢ for each additional book to cover postage and handling. Orders for 5 books or more postage is FREE. Send check or money order only. Allow 3-4 weeks for delivery.

Cost $_____ Name_____

Sales tax*_____ Address_____

Postage _____ City_____

Total $_____ State_____ Zip_____

*The government requires us to collect sales tax in all states except AK, DE, MT, NH and OR.

Prices and availability subject to change without notice.   **8234**

CURRENT CREST BESTSELLERS

☐ **THE MASK OF THE ENCHANTRESS**   24418 $3.25
by Victoria Holt
Suewellyn knew she wanted to possess the Mateland family castle,
but having been illegitimate and cloistered as a young woman, only
a perilous deception could possibly make her dream come true.

☐ **THE HIDDEN TARGET**   24443 $3.50
by Helen MacInnes
A beautiful young woman on a European tour meets a handsome
American army major. All is not simple romance however when she
finds that her tour leaders are active terrorists and her young army
major is the chief of NATO's antiterrorist section.

☐ **BORN WITH THE CENTURY**   24295 $3.50
by William Kinsolving
A gripping chronicle of a man who creates an empire for his family,
and how they engineer its destruction.

☐ **SINS OF THE FATHERS**   24417 $3.95
by Susan Howatch
The tale of a family divided from generation to generation by great
wealth and the consequences of a terrible secret.

☐ **THE NINJA**   24367 $3.50
by Eric Van Lustbader
They were merciless assassins, skilled in the ways of love and the
deadliest of martial arts. An exotic thriller spanning postwar Japan
and present-day New York.